SPEAKERS SOURCEBOOK

Also by Eleanor Doan . . .

A Child's Treasury of Verse

SPEAKERS SOURCEBOOK

ELEANOR DOAN

Ministry Resources Library

Zondervan Publishing House • Grand Rapids, MI

THE SPEAKER'S SOURCEBOOK
Copyright © 1960 by The Zondervan Corporation. Renewed 1988 by the
Zondervan Corporation.

MINISTRY RESOURCES LIBRARY is an imprint of Zondervan Publishing House,
1415 Lake Drive, S.E., Grand Rapids, Michigan 49506.

Library of Congress Cataloging in Publication Data
Doan, Eleanor Lloyd, 1914–
    [Speaker's sourcebook of 4,000 illustrations and quotations for
preachers and other public speakers]
    Speaker's sourcebook / [compiled by] Eleanor Doan.
        p.   cm.
    Reprint. Originally published: Speaker's sourcebook of 4,000 illustra-
tions, quotations, sayings, anecdotes, poems, attention getters, sentence
sermons. Grand Rapids : Zondervan, 1960.
    ISBN 0-310-23751-3
    1. Quotations, English. I. Title.
PN6081.D58   1988
082—dc19   87-31221
                                                                      CIP

Printed in the United States of America

88   89   90   91   92   93 / CH / 10   9   8   7   6   5   4   3   2   1

PLEASE SHARE MY SCRAPBOOK . . .

Most everyone is happy to share his scrapbook. I know that I am. But who would ever think of publishing it? I was sure I never would.

But, here it is.

Like most scrapbooks, its contents came from here and there and everywhere. It was intended to be helpful rather than to be scholarly. The illustrations, quotations, anecdotes, proverbs and poetry, perhaps, will not be found in acknowledged "best volumes," but the sentiments and truths will find lodging in hearts as well as in minds.

Some of the articles were collected during childhood. Numerous items came from friends, others from conversations, from newspapers and periodicals. Many of the classroom illustrations and children's stories are from personal experiences. I honestly do not know the source of all the materials. No claim to originality is made for most of the selections but wherever possible credit is given the author or source. It is regrettable that many fine items are, of necessity, credited "Author Unknown," "Anonymous," "Selected" or "Exchange."

The material in this book was compiled for personal use — to provide illustrative material in an easy-to-use handbook. Others shared it. Then someone suggested that it would be an invaluable aid to teachers, students, Christian workers, pastors, speakers and writers. So it has been fed into typewriters, linotypes and presses, and multiplied many times over. This makes it possible for me to invite you to please share my scrapbook.

ELEANOR DOAN

Glendale, California

OUNCES OF ILLUSTRATION . . .

Everyone at one time or another searches frantically for an attention-getter whether it be an adage, anecdote, illustration, maxim or poem. He is firmly convinced of this truth: "An ounce of illustration is worth a ton of talk." The problem, however, is where to find this "ounce of illustration" in a hurry. Have you found this to be true? If so, this book is your answer.

Attention-getters are many and varied (see the helpful glossary) and success in using them depends upon our understanding their purpose. The words "attention-getters" are self-explanatory. However, besides attracting attention, they are used for the purposes of clinching a truth and giving light. The late Philip E. Howard, Sr., former publisher of *The Sunday School Times*, has given us this fine counsel: "Every good illustration throws light. Every good illustration gives additional light."

Every good illustration gives additional light in an unexpected way. Mr. Howard then summarizes: "An illustration should be opened just as a Christmas package is opened in the home. The tighter the string, the tighter the expectancy, particularly if you can't tell from the shape of the box what is in it."

Every consideration possible should be given to the careful use of attention-getters. They should always be in good taste and should be evaluated as to fitness of subject and range of understanding of audience. Proper timing also is important, as is appropriate telling or expression. Among considerations are two don'ts: (1) Don't antagonize your audience, and (2) don't imitate another person. Never use illustrations for the purpose of telling something interesting or clever. They are helpers only.

"How and where can I find attention-getters?" is a frequently asked question. The answer to the "how" is constant alertness and searching. The answer to "where" is twofold: life itself and reading.

Life about us overflows with resources for stories, illustrations, axioms and anecdotes. Talk with people; pry into their experiences and listen with a pencil in hand. Children will come forth with rare gems of wisdom and unpredictable answers. Teachers will share unusual classroom conversations and experiences. Missionaries will tell thrilling stories for all ages. Parents and neighbors can be more helpful than we realize. Firsthand life experience is indeed an important source of help.

Reading is the second source of real help. Read carefully; read widely. Read missionary papers, biographies, magazines, newspapers. Current news is the best reflector of current life so read with alertness for items which will furnish illustrations. If possible, read with a pair of scissors in hand.

Always keep a little notebook and pencil in your pocket or purse and be prepared to jot down any apt saying, story or illustrative information which you hear or read. Do not trust to memory.

A further question you may ask concerning the gathering of attention-getters is, "How and where should I keep all this material?" Keeping material is as important as gathering it but unfortunately it is usually just kept without any thought as to where or how.

Most everyone has a "Fibber McGee" notebook or desk drawer full of clippings, poetry and similar "things" he wants to keep because someday he will use them. When he does, he looks in the notebook or drawer, shakes his head and says, "Now, where did I put that story or quotation?" Of course he doesn't find it and doesn't use it. But he goes on saving it and hundreds of others, believing that "One of these days I'll sort things out."

Has this ever happened to you? Perhaps you don't have a notebook or drawer, but have assorted boxes under the bed, a spindle in the back of a cupboard or sheaves of papers in assorted envelopes. How can you convert this chaos into an organized handbook? I Corinthians 14:40 gives the answer: "Let all things be done decently and in order."

Have a purpose for saving what you save. Save only what materials you know will be useful to you.

Know where to put what you save. Have a place to put clippings and notes as they accumulate. Decide the method of keeping materials which will best suit your needs. Mark the items as they are saved. Paste materials in notebooks, the size depending upon items saved. The most popular type is a loose-leaf style notebook in which an alphabetizer has been placed. Don't let materials accumulate. Put them into notebooks as soon as possible after they are collected.

Classify what you save. Provide a "table of contents" for each notebook. Keep classification simple and functional. (The index of this book is an example of a practical pattern to follow). Don't serve a system; make it serve you.

The topical method of compiling this book is for the purpose of making it a handbook — usable for innumerable occasions.

In addition to using this book for written or verbal purposes, use it:
1. As a source of quotes for church papers, calendars, bulletin boards.
2. For teacher training poster ideas.
3. For selecting club, class and organization mottoes.
4. For youth bulletins, papers and calendars. Feature in a "Quote Korner" or "Gems of Wisdom" box — it will do more for young people than a ton of talk.

Adapted from *A Little Kit of Teachers' Tools* by Philip E. Howard, Sr., Philadelphia, Pennsylvania, *The Sunday School Times.* Used by permission.

A HELPFUL GLOSSARY . . .

ADAGE — A saying of long established authority and universal appreciation.

ANECDOTE — A brief narrative of curious interest, usually biographical.

APHORISM — A pithy sentence stating a general truth or sentiment or doctrinal truth.

AXIOM — A statement of self-evident truth taken for granted.

CLICHE — A trite or hackneyed expression.

DICTUM — An authoritative statement or dogmatic principle.

ILLUSTRATION — A brief narrative to elucidate a point.

MAXIM — A precept sanctioned by experience and relating especially to the practical concerns of life.

MOTTO — A maxim.

PROVERB — An adage couched, usually, in a homely and vividly concrete phrase.

QUIP — A witty outburst or saying.

SAYING — Any brief current or habitual expression; an axiom.

STORY — An anecdote.

SPEAKERS SOURCEBOOK

A

Ability

When our capabilities are of God, we are never incapable.

———◆———

It is not ability that God wants, but usability.

———◆———

There is a great deal of unmapped country within us.   GEORGE ELIOT

———◆———

Many people have ability, but lack stability.

———◆———

Absence, Absent, Absentee

If absence makes the heart grow fonder, how some people must *love* Sunday school and church.

———◆———

Absent pupils cannot be reached by absent callers.

———◆———

Absence makes the heart go wander.

———◆———

Absent today, lost tomorrow.

———◆———

We have a little grievance:
   We just don't think it's fair
That children come to Sunday school
   But their parents are not there.
Can it be they do not care to hear
   That story old and sweet?
Are they too wise and dignified
   To sit at Jesus' feet?   *P.A.S.S. News*

———◆———

The Absentee

"Someone is absent," the Shepherd said,
   As over my class book He bent His head;
"For several Sundays absent, too,
   So tell Me, teacher, what did you do?"

"I didn't call as perhaps I should,
   I wrote some cards, but they did no good,
I've never heard and she never came,
   So I decided to drop her name."

He answered gravely, "A flock was mine,
   A hundred — no, there were ninety and nine;
For one was lost in the dark and cold;
   So I sought that sheep which had left the fold.

"The path was stony and edged with thorns;
   My feet were wounded, and bruised and torn,
But I kept on seeking, nor counted the cost;
   And, oh, the joy when I found the lost!"

Thus spake the Shepherd in tender tone,
   I looked and lo — I was alone,
But God a vision had sent to me,
   To show His will toward the absentee.
                                    AUTHOR UNKNOWN

———◆———

The Board of Absentees

We are the Board of Absentees;
We attend our church about as we
   please;
We judge it will run of itself, you know,
And, Sundays, we're just too tired to go!

We are the Board of Absentees;
At business meetings our chance we
   seize
To tell exactly how things should be run,
But we lift not a finger to get them done.

We are the Board of Absentees;
We like our drive in the morning breeze;
Of course the budget should all be paid,
"But privately now, I'm in the red."

We are the Board of Absentees;
Men and women of all degrees;
"Shall we give up the church? O never,
   never!"
"Shall we go today?" Well, scarcely ever!

We look for a world far better than this,
A world of peace and of moderate bliss,
A day of right through the Seven Seas—
Just now we're the Board of Absentees!
                        The Christian Register

They won't miss me, said the mother as she repeatedly left her children for rounds of teas and parties. The devil did not "miss" the children either.

They won't miss me, said the soldier as he went A.W.O.L. But he spent thirty days in the guard house after that.

They won't miss me, said the sentry as he slipped away from duty. But the enemy surprised and massacred his comrades that very night.

They won't miss me, said the man on the assembly line, as he slipped away without permission. But the airplane crashed and killed his brother for the lack of a single part.

They won't miss me, said the Christian worker as he shed his responsibilities in a day of crisis, and then he wondered why his country gave way to softness and demoralization.

They won't miss me, said the church member as he omitted worship one Sunday, and then another, for trivial reasons, and then wondered why he no longer enjoyed a victorious Christian life.   *The Baptist Outlook*

———◆———

Private Interpretation of Scripture

I will come into Thy house in the multitude of Thy mercy —
except in summer.
The Lord is in His holy temple —
except in summer.
One thing have I desired of the Lord, that I will seek after;
That I may dwell in the house of the Lord all the days of my life —
except in summer.
God is known in her palaces for a refuge —
except in summer.
How amiable are Thy tabernacles —
except in summer.
My soul longeth, even fainteth for the courts of the Lord —
except in summer.
Preach the word; be instant in season and out of season —
except in summer.

Not forsaking the assembling of ourselves together —
except in summer.
They continued steadfastly in the apostles' doctrine and fellowship,
And in breaking of bread and in prayers —
except in summer.

———◆———

Accidents

One day a young man had an accident — he was struck with a thought.

———◆———

Accidents don't just happen; they are caused!

———◆———

"Did you hear about the terrible accident down town today?" the boy asked.
"No," his friend answered. "What was it?"
"Well, a streetcar ran over a peanut and killed two kernels."

———◆———

Accomplish, Accomplishment

You can get anything done if you don't care who gets the credit.

———◆———

Between the great things we cannot do and the little things we will not do, the danger is that we will do nothing.   H. G. WEAVER

———◆———

The reward of a thing well done is to have done it.   RALPH WALDO EMERSON

———◆———

The world is blessed most by men who do things, and not by those who merely talk about them.   JAMES OLIVER

———◆———

The great doing of little things makes the great life.   EUGENIA PRICE

———◆———

If the mountain won't come to Mohammed, Mohammed will come to the mountain.

———◆———

Those who would bring great things to pass must rise early.   MATTHEW HENRY

———◆———

Specialize in doing what you can't.

14

There is no right way to do a wrong thing.

———♦———

Zacchaeus had short legs, but he outran the crowd when Jesus passed through town.

Short legs will get you there as fast as long legs if you know how to use them.　　DR. BOB JONES, SR.

———♦———

Do the best you can
with what you've got,
where you are.

———♦———

He does most in God's great world who does his best in his own little world.　　THOMAS JEFFERSON

———♦———

If what you did yesterday still looks big to you, you haven't done much today.　　*The Sunday School*

———♦———

If I cannot do great things,
I can do small things in a great way.
　　J. F. CLARKE

———♦———

Unless a man undertakes more than he possibly can do he will never do all that he can.　　HENRY DRUMMOND

———♦———

Free peoples can escape being mastered by others only by being able to master themselves.　　THEODORE ROOSEVELT

———♦———

If people knew how hard I have had to work to gain my mastery, it would not seem wonderful at all.　　MICHELANGELO

———♦———

God will not look you over for medals, degrees or diplomas, but for scars.

———♦———

What most folks need is an alarm clock that will ring when it's time for them to rise to the occasion.

———♦———

An engine of one-cat power running all the time is more effective than an engine of forty-horse power standing idle.　　*The Sunday School*

———♦———

No gains without pains.
　　BENJAMIN FRANKLIN

The fellow who "does it now" has time to do something else while the other fellow is "still thinking about it."

———♦———

Go as far as you can see, and when you get there you will see farther.
　　ORISON SWEET MARDEN

———♦———

The Pessimist says, "It can't be done."
The Optimist says, "It can be done."
The Peptimist says, "I just did it."

———♦———

The greatest things in the world have been done by those who systematized their work and organized their time.
　　ORISON SWEET MARDEN

———♦———

Nobody don't never get nothing for nothing nowhere, no time, nohow.
　　American Proverb

———♦———

I divide the world in three classes —
the few who make things happen,
the many who watch things happen,
the overwhelming majority who have no notion of what happens.
　　NICHOLAS MURRAY BUTLER

———♦———

Footprints in the sands of time were not made sitting down.

———♦———

Accountability

The most frightening fact we have to face: ". . . every one of us shall give account of himself to God." Romans 14:12.

———♦———

Accuracy

Accuracy is better than speed.

———♦———

Accuse, Accuser

A ready accuser may be a self-excuser.

———♦———

He that accuses all mankind of corruption ought to remember that he is sure to convict only one.　　EDMUND BURKE

———♦———

Let us be excusers rather than accusers.

———♦———

Clean your fingers before you point at my spots.　　BENJAMIN FRANKLIN

Adult

When adults act like children, they're
silly.
When children act like adults, they're
delinquent.   *The Kernel*

———◆———

All adults ought to have at least one
job before anyone has more than one
job.

———◆———

Adverse, Adversity

God develops spiritual power in our
lives through pressure of hard places.

———◆———

When any calamity has been suffered, the first thing to be remembered
is, how much has been escaped.
                    SAMUEL JOHNSON

———◆———

God sometimes puts us in the dark
to prove to us that He is light.

———◆———

Adversity

To the thorns of life I'm more indebted
Than am I to the roses sweet;
They will not let me lie inactive
While round me there are tasks to meet.
They spur me on to nobler action,
Nor long allow me quiet ease,
But keep on pricking at my conscience—
And often drive me to my knees.
                    RUTH SMELTZER

———◆———

God gets His best soldiers out of
the highlands of affliction.

———◆———

The school of affliction graduates rare
scholars.

———◆———

Our Heavenly Father never takes
anything from His children unless He
means to give them something better.
                    GEORGE MUELLER

———◆———

To bear other people's afflictions,
everyone has courage and enough to
spare.   BENJAMIN FRANKLIN

———◆———

If God sends us on stony paths He
will provide us with strong shoes.
                    ALEXANDER MACLAREN

My Web of Life

No chance has brought this ill to me;
'Tis God's sweet will, so let it be,
He seeth what I cannot see.
There is a need be for each pain;
And He will one day make it plain
That earthly loss is heavenly gain.
Like as a piece of tapestry
Viewed from the back appears to be
But tangled threads mixed hopelessly;
But in the front a picture fair
Rewards the worker for his care,
Proving his skill and patience rare.
Thou art the workman, I the frame;
Lord, for the glory of Thy name
Perfect Thine image on the same.
                    ANONYMOUS

———◆———

If men can be found faithful in hard
places they can be trusted in high
places.

———◆———

Trial is the school of trust.

———◆———

God pounds you in your soft spots
until you toughen up.   PAUL WHITE

———◆———

God promises a safe landing but not
a calm passage.   *Bulgarian Proverb*

———◆———

The diamond cannot be polished
without friction, nor the man perfected
without trials.   *Chinese Proverb*

———◆———

The brook would lose its song if you
removed the rocks.   FRED BECK

———◆———

Advertise

Advertise

A lion met a tiger
    As they drew beside a pool,
Said the tiger, "Tell me why
    You're roaring like a fool."
"That's not foolish," said the lion
    With a twinkle in his eyes.
"They call me king of all beasts
    Because I advertise."
A rabbit heard them talking
    And ran home like a streak;
He thought he'd try the lion's plan,
    But his roar was just a squeak.

A fox came to investigate —
Had luncheon in the woods,
So when you advertise, my friend,
Be sure you've got the goods.
Exchange

———◆———

The little city boy was on his first real vacation with this father. The two were hiking in the mountains when his daddy pointed out a brilliant rainbow.
"It sure is pretty," said the youngster. "What's it advertising?"

———◆———

Advice

Advice is seldom welcome; and those who want it the most always like it the least.   LORD CHESTERFIELD

———◆———

To profit from good advice requires more wisdom than to give it.
CHURTON COLLINS

———◆———

Advice is like snow; the softer it falls the longer it dwells upon, and the deeper it sinks into the mind.
SAMUEL COLERIDGE

———◆———

Correct your own mistakes by avoiding those of others.

———◆———

Ill customs and bad advice are seldom forgotten.   BENJAMIN FRANKLIN

———◆———

Two things in life I've had and ample: Good advice and bad example.

———◆———

He that won't be counseled can't be helped.   BENJAMIN FRANKLIN

———◆———

It is safer to hear and take counsel than to give it.

———◆———

The best counsel I can give is the advice a friend wrote to a young man who had just been promoted: "Keep on doing what it took to get started."
.JOHN L. MC CAFFERY, *International Harvester*

———◆———

Bride: "How can I keep my wedding ring clean?"
Mother: "Soak gently in dishwater three times a day!"

Timely Advice

If you are *impatient,* sit down quietly and talk with Job.
If you are just a little *strong-headed,* go and see Moses.
If you are getting *weak-kneed,* take a good look at Elijah.
If there is *no song in your heart,* listen to David.
If you are a *policy man,* read Daniel.
If your *faith is below par,* read Paul.
If you are getting *lazy,* watch James.
If you are *losing sight of the future,* climb up the stairs of Revelation and get a glimpse of the promised land.
CHARLES E. FULLER

———◆———

Keep your eye on the ball, your shoulder to the wheel, and your ear to the ground . . . now try to work in that position.

———◆———

Two young children built a clubhouse in their yard. On the wall, in childish lettering is a list of club rules. No. 1 rule reads:
Nobody act big,
Nobody act small,
Everybody act medium.
Voice of Youth

———◆———

Fear less, hope more;
Eat less, chew more;
Whine less, breathe more;
Talk less, say more;
Hate less, love more;
And all good things will be yours.
Swedish Proverb

———◆———

Don't Let Yourself

WORRY when you are doing your best.
HURRY when success depends upon accuracy.
THINK evil of a friend until you have the facts.
BELIEVE a thing is impossible without trying it.
WASTE time on peevish and peeving matters.
IMAGINE that good intentions are a satisfying excuse.
HARBOR bitterness in your soul toward God or man.   *Christ for World Messenger*

Don't Let This Happen to You

There was a man who lived by the side of the road and sold hot dogs.

He was hard of hearing so he had no radio.

He had trouble with his eyes so he read no newspapers.

But he sold good hot dogs.

He put up signs on the highway telling how good they were.

He stood on the side of the road and cried, "Buy a hot dog, Mister?"

And people bought his hot dogs.

He increased his meat and bun orders.

He bought a bigger stove to take care of his trade.

He finally got his son home from college to help out.

But then something happened.

His son said, "Father, haven't you been listening to the radio?

"Haven't you been reading the newspaper?

"There's a big recession on.

"The European situation is terrible.

"The Domestic situation is worse."

Whereupon the father thought, "Well, my son's been to college, he reads the papers and he listens to the radio, and he ought to know."

So the father cut down his meat and bun orders, took down his signs, and no longer bothered to stand out on the highway to sell his hot dogs.

His sales fell overnight.

"You're right, son," the father said to the boy.

"We certainly are in the middle of a big recession."

No vice is so bad as advice.

MARIE DRESSLER

Lucky men need no counsel.

H. G. BOHN

If your head is wax, don't walk in the sun.

BENJAMIN FRANKLIN

Age

Age is a quality of the mind.

Gray hairs are death's blossoms.

Nobody knows the age of the human race, but all agree that it is old enough to know better.

ANONYMOUS

Let your age be measured by spiritual progress.

Eternity

We live in an age which thinks being lost in the woods is a new freedom.

This generation plays everything but safe.

FRED BECK

The Golden Age was never the present age.

BENJAMIN FRANKLIN

The best thing to save for old age is yourself.

National Motorist

One has to grow older to become more tolerant.

GOETHE

As soon as you feel too old to do a thing, do it.

MARGARET DELAND

A man who celebrated his fiftieth wedding anniversary recently, says, "A man is always as young as he feels but seldom as important."

A great many people who are worried about adding years to their life should try adding life to their years.

An old young man will be a young old man.

BENJAMIN FRANKLIN

I Shall Not Mind

I shall not mind
    The whiteness of my hair,
Or that slow steps falter
    On the stair,
Or that young friends hurry
    As they pass,
Or what strange image
    Greets me in the glass —
If I can feel,
    As roots feel in the sod,
That I am growing old to bloom
    Before the face of God.

AUTHOR UNKNOWN

Forty is the old age of youth, fifty is the youth of old age.   VICTOR HUGO

———◆———

Do not resent growing old. Think how much you'd resent being denied the privilege.

———◆———

At 20 years of age the will reigns;
At 30 the wit;
At 40 the judgment.   BENJAMIN FRANKLIN

———◆———

The six ages of man:
  Beef broth,
    Ground steak,
      Sirloin,
        Filet mignon,
      Ground steak,
    Beef broth.

———◆———

Who at twenty knows nothing,
At thirty does nothing,
At forty has nothing.   Italian Proverb

———◆———

How to Grow Old

If you want to be an old man long before your time,
  Never fool with poetry, never make a rhyme.
Never play with children, never skip the rope,
  Never have a good time blowing bubble soap.
Never go a fishing, never pass the ball,
  Never ramble in the woods in summer or in fall.
Never lift your eyes to God, keep 'em looking down,
  Never wear a pleasant smile, always wear a frown.
Never take your time to eat, always overstuff,
  Never have the sense to know when you've had enough.   ALEX RENNIE

———◆———

A birthday is the one time that every woman wants her past forgotten and her present remembered.

———◆———

Grecian ladies counted their age from their marriage, not from their birth.
  HOMER

No woman should ever be quite accurate about her age. It looks so calculating.   OSCAR WILDE

———◆———

Most women not only respect old age, they approach it with extreme caution.

———◆———

When one woman was asked her age she said, "I'm as old as my nose and a little older than my teeth."

———◆———

Alexandre Dumas, in answer to the question, "How do you grow old so gracefully?" replied, "Madam, I give all my time to it."

———◆———

When you begin to notice what a jolly time the young people are having, you're getting old.

———◆———

Middle age is when you're just as young as ever, but it takes a lot more effort.   HAL CHADWICK

———◆———

Definition of B-29: What women in their middle forties wish they could again.

———◆———

The longest period in a woman's life is the 10 years between the time she is 39 and 40.

———◆———

Four

Four is too big for his breeches,
Knows infinitely more than his mother,
Four is matinee idol
To two-and-a-half, his brother.

Four is a lyric composer,
Raconteur extraordinaire,
Four gets away with murder,
Out of line, and into hair.

Where Four is, there dirt is also,
And nails and lengths of twine,
Four is Mr. Fix-it
And all of his tools are mine.

Four barges into everything
(Hearts, too) without a knock
Four will be five on the twelfth of July
And I wish I could stop the clock.
  ELISE GIBBS in Reader's Digest

If you want to know how old a woman is, ask her sister-in-law.

EDGAR W. HOWE

———◆———

A historian says that women used cosmetics in the Middle Ages. They still use cosmetics in the middle ages.

———◆———

Seven Ages of Woman

The infant
The little girl,
The miss.
The young woman,
The young woman,
The young woman,
The young woman.

———◆———

Man's life means
Tender teens,
Teachable twenties,
Tireless thirties,
Fiery forties,
Forceful fifties,
Serious sixties,
Sacred seventies,
Aching eighties,
Shortening breath,
Death,
The Sod,
God.

———◆———

You may be old at 40 and young at 80; but you are genuinely old at any age if:
You feel old;
You feel you have learned all there is to learn;
You find yourself saying, "I'm too old to do that";
You feel tomorrow holds no promise;
You take no interest in the activities of youth;
You would rather talk than listen;
You long for the "good old days" feeling they were the best.

Minnesota State Medical Association

———◆———

Old age is the time when men pay more attention to their food than they do to the waitresses.

ALBERT FLETCHER, *Southern Reporter*

An old-timer is one who remembers when we counted our blessings instead of our calories.

National Motorist

———◆———

Altar

Altars

A man I know has made an altar
Of his factory bench.
And one has turned the counter of his store
Into a place of sacrifice and holy ministry.
Another still has changed his office desk
Into a pulpit desk, from which to speak and write,
Transforming commonplace affairs
Into the business of the King.

A Martha in our midst has made
Her kitchen table a communion table,
A postman makes his daily round
A walk in the temple of God . . .
To all of these each daily happening
Has come to be a whisper from the lips of God,
Each separate task a listening post,
And every common circumstance a wayside shrine.

EDGAR FRANK

———◆———

A family altar leads to an altered life.

The Friendly Messenger

———◆———

The family altar which does not alter the family is not a good family altar.

———◆———

Evening Is Best

I like the evening best
When children say their prayers.
When little tousled towheads
Stumble up the stairs.
I like the birds' soft twitter.
The friendly sounds of night;
A hearth where cherry driftwood
Throws a ruddy light.

HARRIET MARKHAM GILL

———◆———

Ambition

If your pet ambition doesn't mean a "hard row to hoe," it may not have a future worth digging for.

Better to say, "This one thing I do," than to dabble in forty.

It is a sin to do less than your best.
DR. BOB JONES, SR.

I rise early because no day is long enough for a day's work.
JUSTICE BRANDEIS

You draw nothing out of the bank of life except what you deposit in it.

A winner never quits and a quitter never wins.

Nothing is humbler than ambition when it is about to climb.
BENJAMIN FRANKLIN

From a little spark may burst a mighty flame.
DANTE

Stand still and silently watch the world go by — and it will.

There is always room at the top because many of those who get there go to sleep and roll off.
National Motorist

Achievement can be no greater than the plans you make.

After a junior high school class toured the White House, the teacher asked each student to write impressions of the visit. One boy wrote: "I was especially glad to have this opportunity to visit my future home."

Ancestors

It is the general rule, that all superior men inherit the elements of superiority from their mothers.
NICHELET

We used to do things for posterity, but now we do things for ourselves and leave the bill to posterity.
Lutheran Education

As I understand it, heredity is what a man believes in until his son begins to act like a delinquent.
Presbyterian Life

No person can have in-laws without being one.
DR. ALICE SOWERS

A rich relative is described as "the kin we love to touch."

It is a poor tribute to our forefathers to camp where they fell.

Relatives are like sweet potatoes, the best part is under the ground.

Angels

In reviewing the story of Jacob's dream, a Sunday school teacher asked the class, "Why did the angels use the ladder when they had wings?"
One bright pupil quickly replied, "Because they were molting."

Little Hugh had been fascinated about the sermon he had heard on angels. As he was telling a friend about it they got into an argument. The little friend insisted that all angels had wings, but Hugh disagreed.
"It isn't true," insisted Hugh. "Our preacher says that some of them are strangers in underwares."

Anger

The prudent man does not let his temper boil over lest he get into hot water.

Anger is a stone cast into a wasp's nest.
Malabar Proverb

Anger is just one letter short of Danger.

Anger manages everything badly.
STATIUS

Anger is never without a reason, but seldom with a good one.
BENJAMIN FRANKLIN

A husband's wrath spoils the best broth.

Two people ought not to get angry at the same time.

———♦———

Anger is a wind which blows out the lamp of the mind.

———♦———

Animals

One day as we were driving through the country, my small son David spoke up excitedly saying, "Oh, Mother, look at the cow's popsicle." I looked over in a field and saw a cow calmly licking a large block of salt which was placed on a small post on the ground.

HELEN MAC MILLAN in *Christian Home*

———♦———

Me? Owl

In friendship, a rift
Occurs when they've written:
"We're sending a gift
To your children — a kitten."

———♦———

The postman stared doubtfully at the formidable looking animal lying on the doorstep. "What kind of dog is that?" he asked the little old lady.

"I don't rightly know," she said. "My brother sent it from Africa."

"Well," the postman hesitated, "it's the oddest looking dog I've ever seen."

The prim lady nodded her head. "You should have seen it before I cut its mane off."

———♦———

A little boy and his daddy were looking at a litter of puppies, planning to buy one, and the daddy asked the boy which one he wanted. The lad pointed to a pup whose tail was wagging furiously and said, "That one with the happy ending." *Presbyterian Life*

———♦———

Zoo's Who A-B-C

Alligator, beetle, porcupine, whale,
Bobolink, panther, dragonfly, snail,
Crocodile, monkey, buffalo, hare,
Dromedary, leopard, mud turtle, bear,
Elephant, badger, pelican, ox,
Flying fish, reindeer, anaconda, fox,
Guinea pig, dolphin, antelope, goose,
Hummingbird, weasel, pickerel, moose,
Ibex, rhinoceros, owl, kangaroo,
Jackal, opossum, toad, cockatoo,
Kingfisher, peacock, anteater, bat,
Lizard, ichneumon, honeybee, rat,
Mockingbird, camel, grasshopper, mouse,
Nightingale, spider, cuttlefish, grouse,
Ocelot, pheasant, wolverine, auk,
Periwinkle, ermine, katydid, hawk,
Quail, hippopotamus, armadillo, moth,
Rattlesnake, lion, woodpecker, sloth,
Salamander, goldfish, angleworm, dog,
Tiger, flamingo, scorpion, frog,
Unicorn, ostrich, nautilus, mole,
Viper, gorilla, basilisk, sole,
Whippoorwill, beaver, centipede, fawn,
Xantho, canary, pollywog, swan,
Yellowhammer, eagle, hyena, lark,
Zebra, chameleon, butterfly, shark.

HENRY KNIGHT

———♦———

A kindergarten-age lad was deeply grieved because his tiger cat had just died. His mother helped the boy put the cat in a box and bury it. Some weeks later the lad came running into the house excitedly, urging his mother to go outside with him and look up into the tree. Looking down at the boy and his mother was a tiger cat a little larger than the one that had died, but marked the same way.

"There he is, Mommy," the boy said. "See? I planted Tiger and he just growed up."

———♦———

One Sunday afternoon a family was driving out in the country. The children were telling about the Bible story they had heard in Sunday school that morning — David and the giant. Suddenly little Sally interrupted the conversation and pointed to some Holstein cows. "There's some of those Philistines now!"

———♦———

Anxiety

Mistrust the man who finds everything good, the man who finds everything evil, and, still more, the man who is indifferent to everything. LAVATER

The most anxious man in a prison is the governor. GEORGE BERNARD SHAW

———◆———

The beginning of anxiety is the end of faith, and the beginning of true faith is the end of anxiety. GEORGE MUELLER

———◆———

The crosses which we make for ourselves by a restless anxiety as to the future are not crosses which come from God.

———◆———

Anxiety is a word of unbelief or unreasoning dread. We have no right to allow it. Full faith in God puts it to rest. HORACE BUSHNELL

———◆———

Anxiety is like the rust of life, destroying its brightness and weakening its power. A childlike and abiding trust in Providence is its best preventive and remedy.

———◆———

Appearance

A long face and a broad mind are rarely found under the same hat.

———◆———

A dear old Quaker lady, distinguished for her youthful appearance, was asked what she used to preserve her charms. She replied sweetly, "I used for the lips, truth; for the voice, prayer; for the eyes, pity; for the hand, charity; for the figure, uprightness; and for the heart, love." JERRY FLEISHMAN

———◆———

Young Charles, age four, came in for his midmorning glass of fruit juice. It was a warm morning and he had been playing hard. Also, because he liked the treat he had come for, he was juice-conscious.

"Mother," he said, "would you wipe my face with a wet cloth? It is sort of sticky."

"What did you get on it, dear?" his mother asked as she reached for the washcloth.

"Nothin'," he replied in his slow western drawl, "it's just face juice."
Christian Home

Application

"Grandma," asked a youngster, "were you once a little girl like me?"

"Yes, dear."

"Then," continued the child, "I suppose you know how it feels to get an ice cream cone when you don't expect it."

———◆———

One day little Jane was seated alone at a small table while her parents sat with their guests at the large table. This greatly displeased Jane. Before eating, Jane's parents thought it would be nice for Jane to be included in the group although she was seated separately, so father asked her to say the blessing. This was her prayer: "Lord, I thank Thee for this table in the presence of mine enemies. Amen."

———◆———

During the observance of Animal Week the fourth graders told about their kindness to pets. Asked what he had done, one little boy said, "I kicked a boy for kicking his dog."

———◆———

The teacher told the children they could take turns telling a brief story about something exciting. After listening to a few more lengthy stories, Bobby arose, bowed politely and said, "Help!"

———◆———

To live is not to learn, but to apply. LEGOUVE

———◆———

Appreciate, Appreciation

It's better to appreciate things you don't have than to have things you don't appreciate.

———◆———

If you cannot have everything, make the best of everything you have.

———◆———

Next to excellence is the appreciation of it. THACKERAY

———◆———

The chance for appreciation is much increased by being the child of an appreciator. RALPH WALDO EMERSON

23

Argue

Two boys were fighting and the one on the bottom was yelling. At last the mother of the boy on top came out and called her son. He hit the boy on the bottom a few more times and then spit in his eye. The mother said to him when he got up, "Why do you fight all the time? It must be the devil in you."

After a little thought the boy replied, "It may be the devil in me that makes me hit, but spitting in that guy's eye was my own idea."

———

Too many sound arguments are all sound.

———

It is better to debate a question without settling it than to settle it without debate.   JOUBERT

———

To win an argument is to lose a friend.

———

A family jar is no good for preserving the peace.

———

It is a lot easier to get the best of an argument than it is to prove you are right.

———

Many a long dispute among Divines may thus be abridged: It is so: It is not so: It is so: It is not so.
BENJAMIN FRANKLIN

———

Some people are so constituted that they would rather lose a friend than an argument. Be yourself, simple, honest and unpretending, and you will enjoy through life the respect and love of friends.   SHERMAN

———

When nobody disagrees with you, you can assure yourself that you are exceptionally brilliant. Or else you're the boss.

———

The springs of human conflict cannot be eradicated through institutions, but only through the reform of the individual human being.
GENERAL DOUGLAS MAC ARTHUR

To disagree is one thing; to be disagreeable is another.

———

Arithmetic

I was trying to teach arithmetic reasoning when I asked, "If you know the price of seven hats, how would you find the cost of one?"

"Ask the clerk," replied one 10-year-old.   ETHEL FISCHER in NEA Journal

———

Teacher asked Wally how he would divide 10 potatoes equally among 20 people. Wally promptly replied, "I'd mash them."

———

Add to the pleasure of others.
Subtract from another's unhappiness.
Multiply the pleasures of others.
Divide the good things that come your way.

———

Attendance

Simply stopping the leaks in Sunday school attendance would more than triple the number of new members.

———

Little is accomplished if we lose pupils out the back door as fast as we bring them in at the front.

———

Announcing a special meeting the minister said, "Come early if you hope to get a back seat."

———

A minister, out driving, passed a track where a horse race was in progress. His six-year-old son gazed from the window at the crowded stadium. "Oh, Daddy," he exclaimed, "all the pews are filled!"   *Together*

———

I see in your church convention that you discussed the subject, "How to Get People to Attend Church." I have never heard a single address at a farmer's convention on how to get the cattle to come to the rack. We spend our time discussing the best kind of feed.
The Baptist Outlook

Little Johnny came home from Sunday school and told his mother that if he missed three Sundays in a row, teacher would throw him into the furnace. The horrified mother telephoned the teacher at once. "What I said was," the calm teacher explained, "that if any child missed three Sundays in a row, he would be dropped from the register." *Presbyterian Life*

When a man refuses to attend church any day in the week, he is a "Seven Day Absentist."

This Means U!

We cannot spell S U nday without U
We cannot spell ch U rch without U
We cannot spell cens U s without U
We cannot spell s U ccess without U
Our church needs U to help
We are counting on U.
The Sunday School Builder

Ten Reasons for Attending Sunday School

1. From the Standpoint of Godliness:
It teaches the Bible — which is the basis of our faith in God — and leads to Christ as personal Saviour and Lord.
2. From the Standpoint of Education:
It trains the mind and heart along the lines of things eternal.
3. From the Social Standpoint:
It enables one to enjoy the friendship and fellowship of genuine Christians.
4. From the Standpoint of Personality:
It helps to develop the Christian character necessary to face life's problems victoriously.
5. From the Standpoint of Character:
It is the chief aim of the Sunday school to teach us to be examples of the believer in word and deed.
6. From the Standpoint of Interest:
It presents interesting programs for our delight and culture.
7. From the Standpoint of Family:
It has a class for every age, and the whole family can go together and profit by its teaching.

8. From the Standpoint of Service:
It affords simple opportunity to serve God and the Church in activities that are not open elsewhere.
9. From the Standpoint of Immortality:
It turns our eyes heavenward and makes us realize that we must prepare for a life beyond the mortal grave.
10. From the Practical Standpoint:
The hour or so spent in Sunday school each Sunday could not be expended more profitably.
National S.S. Association and Greater Chicago S.S. Association

---

Attention

The true art of memory is the art of attention. SAMUEL JOHNSON

One Sunday morning a man entered the church and sat down near the front with his hat on. Noting the man, one of the ushers spoke to him, asking him if he knew he forgot to remove his hat.

"Yes," the man replied, "I realize I have my hat on. I've been coming to this church for two months and this is the only way I could get anyone to speak to me."

"But, Sir, that's the wrong way to spell *paint*," said the apprentice to his employer.

"Yes, I know," rejoined the other, "but I have a reason for spelling it that way."

He then explained that when he wrote the usual "Wet Paint" sign, passers-by paid little heed and often ruined their clothes, but "Wet Pent" would catch their attention, and while they might laugh at the ignorance of the painter, they remembered to keep away from danger.

Residents of a little village were perturbed because motorists sped through their town at dangerously high speeds, paying no attention to the neat "Drive Slowly" sign posted at the entrance. Finally they dragged a badly wrecked car to the spot and added to the sign the words, "This Might Happen to You." The effect was tremendous.

Even a Sunday school superintendent or teacher might find his suggestions more effective if stated in some unusual way.   *The Sunday School*

Attitude

Often attitudes are kindled in the flame of others' convictions.
                                          LOIS E. LE BAR

It's not the outlook, but the uplook that counts.

They conquer who believe they can.

It is your actions and attitude when you are on your own that reflect what you really are.   MARTIN VANBEE

We should be slower to think that the man at his worst is the real man, and certain that the better we are ourselves the less likely is he to be at his worst in our company.   JAMES M. BARRIE

The best answer to self-consciousness is God-consciousness.   F. B. MEYER

The person who always looks down his nose gets the wrong slant.

The attitude of the individual determines the attitude of the group.

Don't go around with a chip on your shoulder, people might think it came off your head.   *Changing Times*

Automobile

The part of the automobile that causes the most accidents is the nut that holds the steering wheel.

The difference between the driver of a new automobile and the owner of a new automobile is 24 monthly payments.   *Glendale News Press*

Car sickness is that feeling you get every month when the payment falls due.   *American Weiser, Idaho*

A smart aleck stopped at the garage and asked a mechanic: "How do you tell how much horsepower a car has?"

The mechanic replied: "Lift the hood and count the plugs."

A station wagon is something city folks buy when they move to the country so the country folks will know they're from the city.   *Glendale News Press*

Station attendant to beautiful young driver whose new car had two wrinkled fenders: "How much mileage do you get per fender?"

Traffic officer to motorist: "The highway sign '90' means the route number, not the speed limit."

If you want to live to see ninety, don't look for it on the automobile speedometer.

B

Baby, Babies

The great events of this world are not battles and earthquakes and hurricanes. The great events of this world are babies. They are earthquakes and hurricanes.

Young Father: "In your sermon this morning you spoke about a baby being a new wave on the ocean of life."

Minister: "That's right."

Young Father: "Don't you think a fresh squall would have been nearer the truth?"

We haven't all had the good fortune to be ladies; we haven't all been generals, or poets, or statesmen; but when the toast works down to the babies, we stand on common ground. MARK TWAIN

A Baby

That which makes the home happier,
Love stronger,
Patience greater
Hands busier,
Nights longer,
Days shorter,
Purses lighter,
Clothes shabbier,
The past forgotten,
The future brighter. MARION LAWRENCE

Think not that he is all too young to teach,
His little heart will like a magnet reach
And touch the truth for which you have no speech. FROEBEL

A baby is the little rivet in the bonds of matrimony.

Sign on a church's crib room: "Bawl Room."

Infancy conforms to nobody; all conform to it.

Baby Shoes

Often tiny baby feet,
  Tired from their play,
Kick off scuffed-up little shoes
  At the close of day.
And often tired mothers
  Find them lying there,
And over them send up to God
  This fervent, whispered prayer:
"God, guide his every footstep
  In paths where Thou has stood;
God, make him brave; God, make him strong;
  And please, God, make him good!"
And every man must walk a path,
  And every man must choose;
But some forget their mother's prayers
  Over their baby shoes.
MARY HOLMES in The War Cry

It's marvelous how the cry of a little baby in the still of the night evokes wonder. Usually you wonder which one of you will get up. *Changing Times*

Bachelor

A bachelor is one who didn't make the same mistake once.

A bachelor is a man who has cheated some woman out of a divorce.

"I could marry any girl I please," said the young man, "but I don't please any."

A bachelor is a man who can have a girl on his knees without having her on his hands.

A bachelor never gets over the idea that he is a thing of beauty and a boy forever. HELEN ROWLAND

Baptism

A minister was baptizing a six-year-old boy and repeated his name with a "Junior" after it. Instantly he was interrupted in a voice loud enough to fill the great sanctuary.
"It's the third," said the lad, "I'm named after my father and my grandfather, and I have to carry on in their honor, my mother says, but just call me 'Butch,' will you, huh?"

A Presbyterian and a Baptist minister were discussing baptism. After a beautiful dissertation on the subject by the Baptist minister, the Presbyterian minister asked if the Baptist considered a person baptized if he were immersed in water up to his chin. "No," said the Baptist.
"Is he considered baptized if he is immersed up to his nose?" asked the Presbyterian.
Again the Baptist's answer was "No."
"Well, if you immerse him up to his eyebrows do you consider him baptized?" queried the Presbyterian.

27

"You don't seem to understand," said the Baptist. "He must be immersed completely in water — until his head is covered."

"That's what I've been trying to tell you all along," said the Presbyterian, "it's only a little water on the top of the head that counts."

Beauty

Beauty is as beauty does.

———◆———

The best part of beauty is that which no picture can express.

FRANCIS BACON

———◆———

Beauty is only skin deep — but oh, what skin!

———◆———

A woman deserves no credit for her beauty at sixteen but beauty of sixty is her own soul's doing.   ANONYMOUS

———◆———

Beauty belongs to beauty.

———◆———

A plain face is often surprisingly beautiful by reason of an inner light.

HENRY E. WALBERY

———◆———

What is beautiful is good, and who is good will soon also be beautiful.

SAPPHO

Beginnings

A teakettle singing on the stove was the beginning of the steam engine.

A shirt waving on a clothesline was the beginning of a balloon, the forerunner of the Graf Zeppelin.

A spider web strung across a garden path suggested the suspension bridge.

A lantern swinging in a tower was the beginning of the pendulum.

An apple falling from a tree was the cause of discovering the law of gravitation.   Reville

———◆———

Behavior

If you are bent on having a fling, don't forget it carries a sting.

———◆———

Always put off until tomorrow the things you should not do today.

It is not so important to be active, but to be effective.

Six-year-old Bobby's report card showed excellent marks except in deportment.

"Bobby," said his mother, "the teacher has a note attached that says you were a little boisterous."

"Well, what did you expect," bristled Bobby. "Did you think I'd be a little girlsterous?"   *National Parent Teacher*

———◆———

You Tell on Yourself

You tell on yourself by the friends you
    seek,
By the very manner in which you speak,
By the way you employ your leisure
    time,
By the use you make of dollar and
    dime.
You tell what you are by the things
    you wear
By the spirit in which you burdens
    bear,
By the kind of things at which you
    laugh,
By the records you play on the phono-
    graph,
You tell what you are by the way you
    walk,
By the things of which you delight to
    talk,
By the manner in which you bear de-
    feat,
By so simple a thing as how you eat.
By the books you choose from the well-
    filled shelf:
In these ways and more, you tell on
    yourself.
So, there's really no particle of sense,
In an effort to keep up false pretense.
    Selected

———◆———

Always do right. This will gratify some people and astonish the rest.

MARK TWAIN

———◆———

Many a child is spoiled because you can't spank two grandmothers.

Town Journal

———◆———

The man who sows wild oats away from home usually raises cain at home.

Conduct is three-fourths of character, but habits are nine-tenths of conduct. We know character by habits.

———◆———

People may doubt what you say, but they will always believe what you do.

———◆———

What you are speaks so loudly that men cannot hear what you say.

EMERSON

———◆———

It is far better to do well than to say well.

———◆———

All the beautiful sentiments in the world weigh less than a single lovely action.

JAMES RUSSELL LOWELL

———◆———

There probably isn't a business in America that hasn't one or more practices that irritate the public and are not really essential to the business. All our practices need constant examination and appraisal by one whose first precept is that every company action must promote good will and not bad feeling.

KEITH S. MC HUGH

———◆———

Never explain your actions. Your friends don't need it and your enemies won't believe you anyway.

———◆———

A fond mother asked her four-year-old son what the nursery school had taught the pupils that day. Replied the youngster, "They taught the kids who hit, not to hit; and the ones who don't hit, to hit back." *Parents' Magazine*

Belief, Believe, Believers

More persons, on the whole, are humbugged by believing in nothing, than by believing too much.

P. T. BARNUM

———◆———

Believe that you have a thing and you have it.

———◆———

It wasn't Dunninger, but some other mental wizard, who remarked: "Tell me what you believe and I'll tell you what you'll achieve."

What you believe is what you are.

NATHANIEL OLSON

———◆———

Brethren, be great believers. Little faith will bring your souls to heaven, but great faith will bring heaven to your souls. SPURGEON

———◆———

Belief is a truth held in the mind. Faith is a fire in the heart.

JOSEPH FORT NEWTON

———◆———

A good question for an atheist is to serve him a fine dinner, and then ask him if he believes there is a cook.

———◆———

Atheism can never be an institution. It is destitution.

———◆———

Unbelief is not a problem of the intellect but of the will.

———◆———

Believers are not hired servants, supporting themselves by their own work, but children maintained at their Father's expense. HORATIUS BONAR

———◆———

Bible

Seven Wonders of the Word:

1. The wonder of its formation — the way in which it grew is one of the mysteries of time.
2. The wonder of its unification — a library of 66 books, yet one book.
3. The wonder of its age — most ancient of all books.
4. The wonder of its sale — best seller of any book.
5. The wonder of its interest — only book in world read by all classes.
6. The wonder of its language — written largely by uneducated men, yet the best from a literary standpoint.
7. The wonder of its preservation — the most hated of all books, yet it continues to exist. "The word of our God shall stand for ever."

———◆———

While a minister was packing his suitcase he found a little room in it. "So," he told a friend, "there is still enough room for me to pack a guidebook, a lamp, a mirror, a telescope, a book of poems, a number of biographies, a bundle of old letters, a hymn book, a sharp sword, a small library of 30 volumes."

When the friend looked at the small space for all this he asked, "How can you manage all that in the space you have?"

"That is easy," said his friend, "for the Bible contains all of these things."

Gospel Herald

How to Handle the Bible

Get everything out of it,
Do not read anything into it,
Let nothing remain unread in it.

J. A. BENGEL

Seven Wonderful Things in the Bible

1. Peter's hook — to bring up fish.
2. David's crook — to guide the sheep.
3. Gideon's torch — to light the dark places.
4. Moses' rod — to overcome.
5. David's sling — to prostrate giant foes.
6. Brazen serpent — to cure bite of world's snakes.
7. Paul's armor — to be our protection.

Bible Cake

1 cup butter (Judges 5:25)
3½ cups flour (I Kings 4:22)
3 cups sugar (Jeremiah 6:20)
2 cups raisins (I Samuel 30:12)
2 cups figs (I Samuel 30:12)
1 cup water (Genesis 24:17)
1 cup almonds (Genesis 43:11)
6 eggs (Isaiah 10:14)
1 tsp. honey (Exodus 16:31)
  pinch of salt (Leviticus 2:13)
2 tsp. baking powder (I Corinthians 5:6)
  spice to taste (I Kings 10:10)
Follow Solomon's advice for making good boys and girls and you will have a good cake (Proverbs 23:14).

PICKERING

The most desirable time to read the Bible is as often as possible.

Know the Bible in your mind,
Keep it in your heart;
Live it in your life,
Share it with the world.

Bible Society Record

The Books of the Bible

In *Genesis* the world was made by God's creative hand;
In *Exodus* the Hebrews marched to gain the Promised Land;
Leviticus contains the law, holy, and just and good.
Numbers records the tribes enrolled — all sons of Abraham's blood.
Moses in *Deuteronomy*, records God's mighty deeds;
Brave *Joshua* into Canaan's land the host of Israel leads.
In *Judges* their rebellion oft provokes the Lord to smite.
But *Ruth* records the faith of one well pleasing in His sight,
In First and Second *Samuel* of Jesse's son we read.
Ten Tribes in First and Second *Kings* revolted from his seed.
The First and Second *Chronicles* see Judah captive made:
But *Ezra* leads a remnant back by princely Cyrus' aid.
The city wall of Zion, *Nehemiah* builds again,
While *Esther* saves her people from the plots of wicked men.
In *Job* we read how faith will live beneath affliction's rod,
And David's *Psalms* are precious songs to every child of God.
The *Proverbs* like a goodly string of choicest pearls appear,
Ecclesiastes teaches man how vain are all things here.
The mystic *Song of Solomon* exalts sweet Sharon's Rose;
Whilst Christ the Saviour and the King, the "rapt *Isaiah*" shows.
The warning *Jeremiah* apostate Israel scorns;
His plaintive *Lamentations* their awful downfall mourns.

Ezekiel tells in wondrous words of
dazzling mysteries;
While kings and empires yet to come,
Daniel in vision sees.
Of judgment and of mercy, *Hosea* loves
to tell;
Joel describes the blessed days when
God with man shall dwell.
Among Tekoa's herdsmen *Amos* re-
ceived his call;
While *Obadiah* prophesies of Edom's
final fall.
Jonah enshrines a wondrous type of
Christ, our risen Lord,
Micah pronounces Judah lost—lost, but
again restored.
Nahum declares on Nineveh just judg-
ment shall be poured.
A view of Chaldea's coming doom
Habakkuk's visions give;
Next *Zephaniah* warns the Jews to turn,
repent, and live;
Haggai wrote to those who saw the
Temple built again,
And *Zechariah* prophesied of Christ's
triumphant reign.
Malachi was the last who touched the
high prophetic cord;
Its final notes sublimely show the com-
ing of the Lord.

Matthew and *Mark* and *Luke* and *John*
the Holy Gospel wrote,
Describing how the Saviour died — His
life, and all He taught;
Acts proves how God the apostles
owned with signs in every place.
St. Paul, in *Romans*, teaches us how
man is saved by grace.
The apostle, in *Corinthians*, instructs,
exhorts, reproves,
Galatians shows that faith in Christ
alone the Father loves.
Ephesians and *Philippians* tell what
Christians ought to be:
Colossians bids us live to God and for
eternity.
In *Thessalonians* we are taught the
Lord will come from heaven.
In *Timothy* and *Titus*, a bishop's rule
is given.
Philemon marks a Christian's love,
which only Christians know.

Hebrews reveals the Gospel prefigured
by the Law.
James teaches without holiness faith
is but vain and dead.
St. Peter points the narrow way in
which the saints are led.
John in his three epistles on love de-
lights to dwell.
St. Jude gives awful warning of judgment, wrath and hell;
The *Revelation* prophesies of that tremendous day
When Christ — and Christ alone — shall
be the trembling sinner's stay.

AUTHOR UNKNOWN

The Twelve Apostles

Of all the Twelve Apostles,
The Gospels give the names;
First, Andrew, John, and Peter,
Bartholomew and James,
Matthew, and Simon, Thomas,
Were friends both tried and true.
Then Philip, James and Thaddeus,
The traitor Judas, too.
They followed Christ the Master
O'er mountain, shore, and sea,
Samaria, Judea, Perea, Galilee.

AUTHOR UNKNOWN

Bible First Aid Kit

If you find yourself in *sudden trouble
or sorrow*, apply instantly Hebrews
12:5-11 and saturate your heart in
Psalm 23.

If you have *slipped down* and hurt
yourself, Psalm 91 will be found to
greatly benefit.

When that *lonely feeling* steals over the
heart, a good stimulant will be found
in Matthew 11:28-30.

Should you be suffering from *loss of
memory* and cannot call to mind your
blessings, try a good dose of Psalm
103.

In time of *failing strength* and courage, two or three applications of I
John 5:13-15 will be found beneficial.

Whenever you find that *bitter taste* in
your mouth and cannot speak lovingly of others, take a good draught

of I Corinthians 13 and Psalm 34:12, 13.

Some days when your *faith is weak* try the tonic found in Hebrews 11.

———◆———

The Bible contains
The mind of God.
The state of man.
The way of salvation.
The doom of sinners.
The happiness of believers.
Light to direct you.
Food to support you.
Comfort to cheer you.

It is
The traveler's map.
The pilgrim's staff.
The pilot's compass.
The soldier's sword.
The Christian's charter.
A mine of wealth.
A paradise of glory.
A river of pleasure.

Its doctrines are holy.
Its precepts are binding.
Its histories are true.
Its decisions are immutable.
Christ is its grand subject.
Our good its design.
The glory of God its end.

Read it to be wise.
Believe it to be safe.
Practice it to be holy.

Read it slowly, frequently, prayerfully.

It should
Fill the memory.
Rule the heart.
Guide the feet.

It is given you in life,
Will be opened at the Judgment,
And be remembered for ever.

It involves the highest responsibility,
Will reward the greatest labor,
Condemn all who trifle with its sacred contents.

It is "the Word of our God which shall stand for ever." AUTHOR UNKNOWN

The longest telegraphic message ever dispatched was in May, 1881. It carried 180,000 words. It was printed in full that day by the *Chicago Times*, which gave space for the four gospels complete, the Acts and the Epistle to the Romans. "A triumph of publicity," was the verdict of the press. All this was done because the Revised Version of the New Testament in English was on sale that day. In New York 33,000 copies were sold within twenty-four hours.

———◆———

How to Defend the Bible

I am the Bible.
I am God's wonderful library.
I am always — and above all — the Truth.
To the weary pilgrim, I am a good strong Staff.
To the one who sits in black gloom, I am the glorious Light.
To those who stoop beneath heavy burdens, I am sweet Rest.
To him who has lost his way, I am a safe Guide.
To those who have been hurt by sin, I am healing Balm.
To the discouraged, I whisper a glad message of Hope.
To those who are distressed by the storms of life, I am an Anchor, sure and steadfast.
To those who suffer in lonely solitude, I am as a cool, soft Hand resting upon a fevered brow.
Oh, child of man, to best defend me, just *use me!*   Selected

———◆———

The Bible

Century follows century — there it stands.
Empires rise and fall and are forgotten — there it stands.
Dynasty succeeds dynasty — there it stands.
Kings are crowned and uncrowned — there it stands.
Despised and torn to pieces — there it stands.

Storms of hate swirl about it — there it stands.
Atheists rail against it — there it stands.
Profane, prayerless punsters caricature it — there it stands.
Unbelief abandons it — there it stands.
Thunderbolts of wrath smite it — there it stands.
The flames are kindled about it — there it stands. *Selected*

———◆———

The Bible is one of the solid facts of Christianity.

What it is, is not affected by what men think of it.

Changing opinions about the Bible do not change the Bible.

Whatever the Bible was, the Bible is.
And what it is, it has always been.
It is not men's thoughts about the Bible that judge it.

It is the Bible which judges men and their thoughts.

It has nothing to fear but ignorance and neglect.

And the church need have no other fear on its account.

The Bible will take care of itself if . . . *the church will distribute it and get it read.* ROBERT E. SPEER

———◆———

Yet It Lives

Generation follows generation — yet it lives.
Nations rise and fall — yet it lives.
Kings, dictators, presidents come and go — yet it lives.
Hated, despised, cursed — yet it lives.
Doubted, suspected, criticized — yet it lives.
Condemned by atheists — yet it lives.
Scoffed at by scorners — yet it lives.
Exaggerated by fanatics — yet it lives.
Misconstrued and misstated — yet it lives.
Ranted and raved about — yet it lives.
Its inspiration denied — yet it lives.

Yet it lives — as a lamp to our feet.
Yet it lives — as a light to our path.
Yet it lives — as the gate to heaven.
Yet it lives — as a standard for childhood.
Yet it lives — as a guide for youth.
Yet it lives — as an inspiration for the matured.
Yet it lives — as a comfort for the aged.
Yet it lives — as food for the hungry.
Yet it lives — as water for the thirsty.
Yet it lives — as rest for the weary.
Yet it lives — as light for the heathen.
Yet it lives — as salvation for the sinner.
Yet it lives — as grace for the Christian.

To know it is to love it.
To love it is to accept it.
To accept it means life eternal.
AUTHOR UNKNOWN, *from Gideon Magazine*

———◆———

The Ten Commandments in Rhyme

1. Thou no gods shalt have but me.
2. Before no idol bend the knee.
3. Take not the name of God in vain.
4. Dare not the Sabbath day profane.
5. Give to thy parents honor due.
6. Take heed that thou no murder do.
7. Abstain from words and deeds unclean.
8. Steal not, for thou by God art seen.
9. Tell not a willful lie, nor love it.
10. What is thy neighbor's do not covet.
AUTHOR UNKNOWN

———◆———

The Message of the Bible

The Bible is concerned only incidentally with the history of Israel or a system of ethics. The Bible is primarily concerned with the story of redemption of God as it is in Jesus Christ. If you read the Scriptures and miss the story of salvation, you have missed its message and meaning. There have been those who have gone through the Bible and traced the story of Jesus:

In Genesis He is the Seed of the Woman.
In Exodus He is the Passover Lamb.
In Leviticus He is the Atoning Sacrifice.
In Numbers He is the Smitten Rock.
In Deuteronomy He is the Prophet.

33

In Joshua He is the Captain of the Lord's hosts.

In Judges He is the Deliverer.

In Ruth He is the Heavenly Kinsman.

In the six books of Kings He is the Promised King.

In Nehemiah He is the Restorer of the nation.

In Esther He is the Advocate.

In Job He is my Redeemer.

In Psalms He is my All and in All.

In Proverbs He is my Pattern.

In Ecclesiastes He is my Goal.

In the Song of Solomon He is my Satisfier.

In the prophets He is the Coming Prince of Peace.

In the Gospels He is Christ coming to seek and to save.

In Acts He is Christ risen.

In the Epistles He is Christ at the Father's right hand.

In the Revelation He is Christ returning and reigning.　　BILLY GRAHAM

———◆———

How to Read the Bible

Read the Bible, not as a newspaper, but as a home letter.

If a cluster of heavenly fruit hangs within reach, gather it.

If a promise lies upon the page as a blank check, cash it.

If a prayer is recorded, appropriate it, and launch it as a feathered arrow from the bow of your desire.

If an example of holiness gleams before you, ask God to do as much for you.

If the truth is revealed in all its intrinsic splendor, entreat that its brilliance may ever irradiate the hemisphere of your life.　　F. B. MEYER

———◆———

Read Your Bible

1. Slowly, with mind alert.
2. Carefully and with prayer.
3. Expectantly and with anticipation.
4. In a spirit of enjoyment.
5. Eager to respond inwardly.
6. Seeking a personal message.
7. Repeating aloud verses which strike fire.
8. Keeping a definite time each day for reading.
9. Copying out a key verse to carry with you for re-reading through the day.　　*Selected*

———◆———

How to Make the Best Use of the Bible

Read it *through.*
Pray it *in.*
Work it *out.*
Note it *down.*
Pass it *on.*　　PICKERING

———◆———

The Whole Bible Contains

The mind of God.
　The state of man.
　　The doom of sinners.
　　　The happiness of believers.
Its doctrines are holy.
　Its precepts are binding.
　　Its histories are true.
　　　Its decisions are immutable.

———◆———

My Bible and I

We've traveled together, my Bible and I,
Through all kinds of weather, with smile or with sigh!
In sorrow or sunshine, in tempest or calm!
Thy friendship unchanging, my lamp and my psalm.

We've traveled together, my Bible and I,
When life had grown weary and death e'en was nigh!
But all through the darkness of mist or of wrong,
I found there a solace, a prayer and a song.

So now who shall part us, my Bible and I?
Shall isms or schisms or "new lights" who try?
Shall shadow or substance or stone for good bread
Supplant thy sound wisdom, give folly instead?

Oh, no, my dear Bible, exponent of
light!
Thou sword of the Spirit, put error to
flight!
And still through life's journey, until
my last sigh,
We'll travel together, my Bible and I.
Selected

———◆———

Believe it or not: Edgar G. Watts of
North Hollywood, California, age 84,
read the Bible from cover to cover 161
times. He had the use of only one eye
for 55 years.

———◆———

My Bible

Though the cover is worn,
And the pages are torn,
   And though places bear traces of
   tears,
Yet more precious than gold
Is the Book worn and old,
   That can shatter and scatter my fears.

When I prayerfully look
In the precious old Book,
   As my eyes scan the pages I see
Many tokens of love
From the Father above,
   Who is nearest and dearest to me.

This old Book is my guide,
'Tis a friend by my side,
   It will lighten and brighten my way;
And each promise I find
Soothes and gladdens my mind
   As I read it and heed it today.
AUTHOR UNKNOWN

———◆———

Read It Through

I supposed I knew my Bible,
   Reading piecemeal, hit or miss,
Now a bit of John or Matthew,
   Now a snatch of Genesis;
Certain chapters of Isaiah,
   Certain Psalms (the twenty-third),
Twelfth of Romans, first of Proverbs,
   Yes, I thought I knew the Word.
But I found a thorough reading
   Was a different thing to do,
And the way was unfamiliar
   When I read the Bible through.

You who like to play at Bible,
   Dip and dabble here and there,
Just before you kneel a-weary,
   And yawn out a hurried prayer;
You who treat the Crown of Writing
   As you treat no other book —
Just a paragraph disjointed,
   Just a crude, impatient look —
Try a worthier procedure,
   Try a broad and steady view —
You will kneel in very rapture
   When you read the Bible through.
AMOS R. WELLS

———◆———

My Bible

My Bible is not true in spots,
   But true in every sense;
True in its tittles and its jots,
   True in each verb and tense;
True when it speaks of heaven's joy,
   True when it warns of hell;
Its truth is gold without alloy —
   Its source a Springing Well.
KEITH BROOKS

———◆———

My Neighbor's Bible

I am my neighbor's Bible
   He reads me when we meet;
Today he reads me in my home —
   Tomorrow, in the street.
He may be a relative or friend,
   Or slight acquaintance be;
He may not even know my name,
   Yet he is reading me.
And pray, who is this neighbor,
   Who reads me day by day,
To learn if I am living right,
   And walking as I pray?

Oh, he is with me always,
   To criticize or blame;
So worldly wise in his own eyes,
   And "Sinner" is his name.
Dear Christian friends and brothers,
   If we could only know
How faithfully the world records
   Just what we say and do;
Oh, we would write our record plain,
   And come in time to see
Our worldly neighbor won to Christ
   While reading you and me.
The Herald of Light

The Bible

The charter of all true liberty.
The forerunner of civilization.
The moulder of institutions and governments.
The fashioner of law.
The secret of national progress.
The guide of history.
The ornament and mainspring of literature.
The friend of science.
The inspiration of philosophies.
The textbook of ethics.
The light of intellect.
The answer to the deepest human heart hungerings.
The soul of all strong heart life.
The illuminator of darkness.
The foe of superstition.
The enemy of oppression.
The uprooter of sin.
The regulator of all high and worthy standards.
The comfort in sorrow.
The strength in weakness.
The pathway in perplexity.
The escape from temptation.
The steadier in the day of power.
The embodiment of all lofty ideals.
The begetter of life.
The promise of the future.
The star of death's night.
The revealer of God.
The guide and hope and inspiration of man.   BISHOP ANDERSON

------◆------

What Great Men Have Said about the Bible

MATTHEW ARNOLD — To the Bible men will return because they cannot do without it. The true God is and must be preeminently the God of the Bible, the eternal who makes for righteousness from whom Jesus came forth, and whose spirit governs the course of humanity.

NAPOLEON BONAPARTE—The Bible contains a complete series of facts and of historical men, to explain time and eternity, such as no other religion has to offer . . . What happiness that Book procures for those who believe it! What marvels those admire there who reflect upon it!

WILLIAM E. GLADSTONE — There is but one question of the hour: how to bring the truths of God's Word into vital contact with the minds and hearts of all classes of people.

GOETHE — (The universal and most highly cultivated of poets) I consider the Gospels to be thoroughly genuine; for in them there is the effective reflection of a sublimity which emanated from the Person of Christ; and this is as Divine as ever the Divine appeared on earth.

ULYSSES S. GRANT — Hold fast to the Bible as the sheet anchor of your liberties; write its precepts on your heart and practice them in your lives. To the influence of this Book we are indebted for the progress made, and to this we must look as our guide in the future.

HORACE GREELEY — It is impossible to mentally or socially enslave a Bible-reading people.

PATRICK HENRY — This is a Book worth all other books which were ever printed.

HERBERT HOOVER — We are indebted to the Book of books for our ideals and institutions. Their preservation rests in adhering to its principles.

The study of the Bible is a rich post-graduate course in the richest library of human experience.

J. EDGAR HOOVER — Inspiration has been the keynote of America's phenomenal growth. Inspiration has been the backbone of America's greatness. Inspiration has been the difference between defeat and victory in America's wars. And this inspiration has come from faith in God, faith in the teachings of the Sermon on the Mount, and faith in the belief that the Holy Bible is the inspired Word of God.

Reading the Holy Bible within the family circle is more important today than ever before. It draws the family together into a more closely knit unit. It gives each member a faith to live by.

As a small boy I sat at my mother's knee while she read the Bible to me and explained the meaning with the stories as we went along. It served to make the bond of faith between us much stronger. Then, there were those wonderful nights when my father would gather the family around him and read aloud verses from the Bible. This led to family discussions which were interesting, lively and informative. These wonderful sessions left me with an imprint of the power of faith and the power of prayer which has sustained me in trying moments throughout my entire life.

ANDREW JACKSON — The Bible is the rock on which our republic rests.

THOMAS JEFFERSON — The Bible is the cornerstone of liberty.

SIR WILLIAM JONES—The Bible contains more true sensibility, more exquisite beauty, more pure morality, more important history, and finer strains of poetry and eloquence, than can be collected from all other books in whatever age or language they may be written.

ROBERT E. LEE — The Bible is a book in comparison with which all others are of minor importance. In all my perplexities and distress the Bible never failed to give me light and strength.

ABRAHAM LINCOLN — In regard to the great Book, I have only to say that it is the best gift which God has given to man.

WILLIAM MCKINLEY — The more profoundly we study this wonderful Book and the more closely we observe its divine precepts, the better citizens we will become and the higher will be the destiny of our nation.

WILLIAM LYON PHELPS (Called the most beloved professor in America — of Yale University) — I thoroughly believe in university education for both men and women, but I believe a knowledge of the Bible without a college course is more valuable than a college course without the Bible.

JEAN JACQUES ROUSSEAU — The majesty of the Scriptures strikes me with admiration, as the purity of the Gospel has its influence on my heart. Pursue the works of our philosophers with all their pomp of diction, how mean, how contemptible are they, compared with the Scriptures.

GEORGE WASHINGTON — It is impossible rightly to govern the world without God and the Bible.

DANIEL WEBSTER — There is no solid basis for civilization but in the Word of God.

If we abide by the principles taught in the Bible, our country will go on prospering and to prosper.

I make it a practice to read the Bible through once every year.

WOODROW WILSON — A man has deprived himself of the best there is in the world who has deprived himself of this, a knowledge of the Bible.

When you have read the Bible, you will know that it is the Word of God, because you will have found it the key to your own heart, your own happiness, and your own duty.

————◆————

The Christian who is careless in Bible reading is careless in Christian living.
MAX REICH

————◆————

I have read many books, but the Bible reads me.

————◆————

The reason people are down on the Bible is that they're not up on the Bible.
WILLIAM W. AYER

————◆————

The Bible needs less defense and more practice.

————◆————

God's mirror reveals but never cleanses.

The Bible does not need to be rewritten, but reread.

———◆———

For top performance we must refuel daily from the Word.

———◆———

The Bible is an international manifesto.

———◆———

The Ten Commandments and the multiplication table are in no danger of being outmoded.

———◆———

The Bible sure throws a lot of light on the Bible commentaries.   BARNHOUSE

———◆———

Study the Bible to be wise; believe it to be safe; practice it to be holy.

———◆———

Be not miserable about what may happen tomorrow. The same everlasting Father, who cares for you today, will care for you tomorrow and every day. Either He will shield you from suffering or He will give you unfailing strength to bear it.   FRANCIS DE SALES

———◆———

Don't think the Bible is dry inside because it is dusty on the outside.

———◆———

Slip of the tongue by the pastor: "I am well-reversed in the Scriptures."

———◆———

England has two books, the Bible and Shakespeare. England made Shakespeare but the Bible made England.
VICTOR HUGO

———◆———

A young man, after hearing a discussion as to various versions of the Bible, declared, "I prefer my mother's version to any other. She translated it into the language of daily life."

———◆———

A skeptic in London recently said, in speaking of the Bible, that it was quite impossible in these days to believe in any book whose author was unknown. A Christian asked him if the compiler of the multiplication table was known. "No," he answered.

"Then, of course, you do not believe in it?"

"Oh, yes, I believe in it because it works well," replied the skeptic.

"So does the Bible," was the rejoinder, and the skeptic had no answer to make.

———◆———

A lady was mailing a gift of a Bible to a relative. The postal clerk examined the heavy package and inquired if it contained anything breakable. "Nothing," the lady told him, "but the Ten Commandments."

———◆———

When a rich Chinese man came home from a visit to England, he proudly showed his friends a powerful microscope he had bought. But one day he looked at a tiny bit of his dinner rice under the microscope.

Horrors! He saw that tiny living creatures actually crawled all over it. And part of his religion was to eat no animal life.

What did he do? He loved rice. So he simply smashed the microscope!

Foolish, you say? Yes, but no more foolish than the person who rejects the Bible when he sees some things the Bible reveals. "For the word of God . . . is a discerner of the thoughts and intents of the heart" (Hebrews 4:12).   *Sunday School Journal*

———◆———

An infidel said, "There is one thing that mars all the pleasures of my life."

"Indeed!" replied his friend. "What is that?"

He answered, "I am afraid the Bible is true. If I could know for certain that death is an eternal sleep, I should be happy; my joy would be complete! But here is the thorn that stings me. This is the word that pierces my very soul — if the Bible is true, I am lost forever."

———◆———

Some years ago in Italy a missionary lady offered a Bible to a stonemason who was building a wall. He did not want the Bible but finally accepted it. When the lady left the man removed a stone from the wall and placed the Bible in a hollow space.

He then continued building the wall around it, laughing to think how he had fooled her. Not many years after this there was an earthquake which caused many buildings and walls to fall. One dangerous wall was still standing and the workmen were tapping it to make it fall. "Perhaps there is a treasure there," one worker said as he moved part of the stones. There, in the hollow place where the mason had placed the Bible several years before, the workman found the "treasure." He took it home and read it, and was led to love it and to serve God. Indeed he had found a great treasure.

———◆———

We come back laden from our quest
To find that all the sages said
Is in the Book our Mothers read.
WHITTIER

———◆———

Today man sees all his hopes and aspirations crumbling before him. He is perplexed and knows not whither he is drifting. But he must realize that the Bible is his refuge, and the rallying point for all humanity. It is here man will find the solution of his present difficulties and guidance for his future action, and unless he accepts with clear conscience the Bible and its great message, he cannot hope for salvation. For my part, I glory in the Bible.
HAILE SELASSIE, Emperor of Ethiopia

———◆———

Bible (and Children)

Johnny volunteered to review the story of Noah and the Ark for the Sunday school class. "All the animals went into Noah's ark two by two," he said, "except the worms they went in the apples."

———◆———

"What were the names of Noah's three sons, Tommy?" asked his Sunday school teacher.

"I can't remember them exactly," Tommy replied, "but I think one was called Bacon."

"What Bible story did you hear in Sunday school today?" a mother asked Junior.

"Oh, we heard the loafing story," Junior replied.

"Well, that's one I never heard," said the mother. "Tell me about it."

So, Junior told her: "Somebody loafs and fishes."

———◆———

Child: "Mother, what number is this hair I pulled out?"

Mother: "Child, I don't know."

Child: "Well, the Bible says that the hairs of your head are all numbered."
Sunday School Journal

———◆———

The Sunday school teacher asked a little girl if she knew who Matthew was. The answer was no. The teacher then asked if she knew who John was. Again the answer was "no." Finally the teacher asked if she knew who Peter was.

She answered: "I think he was a rabbit."

———◆———

Her Sunday school teacher asked a ten-year-old how Solomon happened to be so wise. "Because," she answered, after due meditation, "he had so many wives to advise him."

———◆———

Charles was telling his friend John about the mystery writing he had learned about in Sunday school.

"It was in the story of Daniel," Charles said. "And a finger wrote some words on the wall of the palace. The king must not have behaved in church as the message was for him."

"What was the message?" asked John.

Happily Charles told him: "Meany, meany, tickle the parson!"

———◆———

One day the Sunday school teacher gave the children a written review of the lesson. Subject: Noah. Laboriously Alfred wrote, but only briefly. He handed in his paper and the teacher read his paper. "You say that Noah went fishing while he was in the ark," commented the teacher, "but gave up after only five minutes. Why did he do that, Alfred?"

"Because," came the prompt reply, "Noah didn't have but two worms."

———◆———

"Joseph was the boy who never had a cold neck," the boy told his mother when she quizzed him about the Sunday school lesson.

"How do you know that?" mother asked.

"Because," replied the lad, "Joseph had a coat of many collars."

———◆———

At a midnight watch service the pastor was conducting a Bible quiz. He asked the question, "Who are the three Johns in the Scriptures?"

One eager ten-year-old volunteered the answer: "First, Second and Third John."

———◆———

During a review one Sunday the teacher asked if the class knew who the twin boys were in the Bible.

"That's easy," said Charles. "First and Second Samuel."

———◆———

After the teacher had told her class they could draw a picture of the Bible story she had told them, she went around to see what the children had done. She noticed that little Sherry hadn't drawn a Bible picture at all, so asked the child to tell the class about her picture.

"This is a car. The man in the front seat is God. The people in the back seat are Adam and Eve. God is driving them out of the Garden of Eden."

———◆———

On another occasion when the teacher let the children "draw" the Bible story they had heard, one little boy drew the picture of an airplane with a pilot in the front seat. The passengers were a man, woman and baby. When asked to tell about his picture, he said:

"This is Pontius the pilot taking Mary and Joseph and Baby Jesus on a flight out of Egypt."

Blessings

To get the blessing we must do the work.

———◆———

Don't count your blessings without praising the Blesser.

———◆———

The private and personal blessings we enjoy, the blessings of immunity, safeguard, liberty, and integrity, deserve the thanksgiving of a whole life.
JEREMY TAYLOR

———◆———

Not only count your blessings, but consider their source. *Eternity*

———◆———

Blood

His blood for my fault;
His robe for my blame.

———◆———

Moody said: "The blood alone makes us safe; the Word alone makes us sure."

———◆———

Boast, Brag, Bluff

Self-brag is half scandal.

———◆———

The man who bragged that he was self-made loved to worship his creator.

———◆———

Nothing in the world is more haughty than a man of moderate capacity when once raised to power. WESSENBURG

———◆———

A show-off never fails to be shown up in a show down.

———◆———

Folks with a lot of brass are seldom polished. PHILIP W. BEMIS

———◆———

A bully's greatest fall is when he stumbles over his own bluff.

———◆———

Great talkers are little doers.
FRANKLIN

———◆———

When a youth was giving himself airs in the theatre and saying, "I am wise for I have talked with many wise men," Epictetus replied, "I too have conversed with many rich men, yet I am not rich."

40

Any party which takes credit for the rain must not be surprised if its opponents blame it for the drought.

DWIGHT W. MORROW

————♦————

He that knows, and knows that he knows, doesn't have to blow and blow.

————♦————

The man who has a right to boast doesn't have to.

————♦————

A Boston salesman visited Texas and heard one particular Texan boasting about heroes of the Alamo who, almost alone, held off whole armies.

"I don't think you ever had anyone so brave around Boston," challenged the Texan.

"Did you ever hear of Paul Revere?" asked the Bostonian.

"Paul Revere?" said the Texan. "Isn't that the guy who ran for help?"

————♦————

Books

Never lend books — no one ever returns them. The only books I have in my library are those people have lent me.

ANATOLE FRANCE

————♦————

Bad books are fountains of vice.

————♦————

Classic: A book which people praise and don't read.

MARK TWAIN

————♦————

Use books as bees use flowers.

————♦————

They borrow books they will not buy.
They have no ethics or religions;
I wish some kind Burbankian guy
Could cross my books with homing
pigeons.

CAROLYN WELLS

————♦————

Who Gives a Book

He who gives a man a book
Gives that man a sweeping look
Through its pages
Down the ages;

Gives that man a ship to sail
Where the far adventures hail
Down the sea
Of destiny!

Gives that man a vision wide
As the skies where stars abide,
Anchored in
The love of him;

Gives that man great dreams to dream,
Sun-lit ways that glint and gleam,
Where the sages
Tramp the ages.

WILLIAM L. STIDGER

————♦————

To a friend who visited Mark Twain, the great man explained the clutter of books on the floor and chairs, "You see, I can't borrow shelves, too."

————♦————

Some books leave us free and some books make us free.

EMERSON

————♦————

Books are but waste paper, unless we spend in action the wisdom we get from thought.

BULIVER

————♦————

If religious books are not widely circulated among the masses in this country and the people do not become religious, I do not know what is to become of us as a nation. And the thought is one to cause solemn reflection on the part of every patriot and Christian. If the truth be not diffused, error will be; if God and His Word are not known and received, the devil and his works will gain the ascendancy; if the evangelical volume does not reach every hamlet, the pages of corrupt and licentious literature will.

DANIEL WEBSTER

————♦————

Books and study are merely the steps of the ladder by which one climbs to the summit; as soon as a step has been advanced, he leaves it behind. The majority of mankind, however, who study to fill their memory with facts, do not use the steps of the ladder to mount upward, but take them off and lay them on their shoulders in order that they may take them along, delighting in the weight of the burden they are carrying. They ever remain below because they carry what should carry them.

SCHOPENHAUER

41

A rare volume is a borrowed book that comes back.

————◆————

Books

Books! Books! Books!
And we thank Thee, God
For the gift of them;
And the lift of them;
  For the gleam in them
  And the dream in them;
For the things they teach
And the souls they reach!
  For the maze of them
  And the blaze of them;
For the ways they open to us
And the rays that they shoot through us.

Books! Books! Books!
And we thank Thee, God
For the light in them;
For the might in them;
  For the urge in them;
  And the surge in them;
For the souls they wake
And the paths they break;
  For the gong in them
  And the song in them;
For the throngs of folks they bring to us
And the songs of hope they sing to us!
WILLIAM L. STIDGER

————◆————

Books are friendly things. Do not count as wasted the hours spent in selecting them. JOHNSON

————◆————

Don't sell your books and keep your diplomas. Sell your diplomas — if you can get anyone to buy them — and keep your books. WALTER PITKIN

————◆————

Boss

The fellow who doesn't need a boss is often the one selected to be one.
Christlife Magazine

————◆————

The boss was pointing out to his secretary several errors she had made during the day, when she interrupted with, "Mr. Jones, it's two minutes past five and you're annoying me on my own time."

Men who complain that the boss is dumb would be out of a job if he were any smarter.

————◆————

If the boss practiced what he preaches, he'd work himself to death.

————◆————

The man who delegates authority must forego the luxury of blowing his top.

————◆————

Boy, Boys

The way to keep a boy out of hot water is to put soap in it.

————◆————

Sons are the anchors of a mother's life. SOPHOCLES

————◆————

Fishing Boy

A little lean boy with a freckled nose
And a fishing pole and two bandaged toes
With his tousled hair looking like ripened wheat
"Tippy-toed" through the back door on kitten-quick feet
And made a beeline for the cookie jar,
In each of his blue eyes a little blue star,
For he knew so exactly what waited for him
When he poked crawfish fingers across the jar's rim.
Round cookies crusted with raisins and spice
Were his favorite kind, and Grandma was nice,
For she left the jar filled for a boy going fishing
And low on the shelf so he needn't stand wishing! ANABEL ARMOUR

————◆————

Jimmy

He is just ten years old.
He is made up of the following ingredients:
  Noise, energy, imagination, curiosity and hunger.
He is the "cute little fellow down the street,"

"That spoiled imp next door," or "My son,"
Depending upon who you are.
He is something to be kept, fed, clothed,
    healthy, happy and out of trouble.
BUT . . .
He is something else, too.
He is tomorrow.
He is the future we are working for:
He is part of the world's most important generation.
Our generation must love them and win them.
His generation will determine whether it was worth doing.
He is one of the most important people in history.
SO . . .
Anyone who influences his life is also a mighty important person.
P.A.A.S News

Only a Boy

His trousers are torn, rolled up to the knee;
A hole in his shirt which he caught on a tree;
But I see a soul for whom Jesus has died,
Clothed in His righteousness, pressed to His side.

I see not labor and hours of prayer
Spent for that freckled-faced naughty boy there,
But I see a Saviour with arms open wide,
Waiting in heaven to take him inside.

I see not freckles, but man fully grown,
A heart filled with God's Word I've carefully sown,
A life speaking forth for the Saviour each day,
O Lord, for this boy I most earnestly pray.

I see not his mischief, but energy bent,
Put to the task where the Lord wants it spent;
O God, make this lively, mischievous boy
A power for Thee, to Thy heart great joy.
MILDRED MORNINGSTAR

The Christian parents' problem is to keep the life of the boy normal — and yet steer him into Christian channels.
Sunday School Journal

A Boy

Nobody knows what a boy is worth,
    A boy at his work or play,
A boy who whistles around the place,
    Or laughs in an artless way.

Nobody knows what a boy is worth,
    And the world must wait and see,
For every man in an honored place,
    Is a boy that used to be.

Nobody knows what a boy is worth,
    A boy with his face aglow,
For hid in his heart there are secrets deep
    Not even the wisest know.

Nobody knows what a boy is worth,
    A boy with his bare, white feet;
So have a smile and a kindly word,
    For every boy you meet.
AUTHOR UNKNOWN

Build

Man builds for a century; the Christian builds for eternity.

Too low they build who build beneath the stars. EDWARD YOUNG

Building a Temple

A builder builded a temple,
He wrought it with grace and skill:
Pillars and groins and arches
All fashioned to work his will.
Men said, as they saw its beauty,
"It shall never know decay,
Great is thy skill, O builder,
Thy fame shall endure for aye."

A teacher builded a temple
With loving and infinite care,
Planning each arch with patience,
Laying each stone with prayer.
None praised her unceasing efforts,
None knew of her wondrous plan;
For the temple the teacher builded
Was unseen by the eyes of men.

Gone is the builder's temple,
Crumbled into the dust;
Low lies each stately pillar,
Food for consuming rust.
But the temple the teacher builded
Will last while the ages roll,
For that beautiful unseen temple
Is the child's immortal soul.

THOMAS CURTIS CLARK

Business

A lot of people never get interested in a thing until they find it is none of their business.

———

A shady business never yields a sunny life.

———

Drive thy business, or it will drive thee.

BENJAMIN FRANKLIN

———

Business circles should be on the square.

———

An institution is the lengthened shadow of an individual.

———

Your chief competition is yourself.

———

A scissors grinder is the only person whose business is good when things are dull.

———

The public business of the nation is the private business of every citizen.

———

The things most people want to know about are usually none of their business.

GEORGE BERNARD SHAW

———

The man who minds his own business usually has a good one.

———

Sign on the window of a men's clothing store that went bankrupt after three months in business: "Opened by Mistake."

———

Running a business without advertising is the same thing as winking at a girl in the dark. You know what you're doing, but she doesn't.

Some years ago a harness dealer had a customer who picked out a fancy saddle for his pony and said, "I'll take it. Please charge it."

After the customer had left, the proprietor asked his bookkeeper to charge the customer with the purchase.

"To whom?" asked the bookkeeper.

"Don't *you* know him?" replied the proprietor. "No," answered the bookkeeper.

"Well," said the proprietor, "only twelve men have ponies in town — send them all a bill." The bookkeeper did. Three of them paid.

WILLIAM WACHER, *The Rotarian*

———

Business Daffynitions

To expedite: this means to confound confusion with commotion.

Under consideration: This means never heard of it.

Reliable source: the guy you just met.

Informed source: the guy who told the guy you just met.

Unimpeachable source: the guy who started the rumor originally.

We are making a survey: we need more time to think of an answer.

Will advise, in due course: if we figure it out, we'll let you know.

AUTHOR UNKNOWN

———

Busy

Some of the busiest people in the world are only picking up the beans they spilled.

———

It isn't enough just to be busy. What are you busy about?

———

The surest way to get a job done is to give it to a busy man. He'll have his secretary do it.

———

Keep busy! It's the cheapest kind of medicine there is on this earth, and one of the best. Don't allow yourself to become upset by the small things that come your way; life is too short to be little! Think and act cheerfully, and you will feel cheerful. Cooperate with the inevitable.

A man never gets too busy to attend his own funeral.

———◆———

A man who is too busy for God is too busy.

———◆———

It is very significant that in every recorded instance the Apostles were busy at their daily work when the Master called them.

Peter and Andrew were fishing;

James and John were mending their nets;

Matthew was sitting at the receipt of custom.

God never visits an idle or unserviceable life.   DAVID SMITH

———◆———

Rush hour: That hour during which traffic is almost at a standstill.

If We Are . . .

too busy to read a book that promises to widen our horizons;

too busy to keep our friendships in good repair;

too busy to maintain a consistent devotional life;

too busy to keep warm, vital loves of our fireside burning;

too busy to conserve our health in the interest of our highest efficiency;

too busy to cultivate the sense of a personal acquaintance with God;

too busy to spend one hour during the week in worship;

too busy to expose ourselves each day to beauty;

too busy to cultivate souls . . .

Then we are indeed *too busy.*

Selected

C

Capital

Capital is what you and I have saved out of yesterday's wages.

———◆———

The strongest objection socialists and communists have against capital is that they don't have any.

Caution

It is better to build a fence around the top of the precipice before the child goes over than it is to build a hospital at the bottom of it.

GYPSY SMITH

———◆———

Sign on a Texas farm fence: Hunters! Don't shoot anything that doesn't move. It may be my hired man.

———◆———

In a discreet man's mouth a public thing is private.   BENJAMIN FRANKLIN

———◆———

To a quick question, give a slow answer.   *Italian Proverb*

It is better to be careful a thousand times than killed once.

———◆———

Watch Your Can'ts and Can's

If you would have some worthwhile plans,
You've got to watch your "can'ts" and "can's."
You can't aim low and then rise high;
You can't succeed if you don't try;
You can't go wrong and come out right;
You can't love sin and walk in light;
You can't throw time and means away
And live sublime from day to day.

You can be great if you'll be good
And do God's will as all men should.
You can ascend life's upward road,
Although you bear a heavy load;
You can be honest, truthful, clean,
By turning from the low and mean;
You can uplift the souls of men
By words and deed, or by your pen.

CAUTION — CHARACTER

So, watch your "can'ts" and watch your
"can's"
And watch your walks and watch your
stands,
And watch the way you talk and act
And do not take the false for fact;
And watch indeed the way you take,
And watch the things that mar or make;
For life is great to every man
Who lives to do the best he can.
The Wesleyan Youth

———♦———

You will be careful,
If you are wise,
How you touch men's religion,
Or credit, or eyes.
BENJAMIN FRANKLIN

Challenge

Be thankful if you have a job a little
harder than you like. A razor cannot
be sharpened on a piece of velvet.

———♦———

Unless we can and do constantly
seek and find ways and means to do
a better job; unless we accept the challenge of the changing times; we have
no right to survive and we shall not
survive. CHESTER O. FISCHER

———♦———

Tackle more than you can do —
Then do it!
Bite off more than you can chew —
Then chew it!
Hitch your wagon to a star,
Keep your seat, and there you are!
AUTHOR UNKNOWN

———♦———

Don't try to think why you can't.
Think how you can.

———♦———

It can't be done,
It never has been done;
Therefore I will do it.

———♦———

Change

We are never two minutes the same,
and still we never change one bit from
what we are. ANATOLE FRANCE

46

Character

Your character is what God knows
you to be. Your reputation is what
men think you are. DR. BOB JONES, SR.

———♦———

Character is what you are in the
dark. DWIGHT L. MOODY

———♦———

Strong foundations are necessary for
a towering structure.

———♦———

You can sell out character but you
can't purchase it.

———♦———

More knowledge may be gained of
a man's real character by a short conversation with one of his servants than
from a formal and studied narrative,
begun with his pedigree and ended
with his funeral. SAMUEL JOHNSON

———♦———

What you are tomorrow, you are
becoming today.

———♦———

To be worth anything, character
must be capable of standing firm upon
its feet in the world of daily work,
temptation and trial; and able to bear
the wear and tear of actual life. Clois-
tered virtues do not count for much.
SAMUEL SMILES

———♦———

Hardship makes character.

———♦———

Thought creates character.
ANNE BESANT

———♦———

You don't make your character in a
crisis; you exhibit it.
OREN ARNOLD, *Presbyterian Life*

———♦———

If men speak ill of you, live so that
no one will believe them.

———♦———

You are what you have been becoming.

———♦———

Much may be known of a man's
character by what excites his laughter.
GOETHE

———♦———

When the ceiling of a man's life is
lower than the heavens, he needs more
room for character expansion.

Every man has in himself a continent of undiscovered character. Happy is he who acts the Columbus to his own soul.   SIR J. STEVENS

The test of your character is what you would do if you knew no one would ever know.   DR. BOB JONES, SR.

Character is made by many acts; it may be lost by a single one.

What thou art in the sight of God, that thou truly art.   THOMAS A' KEMPIS

You can borrow brains, but you cannot borrow character.
DR. BOB JONES, SR.

Character is like a tree and reputation like its shadow. The shadow is what we think of it: the tree is the real thing.   ABRAHAM LINCOLN

What we like determines what we are, and is the sign of what we are; and to teach taste is inevitably to form character.   JOHN RUSKIN

The strength of a nation lies in the character of its citizens.

It is easier and better to build boys than to repair men.

Character is made by what you stand for; reputation by what you fall for.
ROBERT QUILLEN

A man's strength of character may be measured by his ability to control his temper, instead of letting his temper control him.   J. SHERMAN WALLACE

Every human being is intended to have a character of his own; to be what no other is, and to do what no other can do.   WILLIAM ELLERY CHANNING

Charity

Music Lover: "I'm sorry that other engagements prevent my attending your charity concert, but I shall be with you in spirit."

Solicitor: "That's fine! Where would you like your spirit to sit? We have tickets for a half dollar, a dollar, and two dollars."

Let us grant that charity begins at home, but only selfishness will stay there.

Charity gives itself rich; covetousness hoards itself poor.   German Proverb

He who has conferred a kindness should be silent, he who has received one should speak of it.   SENECA

It is not enough to help the feeble up, but to support him after.
SHAKESPEARE

A philanthropist is one who gives it away when he should be giving it back.

Charm

Charm, which means the power to effect work without employing brute force, is indispensable to women. Charm is a woman's strength just as strength is a man's charm.   HAVELOCK ELLIS

Charm is the ability to make someone else think that both of you are pretty wonderful.

Cheer, Cheerful, Cheerfulness

I shall feel until I die a desire to increase the stock of harmless cheerfulness.   CHARLES DICKENS

Wondrous is the strength of cheerfulness, and its power of endurance — the cheerful man will do more in the same time, will do it better, will persevere in it longer, than the sad or sullen.   CARLYLE

The cheerful live longest in years and afterwards in our regards.

Cheerfulness is the window-cleaner of the mind.

What sunshine is to flowers, smiles are to humanity. They are but trifles, to be sure, but scattered along life's pathway, the good they do is inconceivable. ADDISON

Child, Childish, Childlike, Children

We should consider not so much what the child is today as what he may become tomorrow.

Today's unchurched child is tomorrow's criminal. J. EDGAR HOOVER

Train up a child in the way he should go and go that way yourself.

A child is your second chance.

A little child is the only true democrat. HARRIET BEECHER STOWE

A child that is loved has many names. *Hungarian Proverb*

Give me the children until they are seven and anyone may have them afterwards. XAVIER

People who handle other peoples' money are required to account for every cent. Are children less valuable?

Jesus put a child in the midst; many churches put him in the basement.

If you want a garden of good fruit, get the trees young.

If children grew up according to early indications, we would have nothing but geniuses. GOETHE

Kindly interest will do more to attract children than stately majesty. THEO. G. STELZER

If we paid no more attention to our plants than we have to our children, we would now be living in a jungle of weeds.

Our children are the only earthly possessions we can take with us to glory.

Child by child we build our nation. *Prize-winning Slogan*

The more children's fingerprints in a home, the fewer on police records.

The family next door went stork mad; they have eleven children.

Children are natural mimics — they act like their parents in spite of every attempt to teach them good manners.

While men believe in the possibilities of children being religious, they are largely failing to make them so, because they are offering them not a child's but a man's religion — men's forms of truth and men's forms of experience. PHILLIPS BROOKS

A boy is a noise with some dirt on it.

Are All the Children In?

I think oftimes as the night draws nigh
Of an old house on the hill,
Of a yard all wide and blossom-starred
Where the children played at will.
And when the night at last came down,
Hushing the merry din,
Mother would look around and ask,
"Are all the children in?"

'Tis many and many a year since then,
And the old house on the hill
No longer echoes to childish feet,
And the yard is still, so still.
But I see it all as the shadows creep,
And though many the years have been,
Even now, I can hear my mother ask,
"Are all the children in?"

I wonder if, when the shadows fall
On the last short, earthly day,
When we say goodbye to the world outside,
All tired with our childish play,
When we step out into that Other Land

Where mother so long has been,
Will we hear her ask, as we did of old,
"Are all the children in?"

And I wonder, too, what the Lord will
    say,
To us older children of His,
Have we cared for the lambs? Have we
    showed them the fold?
A privilege joyful it is.
And I wonder, too, what our answers
    will be,
When His loving questions begin:
"Have you heeded My voice? Have
    you told of My love?
Have you brought My children in?"

AUTHOR UNKNOWN; *last verse by*
MARION BISHOP BOWER

———♦———

Childhood is like a mirror which re-
flects in afterlife the images presented
to it.   SAMUEL SMILES

———♦———

Nothing is too good for the child.
            GOETHE

———♦———

Good manners require a great deal
of time, as does a wise treatment of
children.   EMERSON

———♦———

Children are poor men's riches.

———♦———

Let every father and mother realize
that when their child is three years of
age, they have done more than half
they will ever do for its character.
            HORACE BUSHNELL

———♦———

Young Things

Give me the bending of the frail and
    fragile stalk,
Give me the tending of the babe that
    learns to walk;
Give me the training of the slim and
    slender vine,
Give me the guiding of the colt that
    learns the line.
Give me the young things, and future
    years will show
All the good care brings, as they shall
    older grow.
LALIA MITCHELL THORNTON, *The Banner*

———♦———

There's nothing thirstier than a child
who has just gone to bed.

The kind of person your child is going to be, he is already becoming.
            Heart-to-Heart Program

———♦———

Those who educate children well
are more to be honored than they who
produce them; for these only gave
them life, those the art of living well.
            ARISTOTLE

———♦———

There's only one pretty child in the
world, and every mother has it.
            Cheshire Proverb

———♦———

Every child born into the world is a
new thought of God, an ever-fresh
and radiant possibility.
            KATE DOUGLAS WIGGIN

———♦———

It is said that the eighteenth century
discovered the man, the nineteenth
century discovered the woman, and the
twentieth century discovered the child.
Now that he is discovered, let's train
him!

———♦———

Recipe for Preserving Children

1 large grassy field
6 children
3 small dogs
A narrow strip of brook with pebbles
Flowers
A deep blue sky

Mix the children with the dogs and
empty into the field, stirring continuously. Sprinkle the field with the deep
blue sky and bake it in a hot sun.
When the children are well browned
they may be removed. They will be
found right for setting away to cool in
a bathtub.   *Childhood Education*

———♦———

Recipe for Raising Children

Love — Oceans of it.
Self Respect — Give generous portions.
Cultural Advantages — Plenty of the
    best available.
Music ⎫
Laughter ⎬ Use generously for seasoning
Play ⎭
Money — Scant and sparingly.
Religion — Use judiciously to thicken;
    makes the best foundation.

CHILDREN

Susannah's Rules for Rearing Children

Susannah Wesley, mother of nineteen, didn't go to textbooks for her theories on child guidance. Though two hundred years old, her rules are still valid today for teaching a child to be obedient and to "cry softly."

1. Allow no eating between meals.
2. Put all children in bed by eight o'clock.
3. Require them to take medicine without complaining.
4. Subdue self-will in a child and thus work together with God to save his soul.
5. Teach each one to pray as soon as he can speak.
6. Require all to be still during family worship.
7. Give them nothing that they cry for, and only that which they ask for politely.
8. To prevent lying, punish no fault which is first confessed and repented of.
9. Never allow a sinful act to go unpunished.
10. Never punish a child twice for a single offense.
11. Commend and reward good behavior.
12. Any attempt to please, even if poorly performed, should be commended.
13. Preserve property rights, even in the smallest matters.
14. Strictly observe all promises.
15. Require no daughter to work before she can read well.
16. Teach children to fear the rod.

Home Life

———◆———

Passing the Buck

The college professor says:
"Such rawness in a student is a shame,
But high school preparation is to blame."
The high school teacher remarks:
"From such youth I should be spared;
They send them up so unprepared."
The elementary school teacher observes:

"A cover for the dunce's stool,
Why was he ever sent to school?"
The kindergarten teacher whispers:
"Never such lack of training did I see!
What kind of person must the mother be?"
The mother replies:
"Poor child, but he is not to blame;
His father's folks were all the same."

GLENN SEELEY, *The Teacher's Treasure Chest*

———◆———

Portrait in Three Lines

Small boy tracing.
Mom erasing
Wall defacing.

IRENE S. SHOEMAKER

———◆———

Some would gather money
Along the path of life.
Some would gather roses
And rest from worldly strife,
But I would gather children
From among the thorns of sin;
I would seek a golden curl
And a freckled, toothless grin.

For money cannot enter
In that land of endless day,
And the roses that are gathered
Soon will wilt along the way.
But, oh, the laughing children,
As I cross the Sunset Sea
And the gates swing wide to heaven,
I can take them in with me.

AUTHOR UNKNOWN

———◆———

Child of the Age

His mind's a flying saucery,
His room a satelloid.
His words are from a glossary
An Einstein would avoid.

He's quite adept in rocketry.
He knows the names of stars.
He's forsworn Davy Crockettry
To plan a trip to Mars.

He boldly deals in distancy.
Fine spacemanship's his mark,
With just one inconsistency —
He's frightened of the dark.

MARY MARGARET MILBRATH *in*
The Wall Street Journal

Children in Church

The little children in each pew are like
  enchanted flowers.
They nod and sway — and yet, they
  plan — across the quiet hours.
And some of them drift into sleep,
  against a mother's breast,
And some of them, in singing hymns,
  find stimulating rest!
Their parents smile and sometimes nod,
  above each curly head,
But, oh, they listen carefully as lesson
  texts are read —
And feeling fingers touch their own,
  like drifting butterflies,
They peer, with heightened tenderness,
  into each other's eyes.

MARGARET SANGSTER

———◆———

An angel passed in his onward flight,
With a seed of love and truth and light,
And cried, O where shall the seed be
  sown —
That it yield most fruit when fully
  grown?
The Saviour heard and He said, as He
  smiled,
Place it for Me in the heart of a child.

ANONYMOUS

———◆———

The Soul of a Child

The soul of a child is the loveliest
  flower
  That grows in the garden of God.
Its climb is from weakness to knowl-
  edge and power,
  To the sky from the clay and the
  clod.
To beauty and sweetness it grows un-
  der care,
  Neglected, 'tis ragged and wild.
'Tis a plant that is tender, but won-
  drously rare,
  The sweet, wistful soul of a child.

Be tender, O gardener, and give it its
  share
Of moisture, of warmth, and of light,
And let it not lack for the painstaking
  care,
  To protect it from frost and from
  blight.

A glad day will come when its bloom
  shall unfold,
It will seem that an angel has smiled,
Reflecting a beauty and sweetness un-
  told
In the sensitive soul of a child.

AUTHOR UNKNOWN

———◆———

Who Wants the Boys and Girls?

God wants the boys, the merry, merry
  boys,
The noisy boys, the funny boys,
  The thoughtless boys;
God wants the boys with all their joys,
That He as gold may make them pure,
And teach them trials to endure;
  His heroes brave, He'd have them
  be,
  Fighting for truth and purity.
  God wants the boys!
God wants the happy-hearted girls,
The loving girls, the best of girls,
  The worst of girls;
God wants to make the girls His pearls,
And so reflect His holy face,
And bring to mind His wondrous grace,
  That beautiful the world may be,
  And filled with love and purity,
  God wants the girls!   AUTHOR UNKNOWN

———◆———

An American couple decided to send
a playpen to a friend in Northern Canada on the arrival of her fourth child.
"Thank you so much for the·pen,"
she wrote. "It is wonderful — I sit in it
every afternoon and read. The children can't get near me."

———◆———

A five-year-old girl was asked by the
minister how many children there were
in her family.
She replied, "Seven."
The minister observed that so many
children must cost a lot.
"Oh, no," the child replied. "We
don't buy 'em, we raise 'em."

Together

———◆———

A woman never stops to consider
how very uninteresting her children
would be if they were some other
woman's.

ROBERT C. EDWARDS

51

Heart of a Child

Whatever you write on the heart of a
  child
  No water can wash away.
The sand may be shifted when billows
  are wild
  And the efforts of time may decay.
Some stories may perish, some songs
  be forgot
  But this graven record—time changes
  it not.
Whatever you write on the heart of a
  child,
  A story of gladness or care
That heaven has blessed or earth has
  defiled,
  Will linger unchangeably there.
                                    Selected

———♦———

Three-year-old Bobby didn't like the
routine of being scrubbed, especially
when soap was applied.
  "Bobby, don't you want to be nice
and clean?" his mother asked.
  "Sure," replied Bobby, "but can't you
just dust me?"

———♦———

Choice, Choose

The granddaughter of Aaron Burr
had gone to an evangelistic service
and given her heart to Christ. That
evening she came to her grandfather
and asked him why he didn't do the
same. His story was a sad one. He
told her that when he was fifteen
years old he had gone to an evangelistic service and walked out without
giving his heart to Christ. Out under
the stars he looked up toward the
heavens and said, "God, if you don't
bother me, I'll never bother you."
  "Honey," he told his little granddaughter, "God kept His part of the
bargain. He's never bothered me. Now
it is too late."

———♦———

Little choices determine habit;
Habit carves and molds character
Which makes the big decisions.

———♦———

Choose: the attainment of man or
the atonement of Christ.   *This Day*

God always gives His best to those
who leave the choice with Him.

———♦———

Choice, not chance, determines human destiny.

———♦———

Christ

Jesus lived that He might die and
died that we might live!

———♦———

If Christ stays, sin goes; if sin stays,
Christ goes.

———♦———

Nature forms us; sin deforms us;
school informs us; but only Christ
transforms us.

———♦———

Christ is no law-giver, but a life-
giver.   LUTHER

———♦———

Christ's limitless resources meet endless needs.

———♦———

Christ is the great central fact in
the world's history; to Him everything
looks forward or backward.   SPURGEON

———♦———

Try the ways of being good, and you
will fail; but try the way of Christ and
you will succeed.   MATTHEW ARNOLD

———♦———

If Socrates would enter the room, we
should rise and do him honor. But if
Jesus Christ came into the room, we
should fall down on our knees and worship Him.   NAPOLEON

———♦———

Jesus Christ forgave voluntarily; He
died vicariously; He arose visibly, and
He lives victoriously.   JIM E. STARK

———♦———

The Lord Jesus Christ loves to reveal
Himself to those who dare to take the
bleak side of the hill with Him.
                              This Day

———♦———

The only person who ever lived before He was born is Jesus Christ.

———♦———

When Jesus Christ has you for anything, then you have Him for everything.   FLEECE

Life of Christ

Virgin Birth
Virtuous Life
Vicarious Death
Victorious Resurrection
Visible Return

————♦————

When I'm on top of the mountain,
He's the bright and morning star.
When I'm on the side of the mountain,
He is the Rose of Sharon.
When I'm in the valley,
He's the lily of the valley.

————♦————

If Christ is the Way, why waste time traveling some other way?

————♦————

Christ sends none away empty but those who are full of themselves.

————♦————

I Met the Master Face to Face

I had walked life's way with an easy
 tread,
Had followed where comforts and
 pleasures led,
Until one day in a quiet place
I met the Master face to face.

With station and rank and wealth for
 my goal,
Much thought for my body but none
 for my soul,
I had entered to win in Life's mad race,
When I met the Master face to face.

I met Him and knew Him and blushed
 to see
That His eyes full of sorrow were fixed
 on me,
And I faltered and fell at His feet that
 day
While my castles melted and vanished
 away.

Melted and vanished, and in their
 place,
Naught else did I see but the Master's
 face;
And I cried aloud, "Oh, make me meet
To follow the steps of Thy wounded
 feet."

My thought is now for the souls of
 men;
I have lost my life to find it again,
E'er since one day in a quiet place
I met the Master face to face.
                                    AUTHOR UNKNOWN

————♦————

Christ is all-sufficient. For the
ARTIST He is the altogether lovely —
 Song of Solomon 5:16.
ARCHITECT He is the chief cornerstone
 — I Peter 2:6.
ASTRONOMER He is the sun of righteous-
 ness — Malachi 4:2.
BAKER He is the living bread — John
 6:51.
BANKER He is the unsearchable riches
 — Ephesians 3:8.
BUILDER He is the sure foundation —
 Isaiah 28:16; I Corinthians 3:11.
CARPENTER He is the door — John 10:9.
EDITOR He is good tidings of great joy
 — Luke 2:10.
ELECTRICIAN He is the light of the world
 John 8:12.
FARMER He is sower and the Lord of
 the harvest — Matthew 13:37; Luke
 10:2.
FLORIST He is the rose of Sharon and
 the lily of the valley — Song of Solo-
 mon 2:1.
JEWELER He is the living precious stone
 — I Peter 2:4.
LAWYER He is the counselor, lawgiver
 and advocate—Isaiah 9:6; I John 2:1.
LABORER He is the giver of rest —
 Matthew 11:28.   SOURCE UNKNOWN

————♦————

The Touch of the Master's Hand

It was battered and scarred, and the
 auctioneer
Thought it scarcely worth the while,
To waste much time on the old violin,
But he held it up with a smile.

"What am I bid for this old violin?
Who will start the bidding for me?
A dollar, a dollar, who'll make it two?
Two dollars, and who'll make it
 three?

"Three dollars once, three dollars twice,
Going for three," but no;

CHRIST — CHRISTIANITY

From the back of the room a gray
    haired man
  Came forward and took up the bow.

Then wiping the dust from the old
    violin,
  And tightening up all the strings,
He played a melody pure and sweet,
  As sweet as the angels sing.

The music ceased and the auctioneer
  With a voice that was quiet and low
Said, "What am I bid for the old
    violin?"
  And he held it up with the bow.

"A thousand dollars, and who'll make
    it two?
  Two thousand, and who'll make it
    three?
Three thousand once, three thousand
    twice,
  Going, and gone," said he.

The people cheered, but some of them
    said,
  "We do not quite understand,
What changed its worth?" Came the
    reply,
  "The touch of the master's hand."

And many a man with his life out of
    tune,
  And battered and scarred with sin,
Is auctioned cheap to a thoughtless
    crowd,
  Much like the old violin.

A mess of pottage, a glass of wine,
  A game, and he shuffles along;
He's going once, and he's going twice,
  He's going and almost gone.

But the Master comes, and the thought-
    less crowd
  Never can quite understand
The worth of the soul, and the change
    that is wrought
  By the touch of the Master's hand.
MYRA BROOKS WELCH

———♦———

He who receives scars for Christ
here will wear stars with Christ there.

Christian, Christianity*

A Christian . . .
is a mind through which Christ thinks.
is a heart through which Christ lives.
is a voice through which Christ speaks.
is a hand through which Christ helps.
F. A. NOBLE

———♦———

The Scriptures give four names
to Christians:
    saints, for their holiness.
    believers, for their faith.
    brethren, for their love.
    disciples, for their knowledge.

———♦———

Two marks of a Christian: giving
and forgiving.
  There are those who are *truly* Christians but not *wholly*, and if not *wholly*, then not *holy*.

———♦———

Only entirely devoted Christians are
entirely happy Christians.

———♦———

Nine per cent of the world's population speak English, but ninety per cent of the Christians speak English.
BOB THOMPSON

———♦———

A Christian is anyone in whom Christ
lives.
EUGENIA PRICE

———♦———

A real Christian is a person who can
give his pet parrot to the town gossip.
BILLY GRAHAM

———♦———

Going to church doesn't make you a
Christian any more than going to a
garage makes you an automobile.
BILLY SUNDAY

———♦———

The devil is willing for a person to
confess Christianity as long as he does
not practice it.   *The Defender*

———♦———

A thirty per cent Christian cannot
be a hundred per cent American.

———♦———

A Christian is a man who knows how
to acquire without cheating, how to
lose without regret, and how to give
without hesitation.

*Also Christian Growth, Christian Life, Christian Living.

54

Some Christians are childish and not childlike.

———◆———

God needs Christians who are separators and not mixers.

———◆———

The Christian who sells out to Christ is always unsatisfied but NOT dissatisfied.

EUGENIA PRICE

———◆———

A Christian, like a candle, must keep cool and burn at the same time.

MERV ROSELL

———◆———

The Christian is the freest of all, slave to none.

LUTHER

———◆———

A Christian should not be a question mark for God, but an exclamation point!

VANCE HAVNER

———◆———

If your Christianity won't work where you are, it won't work anywhere.

VANCE HAVNER

———◆———

A Christian is a blot or a blessing, a blank he cannot be.

This Day

———◆———

Christianity is the one place where surrender brings victory.

———◆———

Christianity begins where religion ends — with the resurrection.

———◆———

Christianity is not a religion, it is a relationship.

DR. THIEME

———◆———

A lot of Christians are like wheelbarrows — not good unless pushed.
Some are like canoes — they need to be paddled.
Some are like kites — if you don't keep a string on them, they fly away.
Some are like footballs — you can't tell which way they will bounce next.
Some are like balloons — full of wind and ready to blow up.
Some are like trailers — they have to be pulled.
Some are like neon lights — they keep going on and off.
Some are like a good watch — open face, pure gold, quietly busy and full of good works.

Slovak Courier

It is not that Christianity fails, but the Christian.

ELD

———◆———

There are but two great dangers for Christianity: that it should become localized, and that it should become institutionalized.

ARNOLD OLSON

———◆———

He who shall introduce into public affairs the principles of primitive Christianity will revolutionize the world.

BENJAMIN FRANKLIN

———◆———

The Christian faith offers
Peace in war,
Comfort in sorrow,
Strength in weakness,
Light in darkness.

WALTER A. MAIER

———◆———

Christianity is like the seafaring life — a smooth sea never made a good sailor.

———◆———

An Old Question

Question: Can I be a Christian without joining the church?
Answer: Yes, it is possible. It is something like being:
A student who will not go to school.
A soldier who will not join an army.
A citizen who does not pay taxes or vote.
A salesman with no customers.
An explorer with no base camp.
A seaman on a ship without a crew.
A business man on a deserted island.
An author without readers.
A tuba player without an orchestra.
A parent without a family.
A football player without a team.
A politician who is a hermit.
A scientist who does not share his findings.
A bee without a hive.

Wesleyan Christian Advocate

———◆———

I envy not the twelve,
Nearer to me is He;
The life He once lived here on earth,
He lives again in me.

———◆———

Christian growth comes not by pouring in, but by giving out.

CHRISTIANITY

Definition of a Christian

He has a mind and he knows it.
He has a will and shows it.
He sees his way and goes it.
He draws a line and toes it.
He has a chance, and takes it,
A friendly hand and shakes it,
A rule, and never breaks it,
If there's no time, he makes it.
He loves the truth, stands by it,
Never, ever tries to shy it,
Whoever may deny it,
Or openly defy it.
He hears a lie and slays it.
He owes a debt and pays it.
And, as I have heard him praise it,
He knows the game and plays it.
He sees the path Christ trod
And grips the hand of God.

ANONYMOUS *from UEA*

There are too many Christians hunting for the things that are IN Christ.

EUGENIA PRICE

God wants spiritual fruit, not religious nuts.

ETHEL WILCOX

God is not looking for ornamental but fruit-bearing Christians.

HAROLD W. ERICKSON

The state of life in a tree is shown by the fruit.

HAROLD W. ERICKSON

Dying men have said, "I am sorry I have been an atheist, infidel, agnostic, skeptic, or sinner," but no man ever said on his deathbed, "I am sorry I have lived a Christian life."

DR. BOB JONES, SR.

You can tell the metal of a Christian when he rubs against the world. The right kind will shine.

The straight and narrow way has the lowest accident rate.

On the "straight and narrow" road, traffic is all one way.

It is not hard to live a Christian life; it is impossible.

There is only one thing to do about anything and that is the right thing.

DR. BOB JONES, SR.

A holy life has a voice. It speaks when the tongue is silent, and is either a constant attraction or a perpetual reproof.

HINTON

You and God make a majority in your community.

DR. BOB JONES, SR.

You can't be religious without religion. You can't be a Christian without Christ. You can't deliver the goods unless you have the goods to deliver. Quit trying to pump water out of a dry well.

DR. BOB JONES, SR.

Live the Christian Life!
Men will admire you,
Women will respect you,
Little children will love you and
God will crown your life with success.
And when the twilight of your life
mingles with the purpling dawn of
eternity
Men will speak your name with
honor
And baptize your grave with tears,
As God attunes for you the evening
chimes.

BILLY SUNDAY

We get no deeper into Christ than we allow Him to get into us.

DR. JOWETT

No man is high-born until he is born from on high.

DR. BOB JONES, SR.

He who walks with God will never be late to his spiritual meals.

The Christian life is not a search for God, but a response to Him.

Eternity

If you will give God your heart He will comb the kinks out of your head.

DR. BOB JONES, SR.

Christianity helps us to face the music, even when we don't like the tune.

PHILLIPS BROOKS

My Neighbor's Bible

I am my neighbor's Bible
He reads me when we meet;
He reads me in my home —
Tomorrow, in the street.
  He may be my relative or friend,
  Or slight acquaintance be;
He may not even know my name
Yet he is reading me.

Youth on the March News

———◆———

His Best

God has His best things for the few
  Who dare to stand the test.
He has His second choice for those
  Who will not have His best.

ANONYMOUS

———◆———

A rather pompous-looking deacon was endeavoring to impress on a class of young boys the importance of living the Christian life.

"Why do people call me a Christian?" the dignitary asked, standing very erect and beaming down upon them.

A moment's pause, then one youngster said: "It may be because they don't know you." *Ladies' Home Journal*

———◆———

A buoy is fastened securely to a rock at the bottom of the sea. The waves splash around it; it floats serenely in its appointed place. The tide rises and falls; it is still there. The Atlantic rollers come racing toward it; it mounts them one by one and rides upon them as they roll past. The tempest descends, the billows rush upon the little buoy, and for a moment it is submerged. But immediately it rises to the surface and is in its place again, unmoved and unharmed.

What a picture of the conquering life! What a power and a privilege for a soul to be able thus to rise lightly above every opponent, every vexation, never to sink into discontentment, never to be overwhelmed with fear and doubt, always to be on top of the fretful sea of life! *S.S. Chronicle*

Little Things

A holy Christian life is made up of a number of small things:
  Little words, not eloquent sermons;
  Little deeds, not miracles of battle
  Or one great, heroic deed of martyrdom;
The little constant sunbeam, not the lightning.

The avoidance of little evils,
  Little inconsistencies, little weaknesses,
  Little follies and indiscretions,
  And little indulgences of the flesh make up
The beauty of a holy life. ANDREW BONAR

———◆———

Not in Vain

To talk with God
No breath is lost —
  Talk on!
To walk with God
No strength is lost —
  Walk on!
To wait on God
No time is lost —
  Wait on! AUTHOR UNKNOWN

———◆———

Christmas

The Night After Christmas

'Twas the night after Christmas,
When all through the house
Not a creature was stirring,
But a hungry gray mouse.
The stockings all empty
On the floor had been flung,
The toys were abandoned,
No carols were sung.
The children were snuggled
All close in their beds,
Held there while Dad
Applied ice to their heads.
And Mama in her kerchief
And I in my cap retired
After midnight to catch
A short nap. When out on the street
There arose such a fuss,
We knew in a moment

It was Dr. Pill's bus.
It rattled and clattered
Like coal in the clink,
His motor was smoking,
His lights on the blink.
His horn had a voice
Like a sledgehammer's blow,
And his four wheels were chugging
Through the new-fallen snow.
He was making his regular
Christmas night call
To check on our pulses,
Our tummies, and all.
As he came up the stairway,
His eyes twinkled bright,
But when our groans reached him,
He cried out "Good Night!"
He bent to his bag,
And the chain 'cross his belly
Shook as he searched
For his old menthol jelly.
He ransacked his satchel
For cough syrup and pills
And enough Analgesique
To cure all our ills.
With a smile on his face,
A quick jerk of his head,
He plastered and pasted
And put all to bed.
He turned on his heel
And cut out the light.
He put on his earmuffs
And pulled out of sight.
We heard him exclaim,
Ere he left us that night,
"Now keep under cover,
Pipe down, and sleep tight!"
RUTH SCOTT HUBBARD, *This Day*

———◆———

The Christmas spirit that goes out with the dried-up Christmas tree is just as worthless.   FRED BECK

———◆———

An older sister was trying to motivate her younger brother to good behavior. "If you are not better, Santa Claus will not stop and see you next week," she told the four-year-old. "He'll pass right over this house."

"What?" said the tot. "Won't he even stop for you?"

Christmas living is the best kind of Christmas giving.   VAN DYKE

———◆———

Some children, all in their early school years, got out of line while putting on a Christmas pageant in church. It was disconcerting.

Thirteen of them were to walk across the stage, each carrying a letter-bearing placard. All together — if they were in correct order and in line — spelled: B-E-T-H-L-E-H-E-M S-T-A-R.

But the "star" bearers got turned around and went in backwards, so to speak, spelling out: B-E-T-H-L-E-H-E-M R-A-T-S!   *Kuna, Idaho*

———◆———

Little Janie was being taught that it was the proper thing to do to write a "thank-you" letter to those persons who sent her gifts at Christmas. She seemed to do pretty well until it came to Aunt Martha's gift. Finally she finished her note which read: "Thank you for your Christmas present. I always wanted a pin-cushion, although not very much."

———◆———

If you hitch your wagon to a star, be sure it is the Star of Bethlehem.

———◆———

The first Christmas that little Linda learned to read she was allowed to distribute the family gifts on Christmas eve. According to the family custom, the one who distributed the gifts could open the first package. After all the gifts were distributed with loving care, Linda kept looking and looking around the tree and among its branches. Finally father asked, "What are you looking for, dear?"

To which Linda replied, "I thought Christmas was Jesus' birthday and I was just wondering where His present is. I guess everyone forgot Him. Did they, Daddy?"

———◆———

Church (Attendance, Membership, etc.)

God puts the church in the world; Satan puts the world into the church.

If the church aims to hit sin it should pull the trigger.   C. GRANT

If you want the church to go on, go to church.

The church is not made up of people who are better than the rest, but of people who want to become better than they are.

Church membership is a poor substitute for real Christianity.

Too many church members are starched and ironed but not washed.
                              VANCE HAVNER

The church cannot remain evangelical in faith unless it remains evangelistic.

An ounce of church is worth a pound of police court.

The church is fairly well supplied with conductors. It shows a shortage of engineers, but an over supply of brakemen.

Any church which is satisfied to hold her own is on the way to the cemetery.
                              This Day

What the church of God needs is men who will talk less and work more.
                              GYPSY SMITH

There is a hotter place than the church in summer.   *Christian Parent*

I am your church. Without *you* I am nothing. If you fail to make an investment in me, I cannot materialize. Invest in me or I will die.

The church must not spend her strength in trifles — in trifles she becomes anemic.   JOWETT

Too many well-meaning people wait for the hearse to bring them to church.
                              Presbyterian Life

The glory of the local church is that it is not local.   *This Day*

The church service is not a convention to which a family should merely send a delegate.

Most churches are full of well-fed saints who need spiritual exercise.

The church is not a dormitory, it is a workshop.

The quickest way to get a church on its feet is to get it on its knees.
                              WILLIAM WARD AYER

The bell calls others to church, but itself never minds the sermon.
                              BENJAMIN FRANKLIN

When church services are over, your service begins.   *This Day*

Many folks think that what a church has is for everyone else.

Church Definitions

Pillars — worship regularly, giving time and money.

Supporters — give time and money if they like the minister and treasurer.

Leaners — use the church for funerals, baptisms and marriages but give no time or money to support it.

Working Leaners — work, but do not give money.

Specials — help and give occasionally for something that appeals to them.

Annuals, or *Easter-Birds* — dress up, look serious and go to church on Easter.

Sponges — take all blessings and benefits, even the sacrament, but give no money to support the church.

Tramps — go from church to church, but support none.

Gossips — talk freely about everyone except the Lord Jesus.

Scrappers — take offense, criticize and fight.

Orphans — are children sent by parents who do not set them an example.

Backsliders—go back and walk no more with Jesus (John 6:66).
                              St. Phillips Society

CHURCH

Some pillars in the church are really nothing but caterpillars.

———◆———

Mr. Lazybones

Died — of spiritual inertia — Samuel Lazybones, Esq., on the fourteenth. The immediate cause of death was paralysis of the spine, induced by long absence from church. His last words were: "A little more sleep, a little more slumber, a little more folding of the hands to sleep." He was a prominent member of the Ancient Order of Adhesive Recalcitrants, and a large concourse of the order, in full regalia, followed his remains. The chaplain delivered an eloquent eulogy and said he had "passed on to rest." *Western Recorder*

———◆———

Recently a blase TV audience was startled into thought when someone read a letter from a girl on the topic: "Why I Go to Church." She said: "I go to church every Sunday so when they carry me in one day, the Lord won't turn and ask, 'Who is it?'" *This Day*

———◆———

The congregation in one church grew so small that when the minister said, "Dearly beloved," the maiden lady thought he was proposing.

———◆———

The following notice was displayed outside a church:

C H ? ? C H

What is missing? F. DODDS

———◆———

Come to Church

1. Come.
2. Come early.
3. Come with your entire family.
4. Take a place near the front.
5. Be devout.
6. Be considerate of the comfort of others.
7. Be kind to strangers — they are the guests of the church.
8. Give a good offering, cheerfully.
9. Never rush for the door after the benediction. *Selected*

Why People Go to Church

Some go to church to take a walk;
Some go to church to laugh and talk;
Some go there to meet a friend;
Some go there their time to spend;
Some go there to meet a lover;
Some go there a fault to cover;
Some go there for speculation;
Some go there for observation;
Some go there to doze and nod;
The wise go there to worship God.
Gospel Herald

———◆———

The retiring usher was instructing his youthful successor in the details of his office. "And remember, my boy, that we have nothing but good, kind Christians in this church — until you try to put someone else in their pew."

———◆———

This is the way the church sometimes looks to the pastor when he goes into the pulpit! The pastor would just as soon preach to a woodpile as to empty benches. He does not find one single bit of inspiration in all the vacant pews!

(Back seats only usually filled)

HOWEVERTHISISREAL-
LYTHEWAYTHECHURCH
OUGHTTOLOOKATEVERY
SERVICE.ANDITWILLIF
EACHONEDOESHISPART
BYCOMINGHIMSELFAND
BRINGINGAFRIENDOR
NEIGHBORORRELATIVE!
THEBESTWAYONEARTH
TO"PEPUP"ANDINSPIRE
THEPREACHERISTOHIDE
ALLTHEEMPTYBENCH-
ESINTHECHURCHWITH
PEOPLEEVERYWEEK.

———◆———

Why Should We Go to Church?

1. Because going to church prepares us for the responsibilities of the week.
2. Because going to church rekindles our spiritual fires.

3. Because going to church affords us the opportunity of expressing our thanks.
4. Because going to church gives us companionship with other believers.
5. Because going to church makes our lives witnesses of our faith.
6. Because going to church enables us to worship God.

———◆———

Lord, what a change within us one
  short hour
Spent in thy presence will prevail to
  make!
What heavy burdens from our bosoms
  take,
What parched grounds revive as with
  a shower!
We kneel, and all around us seems to
  lower;
We rise, and all, the distant and the
  near,
Stands forth a sunny outline brave and
  clear;
We kneel, how weak! We rise, how
  full of power!

RICHARD CHEVENIX TRENCH, *Prayer*

———◆———

I Am Your Church

I am brick, stone, metal, mortar and lath.
I am sanctuary, pews, hymnals, chancel and lectern.
I am classroom, furniture, Bibles, literature, and religious art.
I am boys and girls learning to think, work and play.
I am youth seeking inspiration and guidance.
I am young couples planning to establish a Christian home.
I am the repository of a man's spiritual heritage.
I am the bearer of the evangel of Christ.
I am the custodian of your deepest hopes.
In me there is love and truth, inspiration and instruction, joy and pleasure, help and strength.
In a chaotic and troubled world I hold the answer to its greatest need.

In me there is promise for tomorrow.
In my fellowship you shall find peace.
Whatever else you neglect, do not neglect me.

AUTHOR UNKNOWN

———◆———

If There Were No Churches

If there were no churches there would be:
No church fellowship!
No Sunday schools!
No prayer meetings!
No Christian homes!
No "salt of the earth"!
No "light of the world"!
No gospel preached to lost sinners!
No missionaries sent to the foreign fields!
No "body of Christ" in the world!
No rapture and wedding day of the church to look for!
No training courses for the youth of the land!
No family altars!
No preachers to visit the sad and lonely homes!
No prayers for sinners!
No moral training for boys and girls!
No Christian colleges!
No love for the lost sinner!

AUTHOR UNKNOWN

———◆———

I Am Your Church Office

I feel neglected.
When you are planning to move, you notify every magazine to which you subscribe. You notify all your friends, but you fail to notify me. I am your church office, I feel neglected.
When your class plans to have a meeting, you notify all the members, but fail to tell me. Sometimes you plan to have a meeting in the church, and still you fail to let me know. Sometimes it almost embarrasses me, because I have promised the room you want to use to another group. You see, I am your church office — I feel neglected.
When a member of your family is ill, you seem to manage to call all your friends, except me. I like to know all

CHURCH

our people who are ill, so why don't you call me? I am your church office. I feel neglected!

Christ for the World Messenger

———◆———

Too many board members are just bored members.　　　　ELD

———◆———

The Early Christian Church — a Model Church

It was:
Happy — "had rest," Acts 9:31.
Healthy — "edified" and "walking."
Humble — "in the fear of the Lord."
Holy—"comforted" of the Holy Ghost.
Hearty — multiplied.

———◆———

Pastor Jones in our church had been paying five-year-old Tommy Brown ten cents a week to keep his grandfather awake during the sermon. Last week Tommy didn't deliver, and that night Pastor Jones jumped him. "I know, sir," explained the lad, "but Grandfather pays me fifteen cents to let him sleep."

Presbyterian Life

———◆———

"Johnny, do you know when your church was founded?" asked the pastor.
"Founded?" asked Johnny. "I didn't know it was losted!"

———◆———

Family at Church

Hand in hand, in Sunday dress,
　Parents with their children go,
Asking God their lives to bless,
　Wanting all His love to know.

At the church door families meet,
　Chatting as the spire bells chime,
Telling all upon the street
　Once again it's worship time.

By the pew the father stands,
　Joining them when still are they.
Then, eyes closed and folded hands,
　All together kneel to pray.

Earth has glorious scenes to see;
　Near and far is beauty rare.
But no fairer sight can be
　Than a family joined in prayer.

EDGAR A. GUEST

Some Who Do Not Go to Church

Mr. Speeds will clean his auto,
　Mr. Spurs will groom his horse,
Mr. Gadds will go to Coney,
　With the little Gadds, of course,
Mr. Flite will put carbolic
　On his homing pigeon's perch,
Mr. Weeds will mow his bluegrass,
　Mr. Jones will go to church.

Mr. Cleet will drive a golf ball,
　Mr. Tiller steer his boat,
Mr. Popper, on his cycle,
　Round and round the state will mote.
Mr. Swatt will watch a ball game,
　Mr. Stake and sons will search
Through the bosky woods for mush-
　rooms,
　Mr. Wilks will go to church.

Do you ask me what's the matter?
　Do you wonder what is wrong?
When the nation turns from worship,
　Sermon, prayer and sacred song?
Why do people rush for pleasure,
　Leave religion in the lurch?
Why prefer a padded auto
　To the cushioned pew in church?

Reader, well I know the answer,
　But if I should speak aloud
What I think is the real reason,
　It would queer me with the crowd.
You'll be popular, dear reader,
　When you wield the critic's birch;
You'll be safely in the fashion
　If you blame things on the church.

ANONYMOUS, from *The World's Best Loved Poems*

———◆———

Church Member's Beatitudes

Blessed is he who will not strain at a drizzle and swallow a downpour.
Blessed is he who tries a little harder when all around say: "It cannot be done."
Blessed is he whose program contains a prayer meeting night.
Blessed is the church leader who is not pessimistic.
Blessed is he who loves the church before his business.

Blessed is he who can walk as fast to a religious service as to town.

Blessed is he who invites people to church and comes along himself.

Blessed are those who never gossip about the faults of the church but work to make it better.

————◆————

Dead Weight

I've been a dead weight many years,
  Around the church's neck.
I've let the others carry me
  And always pay the check.
I've had my name upon the rolls,
  For years and years gone by;
I've criticized and grumbled, too;
  Nothing could satisfy.

I've been a dead weight long enough
  Upon the church's back,
Beginning now, I'm going to take
  A wholly different track.
I'm going to pray and pay and work;
  And carry loads instead;
And not have others carry me
  Like people do the dead. ANONYMOUS

————◆————

Ten Commandments for Church-Goers

1. Thou shalt recognize that church-going is a fine art which demands the best preparation of which thou art capable.
2. Thou shalt go to church regularly, for a prescription cannot do thee much good nor be effective if taken only once a year.
3. Thou shalt get in condition for Sunday by refraining from late hours and activities that clash with the will of God during the week, especially on Saturday night.
4. Thou shalt go to church in a relaxed state of body and mind, for the absence of tension is a primary requisite to successful worship.
5. Thou shalt remember that worship in church is not a gloomy exercise, therefore go in a spirit of enjoyment, radiant and happy to enjoy thy religion.
6. Thou shalt sit relaxed in thy pew, for the power of God cannot come to thy personality when thou art rigid and full of tensions.
7. Thou shalt not bring thy problems to church, for six days are sufficient for thee to think upon thy problems, but the church service giveth thee a supreme opportunity to let the peace of God bring thee insight for thy intellectual processes.
8. Thou shalt not bring ill will to church, for the flow of spiritual power is effectively blocked by harboring a grudge against thy neighbor.
9. Thou shalt practice the art of spiritual contemplation by the daily use of Scripture reading and prayer so that thou be not a stranger to the God whose Presence thou canst enter in the sanctuary.
10. Thou shalt go to church expectantly, for great things have happened to those who worship in spirit and truth — and the spiritual miracle can happen unto thee according to thy faith. BENJAMIN F. SWARTZ

————◆————

I Am a Church Member

BECAUSE if no one belonged to church there would be no church to point men to God and heaven.

BECAUSE I cannot ignore my spiritual nature. My soul culture is as necessary as my physical culture.

BECAUSE it benefits me, and enables me to undergird home and democracy with Christianity.

BECAUSE here I can transfer my personal allegiance to Christ in altruistic actions.

BECAUSE others are watching me, and I dare not set an example which will keep them from church.

BECAUSE I need the strength that comes from worship and fellowship with other Christians.

BECAUSE no matter how much I do for Christ it is but little compared with what He did for me.
New Jersey Baptist Bulletin

One day the telephone rang in the clergyman's office of the Washington church which President Franklin Roosevelt attended. An eager voice inquired, "Do you expect the President to be in church Sunday?"

"That," answered the clergyman, "I cannot promise. But we expect God to be there and we fancy that should be incentive enough for a reasonably large attendance." *Together*

Circumstances

If our circumstances find us in God, we shall find God in all our circumstances.

It's not the circumstance that matters, it's your reaction to it.

Don't look to God through your circumstances, look at your circumstances through God.

Civilization

Unless our civilization is redeemed spiritually, it cannot endure materially.
WOODROW WILSON

There is no solid basis for civilization but in the Word of God. DANIEL WEBSTER

What a civilization! The poor man worries over his next meal and the rich man over his last one.

Honesty is not only the best policy, but it is the foundation of civilization.

A Los Angeles teacher training her class in the use of proverbs said, "Cleanliness is next to what?"

A little boy exclaimed, feelingly, "Impossible!" *Christian Herald*

Clothing

The latest thing in men's clothing today is women.

Women who claim they haven't a thing to wear usually need their husband's closets to keep it in. *Town Journal*

I have never seen a badly dressed woman who was agreeable and good-humored. HONORE DE BALZAC

Joe College wrote home and asked his father to send him $100 to buy a suit of clothes. Dad wrote a prompt reply and enclosed $50 with this advice, "Join a fraternity."

Comfort

God does not comfort us that we may be comfortable but that we may be comforters. ALEXANDER NOWELL

It is such a comfort to drop the tangles of life into God's hands and leave them there. C. E. COWMAN

The only comfort that counts is the comfort that results when we do something about the things that make us all uncomfortable. HAROLD W. RUOPP

Would you live with ease,
Do what you ought,
Not what you please.
BENJAMIN FRANKLIN

"Mama, when is God going to send us a blanket?" asked seven-year-old Caryl one day.

"Why do you think God is going to send us a blanket?" asked her mother.

"Because," replied the young daughter, "our Sunday school teacher said that God promised a comforter when Jesus went back to heaven. And Jesus has been in heaven a long time."

A little girl came home from a neighbor's house where her little friend had died.

"Why did you go?" questioned her father.

"To comfort her mother," replied the child.

"What could you do to comfort her?" the father continued.

"I climbed into her lap and cried with her," answered the child. *Selected*

———◆———

Howard Maxwell of Los Angeles had a four-year-old daughter, Melinda, who had acquired a fixation for "The Three Little Pigs" and demanded that he read it to her night after night. Mr. Maxwell, pleased with himself, tape-recorded the story. When Melinda next asked for it, he simply switched on the playback. This worked for a couple of nights, but then one evening Melinda pushed the storybook at her father. "Now honey," he said, "you know how to turn on the recorder."

"Yes," said Melinda, "but I can't sit on its lap."

GENE SHERMAN *in Los Angeles Times*

———◆———

Committee

To be effective, a committee should be made up of three persons. But to get anything done, one member should be sick, another absent.

Chadwick, Illinois Review

———◆———

A committee is a group that keeps minutes but wastes hours.

———◆———

A committee of five usually consists of the man who does the work, three others to pat him on the back, and one to bring in a minority report.

Fort Worth Record-Telegram

———◆———

Blessed is the man who will work on a committee of which he wanted to be chairman.

———◆———

A committee is a group of people who individually can do nothing and who collectively decide nothing can be done.

———◆———

A conference is a way of postponing a decision.

Common Sense

Nothing astonishes men so much as common sense and plain dealing.

RALPH WALDO EMERSON

———◆———

Fads come and go; good sense goes on forever.

———◆———

Common sense is not so common.

VOLTAIRE

———◆———

Horse sense naturally dwells in a stable mind.

———◆———

Common sense is genius in homespun.

A. N. WHITEHEAD

———◆———

It is better to be saved by a lighthouse than by a lifeboat. ERNEST J. KUNSCH

———◆———

"Dad, what do they mean when they say a fellow has horse sense?"

"He can say, 'nay,' son."

———◆———

Always keep the head cool and the feet warm.

———◆———

Better go home and make a net than dive into a pool after fish. *Chinese Proverb*

———◆———

We hardly find any persons of good sense save those who agree with us.

LA ROCHEFOUCAULD

———◆———

Communism

Communism is the devil's imitation of Christianity.

A. W. TOZER

———◆———

Compassion

Compassion will cure more sins than condemnation.

H. W. BEECHER

———◆———

We cannot heal the wounds we do not feel.

S. R. SMALLEY

———◆———

Compensation

It's what we weave in this world that we shall wear in the next.

BISHOP TAYLOR SMITH

———◆———

All too often it's a man's own weaknesses that overpower his strength.

There's a payday for every day — even for the fellow who merely labors under a delusion. *Lutheran Education*

Cheat me once
    Shame for you;
Cheat me twice,
    Shame for me.
Scottish Proverb

Complain

Nagging isn't horse sense.

I had no shoes, and I murmured, till I met a man who had no feet.

Park your grouch outside.

When you feel dog-tired at night, it may be because you growled all day.

Compliment

It is ten to one that when someone slaps you on the back he is trying to make you cough up something.

A pat on the back is all right provided it is administered early enough, hard enough and low enough.

The best way to compliment your wife is frequently. *Changing Times*

Compliments are like perfume to be inhaled but not swallowed. CHARLES CLARK MUNN

Try praising your wife, even if it does frighten her at first. BILLY SUNDAY

Talk to a man about himself and he will listen for hours. DISRAELI

The art of praising is the beginning of the fine art of pleasing.

The same man cannot be both friend and flatterer. BENJAMIN FRANKLIN

A little flattery, now and then, makes husbands out of single men.

Many a man thinks he is being "cultivated" when he's only being trimmed like a Christmas tree. *Lutheran Education*

Approve not of him who commends all you say. BENJAMIN FRANKLIN

A flatterer never seems absurd; the flattered always takes his word. BENJAMIN FRANKLIN

A woman noted for her remarkably ugly face was calling on the minister's wife when the little boy of the house blurted out, "You sure are ugly!"
The horrified mother chided him.
The boy was apologetic. "I only meant it for a joke," he said.
Without thinking, his mother replied, "Well, dear, how much better the joke would have been had you said, 'How pretty you are!'" *Together*

Conceit

People say that he's a self-made man who loves his creator.

A man wrapped up in himself is a pretty small bundle.

Conceit is incompatible with understanding. TOLSTOY

Self-love is often rather arrogant than blind; it does not hide our faults from ourselves, but persuades us that they escape the notice of others. SAMUEL JOHNSON

The person who sings his own praises is quite likely to be a soloist. *The Valve World*

The bigger a man's head gets the easier it is to fill his shoes.

We know more bad things about ourselves than does anyone else, yet no one thinks so highly of us as we do of ourselves. FRANZ V. SCHOENTHAN

One type of inflation is the most dangerous of all — an inflated ego.

Conceited men often seem a harmless kind of men, who by an overweening self-respect relieve others from the duty of respecting them at all.

HENRY WARD BEECHER

A snob is a person who wants to know only the ones who don't want to know him.

Even the conceited bore has one striking virtue — he seldom talks about other people.

The world tolerates conceit from those who are successful, but not from anyone else.

JOHN BLAKE

Forget the "I" stuff. Learn to say "you" and to take the other person's interest into consideration.

Confess, Confession

A man should never be ashamed to own he has been wrong, which is but saying in other words, that he is wiser today than he was yesterday.

ALEXANDER POPE

The confession of evil works is the first beginning of good works.

ST. AUGUSTINE

Confession of sin puts the soul under the blessing of God.

How we love to confess the sins of others.

Last night my little boy confessed to
    me
Some childish wrong;
And kneeling at my knee
He prayed with tears —
"Dear God, make me a man
Like Daddy — wise and strong.
I know You can."
Then while he slept
I knelt beside his bed,
Confessed my sins,
And prayed with low-bowed head,
"O God, make me a child
Like my child here —
    Pure, guileless,
Trusting Thee with faith sincere."

AUTHOR UNKNOWN

Confidence

Confidence is the thing that enables you to eat blackberry jam on a picnic without looking to see if the seeds move.

Optimist: One who finds an opportunity in every difficulty.
Pessimist: One who finds a difficulty in every opportunity.

If you lose confidence in yourself that makes the vote unanimous.

I have held many things in my hands, and I have lost them all; but whatever I have placed in God's hands, that I still possess.

MARTIN LUTHER

Confidence and enthusiasm are the great sales producer.

It's great to believe in oneself, but don't be too easily convinced.

They conquer who believe they can. He has not learned the lesson of life who does not each day surmount a fear.

EMERSON

Conscience

When you have a fight with your conscience and get licked, you win.

Nuggets

A clear conscience is a will of brass.

There is no pillow so soft as a clear conscience.

French Proverb

Small boy's definition of conscience: "Something that makes you tell your mother before your sister does."

National Motorist

Conscience doesn't keep you from doing anything; it just keeps you from enjoying it.

The testimony of a good conscience is worth more than a dozen character witnesses.

CONSCIENCE — CONSECRATION

A man's first care should be to avoid the reproaches of his own heart; his next to escape the censures of the world.   ADDISON

———◆———

A quiet conscience sleeps in thunder, but rest and guilt live far asunder.
BENJAMIN FRANKLIN

———◆———

The best preacher is the heart; the best teacher is time; the best book is the world; the best friend is God.   *Talmud*

———◆———

E'er you remark another's sin, bid your own conscience look within.
BENJAMIN FRANKLIN

———◆———

"Oh, yes," said the Indian, "I know what my conscience is. It is a little three-cornered thing in here," he laid his hand on his heart, "that stands still when I am good; but when I am bad it turns round, and the corners hurt very much. But if I keep on doing wrong, by-and-by the corners wear off and it doesn't hurt any more."
J. ELLIS, *Weapons for Workers*

———◆———

The teacher had given her English class a test. As the teacher began to read off the correct answers, one of the boys changed an answer further down on the paper. This troubled him as he thought the teacher might think he had changed the answer she had just given. He raised his hand and asked what he should do about changing answers after the teacher started reading the correct ones.

"Let your conscience be your guide," the teacher told him.

The boy scratched his head and seemed so puzzled that the teacher asked him what was the matter.

"My conscience can't make up its mind," the boy replied.

———◆———

Consecrate, Consecration

Christ will not take 70 per cent, 90 per cent or 99 per cent. He wants our all.   BILLY GRAHAM

The Lord doesn't want the first place in my life, He wants all of my life.
HOWARD AMERDING

———◆———

"Will you please tell me in a word," said a Christian woman to a minister, "what your idea of consecration is?" Holding out a blank sheet of paper the pastor replied, "It is to sign your name at the bottom of this blank sheet, and let God fill it in as He wills."

———◆———

The greatness of a man's power is the measure of his surrender.
WILLIAM BOOTH

———◆———

It is not a question of who or what you are, but whether God controls you.
DR. J. WILBUR CHAPMAN

———◆———

Surrender

Let me hold lightly
Things of this earth;
Transient treasures,
What are they worth?
Moths can corrupt them,
Rust can decay;
All their bright beauty
Fades in a day.
Let me hold lightly
Temporal things,
I, who am deathless,
I, who wear wings!
Let me hold fast, Lord,
Things of the skies,
Quicken my vision,
Open my eyes!
Show me Thy riches,
Glory and grace,
Boundless as time is,
Endless as space!
Let me hold lightly
Things that are mine —
Lord, Thou hast giv'n me
All that is Thine!
MARTHA SNELL NICHOLSON

———◆———

Dr. Mason of Burma once wanted a teacher to visit and labor among a warlike tribe and asked his converted boatman if he would go. He told him that as a teacher he would receive only four rupees per month whereas as boatman he was then receiving fifteen rupees.

After praying over the matter, the boatman returned to the doctor and the following conversation occurred:

"Well, Shapon," said the doctor, "what have you decided? Will you go for four rupees a month?"

"No, teacher," replied Shapon, "I will not go for four rupees a month but I will go for Christ." *Selected*

———◆———

The Man with a Consecrated Car

He couldn't speak before a crowd;
    He couldn't teach a class;
But when he came to Sunday school
    He brought the folks "en masse."
He couldn't sing to save his life,
    In public couldn't pray,
But always his "jalopy"
    Was crammed on each Lord's Day.

Although he could not sing,
    Nor teach, nor lead in prayer,
He listened well and had a smile
    And he was always there
With all the others whom he brought,
    Who lived both near and far,
And God's work prospered — for he had
    A consecrated car.   AUTHOR UNKNOWN

———◆———

"Use Me"

A beautiful tree stood among many others on a lovely hillside, its stem dark and glossy, its beautiful feathery branches gently quivering in the evening breeze.

As we admired it we became conscious of a gentle rustling of the leaves, and a low murmur was heard: "You think me beautiful and admire my graceful branches, but I have nothing of which to boast; all I have I owe to the loving care of my Master. He planted me in this fruitful hill where my roots, reaching down and dwelling in hidden springs, continually drink of their life-giving water, receiving nourishment, beauty and strength for my whole being.

"The characters on my stem are cut into my very being. The process was painful, but it was my Master's own hand that used the knife, and when the work was finished, with joy I recognized His own name on my stem! Then I knew that He loved me and wanted the world to know I belonged to Him!"

Even as the tree was speaking, the Master Himself stood there. In His hand He held a sharp axe. "I have need of thee," He said. "Art thou willing to give thyself to Me?"

"Master," replied the tree, "I am all Thine own but what use can such as I be to Thee?"

"I need thee," said the Master, "to take My living water to some dry, parched places where there is none."

"But Master, how can I do this? What have I to give to others?"

The Master's voice grew wondrously tender as He replied, "I can use thee if thou art willing. I would fain cut thee down and lop off all thy branches, leaving thee naked and bare; then I would take thee right away from this thy home and carry thee out alone on the far hillside where there will be none to whisper lovingly to thee — only grass and a tangled growth of briers and weeds. Yes, and I would use the painful knife to cut away within thy heart all barriers till there is a free channel for My living water to flow through thee. Thy beauty will be gone; henceforth no one will look on thee and admire thy freshness and grace, but many, many thirsty souls will stoop and drink of the life-giving stream which will reach them so freely through thee. They may give thee no thought, but will they not bless thy Master who has given them His water of life through thee? Art thou willing for this, my tree?"

And the tree replied, "Take and use me as Thou wilt, my Master, if only Thou canst thus bring living water to thirsty souls!"

Adapted from B. E. NEWCOMBE

Content, Contentment

Contentment often serves as a brake on the wheels of progress. God has the correct formula: "Godliness with contentment is great gain."

———

To be content with what we possess is the greatest of all riches.

———

Content makes poor men rich; discontent makes rich men poor.
BENJAMIN FRANKLIN

———

Our idea of a contented man is the one, if any, who enjoys the scenery along the detour.

———

A man from Texas said that he came from the greatest state in the world — the state of contentment.

———

Content is wealth, the riches of the mind; and happy is he who can such riches find.
JOHN DRYDEN

Conversion

I found that I was not only converted, but I was invaded.
EUGENIA PRICE

———

Small boy: "Dad, what is a religious traitor?"
Father: "A man who leaves our church and joins another."
Boy: "And what is a man who leaves his church and joins ours?"
Father: "A convert, son, a convert."
Together

Convict, Conviction

You cannot sell anything you do not believe in.

———

It's always easier to arrive at a firm conviction about a problem after you know what the boss thinks.

———

The strength of a country is the strength of its religious convictions.
CALVIN COOLIDGE

Cook

About the only thing the modern girl can cook as well as her mother is some man's goose.

———

Mother to teenager thinking about marriage: "Now in getting a meal, what is the first and most important thing?"
Daughter: "Find the can opener."

———

Most brides' cooking is a sacrifice: all burnt offerings.

———

As is the cook, so is the kitchen.

———

Cooperate, Cooperation

The mule can't kick and pull at the same time; neither can a church member.

———

The fellow who is pulling the oars usually hasn't time to rock the boat.

———

It's not the way he kicks, but the way he pulls, that makes a mule useful.

———

You can employ men and hire hands to work for you, but you must win their hearts to have them work with you.
TIORIO

———

Cost

Beware of little expenses; a small leak will sink a great ship.
BENJAMIN FRANKLIN

———

The best is always the cheapest.

———

When you have to swallow your own medicine, the spoon seems very large.

———

One father was complaining in the presence of another father of the fact that his son was costing him so much. He had to have money for clothes, books, carfare, lunch, etc. It was a burden.
The other father remarked, "My son does not cost me a dollar. I wish I could spend something on him."

"Why doesn't your son cost you?" asked the first father.

"Because," replied the second father, "we lost him a few months ago."

———♦———

Cost of Following God

It cost Abraham the willingness to yield his only son.

It cost Esther the risk of her life.

It cost Daniel being cast into the den of lions.

It cost Shadrach, Meshach and Abednego being put in a fiery furnace.

It cost Stephen death by stoning.

It cost Peter a martyr's death.

It cost Jesus His life.

Does it cost you anything?   *Challenge*

Courage, Courageous

To see what is right, and not to do it, is want of courage.   CONFUCIUS

———♦———

It is human to stand with the crowd. It is divine to stand alone.

———♦———

Any coward can praise Christ, but it takes a courageous man to follow Him.

———♦———

It takes more courage to face grins than to face guns.

———♦———

Courage is holding on five minutes longer.

———♦———

Those who act faithfully act bravely.

———♦———

Nothing is difficult to the brave.

———♦———

Every time we lose courage, we lose several days of our life.   MAURICE MAETERLINCK

———♦———

Keep your chin up, but don't stick it out.   *KVP Philosopher*

———♦———

The companion virtue of courage is patience.

———♦———

No man in the world has more courage than the man who can stop after he has eaten one peanut.   CHANNING POLLOCK

The man who lacks courage to start, made a finish already.

———♦———

Heroism is the soul's high privilege, and the ranks of those who wear it nobly are always bigger than we know.   *Youth's Companion*

———♦———

One man with courage makes a majority.   ANDREW JACKSON

———♦———

Have courage for the great sorrows of life, and patience for the small ones. And when you have laboriously accomplished your daily task, go to sleep in peace. God is awake.   VICTOR HUGO

———♦———

Courage is the standing army of the soul which keeps it from conquest, pillage and slavery.   HENRY VAN DYKE

———♦———

Courage is knowing what not to fear.   SOCRATES

———♦———

God moves in a mysterious way
His wonders to perform
And plants His footsteps in the sea
And rides upon the storm.

Ye fearful saints, fresh courage take,
The clouds ye so much dread
Are big with mercy and shall break
With blessings on your head.   WILLIAM COWPER

———♦———

Courteous, Courtesy

Nothing costs so little and goes so far as courtesy.

———♦———

Courtesy is contagious.

———♦———

I am a little thing with a big meaning.

I help everyone.

I unlock doors, open hearts, banish prejudice;

I create friendship and good will.

I inspire respect and admiration.

I violate no law.

I cost nothing. Many have praised me; none have condemned me.

I am pleasing to those of high and low degree.

I am useful every moment.

I am courtesy!   ANONYMOUS

71

Courtesy opens every gate and doesn't cost a cent.

———♦———

Hail the small sweet courtesies of life, for smooth do they make the road of it.   LAURENCE STERNE

———♦———

Courtesy is a coin that will pass at par in any nation.

———♦———

Life is short, but there is always time for courtesy.   EMERSON

———♦———

Courtesy can be understood in any language.   ELD

———♦———

Chivalry is a man's inclination to defend a woman against every man but himself.

———♦———

This is the final test of a gentleman: his respect for those who can be of no possible service to him.
WILLIAM LYON PHELPS

———♦———

Coward

Most people are color blind — they think they are blue when they are only yellow.

———♦———

There are no proofs of cowardice.
LAURENCE STERNE

———♦———

The only thing worse than a quitter is the man who is afraid to begin.

———♦———

The coward never started and the weak died along the way.

———♦———

Create, Creation, Creative

The world God made was a beautiful world. The ugliness in it is man's own idea.

———♦———

All This and More

God made the sunlight, but it cannot laugh;
God made the moonbeams, but they cannot smile;
God made the stars, but they cannot play;
God made the endearing fawn, but it cannot sing;
God made the birds, but they cannot hold the heart;
God made music, but it cannot love.
So, God made you, my child.
DORCAS S. MILLER in Gospel Herald

———♦———

While reviewing a Sunday school lesson on the creation story, the teacher asked one junior boy how God created the world.
"With His left hand," replied the boy.
"Why do you say that God created the world with His left hand?" asked the teacher.
"Because," the boy explained, "the Bible says that Jesus is seated at the right hand of God."

———♦———

The kindergarten teacher asked the children what story they would like to hear. Most of the children agreed that they would like to hear about "How God Made the Beautiful World." And so the teacher began and captivated every small child in the room.
"Then God made the lovely sky," she went on, "and for the nighttime He made it dark. And he put the beautiful twinkly stars up in the sky to wink at us and to shine ever so brightly. Then God took some green cheese and made a very beautiful moon and placed it in the nighttime sky with the stars."
At this point one little girl waved her hand so wildly that the teacher asked her what she wanted.
"Well," replied the child, "that part of the story is not true. God made the sun and the moon and the stars on the fourth day and He never made no cows till the fifth day!"

———♦———

A small girl who lived in a remote section of the country was receiving her first Bible instruction at the hands of her elderly grandmother, and the old lady was reading the child the story of the creation. After the story had been finished the little girl seemed lost in thought.

"Well, dear," said the grandmother, "what do you think of it?"

"Oh, I love it. It's so exciting," exclaimed the youngster. "You never know what God is going to do next!"

———◆———

Creeds

A Child's Creed

I believe in God above;
I believe in Jesus' love;
I believe His Spirit, too,
Comes to teach me what to do;
I believe that I must be
True and good, dear Lord, like Thee.

———◆———

A Creed for Everyone

SILENCE when your words would hurt.
PATIENCE when your neighbor's curt.
DEAFNESS when the scandal flows.
THOUGHTFULNESS for others' woes.
PROMPTNESS when stern duty calls.
COURAGE when misfortune falls.
Enos Magazine

———◆———

Crime, Criminal

Some people do not think it is a sin to commit a crime, only to be found out is wrong.

———◆———

The cure of crime is not the electric chair, but the high chair.
J. EDGAR HOOVER

———◆———

Following the lines of least resistance makes men and rivers crooked.
RALPH PIERCE

———◆———

If it is a crime to make a counterfeit dollar, it is ten thousand times worse to make a counterfeit man.   LINCOLN

———◆———

Criminals are home-grown.
J. EDGAR HOOVER

———◆———

Critic, Criticism, Criticize

Constructive criticism is when I criticize you. Destructive criticism is when you criticize me.

You can't make a hit in this world by knocking the other fellow.

———◆———

You shouldn't criticize your wife's judgment . . . look who she married.

———◆———

Did you ever notice that a knocker is always outside of the door?

———◆———

Throwing mud at a good man only soils your own hands.

———◆———

The person who always sweeps before his neighbor's door has never seriously examined his own doorstep.

———◆———

It is well to remember that mansions in the sky cannot be built out of the mud thrown at others.   Evangelist

———◆———

If someone belittles you, he is only trying to cut you down to his size.

———◆———

Some men put anti-knock into their automobiles, when they ought to be taking it themselves.

———◆———

Analyze yourself first — before you criticize another.

———◆———

Knockers belong on a door, not in church.

———◆———

Keep a fair-sized cemetery in your back yard, in which to bury the faults of your friends.   BEECHER

———◆———

If it is painful for you to criticize your friends, you are safe in doing it. But if you take pleasure in it, that's the time to hold your tongue.

———◆———

The stones the critics hurl with harsh intent, a man may use to build his monument.   ARTHUR GUTTERMAN

———◆———

No man can justly censure or condemn another, because indeed no man truly knows another.   SIR THOMAS BROWNE

———◆———

The critic is a person who has you write it, sing it, play it, paint it, or carve it as he would — if he could!

CRITIC

I criticize by creation; not by finding fault.   CICERO

———◆———

Soiling another will never make one's self clean.   TENNYSON

———◆———

Children have more need of models than critics.   JOUBERT

———◆———

A statue has never been set up to a critic.

———◆———

If people speak ill of you, live so that no one will believe them.   PLATO

———◆———

To avoid criticism
say nothing,
do nothing,
be nothing!

———◆———

Search thy own heart; what paineth thee in others in thyself may be.
      J. G. WHITTIER

———◆———

The trouble with most of us is that we would rather be ruined by praise than saved with criticism.
Lutheran Education

———◆———

When It's the Other Fellow

Have you ever noticed?

When the other fellow acts a certain way, he is "ill-tempered"; when you do it, it's "nerves."

When the other fellow is set in his ways, he's "obstinate"; when you are it is just "firmness."

When the other fellow doesn't like your friends, he's "prejudiced"; when you don't like his, you are simply showing that you are a good judge of human nature.

When the other fellow tries to treat someone especially well, he is a "flatterer"; when you try the same thing you are using "tact."

When the other fellow takes time to do things, he is "dead slow"; when you do it, you are "deliberate."

When the other fellow spends a lot he is a "spendthrift"; when you do, you are "generous."

When the other fellow holds too tight to his money, he is "close"; when you do, you are "prudent."

When the other fellow dresses extra well, he's a "dude"; when you do, it is simply "a duty one owes to society."

When the other fellow runs great risks in business, he is "foolhardy"; when you do, you are a "great financier."

When the other fellow says what he thinks, he is "spiteful"; when you do, you are "frank."

———◆———

Take a Walk Around Yourself

When you're criticizing others,
And are finding here and there
A fault or two to speak of,
Or a weakness you can tear;
When you're blaming someone's meanness
Or accusing some of self,
It's time that you went out
To take a walk around yourself.

There's a lot of human failures
In the average of us all,
And lots of grave shortcomings
In the short ones and the tall;
But when we think of evils
Men should lay upon the shelves
It's time that we all went out
To take a walk around ourselves.

We need so oft in this life
This balancing set of scales
Thus seeing how much in us wins
And how much in us fails;
But before you judge another,
Just to lay him on the shelf,
It would be a splendid plan
To take a walk around yourself.
Cincinnati Bulletin

———◆———

Think Twice

Should you feel inclined to censure
Faults you may in others view,
Ask your own heart, ere you venture,
If that has not failings, too.

Let not friendly vows be broken;
Rather strive a friend to gain;
Many a word in anger spoken
Finds its passage home again.

Do not, then, in idle pleasure,
Trifle with a brother's fame,
Guard it as a valued treasure,
Sacred as your own good name.

Do not form opinions blindly,
Hastiness to trouble tends;
Those of whom we thought unkindly
Oft become our warmest friends.

AUTHOR UNKNOWN

Cross

Christ did not bear the cross — He used it.

We do not need culture, but we need Calvary. VANCE HAVNER

The cross is God's plus sign to a needy world.

The Tree

Some people touch a tree and find but
  wood to feed a fire;
Yet, carpenters can feel a floor or sense
  a soaring spire. . . .
The sculptor looks upon its trunk and
  carvings fill the air,
While others come and see the hearts
  which lovers whittled there. . . .

The farmer reaches for its fruit; the
  traveler seeks its shade;
The boy can see a raft of logs on
  streams of flowing jade. . . .
The outdoorsman will think of crafts
  to blunt an ocean's rage;
The pharmacist will see its roots; the
  publisher a page. . . .

The bird finds one beloved branch;
  but mothers see the beds
Wherein at nightfall, they will tuck
  their precious heads. . . .
The artist grasps the golden flame that
  leaves of autumn toss,
And some, whose souls are deep as
  time, can see a Savior's cross.

FRANK H. KEITH

The cross is the only ladder high enough to touch heaven's threshold.

G. D. BOARDMAN

After crosses and losses, men grow humbler and wiser. BENJAMIN FRANKLIN

Taking up your cross is carrying whatever you find is given you to carry as well and stoutly as you can without making faces or calling people to come and look at you. All you have to do is to keep your back straight and not think of what is on it — above all do not boast of what is on it. JOHN RUSKIN

Crowd (also see Courage)

Those who follow the crowd are quickly lost in it. ANONYMOUS

Curiosity, Curious

Curiosity killed a cat; satisfaction brought it back.

The things most people want to know about are usually none of their business. GEORGE BERNARD SHAW

Curiosity is one of the most permanent and certain characteristics of a vigorous intellect.

If you tell the average man there are 278,805,732,168 stars in the universe, he will believe you. But if a sign says, "Fresh Paint" he has to make a personal investigation.

Daily Telegraph, Bluefield, Va.

Customer

Take time to make friends before trying to make customers.

ELMER WHEELER

The seller of liquor is the only man who is ashamed of his best customers.

HERBERT W. THOMSON

The Name Means the Same

The lawyer calls him a client.
The doctor calls him a patient.
The hotel calls him a guest.

The editor calls him a subscriber.

The broadcaster calls him a listener-viewer.

The cooperative calls him a patron.

The retailer calls him a shopper.

The educator calls him a student.

The manufacturer calls him a dealer.

The politician calls him a constituent.

The banker calls him a depositor-borrower.

The sports promoter calls him a fan.

The railroad-airlines calls him a passenger.

The minister calls him a parishioner.

You may give a professional name to the person who buys your product or service, but no matter what you call him, he is always the customer.

Sales Management

Research

Research in the retail field has turned up some startling facts and figures. Of each 100 customers

15 are lost the 1st year, leaving 85.
13 are lost the 2nd year, leaving 72.
11 are lost the 3rd year, leaving 61.
9 are lost the 4th year, leaving 52.
8 are lost the 5th year, leaving 44.
7 are lost the 6th year, leaving 37.
6 are lost the 7th year, leaving 31.
5 are lost the 8th year, leaving 26.
4 are lost the 9th year, leaving 22.
3 are lost the 10th year, leaving 19.

Eighty per cent are lost over a ten-year period. Lost customers can be replaced with new customers, at a national average cost of $20.00 each. And a lot of them can be brought back if you are willing to make the effort and take the time necessary. *Advertising Age*

D

Dark, Darkness

There is not enough darkness in the whole world to put out the light of a single candle. *The Sunday School*

———◆———

Don't curse the darkness — light a candle. *Chinese Proverb*

———◆———

Dead, Death

It is given unto all men once to die — after that the writeup. CARL N. WARREN

———◆———

Fear not death; for the sooner we die, the longer shall we be immortal.

———◆———

We understand death for the first time when He puts His hand upon one whom we love. MME. DE STAEL

———◆———

While some friends were talking about death, one old lady said, "I am not looking for the undertaker, but for the uptaker."

Fruit is not borne by doing, but by dying.

———◆———

For every person who is dead and doesn't know it, there are ten living and don't know it.

———◆———

When Robert Ingersoll died, the printed notice of his funeral said, "There will be no singing."

———◆———

More people commit suicide with a fork than with any other weapon.

———◆———

Francis of Assisi, hoeing his garden, was asked what he would do if he were suddenly to learn that he was to die at sunset that day. He said, "I would finish hoeing my garden."

———◆———

If you would not be forgotten as soon as you are dead, either write things worth reading or do things worth writing. BENJAMIN FRANKLIN

When a man dies he clutches in his hands only that which he has given away in his lifetime. ROUSSEAU

———◆———

When death comes to me it will find me busy, unless I am asleep. If I thought I was going to die tomorrow, I should nevertheless plant a tree to-day. STEPHEN GIRARD

———◆———

Die when I may, I want it said of me by those who knew me best, that I always plucked a thistle and planted a flower where I thought a flower would grow. ABRAHAM LINCOLN

———◆———

It was a truly human tombstone which bore the inscription, "I expected this, but not just yet."

———◆———

Death takes no bribes. BENJAMIN FRANKLIN

———◆———

They were burying a rather unsavory character who had never been near a place of worship in his life. The services were being conducted by a minister who had never heard of him.

Carried away by the occasion, he poured on praise for the departed man. After ten minutes of describing the late lamented as a father, husband and boss, the widow, whose expression had grown more and more puzzled, nudged her son and whispered:

"Go up there and make sure it's Papa." *National Motorist*

———◆———

At the last moment, a minister was asked to preach a funeral sermon for another minister who had suddenly become ill.

Realizing he had forgotten to ask if the deceased had been a man or woman, he frantically tried to catch a mourner's eye. Finally succeeding, he pointed to the casket and whispered, "Brother or sister?"

"Cousin," came the faint reply. *Together*

Debt

The surest way to have the world beat a path to your door is to owe everyone money.

———◆———

Out of debt, out of danger.

———◆———

If you are in debt, someone owns part of you.

———◆———

Men in debt are often stoned.

———◆———

Creditors have better memories than debtors. BENJAMIN FRANKLIN

———◆———

No one can live without being a debtor; no one should live without being a creditor. N. J. PANIN

———◆———

Industry pays debts, despair increases them.

———◆———

Decide, Decision

Decision determines destiny. Eternity — where?

———◆———

Some people decide to be saved at the eleventh hour, and die at ten-thirty.

———◆———

Our decisions must be based on what's right, not who is right.

———◆———

Sunday morning test: Auto or ought to?

———◆———

Learn to say "no!" It will be of more use to you than to be able to read Latin. CHARLES H. SPURGEON

———◆———

History is made whenever you make a decision.

———◆———

One day a farmer hired a man. He asked him to paint the barn. He estimated it would take three days — the man did it in one day. Then he asked him to cut up a pile of wood. He estimated that would take four days — the man did it in one day. Then he asked the man to sort a pile of potatoes. He wanted them divided into three groups: one pile that he could

77

use for seed potatoes; one pile that he could use to sell; one pile to use to feed the hogs. He estimated that he would do that in one day. At the end of the day he went to see the man to see how he had done and found three little groups. He hadn't even started on the pile. He asked what was wrong and the man said, "I can work, but I can't make decisions."

Deeds

Deeds are better than words.

To remind a man of the good turns you have done him is very much like a reproach.   DEMOSTHENES

Some men are known by their deeds, others by their mortgages.

Well done is better than well said.
          BENJAMIN FRANKLIN

Sometimes when I consider what tremendous consequences come from little things — a chance word, a tap on the shoulder, or a penny dropped on a newsstand — I am tempted to think . . . there are no little things.   BRUCE BARTON

Defeat

If you think you are beaten, you are;
If you think you dare not, you don't,
If you'd like to win but you think you can't
It's almost a cinch you won't.

If you think you'll lose, you're lost,
For out of the world we find
Success begins with a fellow's will
It's all in the state of mind.

If you think you're outclassed, you are;
You've got to think high to rise
You've got to be sure of yourself before
You can ever win a prize.

Life's battles don't always go
To stronger or faster men
But soon or late the man who wins
Is the one who thinks he can.
          AUTHOR UNKNOWN

Defeated

I meant to study all the week
And very carefully prepare.
I meant to kneel — yes, every day
And bear each pupil up in prayer.
But I was weary and I found
So many things that I must do —
Important things that could not wait —
The week was gone before I knew.

I meant to visit several homes,
And mail some cards to absentees
To let them know that they were missed,
For such a word is sure to please,
And often brings them quickly back.
But somehow every day went by,
And not a single card I sent.
And now I ask, "Why didn't I?"

So this morning when I rose
I tried to study while I ate.
I briefly read my quarterly,
And hurried out, five minutes late.
I found them singing, and I dropped
Breathless, ashamed, into my seat,
For I intended to be there
That I the earliest child might greet.

Time for the lessons, and a group
Of eager voices beg their turn
To quote by heart the memory verse
Which I, alas, forgot to learn.
And so I stumbled through the hour,
And built with stubble, hay, and wood —
Instead of gold and precious stones
And silver, as His servants should.

"Go feed my lambs," was His command,
And shall I hope for them to live
On little morsels such as this,
When mighty feasts are mine to give?
"Forgive me, Lord, that I should treat
Thy Word in such a shameful way,
And may I never stand again
Defeated, as I've done today."
          AUTHOR UNKNOWN

Defeat comes not so much from physical effects, as from a state of mind which makes men reduce or cease from their efforts.
          GEN. CHARLES P. SUMMERALL

You are never defeated unless you defeat yourself.

———◆———

Definitions

Amateur Carpenter — A carpenter who resembles lightning. He never strikes twice in the same place.

———◆———

Ambiguity — is like a blind man looking in a dark room for a black cat that isn't there.

———◆———

Baby Sitter — Someone you pay to watch your television set while your kids cry themselves to sleep.

———◆———

Bore — One who talks about himself while you want to talk about yourself.

———◆———

Candor — What a woman thinks about another woman's gown. Tact is what she says about it.
The Cynic's Dictionary

———◆———

Celebrity — The advantage of being known to people who don't know you.
CHAMFORT

———◆———

Coordinator — One who can bring organized chaos out of regimented confusion.

———◆———

Depression — A period when you can't spend money you don't have.

———◆———

Draw — The result of a battle between a dentist and a patient.

———◆———

Electrician — A man who wires for money.

———◆———

Homiletics — The studying of sanctified salesmanship.

———◆———

Hospital — A place where people who are run down wind up.

———◆———

Individual — A person with the rough edges still showing.

———◆———

Nuisance — Is the right person in the wrong place.

Office Filing — Is an orderly system of misplacing important papers.

———◆———

Pattern — Is a picture of what the story is going to be.

———◆———

Penury — Wages of the pen.
WILLIAM DEAN HOWELLS

———◆———

Perfume Counter — Where people talk scents.
Changing Times

———◆———

Perfectionist — One who takes great pains and gives them to other people.
Changing Times

———◆———

Public Officials — The trustees of the people.
GROVER CLEVELAND

———◆———

Steam — Water turning crazy with the heat.

———◆———

Upper Crust — A few crumbs held together with a little dough.

———◆———

Waitress — A girl who thinks money grows on trays.
Whitehall Wisconsin Times

Deliberate

He who hesitates is lost.

———◆———

Act in haste, repent at leisure.

———◆———

That done with deliberation is done quickly enough, and better; what is made in haste is unmade as quickly.

———◆———

Delinquent

There would be less juvenile delinquency if parents led the way instead of pointing to it.

———◆———

We wonder sometimes whether the conversion of so many woodsheds into garages hasn't had something to do with the alarming increase of juvenile delinquencies.
ROY G. ROBINSON, *The Sunday School*

Teenager: "Mother, where did you learn all the things you tell me not to do?"

Prisons are a monument to neglected youth.

————◆————

Juvenile delinquents are other people's children.

————◆————

Most children who get classified as delinquents come from homes that have failed. It is their parents who are delinquent — either too poor to care for the child, or mentally or morally deficient, or have criminal tendencies themselves. Parents fail by neglect, ignorance, and unwillingness or inability to direct their children. They don't want to, they don't know how, or they can't — because of poverty, hopelessness, or some other cause.

1954 Annual Report, St. Louis Police Dept.

————◆————

If we can keep our adolescents in Sunday school, we will close our courts and fill our churches.

————◆————

Ninety per cent of most youth problems are adult. DR. LOUIS EVANS

————◆————

Adult Delinquency

Fathers and mothers, listen to me!
  Who is to blame for delinquency —
You or your untrained girl or boy
  Who turned to crime in search of joy?

Do you delight in obeying God?
  And train your child with reproof and rod?
Or does he grow from a babe to youth,
  Devoid of the knowledge of Christian truth?

Do you take your children to Sunday school
  To learn of God and the Golden Rule?
Or are they sent to a picture show
  Where most delinquent children go?

They learn of crime and of sinful lust,
  But not of Christ whom they ought to trust.
They learn to lie and to steal and kill
  But not to love and to do God's will.

Who is to blame — you or the child,
  If he turns to crime and becomes defiled?
Who should go to the prison cell,
  The rope or the chair, and a burning hell?

God is your Judge in heaven above,
  He bids you repent and in His grace and love
To turn from your careless, wicked way,
  And to start to study His Word and pray.

Forsake the world and the social whirl,
  And go to church with your boy and girl,
O parents, pause and listen to me,
  For *you* are the cause of delinquency!

DWIGHT C. RITCHIE

————◆————

Democracy, Democratic

Democracy means not "I am as good as you are," but "You are as good as I am." PARKER

————◆————

Democracy becomes a government of bullies tempered by editors. EMERSON

————◆————

Rule of the majority in America has been successful only to the extent that the majority has constantly recognized the rights of the minority.

————◆————

A democratic country: a place where people say what they think without thinking.

————◆————

A democracy is a country in which everyone has an equal right to feel superior to the other fellow.

————◆————

Denominations

The Salvation Army picks a man up.
The Baptists washes him up.
The Methodists warm him up.
The Episcopalian introduces him to society.

————◆————

Our denominational fences should be low enough to permit us to shake hands.

Depend, Dependence, Dependent

Dependence is a poor trade to follow.

———◆———

The sturdy oak is just an acorn that held its ground!

———◆———

God depends upon our dependence upon Him.

———◆———

Shipwrecked on God!

Shipwrecked on God! of all else forsaken,
All hope of help from every source has fled.
'Tis then and only then we find the Rock
Beneath us that wrecked our keel and stranded
Us on God. Shipwrecked on God! 'Tis not till
Then we know Him. 'Tis not till then we trust
Him to the uttermost. 'Tis not till then
We prove Him all sufficient and feed upon
His bread alone. Release thy hold of all
That binds thee to another; let shore-lines
Go, and dare the swelling tide; it will but
Bear thee safely into heaven, and land
Thee safe upon the Rock, shipwrecked on God.

Shipwrecked on God! O blessed place of safety.
Shipwrecked on God! No greater place of rest.
Shipwrecked on God! All shore-lines broke asunder
With nothing left in all the universe but God.
Shipwrecked on God! Then face to face we see
Him, with naught between to dim the vision
Of His Love. 'Tis then we learn the secret
Of Redemption, when we have nothing left

In earth or heaven — but God. Shipwrecked on God!
'Tis then we learn to know Him, as heart meets
Heart in unison of love; then no more
Twain, but married to another — He whom
God gave from out the bosom of His Love.
Shipwrecked on God! 'Tis not till then we vanish.
'Tis not till then we find we're hid with Christ in God,

And cease from all our trying and our struggling,
To find at last that Christ is all in all.
Shipwrecked on God! No land in sight to flee
To, where height and depth cannot be reached or
Length or breadth be spanned; we sink into the
Mighty sea of God's Own fullness, to find
That nothing else remains — but Him, the Christ of God.
Shipwrecked on God! With naught but Christ remaining,
I find Him Life and Breath, Environment —
Yea, all! I've ceased from all my trying and
My toiling; I've entered into rest to
Toil no more. He lives His Life while I abide
Within Him, and now "For me to live is Christ" forevermore.

CECILIA M. BARTON

———◆———

Desire

'Tis easier to suppress the first desire than to satisfy all that follows it.

BENJAMIN FRANKLIN

———◆———

Life is a continuous struggle to keep one's earning capacity up to one's yearning capacity.

———◆———

If you get what you wanted, you'll be fortunate. If you want what you get, you'll be happy.

Many a man has been led astray by following his own inclinations.

———◆———

Essentials

Give me work to do;
Give me health;
Give me joy in simple things.
Give me an eye for beauty,
A tongue for truth,
A heart that loves,
A mind that reasons,
A sympathy that understands;
Give me neither malice nor envy,
But a true kindness
And a noble common sense.
At the close of each day
Give me a book,
And a friend with whom
I can be silent.   AUTHOR UNKNOWN

———◆———

Destination, Destiny

The future destiny of the child is always the work of the mother.
                              NAPOLEON

———◆———

Methods of locomotion have improved greatly in recent years, but places to go remain about the same.
                              DON HEROLD

———◆———

Sad Story

The curfew tolls the knell of parting day,
A line of cars winds slowly o'er the lea.
A hiker plods his absent-minded way,
And leaves the world quite unexpectedly.   AUTHOR UNKNOWN

———◆———

Choice, not chance, determines human destiny.

———◆———

Determination, Determine

Satisfy your want and wish power by overcoming your can't and won't power with can and will power.
                         WM. J. H. BOETCHER

———◆———

When it is definitely settled that a thing can't be done, watch someone do it.

Nothing turns out right unless someone makes it his job to see that it does.

———◆———

Attempt great things for God; expect great things from God.   WILLIAM CAREY

———◆———

Our grand business is not to see what lies dimly at a distance, but to do what lies clearly at hand.

———◆———

The woman who is determined to be respected can be so in the midst of an army of soldiers.

———◆———

You

All that stands between your goal
And the deeds you hope to do,
And the dreams which stir your restless
    soul —
Is you!

The way is rough and the way is long,
And the end is hid from view,
But the one to say if you shall be
    strong —
Is you!   Mac-Sim-Ology

———◆———

It is not life that counts but the fortitude you bring to it.
                         JOHN GALSWORTHY

———◆———

If you have plenty of push you will not be bothered by a pull.

———◆———

When you get to the end of your rope, tie a knot and hang on.

———◆———

Determination

I am only one, but I am one;
I cannot do everything,
But I can do something,
What I can do I ought to do,
And what I ought to do
By God's grace I will do.   Listen

———◆———

The man who, when given a letter to Garcia, quietly takes the missive, without asking any idiotic questions, and with no lurking intention of chucking it into the nearest sewer, or of doing aught else but deliver it, never gets "laid off" nor has to go on strike for higher wages. Civilization is one long, anxious search for just such individuals. Anything such a man asks shall be granted; his kind is so rare that no employer can afford to let him go. He is wanted in every city, town and village — in every office, shop and store and factory. The world cries out for such; he is needed and needed badly — the man who can "carry a message to Garcia."   ELBERT HUBBARD

Behold the turtle. He makes progress only when he sticks his neck out.
JAMES BRYANT CONANT

You cannot prevent the birds from flying overhead but you can prevent them from making a nest in your hair.

Some people will never be convinced that they are on the right course until they have explored all the wrong ones.
Lutheran Education

Among the students of one of our well-known colleges some years ago was a young man who was obliged to walk with crutches. He was a stumbling, homely sort of human being but he was a genius for intelligence, friendliness and optimism.

During his four years in college, this crippled young man won many scholastic honors. During all that time his friends, out of consideration and respect, refrained from questioning him about the cause of his deformity but one day his pal made bold to ask him the fateful question.

"Infantile paralysis," was the brief answer.

"Then, tell me," said the friend, "with a misfortune like that, how could you face the world so confidently and without bitterness?"

The young man's eyes smiled and he tapped his chest with his hand. "Oh," he replied, "you see, it never touched my heart."   *The Message*

Be the Best of Whatever You Are

If you can't be a pine on the top of the hill,
Be a scrub in the valley — but be
The best little scrub by the side of the rill;
Be a bush if you can't be a tree.

If you can't be a bush, be a bit of the grass,
And some highway happier make;
If you can't be a muskie then just be a bass —
But the liveliest bass in the lake!

We can't all be captains, we've got to be crew,
There's something for all of us here,
There's big work to do and there's lesser to do,
And the task we must do is the near.

If you can't be a highway, then just be a trail,
If you can't be the sun, be a star;
It isn't by size that you win or you fail —
Be the best of whatever you are!
DOUGLAS MALLOCH

A pound of determination is worth a ton of repentance.

Devil

The devil's meal is all bran.

Idleness is the devil's workshop.

The devil comes because the house is empty.

Satan contests every soul that accepts Christ as Saviour.   GORDON VAN ROOY

Devil or Jesus

DEVIL	JESUS
EVIL wrought	EFFECTED on
VILE temptation and	Calvary
	SALVATION for
ILL brought	UNDONE
LYING still.	SINNERS.

Matthew 4:1-11; 6:24

When the devil calls, let Jesus answer the door.

————◆————

The devil has no happy old men.

————◆————

The old idea that children must sow their wild oats and go to the devil before they can come to Christ is contrary to Christian experience, is not warranted by Scripture and is not in accord with the teachings of Jesus.
SENSABAUGH

————◆————

Two boys were walking home from Sunday school. They had had a lesson that morning on the devil.
"What do you think of this devil business?" one boy asked the other.
"Well," the other boy replied, "you know how Santa Claus turned out — it is either your mother or your dad."

————◆————

The little girl couldn't quite remember the correct words of the memory verse, "Resist the devil and he will flee from you," but she got the idea. Her version: "Tell the devil to get out and he's got to go!"

————◆————

The devil's best work is done by many who claim to love the Lord.

————◆————

The devil is never too busy to rock the cradle of a sleeping backslider.

————◆————

Devotion

Devotional life, like muscle, develops with exercise.

————◆————

If we do not come apart, we will come apart.

————◆————

When you are so devoted to doing what is right that you press straight on and disregard what men are saying about you, there is the triumph of moral courage.
PHILLIPS BROOKS

————◆————

Difficult, Difficulty

Good manners and soft words have brought many a difficult thing to pass.
AESOP

Difficulties are stepping stones to success.

————◆————

There are three things difficult: to keep a secret, to suffer an injury, to use leisure.
VOLTAIRE

————◆————

Some folks look to God through their difficulties;
Some look at their difficulties through God.

————◆————

The people we have the most trouble with is ourselves.

————◆————

All things are difficult before they are easy.

————◆————

Difficulties are things that show what men are.
EPICTETUS

————◆————

Difficulties are God's errands; and when we are sent upon them we should esteem it a proof of God's confidence as a compliment from Him.
HENRY WARD BEECHER

————◆————

Most of the shadows of life are caused by standing in our own sunshine.
EMERSON

————◆————

Often the thrill of life comes from the difficult work well done.

————◆————

It Is Hard

To forget
To apologize
To save money
To be unselfish
To avoid mistakes
To keep out of a rut
To begin all over again
To make the best of all things
To keep your temper at all times
To think first and act afterwards
To maintain a high standard
To keep on keeping on
To shoulder blame
To be charitable
To admit error
To take advice
To forgive
But it pays!

The greater the difficulty, the more glory in surmounting it. Skillful pilots gain their reputation from storms and tempests.

EPICURUS

Diplomat

A diplomat is a person who remembers a woman's birthday but forgets her age.

Disappoint, Disappointments

Life's disappointments are veiled love's appointments.

C. A. FOX

Disappointments should be cremated and not embalmed.

We can praise our Heavenly Father that sorrows and disappointments are not meant to disfigure but to transform us.

The most disappointed people in the world are those who get just exactly what is coming to them and no more.

Blessed is he that expects nothing, for he shall never be disappointed.

Discipline

Depend upon divine displacement rather than self-discipline.

DR. ROBERT B. MUNGER

Discipline: Before you flare up at your child's faults, take time to count ten . . . ten of your own.

The handwriting on the wall usually means someone's going to get a spanking.

God is more interested in making us what He wants us to be than giving us what we ought to have.

WALTER L. WILSON

Teacher: "This is the fifth time this week that I have had to punish you. What have you to say, Charles?"
Charles: "I'm glad it's Friday!"

Today's dilemma: "Everything in the modern home is controlled with a switch except the child."

A teacher left her class one day and on returning found all the children sitting in profound silence with their arms folded. She was not only surprised at such silence, but bewildered and asked for an explanation. A little girl arose and said:
"Teacher, you told us one day if you ever left the class room and came back and found all of us sitting perfectly silent, you would drop dead."

A switch in time saves crime.

ROY B. NEWELL

When a mother was disciplining her small boy, he begged, "Don't say 'must,' Mother. It makes me feel 'won't' all over."

When the archaeologists were digging in the ruins of Nineveh they came upon a library of plaques containing the laws of the realm. One of the laws reads, in effect, that anyone guilty of neglect would be held responsible for the result of his neglect. . . . If you fail to teach your child to obey, if you fail to teach him to respect the property rights of others, *you and not he* are responsible for the result of your neglect.

WILLIAM TAIT, *Is It Juvenile or Adult Delinquency*

Three-year-old Bobby insisted in standing up in his highchair although mother had admonished him to remain seated then emphasized her admonishment by twice reseating him. After the third time little Bobby remained seated but looked at his mother searchingly and said, "Mommy, I'm still standing up inside."

Discourage, Discouragement

Ten rules for getting rid of the blues: Go out and do something for someone else — and repeat it nine times.

Selected

85

DISCOURAGEMENT

One cause for depression in people is hunger for appreciation.

Church Management

———◆———

You can tell how big a man is by observing how much it takes to discourage him.

———◆———

Don't despair. Even the sun has a sinking spell every night, but it rises again in the morning.

———◆———

Keep Scrappin'

When you're sick and you think, What's the use?
And you're tired, discouraged, afraid;
And you keep asking why they don't let you die
And forget the mistakes you have made;
When you're chuck full of pain and you're tired of the game,
And you want to get out of it all —
That's the time to begin to stick out your chin
And fight with your back to the wall!

When you've done all you can to scrap like a man
But you can't keep your head up much more;
And the end of the bout leaves you all down and out,
Bleeding, and reeling, and sore;
When you've prayed all along for the sound of the gong
To ring for the fight to stop —
Just keep on your feet and smile at defeat;
That's the real way to come out on top!

When you're tired of hard knocks and you're right on the rocks,
And nobody lends you a hand;
When none of your schemes, the best of your dreams,
Turn out in the way you'd planned,
And you've lost all your grit and you're ready to quit
For life's just a failure for you,
Why, start in again and see if all men
Don't call you a man through and through.   AUTHOR UNKNOWN

The One Who Stubbed His Toe

Did you ever meet a youngster who had been an' stubbed his toe,
An' was settin' by the roadside, just a-cryin' soft and low,
A-holdin' of his dusty foot, so hard and brown and bare,
Tryin' to keep from his eyes the tears a-gatherin' there?
You hear him sort o' sobbin' like, an' sniffin' of his nose;
You stop and pat him on the head an' try to ease his woes,
You treat him sort o' kind like, an' the first thing that you know,
He's up and off a-smilin' — clean forgot he's stubbed his toe.
Now, 'long the road of life you'll find a fellow goin' slow,
An' like as not he's some poor man who's been and stubbed his toe;
He was makin' swimmin' headway till he bumped into a stone,
An' his friends kept hurryin' onward an' left him there alone;
He's not sobbin', he's not sniffin', he's just too old for cries,
But he's grievin' just as earnest, if it only comes in sighs.
An' it does a lot of good sometimes to go a little slow,
An' speak a word of comfort to the man who stubbed his toe.
Today, you're bright and happy in the world's sunlight and glow,
An' tomorrow you're a-freezin' and trudgin' thro the snow,
The time you think you've got the world the tightest in your grip
Is the very time you'll find that you're the likeliest to slip.
So it does a lot o' good sometimes to go a little slow,
An' speak a word o' comfort to the man who's stubbed his toe.

AUTHOR UNKNOWN

———◆———

Do not get discouraged; it may be the last key in the bunch that opens the door.   STANAIFER

86

The surest way to petrify the human heart is to awaken feelings and give it nothing to do.

———◆———

Depression, gloom, pessimism, despair, discouragement — these slay ten human beings to every one murdered by typhoid, influenza, diabetes, or pneumonia. If tuberculosis is the great white plague, fear is the great black plague. Be cheerful!   DR. FRANK CRANE

Discover, Discovery

Discover

I cannot invent
New things,
Like the airships
Which sail
On silver wings;
But today
A wonderful thought
In the dawn was given,
And the stripes on my robe,
Shining from wear,
Were suddenly fair,
Bright with a light.
Falling from Heaven —
Gold and silver and bronze
Light from the windows of Heaven.
　And the thought
　Was this:
　That a secret plan
　Is hid in my hand,
　That my hand is big
　Big.
　Because of this plan.
　　That God,
　　Who dwells in my hand,
　　Knows this secret plan
　　Of the things He will do for the world.
　　Using my hand!   TOYOHIKO KAGAWA

———◆———

Disposition

All the world's a camera; look pleasant, please!

———◆———

A smile doesn't look good on some faces but a kind disposition wins friends everywhere.

Half of the secret of getting along with people is consideration of their views; the other half is tolerance in one's own views.   DAVID FRAHMAN

———◆———

Uneasy lies the head that wears the frown.

———◆———

Sour godliness is the devil's religion.   JOHN WESLEY

———◆———

When dressing, don't forget to put on a smile.

———◆———

If not actually disgruntled, he was far from being gruntled.   P. G. WODEHOUSE

———◆———

It's easy to smile when someone cares.

———◆———

All people smile in the same language.

———◆———

Who can tell by computation,
The true value of a smile;
You'll save many a situation,
E'en though humble be your station;
By the simple application
　　Of a *smile*.   PETER AULD

———◆———

Let Us Smile

The thing that goes the farthest toward
　Making life worthwhile,
That costs the least and does the most,
　Is just a pleasant smile.
The smile that bubbles from a heart
　That loves its fellow men,
Will drive away the clouds of gloom,
　And coax the sun again;
It's full of worth and goodness, too,
　With manly kindness blent,
It's worth a million dollars, and
　It doesn't cost a cent.

There is no room for sadness
　When we see a cheery smile
It always has the same good look —
　It's never out of style;
It nerves us on to try again
　When failure makes us blue,
The dimples of encouragement
　Are good for me and you;

It pays a higher interest
  For it is merely lent,
It's worth a million dollars and
  It doesn't cost a cent. AUTHOR UNKNOWN

———◆———

Divorce

Why divorce? What is needed is not a change *of* partners but a change *in* partners. *Family Altar Crusader*

———◆———

Divorce is the hash made from domestic scraps.

———◆———

Doctor

He's the best physician that knows the worthlessness of the most medicines.

———◆———

God heals and the doctor takes the fee. BENJAMIN FRANKLIN

———◆———

Zeke has finally figured out what the doctor's scribbling means on a prescription blank. He says it is a message for the druggist saying: "I got my $5.00, now he's all yours." *Glendale News Press*

———◆———

Those Medics

If you're fat or if you're thin,
If your toes are turning in,
If you've bunions on your shin —
  It's your tonsils!

If your hair is falling out
If you're suffering from the gout,
If you're getting far too stout
  It's your adenoids!

If your dome is turning gray,
And you can't eat bales of hay,
If you're failing day by day —
  It's your teeth!

Pain in thumb, or ache in toe,
When to "Doc" you sadly go,
He will say his little piece —
  "Tonsils, adenoids, or your teeth!"
                        AUTHOR UNKNOWN

———◆———

Doubt

Doubt sees the obstacles;
Faith sees the way.
Doubt sees the darkest night,

Faith sees the day!
Doubt dreads to take a step;
Faith soars on high,
Doubt questions, "Who believes?"
Faith answers, "I!" *The Good News*

———◆———

When in doubt, don't.

———◆———

Dreams

Dreams are as true today as they were a hundred years ago. *Dutch Proverb*

———◆———

It isn't a bad thing to be a dreamer, provided you are awake when you dream.

———◆———

Some people find life an empty dream because they put nothing into it.

———◆———

Don't part with your illusions.
When they are gone you may still exist,
But you cease to live. SWIFT

———◆———

You have to stay awake to make dreams come true.

———◆———

Drive, Driver, Driving

His fuel was rich,
His speed was high;
He parked in a ditch
To let the curve go by.

———◆———

Some people drive as though determined that no accident will be prevented if they can help it.

———◆———

Perhaps

If you can drive a car when all about
  you
  The homeward rush is on at five
  o'clock,
And know you're right when all the
  family doubt you,
  And red lights flag you down at
  every block.
If you can trust your instinct to inform
  you
  Which way the guy in front intended
  to turn,

Though he hasn't given any sign to warn you
  Excepting that his stop light starts to burn;
If you're content to drive the speed that's safest.
  Regardless of the speed by law allowed,
And, knowing you are good, can still give credit
  To those who are with greater skill endowed;
If you can use your horn and not abuse it
  When those in front are creeping like a snail —
The boulevard is yours, to have and use it.
  And what is more, you may keep out of jail!   AUTHOR UNKNOWN

Sing While You Drive

At 45 miles per hour, sing:
  "Highways Are Happy Ways."

At 55 miles per hour, sing:
  "I'm But a Stranger Here, Heaven Is My Home."

At 65 miles per hour, sing:
  "When the Roll Is Called Up Yonder, I'll Be There."

At 85 miles per hour, sing:
  "Lord, I'm Coming Home."

Two motorists met on a street too narrow for both cars to pass.
  "I'll never back up for an idiot," yelled one driver.
  "That's all right," said the other shifting into reverse, "I always do."

When you feel that the motorist ahead of you is proceeding at a snail's pace, check your speedometer. A snail's pace, according to the University of Maryland scientist, is .000363005 miles per hour.   *Executive Digest*

If you drink, don't drive; if you drive, don't drink.

A tree is something that will stand by the side of the road for fifty years and then suddenly jump in front of a woman driver.

The biggest problems for the road safety campaigns are the urban, suburban and bourbon drivers.   *Record, Treynor, Iowa*

Reckless automobile driving arouses the suspicion that much of the horse sense of the good old days was possessed by the horse.   ANONYMOUS

Natives who beat drums to beat off evil spirits are objects of scorn to smart American motorists who blow horns to break up traffic jams.   *National Motorist*

Duty

Duty makes us do things well, but love makes us do them beautifully.   PHILLIPS BROOKS

He who is false to present duty breaks a thread in the loom, and will find the flaw when he may have forgotten the cause.   H. W. BEECHER

Count your obligations,
Name them one by one,
And it will surprise you
What the Lord wants done!

The duty of the many should not be the task of the few.

Duty is not beneficial because it is commanded, but it is commanded because it is beneficial.   BENJAMIN FRANKLIN

A sense of duty pursues us ever. It is omnipresent, like the Deity.

For duty must be done; the rule applies to everyone.   W. S. GILBERT

E

Easter

The great Easter truth is not that we are to live newly after death — that is not the great thing — but that we are to be new here and now by the power of the resurrection; not so much that we are to live forever as that we are to, and may, live nobly now because we are to live forever. PHILLIPS BROOKS

———◆———

Christ died for you but you can live for Him.

———◆———

The value of Easter Sunday attendance cannot be evaluated until attendance is taken the following Sunday.

———◆———

Let us place more emphasis on the Easter heart than the Easter hat.

———◆———

The empty tomb proves Christianity, but an empty church denies it.

———◆———

The stone at Jesus' tomb was a pebble to the Rock of Ages inside.
FRED BECK

———◆———

The kindergarten-age child came home from Sunday school Easter Sunday and told his mother he could understand about Christ but not about the roses and asked his mother, "Why was Christ a rose?"

———◆———

Eat, Eating

Hunger is good kitchen meat.

———◆———

Hunger is the best sauce.

———◆———

A good dinner is better than a fine coat.

———◆———

The old-fashioned housewife's menus were carefully thought out. The modern housewife's are carefully thawed out. *Changing Times*

More people commit suicide with a fork than any other weapon.

———◆———

One first grade class in public school was marching past the room of another first grade class where the children were singing a prayer song with their heads bowed and hands clasped. As the children marched on past the room and to the cafeteria one boy said to his teacher, "I know why they were praying. They were hoping they wouldn't have spinach today."

———◆———

I eat my peas with honey,
I've done so all my life,
It makes the peas taste funny,
But it keeps them on my knife.

———◆———

Someone has said that the writer of Psalm 91 must have been speaking at a luncheon club when he wrote about the "Destruction that wasteth at noon day." Perhaps he referred to banquets when he spoke of "The pestilence that walketh in darkness."
CHARLES F. BANNING *in Church Management*

———◆———

Diet for Every Man

Jam — for car conductors.
Cereals — for novelists.
Mincemeat — for autoists.
Beets — for policemen.
Pie — for printers.
Corn — for chiropodists.
Starch — for henpecked husbands.
Gumdrops — for dentists.
Taffy — for after-dinner speakers.
Dough — for insurance company presidents. ANONYMOUS

———◆———

"Tommy," said the teacher, "can you tell us what is meant by nutritious food?"

"Yes'm," said Tommy, "it's food what ain't got no taste to it."

Young Charles, age four, came in for his midmorning glass of fruit juice. It was a warm morning and he had been playing hard. Also, because of the treat he had come for, he was very juice-conscious.

"Mother," he said, "would you wipe my face with a wet cloth? It is sort of sticky."

"What did you get on it, dear?" his mother asked as she reached for the washcloth.

"Nothin'," he replied in his slow western drawl, "it's just face juice."

F. M. MORTON in *Christian Home*

Parsley is the food you push aside to see what is under it.

PAUL H. GILBERT, *Seattle Times*

The new minister was a bachelor, and when he helped himself to the biscuits for the third time he looked across the table at the hostess' small daughter. She was staring at him with round eyes.

"I don't often have such a good supper as this, my dear," he told her.

"We don't either," said the little girl. "I'm glad you came."

MRS. J. C. FRY in *Together*

Summer advice to all eaters: If you are thin, don't eat fast. If you are fat, don't eat. Fast!

Presbyterian Life

Diner: "What sort of bird is this?"
Waiter: "It's a wood pigeon, sir."
Diner: "I thought so. Get me a saw."

On eating an apple
And finding inside
A hole deeply burrowed
But unoccupied,
Don't pity yourself
As you frantically squirm,
But think of the worry
You've given the worm.

WILLIAM W. PRATT

'Twas in a restaurant they met,
Brave Romeo and Juliet;
He had no dough to pay his debt,
So Romeo'd what Juli 'et.

To lengthen thy life, lessen thy meals.

BENJAMIN FRANKLIN

Eat to live, and do not live to eat.

BENJAMIN FRANKLIN

Rare: The way you get a steak when you order it well-done.

EVAN ESAR, *Comic Dictionary*

Diet: Something to take the starch out of you.

Pathfinder

Sandwich Spread: What you get from eating between meals.

EARL WILSON

Army Food: The spoils of war.

Hudson Newsletter

Economics, Economy

In the family as in the state the best source of wealth is economy.

With economy few need be poor.

Economy is the household mint.

An economist reports that Jones is having a tough time keeping up with himself.

An economist is a man who plans something which should be done with the money someone else made.

Some men's idea of practicing economy is to preach it daily to their wives.

He that buys by the penny, maintains not only himself, but other people.

BENJAMIN FRANKLIN

Someone has said our economic situation is one where this generation pays the debts of the last generation by issuing bonds for the next generation.

This Day

Education

Education is learning a lot about how little you know.

EDUCATION

Degrees

M.A. for master of action
D.D. for a doctor of doing
M.A. for a missionary artist
B.A. for a bachelor assimilator

———◆———

By the time a child is seven he has received three-fourths of his basic education.

———◆———

A college student in his four years does not make proportionately a fraction of the progress the well-trained infant does in his first two years.   ERNEST M. LIGNON

———◆———

A child educated only at school is an uneducated child.   SANTAYANA

———◆———

Never let your studies interfere with your education.

———◆———

Once I was a tadpole a-beginning to begin,
Next I was a toad-frog with my tail tucked in,
Then I was a monkey in a banyan tree.
But look at me now, I'm a Ph.D.

———◆———

It takes diplomacy to get a diploma.

———◆———

A college education never hurt anyone who was willing to learn something afterwards.

———◆———

The thing that surprises a college man the most when he gets out into the world is how much uneducated people know that he doesn't know.

———◆———

Young people can go to college now and pay later. Like Pop always said, you have to give a lot of credit to a fellow who wants to get ahead.   *Changing Times*

———◆———

A young man who had just received his degree from college rushed out and said, "Here I am, world; I have my A.B."
The world replied: "Sit down, son, and I'll teach you the rest of the alphabet."

Some men go to college to learn to express their ignorance in scientific terms.

———◆———

The time education rings up a score is when you can't spell round the kids anymore.   PAT CUNNINGHAM *in Christian Home*

———◆———

To educate a man in mind and not in morals is to educate a menace to society.   THEODORE ROOSEVELT

———◆———

Perhaps the most valuable result of all education is the ability to make yourself do the thing you have to do when it has to be done, whether you like it or not.   HUXLEY

———◆———

Secular education can make men clever, but it cannot make them good.

———◆———

All who have meditated on the art of governing mankind have been convinced that the fate of empires depends on the education of youth.   ARISTOTLE

———◆———

By education I mean that training in excellence from youth upward which makes a man passionately desire to be a perfect citizen, and teaches him to rule, and to obey, with justice. This is the only education which deserves the name. That other sort of training which aims at acquiring wealth or bodily strength is not worthy to be called education at all.   PLATO

———◆———

It now costs more to amuse a child than it once did to educate his father.

———◆———

Education should include knowledge of what to do with it.

———◆———

'Tis education forms the common mind:
Just as the twig is bent, the tree's inclined.   POPE

———◆———

Education does not mean teaching people to know what they do not know; it means teaching them to behave as they do not behave.   MARK TWAIN

The heart of education is the education of the heart.

———◆———

Education is the mirror of society.

ELD

To *look* is one thing. To *see* what you look at is another. To *understand* what you see is a third. To *learn* from what you understand is still something else. But *to act* on what you learn is what really matters. *Educator's Dispatch*

———◆———

Three steps in Christian education:
To know
To will
To do.

———◆———

It is said that Protestant boys and girls receive 52 hours of religious instruction a year; Jewish boys and girls receive 325 hours of religious instruction a year and Roman Catholics receive 200 hours a year. Due to tardincss, untrained Sunday school teachers, absences, poor lesson materials and surroundings it is said that even the 52 hours of instruction actually only average about 17 hours per year. *Selected*

———◆———

When the farmer boy explained to another about the special speaker at his church he puzzled over the letters Ph.D. after the speaker's name. Then he explained that it meant "Post-hole digger." ———◆———

Father: "I'm worried about your being at the bottom of the class."
Son: "Don't worry, Pop, they teach the same stuff at both ends."

———◆———

"Oh, I know a few things!" exclaimed the haughty senior.
"Well, you haven't anything on me," retorted the freshman confidently; "I guess I know as few things as anyone."

———◆———

"Why were you kept in after school?" the father asked his son.
"I didn't know where the Azores were," replied the son.
"In the future," said father, "just remember where you put your things."

Effort

There is a great distance between "said" and "done."

———◆———

The top is reached by topping yesterday's effort.

———◆———

The mode by which the inevitable comes to pass is effort. JUSTICE HOLMES

———◆———

Those who try to do something and fail are infinitely better than those who try to do nothing and succeed at it.

———◆———

Little Janie was trying to dress herself.
"Mother," she said after a long period of effort, "I guess you'll have to button my dress. The buttons are behind and I'm in front." *National Motorist*

———◆———

Ego, Egotism

Egotism has been described as just a case of mistaken nonentity. *Toastmaster*

———◆———

A high brow is a person educated beyond his own intelligence.
Ladies' Home Journal

———◆———

The egotist is an I specialist.

———◆———

You can always tell an egotist, but unfortunately you can't tell him much.

———◆———

An egotist is one who thinks that if he hadn't been born, people would wonder why. *Changing Times*

———◆———

When a man is wrapped up in himself, he makes a pretty small package.
JOHN RUSKIN

———◆———

Big shots are usually small shots who kept on shooting.

———◆———

Employ, Employer, Employment

The following notice was posted in a Chicago store in 1858:
This store will be open from 6 a.m. to 9 p.m. the year round.

On arrival each morning, store must be swept, counters, shelves, and show-cases dusted. Lamps must be trimmed, pens made, a pail of water and a bucket of coal brought in before break-fast.

The employee who is in the habit of smoking Spanish cigars, being shaved at the barber's, going to dances and other places of amusement, will surely give his employer reason to be suspicious of his integrity.

Each employee must pay not less than $5.00 per year to the church and must attend Sunday school regularly.

Men employees are given one eve-ning a week for courting, and two if they go to prayer meeting.

After 14 hours of work, leisure hours should be spent mostly in reading.

———◆———

Thomas Jefferson said in hiring men that he considered these three items:
1. Is he honest?
2. Will he work?
3. Is he loyal?

———◆———

Encourage, Encouragement

Each time we meet, you always say
    Some word of praise that makes me gay.
You see some hidden, struggling trait,
    Encourage it and make it great.
Tight-fisted little buds of good
    Bloom large because you said they would.
A glad, mad music in me sings;
    My soul sprouts tiny flaming wings.
My day takes on a brand-new zest.
    Your gift of praising brings my best,
Revives my spirit, flings it high;
    For God loves praise, and so do I.
            AUTHOR UNKNOWN

———◆———

God keeps his choicest cordials for our deepest faintings.   C. E. COWMAN

———◆———

The blue of heaven is larger than the clouds.

———◆———

Correction can help, but encourage-ment can help far more.

There is no high hill but beside some deep valley. There is no birth without a pang.   DAN CRAWFORD

———◆———

The Sermon on the Mount can lift us out of the Valley of Depression.

———◆———

Correction does much, but encour-agement does more. Encouragement coming after censure is the sun after a shower.   J. WOLFGANG GOETHE

———◆———

"What I need most," wrote Emerson, "is something to make me do what I can." One of the most rewarding ex-periences you can ever have is to be that "something" for someone — to be the catalyst that dispels inertia and brings out the best in someone you know. The thing that brings out the best in most people is encouragement, and you — no matter what your cir-cumstances are — can provide those around you with this precious morale plasma. Think encouraging thoughts, speak encouraging words, and, most important of all, adopt an air of con-fident expectancy toward those you are trying to help. Be genuinely interested, let your attitude be more eloquent than your words. In this way, you can be, in truth, a "best" friend. There is no happiness quite comparable to the happiness you can earn in this way.
          Whatsoever Things

———◆———

There's Hope for the Rest of Us

Napoleon was number forty-two in his class. (Wonder who the forty-one were ahead of him?)

Sir Isaac Newton was next to the lowest in his form. He failed in geom-etry because he didn't do his problems according to the book.

George Eliot learned to read with great difficulty, giving no promise of brilliance in her youth.

James Russell Lowell was suspended from Harvard for complete indolence.

Oliver Goldsmith was at the bottom of his class.

James Watt was the butt of jokes by his schoolmates.

Endurance, Endure

The battle against evil is difficult, not so much because of the action required, but because of the endurance necessary to achieve victory.

———◆———

Flowers that last have deep roots and bloom late. Things that endure grow slowly.

———◆———

If there is anything that cannot bear free thought, let it crack.

WENDELL PHILLIPS

When some people yell for tolerance, what they really want is special privilege.

Garner (Iowa) Leader

Enemies, Enemy

Speak well of your enemies. You made them.

———◆———

My enemies are my friends who don't know me.

———◆———

If we would read the secret history of our enemies, we would find in each man's life a sorrow and suffering enough to disarm all hostility.

LONGFELLOW

The only satisfactory way to make people do things is to make them want to do them. Enemies are never truly conquered until their friendship is won.

WILFERD PETERSON

Love your enemies, for they tell you your faults.

BENJAMIN FRANKLIN

Love your enemy — it will drive him nuts.

———◆———

Enthusiasm

Enthusiasm is the best protection in any situation. Wholeheartedness is contagious. Give yourself, if you wish to get others.

DAVID SEABURY, *Good Business*

———◆———

You cannot kindle a fire in any other heart until it is burning within your own.

ANONYMOUS

In order to do great things, one must be enthusiastic.

DE ROUVROY

———◆———

The worst bankrupt in the world is the man who has lost his enthusiasm.

———◆———

Enthusiasm is unmistakable evidence that you're in love with your work.

———◆———

Enthusiasm is the fever of reason.

———◆———

When a man is enthusiastic about hard work, the chances are that he's an employer.

HAL CHADWICK

———◆———

We act as though comfort and luxury were the chief requirements of life, when all that we need to make us really happy is something to be enthusiastic about.

CHARLES KINGSLEY

———◆———

If you can give your son only one gift, let it be enthusiasm.

BRUCE BARTON

———◆———

Enthusiasm is the genius of sincerity, and truth accomplishes no victories without it.

BULWER-LYTTON

———◆———

Environment

You can take a boy out of the country but you can't take the country out of the boy.

———◆———

God is not interested in changing environment but in renewing men.

MALCOLM R. CRONK

———◆———

Epitaphs

It is said that on the tomb of Confucius are the words, "He taught for 10,000 years."

On your tomb can it be said, "He taught for eternity"?

———◆———

The marks on the grave of a guide who died while climbing the Alps were: "He died climbing." On the tomb of a Christian astronomer were these words (by his partner): "We have gazed too long at the stars together to be afraid of the night."

Here is the original epitaph of Benjamin Franklin:

The body of B. Franklin
Printer
Like the cover of an old book
Its contents torn out
And stript of its lettering and gilding
Lies here food for worms.
But the work shall not be wholly lost
For it will, as he believes, appear
once more
In a new and more perfect edition
Corrected and amended
By the Author.

———♦———

Even a tombstone will say good things about a fellow when he is down.

———♦———

Better a little "taffy" while they are living than so much "epitaphy" when they're dead.

———♦———

These words are on the grave of a scientist who died at the age of 85: "He died learning."

———♦———

Live so that the man who carves your epitaph on the tombstone won't feel like a prevaricator.

———♦———

Epitaph on a grave: "All dressed up and no place to go."

———♦———

This man died at 30; he was buried at 70.

———♦———

Original inscription on tombstone:
Remember, friend, when passing by,
As you are now, so once was I.
As I am now, soon you will be,
Prepare for death and follow me.

Added comment to inscription:
To follow you I'm not content.
Until I know which way you went.

———♦———

Error

A man should never be ashamed to own he has been in the wrong, which is but saying, in other words, that he is wiser today than he was yesterday. ALEXANDER POPE

Eternal, Eternal Life, Eternity

Eternal life begins with salvation.

———♦———

Join thyself to the eternal God, and thou shalt be eternal. AUGUSTINE

———♦———

He who provides for this life, but takes no care for eternity, is wise for a moment, but a fool forever. TILLOTSON

———♦———

He who has no vision of eternity will never get a true hold of time. CARLYLE

———♦———

There is only one way to get ready for immortality, and that is to love this life and live it as bravely and faithfully and cheerfully as we can.
HENRY VAN DYKE

———♦———

Over the triple doorway of the Cathedral of Milan there are three inscriptions spanning the splendid arches. Over one is carved a beautiful wreath of roses, and underneath is the legend, "All that pleases is but for a moment."
Over the other is sculptured a cross, and these are the words beneath: "All that troubles is but for a moment." But underneath the great central entrance in the main aisle is the inscription, "That only is important which is eternal."

———♦———

Ethics

A four-way test of business ethics:
1. Is it the truth?
2. Is it fair to all concerned?
3. Will it build goodwill and better friendships?
4. Will it be beneficial to all concerned?

———♦———

"Ethics," the man told his son, "is vital to everyday living. For example, today an old friend paid me back a loan with a new hundred-dollar bill. As he was leaving I discovered he'd given me two bills stuck together. Immediately a question of ethics arose: Should I tell your mother?"

Evangelism, Evangelistic

Before reaching the uttermost we must keep Jerusalem uppermost in mind.

———✦———

We have a Samaria vision but only a Jerusalem zeal.

———✦———

You can't emphasize the Bible unless you have pupils.

———✦———

You say you don't believe in magnifying numbers and perhaps that's why you don't have them.

———✦———

Personal evangelism is a collision of souls. In the Book of Acts the Christians went after souls and got them.

———✦———

When a child is old enough to knowingly sin he is old enough to savingly believe.

———✦———

It is easier to win an entire family than it is to win them as individuals.
HARRY DENMAN

———✦———

Reach all you can, teach all you reach, win all you teach, train all you win, enlist all you train.

———✦———

The monument I want after I am dead is a monument with two legs going around the world — a saved sinner telling about the salvation of Jesus Christ. D. L. MOODY

———✦———

The Lord, our gentle shepherd, stands,
  With all engaging charms,
Hark! how He calls the tender lambs,
  And folds them in His arms.

"Permit them to approach," He cries,
  "Nor scorn their humble name,
For 'twas to bless such souls as these
  The Lord of angels came."

We bring them, Lord, in thankful hands,
  And yield them up to Thee;
Joyful that we ourselves are Thine;
  Thine let our offspring be. *Selected*

We never move people until we are moved.

———✦———

The only ladder to heaven is the cross.

———✦———

The only thing a man can really gain before he dies is heaven.

———✦———

Evil

No man is justified in doing evil on the grounds of expediency.
THEODORE ROOSEVELT

———✦———

For evil to triumph, it is only necessary for good men to do nothing.
EDMUND BURKE

———✦———

Some of your hurts you have cured,
  And the sharpest you still have survived,
But what torments of grief you endured
  From evils which never arrived.
EMERSON

———✦———

Exaggerate, Exaggeration

A fish is an underwater creature that grows fastest between the time it is caught and the time the fisherman describes it to his friends.

———✦———

A woman approached evangelist Billy Sunday after one of his sermons and asked pensively, "I wonder if you can help me? I have a terrible habit of exaggeration."

"Certainly, madam," replied Sunday. "Just call it lying!"

———✦———

Example

There is just one way to bring up a child in the way he should go and that is to travel that way yourself.
ABRAHAM LINCOLN

———✦———

One example is worth a thousand precepts.

———✦———

How many people have made you homesick to know God?

The Little Chap

A careful man I ought to be —
A little fellow follows me.
I do not dare to go astray,
For fear he'll go the selfsame way.

I cannot once escape his eyes.
What'er he sees me do, he tries.
Like me, he says he's going to be —
The little chap who follows me.

He thinks that I am good and fine,
Believes in every word of mine.
Wrong steps by me he must not see —
The little fellow who follows me.

I must remember as I go,
Through summer's sun and winter's
    snow,
I'm building for the years to be,
The little chap who follows me.

ANONYMOUS

Men who won't read the Bible will read "living epistles."

I'd rather see a sermon, than hear one
    any day:
I'd rather one should walk with me,
    than merely show the way;
The eye's a better pupil, and more will-
    ing than the ear,
Fine counsel is confusing but exam-
    ple's always clear.
And best of all the preachers, are the
    men who live their creeds,
For to see good put in action is what
    everybody needs.
I soon can learn to do it, if you'll let
    me see it done;
I can see your hands in action, but
    your tongue too fast may run.
And the lectures you deliver may be
    very fine and true;
But I'd rather get my lesson by observ-
    ing what you do;
For I may not understand you and the
    high advice you give.
But there's no misunderstanding how
    you act and how you live.

EDGAR A. GUEST

Children you teach are now becoming what you are going to be.

A good example is worth a thousand sermons.

Of all commentaries upon the Scriptures, good examples are the best and liveliest.

JOHN DONNE

A pint of example is worth a gallon of advice.

An ounce of practice is worth a pound of preach.

"When I was a little child," the sergeant sweetly addressed his men at the end of an exhaustive hour of drill, "I had a set of wooden soldiers. There was a poor little boy in the neighborhood and after I had been to Sunday school one day and listened to a stirring talk on the beauties of charity, I was soft enough to give them to him. Then I wanted them back and cried, but my mother said: 'Don't cry, Johnnie; some day you'll get your wooden soldiers back.'

"And believe me, you lop-sided, mutton-headed, goofus-brained set of certified rolling pins, that day has come!"

There are four classes of men:
1. He who knows not, and knows
   not he knows not,
      He is a fool; shun him.
2. He who knows not, and knows
   he knows not,
      He is simple, teach him.
3. He who knows, and knows not
   he knows,
      He is asleep; waken him.
4. He who knows, and knows he
   knows,
      He is wise; follow him.

AUTHOR UNKNOWN

Excuse, Excuses

Let us be excusers rather than accusers.

The man who is good for excuses is good for nothing else.

BENJAMIN FRANKLIN

The worst buy is an alibi.

Then there were the two Sunday fishermen who heard bells ringing in the distance. One said, contritely, "You know, Sam, we really ought to be in church." Sam re-baited his hook and answered, "Well, I couldn't go, anyway. My wife is sick."

Presbyterian Life

You may often make excuses for another, never to yourself.

PUBLILIUS SYRUS

Executive

An executive is one who makes an immediate decision and is sometimes right.

It is a safer thing any time to fol- a man's advice rather than his example.

JOSH BILLINGS

A consultant is an executive who can't find another job. HENRY W. PLATT

The man who delegates authority must forego the luxury of blowing his top. *Nation's Business*

He that multiplieth the doers is greater than he that doeth the work.

JOHN R. MOTT

They that govern the most make the least noise.

A good executive is simply a man who can set up an organization that can run efficiently without him.

Experience

Experience is not what happens to a man; it is what a man does with what happens to him. HUXLEY

One thorn of experience is worth a whole wilderness of warning. LOWELL

Experience may not be worth what it costs, but I can't seem to get it for any less. *Presbyterian Life*

Experience is the mother of science.

Past experience should be a guide post, not a hitching post.

There is no free tuition in the school of experience.

Experience is what you get while you are looking for something else.

There are no vacations from the school of experience.

Experience keeps a dear school, yet fools will learn in no other.

BENJAMIN FRANKLIN

Experience is a good teacher but it is very costly.

Expert

An expert is any little spurt away from home.

An expert is a little drip under pressure.

An expert is one smart enough to tell you how to run your own business but too smart to start one of his own.

An expert — a big shot — small caliber, big bore.

1st neighbor: "My husband is an efficiency expert in a large office."
2nd neighbor: "What does an efficiency expert do?"
1st neighbor: "Well, if we women did it, they'd call it nagging."

Express, Expression

Of all the things you wear, your expression is the most important.

As soon as you move one step up from the bottom, your effectiveness depends on your ability to reach others through the spoken or written word. This ability to express oneself is perhaps the most important of all skills a man can possess.

PETER BRUCKNER *in Fortune*

F

Facts

An eminent English editor said, "Opinion is free, but facts are sacred."

———◆———

Facts do not change; feelings do.

———◆———

You can tell how many seeds are in an apple, but you cannot tell how many apples are in a seed.

———◆———

The modern 7-inch-long lead pencil can draw a line 35 miles in length; it can write an average of 45,000 words; and it can take an average of 17 sharpenings.

———◆———

An ounce of fact means more than a ton of argument.   MARTIN VANBEE

———◆———

There are 44,379,000 children under 14 living in homes where both parents are of the same faith, and 4,148,000 in homes where there is a mixed marriage or where one partner has "no religion."

———◆———

Eighty per cent of the heads of the science departments of the great universities of the United States say grace at the table in their homes. This was the observation of an eminent scientist from New Zealand who visited these United States scientists during his six months tour of scientific institutions here.

———◆———

Fail, Failure

Life's greatest failure is failing to be true to the best you know.

———◆———

One seldom meets a man who fails at doing what he likes to do.

———◆———

It isn't that we fail when we try, but that we fail to try!
DR. HENRIETTA C. MEARS

Our greatest glory consists not in never failing, but in rising every time we do fail.

———◆———

Failure can become a weight or it can give you wings.

———◆———

Failure is the only thing that can be achieved without much effort.

———◆———

Failure is the line of least persistence.
STEPHANIE MARTINO

———◆———

It is no disgrace to fail when trying. The one time you don't want to fail is the last time you try.
CHARLES F. KETTERING

———◆———

You can achieve one very important thing without effort — failure.

———◆———

Formula for failure: Try to please everyone.   HERBERT BAYARD SWOPE

———◆———

No man ever fails until he fails on the inside.

———◆———

The world of failure is divided north and south by lines of lassitude, east and west by lines of loungitude.

———◆———

Some of the "room at the top" is created by the men who go to sleep there and fall off.

———◆———

It is at night that the astronomers discover new worlds. It is often in the night of failure that men discover the light of a new hope.

———◆———

Most failures begin in failure to try.

———◆———

We need to teach the highly educated person that it is not a disgrace to fail and that he must analyze every failure to find its cause. He must learn how to fail intelligently, for failing is one of the greatest arts in the world. CHARLES F. KETTERING

———♦———

Failure is only the opportunity to begin again, more intelligently. HENRY FORD

Faith, Faithful, Faithfulness

The greatest victories are the victories of faith. It is not so much what we can do that counts, but what we can trust God to do.

———♦———

Faith in God sees the invisible, believes the incredible, and receives the impossible.

———♦———

"Daddy, may I have a cat?" kindergarten-age Peggy asked her father.

"Yes," replied her father, "but not until we move into a larger home."

"Daddy, may I have two cats?" asked the eager little girl.

"Yes, you may have two cats, or three or four cats if you wish," he answered, sure that the family would not be moving. But the inevitable happened and the family moved into a spacious home with an over-sized yard. Daddy had forgotten about the promised cats, but not Peggy. And she kept pressing her father, who made excuses. Peggy, however, was hopeful and believed the day would come when she could have a cat, or two or three . . . but one night she decided to change her prayer. Instead of praying that she would soon have the promised cat, she said, "Thank You, God, for sending me a cat."

"Peggy, why did you say that to God?" her older sister asked her when putting her to bed.

"Well," the little miss replied, "I thought that if I thanked God He would be embarrassed and send the cats."

The next day Peggy was playing out in the back yard and chanced to go into the tool shed. There she found an old mother cat and a litter of baby kittens. Of course no one in the family knew about the cat family or when the mother cat chose her home, but Peggy maintained it was a good thing she had embarrassed God!

———♦———

One day a man went running and puffing into the railroad station to catch a train, but missed it. He looked at his watch and said, "Watch, I had a lot of faith in you." A friend overheard him and said, "Don't you know that faith without works is dead?"

———♦———

The steps of faith fall on the seeming void and find rock beneath. JOHN GREENLEAF WHITTIER

———♦———

Faith is belief in action.

———♦———

You will never learn faith in comfortable surroundings. A. B. SIMPSON

———♦———

Faith honors God;
God honors faith.

———♦———

Faith is a lively, richless confidence in God. MARTIN LUTHER

———♦———

F - orsaking
A - ll
I
T - ake
H - im

———♦———

Religious faith is not a final goal to be reached, but a highway to be traveled.

———♦———

Living without faith is like driving in the fog.

———♦———

Faith is the one great moving force which we can neither weigh in the balance nor test in the crucible. SIR WILLIAM OSLER

———♦———

Faith is the pencil of the soul that pictures heavenly things. T. BURBRIDGE

———♦———

A little boy was crossing the ocean with his father, who was captain of the ship, when they ran into a storm. The waves tossed the ship about like a cork and everyone was stricken with fear. But the boy sat still, with his eyes directed toward a certain spot.

He sat there quite unperturbed as the ship was being dashed about by the waves. Someone asked him if he were not afraid, and he answered:

"I have my eye on that little window, and through that window I can see the bridge, and on that bridge is my father. My father is the captain of the ship, and he has taken it through many storms."

———◆———

Faith is to believe what we do not see, and the reward of this faith is to see what we believe.　　ST. AUGUSTINE

———◆———

The Christian faith offers peace in war, comfort in sorrow, strength in weakness, and light in darkness.
　　　　　　　　　　WALTER A. MAIER

———◆———

Faith is the link that binds our nothingness to almightiness.

———◆———

Faith either removes mountains or tunnels through.

———◆———

Faith that is sure of God is the only faith there is.　　OSWALD CHAMBERS

———◆———

Faith contains belief, but belief is not the whole of faith.　　*Eternity*

———◆———

There are a thousand ways of pleasing God, but not one without faith.

———◆———

Small faith may take you to heaven but great faith may bring heaven to you.

———◆———

Faith ends where worry begins and worry ends where faith begins.

———◆———

Faith, like light, should always be simple and unbending; while love, like warmth, should beam forth on every side, and bend to every necessity of our brethren.　　LUTHER

———◆———

While reason is puzzling herself about the mystery, faith is turning into her daily bread and feeding on it thankfully in her heart of hearts.
　　　　　　　　　　F. D. HUNTINGTON

I cannot explain the wind, but I can hoist a sail.

———◆———

The most precious things are near at hand, without money and without price. All that I have ever had, may be yours by stretching forth your hand and taking it.　　JOHN BURROUGHS

———◆———

Faith does not demand miracles but often accomplishes them.

———◆———

Credit is applied faith.

———◆———

When faithfulness is most difficult, it is most necessary.

———◆———

Faith is what made the little girl take an umbrella to a prayer meeting called especially to pray for rain. Grownups wore sun glasses.

———◆———

Faith's answer to the question "How?" is one word, "God!"

———◆———

Faith does not eliminate foresight.

———◆———

Fame

Fame and fortune never got any man to heaven.

———◆———

The man who wakes up and finds himself famous hasn't been asleep.

———◆———

No one ever traveled the road to fame on a pass.

———◆———

Family

The family that prays together, stays together.

———◆———

A family jar is no good for preserving the peace!

———◆———

There is just as much authority in the family today as there ever was — only now the children exercise it.

———◆———

He that has no fools, knaves nor beggars in his family must have been begot by a flash of lightning
　　　　　　　　　　THOMAS FULLER

The family is like a book,
The children are the leaves,
The parents are the covers
That protective beauty gives.
At first the pages of the book
Are blank and purely fair,
But time soon writes its memories
And paints its pictures there.
Love is the little golden clasp
That bindeth up the trust.
Oh, break it not, lest all the leaves
Shall scatter and be lost.
AUTHOR UNKNOWN

———♦———

Every family tree has some sap in it.

———♦———

Fanatic, Fanaticism

Fanaticism is redoubling your effort
when you have forgotten your aim.

———♦———

Father

My Dad

He couldn't speak before a crowd;
He couldn't teach a class;
But when he came to Sunday school
He brought the folks en masse.

He couldn't sing to save his life,
In public couldn't pray;
But always his jalopy was just
Crammed on each Lord's day.

And although he couldn't sing,
Nor teach, nor lead in prayer,
He listened well, he had a smile,
And he was always there
With all the others whom he brought
Who lived both far and near —
And God's work prospered, for
I had a consecrated dad.   *Selected*

———♦———

Fatigue

Fatigue is the devil's best weapon.

———♦———

Fault, Faults

I see no fault that I might not have
committed myself.   GOETHE

———♦———

Next time you are tempted to pick
out the faults in your brother, take
time to count ten — ten of your own.

Faults are thick when love is thin.

———♦———

The greatest fault is to be conscious
of none.   CARLYLE

———♦———

Blaming your faults on your nature
does not change the nature of your
faults.   ANONYMOUS

———♦———

You can bear your own faults, why
not a fault in your wife?
BENJAMIN FRANKLIN

———♦———

Wink at small faults — remember
thou hast great ones.   BENJAMIN FRANKLIN

———♦———

Make sure that however good you
may be, you have some faults; that
however dull you may be, you can
find out what they are; and that however slight they may be, you had
better make some patient effort to get
rid of them.

———♦———

How few there are who have courage enough to own their faults, or
resolution enough to mend them!
BENJAMIN FRANKLIN

———♦———

Women's faults are many,
Men have only two:
Everything they say, everything they
do.

———♦———

When you are looking for faults to
correct, look in the mirror.

———♦———

Favors

Any person who accepts favors from
others is placing a mortgage on his
peace of mind.

———♦———

Fear

If you fear that people will know,
don't do it.

———♦———

Nothing in life is to be feared, it is
only to be understood.

———♦———

Keep your fears to yourself, but
share your courage with others.
ROBERT LOUIS STEVENSON

Fear always springs from ignorance.

EMERSON

———◆———

Fear of failure is the father of failure.

———◆———

Fear is unbelief parading in disguise.

———◆———

Don't be afraid of the day you have never seen.   *English Proverb*

———◆———

"He lies there that never feared the face of man," so mused the Regent Morton over the open grave of John Knox. To fear God and to fear nothing else in God's universe — this, indeed, is to be a man.   JOHN ROADMENDER

Feelings

It is with feelings as with waters, the shallow murmur, but the deep are dumb.   RALEIGH

———◆———

We often dislike a people not for what they are but for what we are.

ANONYMOUS

———◆———

Someone asked Luther, "Do you feel sure that you have been forgiven?"

He answered, "No, but I'm as sure as there's a God in heaven."

———◆———

For feelings come, and feelings go,
And feelings are deceiving,
My warrant is the Word of God
Naught else is worth believing.

Selected

———◆———

Emotion rises out of truth; emotionalism is poured on to it.

Fellowship

Fellowship with God means warfare with the world.   CHARLES E. FULLER

———◆———

Most Christians do not have fellowship with God; they have fellowship with each other about God.

PARIS REIDHEAD

———◆———

Fire

It is not enough to light a fire; you must put fuel on it.

Flag

We all love that flag. It gladdens the heart of the old and the young, and it shelters us all. Wherever it is raised, on land or sea, at home or in our distant possessions, it always stands for liberty and humanity; and wherever it is assaulted the whole nation rises up to defend it.   WILLIAM MC KINLEY

———◆———

A flag neglected means flagging patriotism.

———◆———

Flowers

It is better to bring a cheap bouquet
To a living friend this very day,
Than a bushel of roses,
To lay on his casket when he's dead.

AUTHOR UNKNOWN

———◆———

The church-nursery school teacher had placed a lovely bouquet of daffodils on a table in the nursery room. When little Sandra came into the room she was fascinated by the flowers and said to her teacher, "Aren't these pretty telephones God made? I think I'll call God up and say, 'Thank you for the pretty flowers.'"

———◆———

Fool, Fools, Fooling

Oh what a tangled web we weave
When first we practice to deceive.

———◆———

Who has deceived thee so oft as thyself.   BENJAMIN FRANKLIN

———◆———

It is never wise to argue with a fool. Bystanders don't know which is which.

———◆———

All are not fools that look so.

———◆———

Any fool can criticize, condemn and complain — and generally does.

———◆———

A fool tells us what he will do; a boaster what he has done; the wise man does it and says nothing.

———◆———

You can't fool all the people all the time. Some of them are fooling you.

A magician was sailing the Pacific right after World War II, entertaining the passengers. With each amazing feat of magic, a parrot, who perched on his shoulder would squawk, "Faker, faker." No matter what the magician did, rabbits out of hats, vanishing bird cage and all, he would repeatedly cry, "Faker, faker." The magician and parrot became bitter enemies. Finally the magician promised that he would do a trick that would out-Houdini Houdini. The night came, the wand was waved, the "woofle dust" was sprinkled. At that minute the ship hit a floating mine, which blew the ship to pieces. The next morning, on a make-shift life raft, the parrot was perched at one end, the magician at the other. Finally the parrot hopped over and said, "O.K. Buddy, you win, but what did you do with the ship?"

The family of fools is ancient.
BENJAMIN FRANKLIN

Fools are never uneasy. Stupidity is without anxiety.
GOETHE

Forget

What a grand world this would be if we could forget our troubles as easily as we forget our blessings.
Tips

Always remember to forget
The things that made you sad,
But never forget to remember
The things that made you glad.

If you were busy being true
To what you knew you ought to do,
You'd be so busy you'd forget
The blunders of the folks you met.
ANONYMOUS

"Did you forget your memory verse, Johnny?" the teacher asked when he did not say it.

"Oh, no," replied Johnny. "I didn't learn it. I can't forget what I didn't learn."

Forgive, Forgiveness

Christ can forgive any trespass. He can overlook none.

Pardon others often, thyself seldom.

He who forgives ends the quarrel.

He who cannot forgive others breaks the bridge over which he must pass himself.
GEORGE HERBERT

It is usually easier to forgive an enemy than a friend.

Doing an injury puts you below your enemy;
Revenging one makes you but even with him;
Forgiving it sets you above him.
BENJAMIN FRANKLIN

They never pardon who commit the wrong.
JOHN DRYDEN

Forgiveness is man's deepest need and highest achievement.
HORACE BUSHNELL

Forgive and forget. When you bury a mad dog, don't leave his tail above the ground.
SPURGEON

Forgiveness is more than the remission of penalty; it should mean the restoration of a broken fellowship.

Fortune

Fortune does not so much change men as it unmasks them.

It is no use to wait for your ship to come in, unless you have sent one out.
Belgian Proverb

As pride increases, fortune declines.
BENJAMIN FRANKLIN

He that waits upon fortune is never sure of a dinner.
BENJAMIN FRANKLIN

105

Free, Freedom

Freedom is not a question of doing as we like but doing as we ought.

———◆———

You should never wear your best trousers when you go out to fight for freedom and truth.   HENRIK IBSEN

———◆———

Freedom is only a word until you have been close to losing it.

———◆———

Freedom is not worth having if it does not include the freedom to make mistakes.   GANDHI

———◆———

The greatest glory of a freeborn people is to transmit that freedom to their children.   WILLIAM HARVARD

———◆———

Freedom of religion does not mean freedom from religion.
          N. Y. Supreme Court

———◆———

In a free country there is much clamor with little suffering; in a despotic state there is little complaint but much suffering.   CARUOT

———◆———

There are two freedoms — the false, where a man is free to do what he likes; the true, where a man is free to do what he ought.   CHARLES KINGSLEY

———◆———

Friends, Friendship

A friend is someone who will make us do what we can when we are saying we can't.   EMERSON

———◆———

There are three faithful friends — an old wife, an old dog and ready money.
          BENJAMIN FRANKLIN

———◆———

Friendship is a disinterested commerce between equals.   OLIVER GOLDSMITH

———◆———

The only way to have a friend is to be one.   EMERSON

———◆———

There's happiness in little things,
There's joy in passing pleasure.
But friendships are, from year to year,
The best of all life's treasure.

Every friend lost pushes you one step closer to the brink of character bankruptcy.

———◆———

God evidently does not intend us all to be rich, or powerful or great, but He does intend us all to be friends.
          EMERSON

———◆———

Lord Brooke was so delighted with the friendship of Sir Philip Sydney that he ordered to be engraved upon his tomb nothing but this — "Here lies the friend of Sir Philip Sydney."

———◆———

An open foe may prove a curse; but a pretended friend is worse.
          BENJAMIN FRANKLIN

———◆———

He that lieth down with dogs, shall rise up with fleas.   BENJAMIN FRANKLIN

———◆———

Friendships cemented together with sin do not hold.

———◆———

The best way to keep your friends is not to give them away.

———◆———

Friendship is a responsibility, not an opportunity.

———◆———

Most of us are so busy trying to get something else that we can't enjoy what we have.   Friendly Thoughts

———◆———

I do with my friends as I do with books. I would have them where I can find them but seldom use them.
          RALPH WALDO EMERSON

———◆———

Friendship increases by visiting friends, but by visiting seldom.
          BENJAMIN FRANKLIN

———◆———

True friendship is a plant of slow growth, and must undergo and withstand the shocks of adversity before it is entitled to the appellation.
          GEORGE WASHINGTON

———◆———

Happy is the house that shelters a friend.   RALPH WALDO EMERSON

———◆———

Be slow in choosing a friend, slower in changing.   BENJAMIN FRANKLIN

The only safe and sure way to destroy an enemy is to make him your friend.

————♦————

The quickest way to wipe out friendship is to sponge on it.

————♦————

Life has no blessing like a prudent friend.

————♦————

The wisest man I have ever known once said to me, "Nine out of every ten people improve on acquaintance," and I have found his words true.

FRANK SWINNERTON

————♦————

A brother may not be a friend, but a friend will always be a brother.

BENJAMIN FRANKLIN

————♦————

The higher style we demand of friendship, the less easy to establish it with flesh and blood.

RALPH WALDO EMERSON

————♦————

If you were another person would you like to be a friend of yours?

————♦————

Friendship does not mean knowing all about a person. It is knowing him.

DR. HENRIETTA C. MEARS

————♦————

Ever notice how a dog wins friends and influences people without reading books?

Vidette, Iuka, Miss.

————♦————

Do good to thy friend to keep him, to thy enemy to gain him.

BENJAMIN FRANKLIN

————♦————

If a man does not make new acquaintances as he passes through life, he will soon find himself left alone. A man should keep his friendships in constant repair.

JOHNSON

————♦————

A true friend unbosoms freely, advises justly, assists readily, adventures boldly, takes all patiently, defends courageously, and continues a friend unchangeable.

WILLIAM PENN

————♦————

When befriended, remember it; when you befriend, forget it.

BENJAMIN FRANKLIN

Friendship is a treasure ship anyone can launch.

————♦————

Oh, the comfort, the inexpressible comfort of feeling safe with a person; having neither to weigh thoughts nor measure words, but to pour them all out, just as they are, chaff and grain together, knowing that a faithful hand will take and sift them, keep what is worth keeping, and then, with the breath of kindness, blow the rest away.

GEORGE ELIOT

————♦————

Cultivate the qualities you desire in a friend because someone is looking for you as their friend.

————♦————

I never considered a difference of opinion in politics, in religion, in philosophy, as cause for withdrawing from a friend.

THOMAS JEFFERSON

————♦————

A thirteen-year-old girl's definition: A friend is one in front of whom you can be your own true self.

————♦————

Friendship cannot live without ceremony, nor without civility.

BENJAMIN FRANKLIN

————♦————

A friend is a present you give yourself by being friendly.

Home Life

————♦————

It's a Funny Thing But True

It's a funny thing but true,
The folks you don't like, don't like you.
I don't know why this should be so
But just the same I always know,
That when I'm sour, friends are few,
When I'm friendly, folks are, too.
I sometimes get up in the morn,
Awishin' I was never born,
And then I make cross remarks, a few,
And then my family wishes, too,
That I had gone some other place,
But then I change my little tune,
And sing and smile,
And then the folks around me sing
    and smile.
I guess 'twas catching all the while.
It's a funny thing but true,
The folks you like, they sure like you!

AUTHOR UNKNOWN

107

I know I've never told you
In the hurried rush of days
How much your friendship helps me
In a thousand little ways;
But you've played such a part
In all I do or try to be,
I want to tell you thank you
For being friends with me. ANONYMOUS

————◆————

You can make more friends in two months by becoming interested in other people than you can in two years by trying to get other people interested in you. DALE CARNEGIE

————◆————

Abraham Lincoln was once taken to task by an associate for his attitude toward his enemies: "Why do you try to make friends of them? You should try to destroy them."

Lincoln replied gently, "Am I not destroying my enemies when I make them my friends?"

————◆————

We do not make friends
    As we do houses,
But discover them
    As we do the arbutus,
Under the leaves of our lives,
Concealed in our experience. RADER

If you are an archer,
    And friendship your date,
Take aim very carefully —
    Don't pierce the wrong heart.

For friendship misplaced
    Is bound to bring sorrow;
Perhaps not today,
    But most surely tomorrow.

————◆————

Friends

The joy of being friends is just
A simple code of faith and trust,
A homey comradeship that stays
The threatened fear of darker days;
The kind of faith that brings to light
The good, the beautiful, and bright;
And best and blest, and true and rare —
Is having friends who love and care! AUTHOR UNKNOWN

————◆————

Future

The best thing about the future is that it comes only one day at a time.

————◆————

My interest is in the future because I am going to spend the rest of my life there. CHARLES F. KETTERING

G

Genius

It is necessary to be almost a genius to make a good husband. BALZAC

————◆————

Doing easily what others find difficult is talent; doing what is impossible is genius. AMIEL

————◆————

Common sense is instinct, and enough of it is genius. G. B. SHAW

————◆————

Genius without education is like silver in the mine. FRANKLIN

————◆————

Genius is only the power of making continuous effort. ELBERT HUBBARD

We'd have a generation of geniuses if all our children were as brilliant in school and as well-behaved at home as we parents think we remember being.

————◆————

A genius is a man seen driving his own car when his son and daughter are home from college. Town Journal

————◆————

If we are to have genius we must put up with the inconvenience of genius, a thing the world will never do; it wants geniuses, but would like them just like other people. GEORGE MOORE

Girls

A little girl is many things . . .
 To Grandma, she's an angel,
 To Daddy, she's a flirt,
 To the boy next door, she's an awful
  pest
 With her face all covered with dirt.
 To Mommy she is all these things
 And a miniature woman, too,
 But they don't suspect for a minute . . .
 What their little girl is to you. . . .
To you, her teacher, a little girl is a
sponge soaking up knowledge. In her
you see the promise of a bright future
which you have the chance to help
mold. If she's selfish, you teach her to
share; if she fibs, you teach her truth.
If she is insecure, you do your best to
give her confidence. Through her Sunday school work you discover talents
seldom recognized or understood by
her parents. These you encourage and
develop to the satisfaction of you both.
To you, little girls and little boys are
individuals, and you give them many
attentions above and beyond the cur-
ricular call of duty.   AUTHOR UNKNOWN

———◆———

A girl who knows all the answers has
been asked all the questions.

———◆———

The Taking Girl

She took my hand in sheltered nooks,
She took my candy and my books,
She took the lustrous wrap of fur,
She took those gloves I bought for her,
She took my words of love and care,
She took my flowers, rich and rare,
She took my ring with tender smile,
She took my time for quite a while,
She took my kisses, maid so shy —
She took, I must confess, my eye,
She took whatever I would buy,
And then she took the other guy!

———◆———

Give, Giving, Gifts

Every gift, though it be small, is in
reality great if given with affection.
                                    PINDAR

Who gives himself, with his alms, feeds
  three,
Himself, his hungering neighbor, and
  Me.   *The Vision of Sir Launfal*

———◆———

Old Deacon Horner, sat in a corner
As the contribution box passed by;
Sweetly content, he dropped in a cent,
And said, "What a good churchman
  am I."

———◆———

A gift is never lost; only what is
selfishly kept impoverishes.

———◆———

When God sends the dawn, he sends
it for all.   CERVANTES

———◆———

The most expensive gift is the gift
of gab.

———◆———

Be not niggardly of what costs thee
nothing, as courtesy, counsel and countenance.   BENJAMIN FRANKLIN

———◆———

Generosity does not come naturally;
it must be taught.

———◆———

Treasure in heaven is laid up only
as treasure on earth is laid down.

———◆———

The Greatest Gift — John 3:16

GOD . . . . The Greatest Lover
SO LOVED . . . . The Greatest Degree
THE WORLD . . . . The Greatest Company
THAT HE GAVE. . . . . . The Greatest Act
HIS ONLY
 BEGOTTEN SON . . . . The Greatest Gift
THAT WHO-
 SOEVER . . . The Greatest Opportunity
BELIEVETH . . . . The Greatest Simplicity
IN HIM . . . . . . The Greatest Attraction
SHOULD NOT
 PERISH . . . . The Greatest Promise
BUT . . . . The Greatest Difference
HAVE . . . . The Greatest Certainty
EVERLASTING
 LIFE . . . . The Greatest Possession

———◆———

The hand that gives, gathers.

———◆———

Give what you have; to someone it
may be better than you dare to think.
                              LONGFELLOW

GIVING

Our Heavenly Father never takes anything from His children unless He means to give them something better.
GEORGE MUELLER

———◆———

Some Christians give to the Lord's work weekly; others just give weakly.

———◆———

To whom much is given, much is expected.

———◆———

The minister of a small church believed some practical joker was joshing him as I.O.U.'s began to appear in the collection plate. But one Sunday night weeks later the collection included an envelope containing bills equal to the total of the I.O.U.'s.

After that, the parson could hardly wait to see what amount the anonymous doner had promised. The range in contributions was from five to fifteen dollars — apparently based on what the donor thought the sermon to be worth — for there came a Sunday when the collection plate brought a note reading, "U.O. Me $5."
Pathfinder

———◆———

A government income tax inspector visited a clergyman and expressed a desire to see his church. The clergyman beamed with pleasure at the request. Afterwards he asked the inspector what he thought of it.

"Frankly, I'm a bit disappointed," said the government man. "After looking at the income tax returns of your parishioners and the fine gifts they claim to your church, I had come to the conclusion that the aisles must be paved with gold."

———◆———

There are three kinds of givers — the flint, the sponge and the honeycomb.

To get anything out of a flint you must hammer it. And then you get only chips and sparks.

To get water out of a sponge you must squeeze it, and the more you use pressure, the more you will get.

But the honeycomb just overflows with its own sweetness. *The Evangel*

Whatever is offered to the Lord, broken in His hands, and given to the multitude, is sufficient for the need.
V. RAYMOND EDMAN

———◆———

You may give without loving, but you can't love without giving.

———◆———

The Lord takes notice, not only of what we give, but of what we have left.

———◆———

Think It Over:

God made the sun — it gives.
God made the moon — it gives.
God made the stars — they give.
God made the air — it gives.
God made the clouds — they give.
God made the earth — it gives.
God made the sea — it gives.
God made the trees — they give.
God made the flowers — they give.
God made the fowls — they give.
God made the beasts — they give.
God made the Plan — He gives.
God made man — He . . .? *Selected*

———◆———

Do your givin'
While you're livin'
Then you're knowin'
Where it's goin'.

———◆———

There is more power in the open hand than in the clenched fist.
HERBERT N. CASSON

———◆———

Some people give according to their means and others according to their meanness.

———◆———

Once there was a Christian, he had a
  pious look.
His consecration was complete, except
  his pocketbook.
He'd put a nickel in the plate,
Then with might and main,
He'd sing, "When we asunder part, it
  gives us inward pain."
He dropped a nickel in the plate, meekly raised his eyes
Glad the weekly rent was paid for a
  mansion in the skies.
Western Messenger

Don't give till it hurts: Give a little more . . . give till it feels good.

———◆———

You can't outgive God.

———◆———

You cannot get without giving.

———◆———

A lady was filling a box for India when a child brought her a penny. With it the lady bought a tract to put in the box. The tract was at length given to a Burmese chief, and it led him to Christ. The chief told the story of his Saviour and his great happiness to his friends. They also believed, and cast away their idols. A church was built there. A missionary was sent, and fifteen hundred were converted from heathenism. All of these wonderful changes were the result of that little seed.   SOURCE UNKNOWN

———◆———

Give a penny and hear it squeal
Give a quarter and hear it speak
But if you'd hear a real live holler
Drop on the plate a silver dollar.

———◆———

A steward in a church asked a member for a contribution, and the member said that he didn't have any money to give. The steward said, "Brother, we only have two kinds of members in our church. Those who give to the church and those the church gives to . . . and right now we'll start helping you."
Result: The steward got a sizable donation.

———◆———

Don't give from the top of your purse but from the bottom of your heart.

———◆———

A pig was lamenting his lack of popularity. He complained to the cow that people were always talking about the cow's gentleness and kind eyes, whereas his name was used as an insult. The pig admitted that the cow gave milk and cream, but maintained that pigs gave more. "Why," the animal complained, "we pigs give bacon and ham and bristles and people even pickle our feet. I don't see why you cows are esteemed so much more."
The cow thought awhile and said gently: "Maybe it's because we give while we're still living."

———◆———

The best thing to give . . .
to your enemy is forgiveness;
to an opponent, tolerance;
to a friend, your heart;
to your child, a good example;
to a father, deference;
to your mother, conduct that will
make her proud of you;
to yourself, respect;
to all men, charity.   LORD BALFOUR

———◆———

Wife to husband on Christmas morning: "You angel! Just what I need to exchange for just what I wanted."

———◆———

Do you know what the buffalo on the nickel said to the offering plate? "I need a little green stuff to feed on."

———◆———

A small boy observed his mother put a penny on the offering plate at the morning service. On the way home from church, she freely criticized the poor sermon they had heard. "But, Mother," said the boy, "what could you expect for a penny?"

———◆———

If you train up a child to give pennies, when he is old he will not depart from it.

———◆———

May God forbid that we should present our gifts and withhold ourselves.

———◆———

Minister to congregation: "This morning we will worship the Lord in silent prayer, followed by a silent offering. It will fall even more silently if you fold it."

———◆———

When the collection plate was passed, the little old lady began fumbling in her purse. The nearer the ushers approached, the more frantically she searched her bag. Finally, noticing her plight, the little boy sitting nearby slid over and nudged her.

"Here lady," he told her. "You take my dime. I can hide under the seat."

Together

———◆———

While a minister was announcing that a missionary offering would be taken, one man in the congregation said he would not give because he did not believe in missions.

"All right then," said the minister, "take some of the offering out of the plate because it is for the heathen."

———◆———

A practical demonstration of love for God needs to be made by way of the collection plate.

———◆———

To Pledge or Not to Pledge

To pledge or not to pledge —
That is the question.
Whether 'tis nobler in a man
To take the Gospel free
And let another foot the bill,
Or sign a pledge and pay toward
Church expense!
To give, to pay — aye, there's the rub,
To pay —
When on the free-pew plan a man
May have
A sitting free and take the Gospel, too,
As though he paid, and none be aught
The wiser
Save the church committee who —
Most honorable men — can keep a secret!
"To err is human," and human, too, to buy
At cheapest rate. I'll take the Gospel so!
For others do the same — a common rule!
I'm wise; I'll wait, not work —
I'll pray, not pay,
And let the other fellow foot the bills,
And so I'll get the Gospel free,
You see!

AUTHOR UNKNOWN

Goals

Knowing what our goal is and desiring to reach it doesn't bring us closer to it. Doing something does! ELD

———◆———

For finding the best in life:
Go!
Keep going!
Help someone else to go!

———◆———

Are you a pilgrim or a vagrant? A pilgrim is one who is traveling to a certain place. A vagrant is a mere stroller, with no settled purpose or goal. T. C. INNES

———◆———

Education teaches a student good marksmanship before he takes aim at his goal in life.

———◆———

Set your goal high. You may not reach it, but you'll put on muscle climbing toward it.

———◆———

You must have long-range goals to keep you from being frustrated by short-range failures. CHARLES C. NOBLE

———◆———

There is only one way of seeing things rightly, and that is seeing the whole of them. JOHN RUSKIN

———◆———

Aim at the unattainable so that your work will have an ideal direction even though it never achieves perfection.

EMERSON

———◆———

One of the best marksmen in the country was passing through a small town and everywhere he saw evidence of amazing shooting. On trees, on walls, on fences, and on barns were countless targets with a bullet hole in the exact center of the bull's-eye. So the man sought out the person responsible for this great marksmanship.

"This is the most wonderful shooting I have ever seen," the man said. "How in the world did you do it?"

"Easy as pie," replied the marksman, "I shot first and drew the circles afterwards." *National Motorist*

You don't hit anything unless you aim at it.

There are two words we ought to keep in mind: today and that day.

Our objectives are not set on what we have done, they are not set on what we would like to do; they are set on what we ought to do.

If we could first know where we are, and whither we are tending, we could better judge what to do and how to do it. ABRAHAM LINCOLN

It may be a long way to a goal, but it is never far to the next step toward the goal.

The first two letters of the word goal spell GO. ELD

The great thing in this world is not so much where we stand as in what direction we are moving.
OLIVER WENDELL HOLMES

Men, like tacks, are useful if they have good heads and are pointed in the right direction.

If you haven't figured out where you are going, you're lost before you start.

God

Reach up as far as you can, and God will reach down all the way.
BISHOP VINCENT

It is easier for God to do a difficult thing than an easy thing.

I have lived a long time and the longer I live the more convincing proofs I see that God governs in the affairs of men. BENJAMIN FRANKLIN

"Tell me," said a philosopher, "where is God?"
"First tell me," said the other, "where He is not." ANONYMOUS

We must accept the existence of a Creator in order to accept our American way of life because He is the source of our Freedom. If there is no God then the Communists are right. If there's a God, the American way is right. *American Childhood*

God must first do something *for* us and *in* us, before He can do something *through* us.

When God measures men He puts the tape around the heart, not the head.

We are all dangerous folk without God's controlling hand. W. W. AYER

God can do without us, but we cannot do without Him.

All God's giants have been weak men who did great things for God because they reckoned on His being with them. J. HUDSON TAYLOR

God has given us a will to choose His will. DR. HENRIETTA C. MEARS

The Lord's choice is always choice.

Even as you can't outrun God when you dodge His will, it is equally impossible to outrun His care when you are in His will. CAL GUY, *The Teacher*

The most important thing in the world is not to know the Lord's will but to know the Lord. WALLACE BOYS

God's way becomes plain when we walk in it. *This Day*

The mystery of godliness is God humbling Himself to become man. The mystery of iniquity is man exalting himself to become God. A. J. GORDON

God can give Himself to us only in the measure in which we give ourselves to Him.

Sour godliness is the devil's religion.
JOHN WESLEY

———◆———

Unless there is within us that which is above us, we shall soon yield to that which is about us.   PETER FORSYTHE

———◆———

God is the answer . . .
When you have sinned and need forgiveness;
When you are about to make a decision;
When you feel ill toward another;
When you think you are better than other people;
When your home is at the point of breaking;
When your marriage begins to waver;
When your children begin to lose respect for you;
When you want to live a life of triumph and joy — for here and hereafter.   *Bethel Methodist Church News*

———◆———

A theological school instructor shared a seat with a small boy on a shuttle train. The boy was holding a Sunday school book.

"Do you go to Sunday school, my boy?" asked the man in a friendly way.

"Yes, sir."

"Tell me, my boy," continued the man, thinking to have some fun with the lad, "tell me where God is, and I'll give you an apple."

The boy looked up sharply at the man and promptly replied, "I will give you a whole barrel of apples if you tell me where He is not."

———◆———

A man met a boy on a country road with a basket of bread on his arm. "What have you in that basket, my boy?" asked the man.

"Bread, sir."

"Where did you get that bread?"

"From the baker, sir."

"And where did he get the flour?" asked the man.

"From the farmer, sir."

"And where did the farmer get the flour?" continued the man.

"From seed, sir."

"And where did he get the seed?" persisted the man.

The boy paused, then exclaimed in an awe-struck voice, "From God, sir!"

Yes, behind each loaf of bread is God!

———◆———

God's Way

God moves in a mysterious way,
His wonders to perform;
He plants His footsteps in the sea,
And rides upon the storm.

Deep in unfathomable mines
Of never-failing skill,
He treasures up His bright designs
And works His sov'reign will.

Ye fearful saints, fresh courage take,
The clouds ye so much dread
Are big with mercy, and shall break
In blessing on your head.

Judge not the Lord by feeble sense,
But trust Him for His grace;
Behind a frowning providence
He hides a smiling face.

His purposes will ripen fast,
Unfolding every hour;
The bud may have a bitter taste,
But sweet will be the flower.

Blind unbelief is sure to err,
And scan His work in vain;
God is His own interpreter,
And He will make it plain.
COWPER, 1779

———◆———

Good, Good Will, Good Works

Do all the good you can,
By all the means you can,
In all the ways you can,
In all the places you can,
At all the times you can,
To all the people you can,
As long as ever you can.
JOHN WESLEY

———◆———

The value of our good is not measured by what it costs us but by the amount of good it does the one concerned.

If "God" is taken out of "good" nothing (o) is left.

———♦———

What is serving God?
'Tis doing good to man.

———♦———

There is so much good in the worst of us,
And so much bad in the best of us,
That it ill becomes any of us
To find fault with the rest of us.

———♦———

The man who tries to keep a book account of the good he does never does enough good to pay for the binding of the book.
WILLIAM JENNINGS BRYAN

———♦———

I'd rather be a good man than a brilliant man.
HAROLD L. LUNDQUIST

———♦———

When you are good to others you are always best to yourself.

———♦———

Little Things

Little drops of water, little grains of sand,
Make the mighty ocean and the pleasant land;
So the little moments, humble though they be,
Make the mighty ages of eternity.

So our little errors lead the soul away
From the path of virtue, far in sin to stray.
Little deeds of kindness, little words of love,
Help to make earth happy like the heaven above. JULIA FLETCHER CARNEY

———♦———

I shall pass through this world but once. Any good therefore that I can do or any kindness that I can show to any human being, let me do it now. Let me not defer or neglect it, for I shall not pass this way again.

———♦———

Worth, true worth, rarely needs a megaphone to announce its presence. There are no arrows pointing the way to the sun.

Good, the more communicated, the more abundant grows.
MILTON

———♦———

Goodness consists not in the outward things we do, but in the inward things we are. To be good is the great thing.
E. H. CHAPIN

———♦———

You are expected to make good—not to make excuses.

———♦———

He who stops being better stops being good.
OLIVER CROMWELL

———♦———

Somehow, the better we are, the better the people are that we meet.

———♦———

Good, better, best;
Never let it rest
Till your good is better,
And your better best.
Old Maxim

———♦———

Good will is the one and only asset that competition cannot understand or destroy.
MARSHALL FIELD

———♦———

The most precious thing anyone can have is the good will of others. It is something as fragile as an orchid— and as beautiful. As precious as a gold nugget and as hard to find. As powerful as a great turbine and as hard to build—as wonderful as youth and as hard to keep.
AMOS PARISH

———♦———

Spurgeon once said that one might better try to sail the Atlantic in a paper boat, than try to get to heaven on good works.

———♦———

The best minds that accept Christianity as a divinely inspired system believe that the great end of the Gospel is not merely the saving, but the educating of men's souls, the creating within them of holy disposition, the subduing of egotistical pretentions, and the perpetual enhancing of the desire that the will of God—a will synonymous with goodness and truth—may be done on earth.
GEORGE ELIOT

GOSPEL

Gospel

That the Gospel is to be
opposed is inevitable —
disbelieved is to be expected —
But that it should be made
dull is intolerable!   GERALD KENNEDY

———◆———

The Gospel breaks hard hearts and
heals broken hearts.

———◆———

The good news is that God meets us
where we are, because we cannot rise
to where He would have us be.

———◆———

Christ came, not to preach the Gospel, but that there might be a Gospel
to preach.   DR. GRIFFETH THOMAS

———◆———

The Gospel According to You

There's a sweet old story translated
for men,
But writ in the long, long ago,
The Gospel according to Mark, Luke
and John
Of Christ and His mission below.

Men read and admire the Gospel of
Christ,
With its love so unfailing and true;
But what do they say, and what do
they think,
Of the gospel "according to you"?

'Tis a wonderful story, that gospel of
love,
As it shines in the Christ life divine;
And, oh, that its truth might be told
again
In the story of your life and mine!

Unselfishness mirrors in every scene;
Love blossoms on every sod;
And back from its vision the heart
comes to tell
The wonderful goodness of God.

You are writing each day a letter to
men;
Take care that the writing is true;
'Tis the only gospel that some men will
read —
That gospel according to you.
   AUTHOR UNKNOWN

G - lad Tidings
O - ffer Pardon
S - alvation
P - eace
E - ternal Life
L - asting Joy

———◆———

Run, John, and live! the Law com-
mands,
Yet gives me neither legs nor hands.
A better note the Gospel brings,
It bids me fly — and gives me wings.

———◆———

There is only one Gospel. It is for
the whole man, his family, his community, his neighbor, his nation, his
world.   HERBERT GEZORK

———◆———

It is not nearly so important that
we send sputniks around the globe as
that we should send the message of
Christ around the world.
   The Sunday Bulletin

———◆———

Another version of
The Gospel According to You

"You are our epistle, written in our
hearts, known and read of all men."

The Gospels of Matthew, Mark, Luke
and John,
Are read by more than a few,
But the one that is most read and
commented on
Is the gospel according to *you.*

You are writing a gospel, a chapter
each day
By things that you do and words that
you say,
Men read what you write, whether
faithless or true.
Say, what is the gospel according to
you?

Do men read His truth and His love
in your life,
Or has yours been too full of malice
and strife?
Does your life speak of evil, or does
it ring true?
Say, what is the gospel according to
you?   AUTHOR UNKNOWN

116

You can't spell Gospel without Go.
Nor Pray without Pay, you know.
But if we put them together and pray
and pay
The Gospel will go to lands far away.
The Tower of St. Paul

Gossip

Gossip is the art of saying nothing and leaving nothing unsaid.

A great many people, like cats, lick themselves with their tongues.

It is well to remember that mansions in the sky cannot be built out of the mud thrown at others. *Evangelist*

Gossiping and lying go hand in hand.

A little girl explained that the teacher had said: "Go into all the world and preach the gossip."

A gossip is a person with a keen sense of rumor.

Gossip is like mud thrown against a clean wall; it may not stick, but it leaves a mark.

If you say nothing, no one will repeat it.

It's easier to float a rumor than to sink one!

The Shady Dozen

"I heard. . . ."
"They say. . . ."
"Everybody says. . . ."
"Have you heard . . .?"
"Did you hear . . .?"
"Isn't it awful . . .?"
"People say. . . ."
"Did you ever . . .?"
"Somebody said . . ."
"Would you think . . .?"
"Don't say I told you . . ."
"Oh, I think it is terrible. . . ."
The Outlook

When it comes to spreading gossip it seems that the female of the species is much faster than the mail.
Glendale News Press

The difference between gossip and news is whether you hear it or tell it.

Four preachers met for a friendly gathering. During the conversation one preacher said, "Our people come to us and pour out their hearts, confess certain sins and needs. Let's do the same. Confession is good for the soul." In due time they agreed. One confessed he liked to go to the movies, and would sneak off when away from his church. The second confessed to liking to smoke cigars, and the third one confessed to liking to play cards. When they came to the fourth one, he wouldn't confess. The others pressed him, saying, "Come now, we confessed ours, what is your secret sin or vice?"

Finally he answered, "It is gossiping and I can hardly wait to get out of here."

I Know Something Good About You

Wouldn't this old world be better
If the folks we met would say,
"I know something good about you!"
And then treat us just that way?

Wouldn't it be fine and dandy,
If each handclasp, warm and true,
Carried with it this assurance,
"I know something good about you?"

Wouldn't life be lots more happy,
If the good that's in us all
Were the only thing about us
That folks bothered to recall?

Wouldn't life be lots more happy,
If we praised the good we see?
For there's such a lot of goodness
In the worst of you and me.

Wouldn't it be nice to practice
That fine way of thinking, too;
You know something good about me;
I know something good about you?
ANONYMOUS

117

Government

In rivers and bad governments, the lightest things swim at the top.
BENJAMIN FRANKLIN

———◆———

Government is impossible where moral character is wanting.

———◆———

While just government protects all in their religious rites, true religion affords government its surest support.
GEORGE WASHINGTON

———◆———

Accepting government aid is like taking drugs — pleasant at first, habit-forming later, damning at last.
W. W. WARD

———◆———

It used to be that when you said a man had gone to his everlasting rest, it didn't mean he had landed a job with the government.

———◆———

Grace

The higher a man is in grace, the lower he will be in his own esteem.
SPURGEON

———◆———

Graduation

A father, attending his son's graduation exercises from college, was heard to remark, "Well, I worked my way through college, and now I have just finished working my son's way through."
The Watchman Examiner

———◆———

Graduation Means:

G - oing forward
R - eady to
A - ccept God's will —
D - etermined to
U - nderstand His Word —
A - lert to
T - emptations —
I - nterested in
O - thers
N - ever forgetting that Christ is my helper.   ELD

———◆———

All that stands between the graduate and the top of the ladder is the ladder.

Great, Greatness

Greatness stands on a precipice.

———◆———

To be great is to be misunderstood.

———◆———

A great man is great until he finds it out; then he is a danger and a nuisance.

———◆———

Great men are known by their deeds — the rest of us by our mortgages.

———◆———

The great man is the man who does a thing for the first time.
ALEXANDER SMITH

———◆———

There never was any heart truly great and gracious that was not also tender and compassionate.   SOUTH

———◆———

No man is small who does a small job in a great way.

———◆———

I will expect great things from God, and I will attempt great things for God.
WILLIAM CAREY

———◆———

The Greatest of All

My greatest loss, to lose my soul.
My greatest gain, Christ as my Saviour.
My greatest object, to glorify God.
My greatest price, a crown of glory.
My greatest work, to win souls for Christ.
My greatest joy, the joy of God's salvation.
My greatest inheritance, heaven and its glories.
My greatest neglect, the neglect of so great salvation.
My greatest crime, to reject Christ the only Saviour.
My greatest privilege, power to become a child of God.
My greatest bargain, to lose all things to win Christ.
My greatest profit, godliness in this life and that to come.
My greatest peace, the peace that passeth understanding.
My greatest knowledge, to know God and Jesus Christ whom He hath sent.
AUTHOR UNKNOWN

There is in every man something greater than he had begun to dream of. Men are nobler than they think themselves. PHILLIPS BROOKS

Go as far as you can see, and when you get there you will see farther.

The greatest things in the world have been done by those who systematized their work and organized their time. ORISON SWEET MARDEN

Grow, Growth

To grow tall spiritually, a man first must learn to kneel.

As we grow better we meet better people. ELBERT HUBBARD

When Longfellow was well along in years, his head as white as snow, but his cheeks as red as a rose, an ardent admirer asked him how it was that he was able to keep so vigorous and write so beautifully. Pointing to a blooming apple tree nearby, he replied: "That apple tree is very old, but I never saw prettier blossoms upon it than those it now bears. The tree grows a little new wood every year, and I suppose it is out of that new wood that those blossoms come. Like the apple tree, I try to grow a little new wood every year." And what Longfellow did, we all ought to do.

Guide, Guidance

If God has called you, don't look over your shoulder to see who is following you.

When God shuts and bolts the door, don't try to get in through the window.

If you would have God's guidance, you must listen as well as talk to the guide. ELD

I know not the way God leads me, but well do I know my Guide. MARTIN LUTHER

Guilt, Guilty

Guilt is always suspicious.

H

Habit, Habits

We Cannot
Sow bad habits and reap a good character;
Sow jealousy and hatred and reap love and friendship;
Sow dissipation and reap a healthy body;
Sow deception and reap confidence;
Sow cowardice and reap courage;
Sow neglect of the Bible and reap a well-guided life. AUTHOR UNKNOWN

It is easier to prevent bad habits than to break them.

Choose the best life, habits will make it pleasant.

Every bad habit acquired by a person actually places a chattel mortgage on his personality.

Habits shape personality — encourage the Sunday school habit.

One good way to break a bad habit: drop it! C. GRANT

Happy, Happiness

Happiness is beneficial for the body but it is grief that develops the power of the mind. MARCEL PROUST

Those who bring sunshine into the lives of others cannot keep it from themselves. J. M. BARRIE

119

HAPPINESS

The first steps to happiness are the church steps.

———

Happiness is found not in reward but in honorable effort.

———

"You should do something every day to make other people happy," one person said to another, "even if it's only to leave them alone."

———

To be happy at home is the ultimate result of all ambition. SAMUEL JOHNSON

———

Folks are generally as happy as they make up their minds to be. ABRAHAM LINCOLN

———

Rules for Happiness

Something to do,
Some one to love,
Something to hope for. KANT

———

The happiness of your life depends upon the character of your thoughts. MARCUS AURELIUS

———

Some people bring happiness wherever they go; others whenever they go.

———

Happiness is a butterfly, which when pursued is always just beyond your grasp, but which if you will sit down quietly will light upon you. HAWTHORNE

———

To be happy with a man you must understand him a lot and love him a little. To be happy with a woman you must love her a lot and not try to understand her at all. HELEN ROWLAND

———

Happiness is not the end of life; character is. H. W. BEECHER

———

Rule for Happiness

1 cup filled to overflowing with
Industry
Concentration
Enthusiasm
1 pinch of spice
1 pinch of sand
Served with sauce of smiles.

The Constitution guarantees only the right to the pursuit of happiness and not the ability to catch it.

———

Happiness is in the heart, not in the circumstances.

———

An effort made for the happiness of others lifts us above ourselves. Happiness isn't so much a matter of position as it is of disposition. Many a train of thought is just a string of empties.

———

The days that make us happy make us wise. JOHN MASEFIELD

———

Many persons have a wrong idea about what constitutes true happiness. It is not attained through self-gratifications, but through fidelity to a worthy purpose. HELEN KELLER

———

Happiness consists in being happy with what we have got and with what we haven't got. SPURGEON

———

You cannot build your happiness on someone else's unhappiness.

———

Plant Happiness

First plant five rows of peas:
Perseverance,
Presence,
Preparation,
Promptness,
Purity.
Next plant three rows of squash:
Squash gossip,
Squash criticism and
Squash indifference.
Then five rows of lettuce:
Let us be faithful to duty.
Let us be unselfish and loyal.
Let us be true to our own obligations.
Let us love one another.
No garden is complete without turnips:
Turn up for important meetings.
Turn up with a smile.
Turn up with new ideas.
Turn up with determination to make everything count for something good and worthwhile.
AUTHOR UNKNOWN

Happiness has no reason. It is not to be found in the facts of our lives, but in the color of the light by which we look at the facts.

———◆———

Society is so interwoven that no individual can attain real happiness alone.

———◆———

Be Happy

Life is too short to be sad in,
To carry a grouch or be mad in,
'Tis made to be happy and glad in,
So let us be friends and be happy!

Friends are too scarce to be sore at,
To gloom and to glower and roar at,
They're made to be loved and not
   "swore at,"
So let us be friends and be happy!

Love is the store we should lay in,
Love is the coin we should pay in,
Love is the language to pray in,
So fill up with love and be happy.
       CLARA COLBURN WOUTERS

———◆———

Happiness is no easy matter; 'tis very hard to find it within ourselves, and impossible to find it anywhere else.
       CHAMFORT

———◆———

After all, it is not what is around us, but what is in us; not what we have, but what we are, that makes us really happy.
       GEIKE

———◆———

God evidently does not intend us all to be rich, or powerful, or great, but He does intend us all to be friends.
       EMERSON

———◆———

If you make children happy now, you will make them happy twenty years hence by the memory of it.
       KATE DOUGLAS WIGGIN

———◆———

Happiness can be built only on virtue, and must of necessity have truth for its foundation.
       COLERIDGE

———◆———

No human being can come into this world without increasing or diminishing the sum total of human happiness.
       ELIHU BURRETT

If our lives are in harmony with the world, they are out of harmony with God.
       WENDELL P. LOVELESS

———◆———

You can be happy by yourself but you can be happier with someone else.

———◆———

Labor and trouble one can always get through alone, but it takes two to be glad.
       IBSEN

———◆———

It's the counterfeit of happiness that costs the most.

———◆———

True happiness comes from the knowledge that we are some use in this world.

———◆———

The office of government is not to confer happiness but to give men opportunity to work out happiness for themselves.
       WILLIAM ELLERY CHANNING

———◆———

The story is told of a king who had an unhappy little son. The prince had everything he could wish for — pony, toys, even a yacht to sail in the lake. Still he was unhappy.

One day the king consulted a wise old man about his son. The old man took a piece of paper and wrote on it some words in invisible ink. He told the king to hold the paper between his eyes and a lighted candle that night and he would be able to read the words.

That night the king lit a candle and held the paper before it. Here was the message:

"The secret of true happiness is to do a little kindness to someone every day."

———◆———

Where Is Happiness?

Not in unbelief — Voltaire was an infidel of the most pronounced type. He wrote: "I wish I had never been born."

Not in pleasure — Lord Byron lived a life of pleasure, if anyone did. He wrote: "The worm, the canker and the grief are mine alone."

Not in money — Jay Gould, the American millionaire, had plenty of that.

When dying, he said: "I suppose I am the most miserable man on earth."

Not in possession and fame — Lord Beaconsfield enjoyed more than his share of both. He wrote: "Youth is a mistake, manhood a struggle, old age a regret."

Not in military glory — Alexander the Great conquered the known world of his day. Having done so, he wept in his tent, because, as he said, "There are no more worlds to conquer."

Where, then, is happiness found? The answer is simple: "In Christ alone." He said: "I will see you again and your heart shall rejoice, and your joy no man taketh from you" (John 16:22).   MARCARTNEY

———♦———

Some years ago a newspaper offered a prize for the best definition of "money." Out of hundreds who competed, the winner submitted the following:

"Money is a universal provider of everything but happiness; and a passport everywhere but to heaven."

———♦———

Harmony

There is a unique harmony in the Bible. Compare, for example, the first two and the last two chapters:
In GENESIS the earth is created;
In REVELATION it passes away.
In GENESIS the sun and moon appear;
In REVELATION there is no need of the sun or moon.
In GENESIS there is a garden, the home of a man;
In REVELATION there is a city, the home of the nations.
In GENESIS we are introduced to Satan;
In REVELATION we see his doom.
In GENESIS we hear the first sob and see the first tear;
In REVELATION we read: "God shall wipe away all tears from their eyes."
In GENESIS the curse is pronounced;
In REVELATION we read: "There shall be no more curse."   *Selected*

Haste, Hurry

Haste makes waste.
                    BENJAMIN FRANKLIN

———♦———

Why is it that people who don't know whether they are coming or going are usually in such a big hurry to get there?

———♦———

He that riseth late, must trot all day, and shall scarce overtake his business at night.   BENJAMIN FRANKLIN

———♦———

Haste Is Waste

No doubt a nervous speed or hurry
Can bring about a senseless worry
That grows into a fretful flurry
For haste.

Whoever dashes yon and hither
May watch his cherished plans all wither
And find that any kind of dither
Is waste.   MARJORIE LINDSEY BREWER,
                    The Baptist Standard

———♦———

Hate

It is better to take many injuries than to give one.   BENJAMIN FRANKLIN

———♦———

Health

Without health all men are poor.

———♦———

Health is better than wealth.

———♦———

Prayer for Health

Lord, look with pity on my pain,
And soon my strength restore,
And grant me life and health again,
To serve Thee evermore.
                    AUTHOR UNKNOWN

———♦———

Heart, Hearts

A merry heart goes all the day, a sad tires in a mile.   SHAKESPEARE

———♦———

The head has not heard until the heart has listened.

———♦———

A new heart creates a new life.

The world is shrinking faster than the human heart is expanding.

MARION F. MOORHEAD

———♦———

Carve your name on hearts and not on marble.

C. H. SPURGEON

———♦———

In vacation Bible school little four-year-old Mary insisted on placing her hand on the top of her head while the group said the pledge to the American flag. When her teacher asked her why she did this she replied:

"Well, that's where my heart is. Mother always put her hand on the top of my head and says, 'Bless your little heart, Mary.'"

———♦———

Little Susan, four years old, returned from Sunday school with her offering money.

"Why didn't you give your money in the offering today, dear?" her mother asked.

"Because our teacher told us that if we love Jesus He comes and lives in our hearts. And you told me never to put money in my mouth. So I didn't know what to do. If I gave my money to Jesus I would have to swallow it."

———♦———

Heathen

Heathenness is all ungodliness.

———♦———

Heaven

You can't get into heaven by naturalization papers.

———♦———

God may not give us an easy journey to the Promised Land, but He will give us a safe one.

BONAR

———♦———

When we go to heaven we will go heart-first, not head-first.

———♦———

When traveling by plane, the minister said, "If I go down, I go up."

———♦———

A little boy, caught in mischief, was asked by his mother: "How do you expect to get into heaven?"

He thought a minute, and then said:

"Well, I'll just run in and out and keep slamming the door till they say, 'For goodness' sake, come in or stay out,' then I'll go in."

Christian Herald

———♦———

It is our main business in this world to secure an interest in the next.

———♦———

If you are seated in heavenly places, sit still.

———♦———

"And," concluded the Sunday school teacher, "If you are a good boy, Tommy, you will go to heaven and have a crown of gold on your head."

"Not me!" said Tommy, "I had one of those things put on a tooth once."

———♦———

A Man May Go to Heaven

Without health,
Without wealth,
Without fame,
Without a great name,
Without learning,
Without big earning,
Without culture,
Without beauty,
Without friends.
Without 10,000 other things.
But he can
Never go to heaven
Without Christ.

PHA

———♦———

"How is your wife?" the man asked a friend he hadn't seen for years.

"She's in heaven," replied the friend.

"Oh, I'm sorry." Then he realized that was not the thing to say, so he added, "I mean, I'm glad." And that was even worse. He finally came out with, "Well, I'm surprised."

Christian Herald

———♦———

A big advertising man had a small daughter who came home from Sunday school one day carrying a bundle of pamphlets and cards.

"And what do you have there?" asked the man.

"Oh, nothing much," answered the little girl. "Just some ads about heaven."

A preacher was asked if a man who learned to play a cornet on Sunday would go to heaven. The preacher's cryptic reply was: "I don't see why he shouldn't . . . but . . ." after a pause, "I doubt whether the man next door will."

———♦———

Hell

It does not require a decision to go to hell.

———♦———

A true fear of hell has sent many a soul to heaven.

———♦———

Help, Helpful

For a web begun, God sends thread.
Italian Proverb

———♦———

Help thyself and heaven will help thee.

———♦———

Where God's finger points, there God's hand will make the way.

———♦———

A candle loses nothing by lighting another candle. ANONYMOUS

———♦———

Consider

Is anybody happier
  Because you passed his way?
Does anyone remember
  That you spoke to him today?
This day is almost over,
  And its toiling time is through;
Is there anyone to utter now,
  A friendly word for you?

Can you say tonight in passing,
  With the day that slipped so fast,
That you helped a single person,
  Of the many that you passed?
Is a single heart rejoicing,
  Over what you did or said?
Does one whose hopes were fading
  Now with courage look ahead?

Did you waste the day, or lose it?
Was it well or poorly spent?
Did you leave a trail of kindness,
Or a scar of discontent? ANONYMOUS

Bearing one another's burdens is different from bearing down on them.

———♦———

There is no exercise better for the heart than reaching down and lifting people up. JOHN ANDREW HOLMER

———♦———

A mother was telling her six-year-old son about the Golden Rule. "Always remember," she said, "that we are here to help others."

The youngster mulled this over for a minute and then asked, "Well, what are the others here for?" *Christian Herald*

———♦———

God helps them that help themselves.
BENJAMIN FRANKLIN

———♦———

Life is short and we have never too much time for gladdening the hearts of those who are traveling the dark journey with us. *Amiel's Journal*

———♦———

One day a teacher asked her first-graders what they did to help at home. They took turns giving such answers as "dry dishes," "feed the dog," and "make my bed." She noticed that Johnny hadn't spoken, so she asked him to tell what he did.

After hesitating a moment, he replied, "Mostly I stay out of the way."
The Instructor

———♦———

History

The worst thing about history is that every time it repeats itself the price goes up. *Pillar in Coronet*

———♦———

It is only world history that repeats itself. Your private history is repeated by the neighbors.

———♦———

Christ is the great central fact in the world's history; to Him everything looks forward or backward.
CHARLES E. SPURGEON

———♦———

In the last four thousand years of history, there have been but 268 years entirely free of war. *Coronet*

A great man does not make his place in history. He finds it and fills it.

FRANK NELSON

------◆------

The highways of history are strewn with the wreckage of nations that forgot God.

------◆------

Holy, Holiness

Holiness is wholeness — the whole of Christ in the whole life.

------◆------

Holiness vanishes when you talk about it, but becomes gloriously conspicuous when you live it.

------◆------

A holy life has a voice. It speaks when the tongue is silent, and is either a constant attraction or a perpetual reproof.

HINTON

------◆------

Holy Spirit

He who has the Holy Spirit in his heart and the Scripture in his hands has all he needs.

ALEXANDER MACLAREN

------◆------

My human best filled with the Holy Spirit makes a good motto.

Sunday School Journal

------◆------

No one wants to see an old barn, but everyone likes to see the old barn burn.

DR. HENRIETTA C. MEARS

------◆------

The Holy Spirit is God at work.

D. L. MOODY

------◆------

The Fruits of the Spirit

In newspaper English, Galatians 5:22, 23 would read something like this: "The fruit of the Spirit is an affectionate, lovable disposition, a radiant spirit and a cheerful temper, a tranquil mind and a quiet manner, a forbearing patience in provoking circumstances and with trying people, a sympathetic insight and tactful helpfulness, generous judgment and a big-souled charity, loyalty and reliableness under all circumstances, humility that forgets self in the joy of others, in all things self-mastered and self-controlled, which is the final mark of perfecting."

Home

Home should be more than a filling station.

DR. W. W. AYER

------◆------

It takes a hundred men to make an encampment, but one woman can make a home.

------◆------

Be it ever so humble, nobody stays home.

------◆------

Home is where the mortgage is.

------◆------

Home Blessing
Bless our home,
   Our lives, our friends
With love that, Lord,
   On Thee depends.   Amen.

------◆------

Recipe for a Happy Home

To 3 cups of love and 2 cups of understanding add 4 teaspoons of courtesy and 2 teaspoons each of thoughtfulness and helpfulness. Sift together thoroughly, then stir in an equal amount of work and play. Add 3 teaspoons of responsibility. Season to taste with study and culture, then fold in a generous amount of worship. Place in a pan well greased with security and lined with respect for personality. Sprinkle lightly with a sense of humor. Allow to set in an atmosphere of democratic planning and of mutual sharing. Bake in a moderate oven. When well done, remove and top with a thick coating of Christian teachings. Serve on a platter of friendliness garnished with smiles.

PAULINE AND LEONARD MILLER

------◆------

Dry bread at home is better than roast meat abroad.

------◆------

Home — the place where the great are small and the small are great.

------◆------

The home can be the strongest ally of the Sunday school or its greatest enemy, depending on the parents.

------◆------

Only the home can found a state.

JOSEPH COOK

What a Real Home Is

A Real Home is a gymnasium. The ideal of a healthy body is the first one to give a child.

A Real Home is a lighthouse. A lighthouse reveals the breakers ahead and shows a clear way past them.

A Real Home is a playground. Beware of the house where you "dassn't frolic" — there mischief is brewing for someone.

A Real Home is a workshop. Pity the boy without a kit of tools or the girl without a sewing basket. They haven't learned the fun of doing things — and there is no fun like that.

A Real Home is a forum. Honest, open discussion of life's great problems belongs originally in the family circle.

A Real Home is a secret society. Loyalty to one's family should mean keeping silent on family matters — just this and nothing more.

A Real Home is a health resort. Mothers are the natural physicians.

A Real Home is a cooperative league. Households flourish where the interests of each is made the interest of all.

A Real Home is a business concern. Order is a housewife's hobby. But order without system is a harness without the horse.

A Real Home is a haven of refuge. The world does this for us all: it makes us hunger for a loving sympathy and a calming, soothing touch.

A Real Home is a temple of worship.
EDWARD PURINTON, *Covenanter Witness*

————◆————

Home

"What makes a home?"
I asked my little boy.
And this is what he said,
"You, Mother,
And when Father comes,
Our table set all shiny,
And my bed,
And, Mother, I think it's home,
Because we love each other."
You who are old and wise,
What would you say
If you were asked the question?
Tell me, pray
Thus simply as a little child, we learn
A home is made from love.
Warm as the golden hearthfire on the floor,
A table and a lamp for light,
And smooth white beds at night —
Only the old sweet fundamental things.
And long ago I learned —
Home may be near, home may be far,
But it is anywhere that love
And a few plain household treasures are.
AUTHOR UNKNOWN

————◆————

Little Alice was allowed to sit in her mother's place at the dinner table one evening when her mother was absent. Her slightly older brother, resenting the arrangement, sneered, "So you're the mother tonight. All right, how much is two times seven?"

Without a moment's hesitation, Alice replied nonchalantly, "I'm busy. Ask your father." *Teens*

————◆————

Recipe for a Home

Half a cup of friendship
  And a cup of thoughtfulness,
Creamed together with a pinch
  Of powdered tenderness.

Very lightly beaten
  In a bowl of loyalty,
With a cup of faith, and one of hope,
  And one of charity.

Be sure to add a spoonful each
  Of gaiety-that-sings.
And also the ability
  To-laugh-at-little-things.

Moisten with the sudden tears
  Of heartfelt sympathy;
Bake in a good-natured pan
  And serve repeatedly. *Christian Home*

————◆————

Honest, Honesty

Honesty is the best policy, especially when you want to borrow your policy.

————◆————

The whole art of government consists in the art of being honest.
THOMAS JEFFERSON

It matters not what you do —
Make a nation or a shoe;
For he who does an honest thing
In God's pure sight is ranked a king.

JOHN PARNELL

The badge of honesty is simplicity.

It is often surprising to find what heights may be obtained merely by remaining on the level.

When a man gets in the straight way, he finds there is no room for crooked dealings.

The Presbyterian

An honest man will receive neither money nor praise that is not his due.

BENJAMIN FRANKLIN

Hope

Get a Transfer

If you are on a gloomy line,
Get a transfer.
If you're inclined to fret and pine,
Get a transfer.
Get off the track of Doubt and Gloom,
Get on a Sunshine Train, there's room.
Get a transfer.
If you are on the Worry Train,
Get a transfer.
You must not stay there and complain;
Get a transfer.
The Cheerful Cars are passing through,
And there is lots of room for you,
Get a transfer.
If you are on the Grouchy Track,
Get a transfer.
Just take a Happy Special back,
Get a transfer.
Jump on the train and pull the rope,
That lands you at the Station Hope,
Get a transfer.

Canadian Baptist

Hope is as cheap as despair.

Living on hope is a slim diet.

We promise according to our hopes, and perform according to our fears.

LA ROCHEFOUCAULD

When hope is alive, the night is less dark; the solitude less deep, fear less acute.

Hospitality

Hospitality should have no other nature than love.

DR. HENRIETTA C. MEARS

Human, Humanity, Human Nature

After all, there is but one race — humanity.

GEORGE MOORE

Who lives for humanity must be content to lose himself.

O. B. FROTHINGHAM

Human nature is the same all over the world; but its operations are so varied by education and habit that one must see it in all its dresses.

LORD CHESTERFIELD

Humble, Humility

Only if man strikes rock bottom in the sense of his own nothingness will he strike the Rock of Ages.

If we do not learn humility, we will learn humiliation.

The only way up is down on your knees.

Meekness is not weakness, but strength harnessed for service.

The smaller we are the more room God has.

I believe the first test of a truly great man is his humility.

JOHN RUSKIN

To be humble to superiors is duty, to equals courtesy, to inferiors nobleness.

BENJAMIN FRANKLIN

It is no humility for a man to think less of himself than he ought, though it might rather puzzle him to do that.

SPURGEON

A mountain shames a molehill until both are humbled by the stars.

AUTHOR UNKNOWN

Humility is to make a right estimate of oneself.

SPURGEON

Humility is such a frail and delicate thing that he who dares to think that he has it, proves by that single thought that he has it not.

IVAN O. MILLER

Nothing sets a person so much out of the devil's reach as humility.

JONATHAN EDWARDS

The humblest citizen of all the land, when clad in the armor of a righteous cause, is stronger than all the hosts of error.

WILLIAM JENNINGS BRYAN

The dogmas of the quiet past are inadequate to the stormy present. The occasion is piled high with difficulty, so we must rise with the occasion. As our case is new, so we must think anew and act anew. We must disenthrall ourselves.

ABRAHAM LINCOLN, 1862

Humor

A good thing to have up your sleeve is a funny-bone.

Asked to define "medieval," a college freshman wrote, "partly bad."

Funny?

As soon as day begins to dawn
The meadow lark starts singing.
As soon as evening comes a star —
The angel's lamp starts swinging.
As soon as I am in the tub
The telephone starts ringing!

Student Boners

Scalped potatoes are a tasty dish.
Chicken is the most wildly eaten food in America.
Pyrenees are tombs the Egyptians are buried in.
The three departments of government are Alaska, Maryland, Greece.

Bribery is having more than one wife.
Strategy is the studying of the moon and stars.
A plebiscite is a trader or rat, as you might call him.
The duties of a squire are to take care of a knight's armor.
Louis Pasteur discovered germs and apple cider.

NEA Journal

From School Examinations!

Poise is the way a Dutchman says boys.
Esquinox is a wild animal that lives in the Arctic.
Rabbi is plural for rabbit.
Copernicus invented the cornucopia.
Etiquette teaches us how to be polite without trying to remember to be.
In the stone age all the men were ossified.
The climax of a story is where it says it is to be continued.
Prohibition means a very dry state to be in.
Buttress is a butler's wife.
A gulf is a dent in a continent.
Conservation means doing without things we need.
If Ponce de Leon hadn't died before he found the fountain of youth, he wouldn't have died.

Whatever trouble Adam had,
  No man in days of yore
Could say, when Adam cracked a joke,
  "I've heard that one before."

Husband

"If you were to lose your husband," the insurance salesman asked the young housewife, "what would you get?"
She thought for a moment, then: "A parakeet."

I should like to see any kind of a man, distinguishable from a gorilla, that some good and even pretty woman could not shape a husband out of.

OLIVER WENDELL HOLMES

One of a husband's tougher problems in life is getting back some of his take-home pay after he takes it home.

———◆———

Husband to wife: "Did you see that pretty girl smile at me?"
Wife: "That's nothing, the first time I saw you I laughed out loud."

———◆———

Irate husband: "Light bill, water bill, gas bill, milk bill — you've got to quit this wild spending!"

Hypocrisy, Hypocrite

Don't stay away from church because there are so many hypocrites; there is always room for one more.

———◆———

Certainly there are hypocrites in the church, for any church is but a gathering of sinful people. And what better place for us to be? *Presbyterian Life*

———◆———

The devil is helped most by the inconsistent Christian.

I

Idea, Ideas

Getting an idea should be like sitting on a pin; it should make you jump up and do something. SIMPSON

———◆———

The reason that so many good ideas die is that they cannot stand solitary confinement.

———◆———

Ideas are funny things, they do not work unless you do.

———◆———

Many ideas grow better when transplanted into another mind than in the one where they sprang up.
OLIVER WENDELL HOLMES

———◆———

Some folks entertain ideas; others work them.

———◆———

Ideas rule life and in the long run shape the ages.

———◆———

There is something inevitable about an idea whose hour has struck.
GOETHE

———◆———

You have to hatch ideas, and then hitch them. EMERSON

———◆———

The man who is set in his ways doesn't hatch new ideas.

———◆———

No big ideas ever came from swelled heads!

Ideas are like weapons. Men possess thoughts, but ideas possess men.
MAX LERNER

———◆———

He who wishes to fulfill his mission in the world must be a man of one idea that is one of the great overmastering purposes, overshadowing all his aims, and guiding and controlling his entire life. BATES

Ideal, Ideals

Those who live on a mountain have a longer day than those who live in a valley.

———◆———

Idle, Idleness

Business may be troublesome, but idleness is pernicious.

———◆———

Busybodies never have anything to do.

———◆———

Idle folks take the most pains.

———◆———

Be always ashamed to catch thyself idle. BENJAMIN FRANKLIN

———◆———

Too much idleness, I have observed, fills up a man's time much more completely, and leaves him less his own master, than any sort of employment whatsoever. EDMUND BURKE

The idler does not waste time; he merely wastes himself.   *The Defender*

Idolatry, Idols

When God comes in the idols tumble down.

Ignorance, Ignorant

To be conscious that you are ignorant is a great step to knowledge.

———

Seems like people who know the least know it mighty fluently.
Lutheran Education

———

The man who cheapens himself in public is sure to be marked down by his neighbors.

———

One of the speakers at a church conference was haranguing against higher education and the universities. He closed his speech with pious gratitude that he had never been corrupted by contact with learning and college.

The next speaker was an erudite bishop. He peered at the anti-education man and then rumbled, "Do I understand that Mr. Dobson is thankful for his ignorance?"

"Well, yes," was the answer. "You can put it that way if you like."

The bishop beamed at his solemn audience and when he spoke his voice was like a benediction. "All I have to say," he intoned, "is that this man has a great deal, a very great deal to be thankful for."   *Coronet*

Ill, Illness

A cold is both positive and negative. Sometimes the eyes have it, sometimes the nose.

———

Many people who review their illness are really giving an organ recital.

———

Wife to husband sick in bed: "It's a sympathy card from your secretary to me."

I enjoy convalescence. It is the part that makes the illness worthwhile.
G. B. SHAW

———

A disease known is half cured.

———

Diseases are taxes on pleasure.

———

Illustrations

One illustration is worth a ton of chalk.

———

Illustrations in a story are like sunshine streaming through a window.

———

Never state a fact if you can bring the fact to life with an illustration.

———

Illustrate, but don't illustrate the obvious.

———

We needs must illustrate the greater by the analogy of the less, but your illustration must not belittle you the theme.

———

"I want you to look at this picture," said the Sunday school teacher. "It illustrates today's lesson. Lot was told to take his daughters and wife, and flee out of Sodom. Here are Lot and his daughters, with his wife just behind them. There is Sodom in the background. Does anyone have any questions about the picture?"

Came a voice from the back of the room: "Where is the flea?"   *Together*

———

Teaching a Sunday school class without the use of illustrations to explain the lesson is like building a house with no windows to let the light in. The well-constructed house has both walls and windows — walls for strength and protection, and windows for light. And is not good teaching something like building a house?

Who would build a house without windows? And who would build a house with all windows? Both windows and walls are needed in every house. In much the same way teaching needs the solid structure of Biblical truths to

provide for the safety and salvation of young lives as well as selected illustrations and stories which emphasize and illumine those truths.
W. G. MONTGOMERY *in Sunday School World*

Imagination, Imagine

What is now proved was once only imagined.
WILLIAM BLAKE

Solitude is as needful to the imagination as society is wholesome for the character.
JAMES RUSSELL LOWELL

Do not let work divorce itself from imagination.

Grandmother saw Billy running around the house slapping himself and asked him why.
"Well," said Billy, "I just got so tired of walking that I thought I'd ride my horse for a while."

Unless a man constantly keeps a partition between his imagination and his facts, he is in danger of becoming just an ordinary liar.

Imitate, Imitation

Don't worry because a rival imitates you. As long as he follows in your tracks he can't pass you.

The young heroes, aged 10 to 14, were being honored for rescuing a comrade who had fallen through the ice. "Did you think of the idea of forming a human chain, or did you learn that in Scout work?" they were asked.
"Oh, that," piped one. "I saw it in a comic book."

A devoted father (who was a Sunday school superintendent) asked his young son, "What are you going to be when you grow up?"
The admiring son, without hesitation answered, "I'm going to be a Sunday school superintendent."

There is much difference between imitating a good man, and counterfeiting him.
BENJAMIN FRANKLIN

Important

Important Things

The things that count are never weighed on scales
Nor measured by the dollar's gruesome face;
They are the friendly smile that never fails,
The handclasp that no bribery can replace.
The things that count are not of mansion size,
Nor lined with jeweled satin nor brocade;
They are the simple trust in children's eyes
And prayer that helps the person who has prayed.
The things that count are courage in distress
And hope that shines as brightly as a star
And vision and humility that bless
With God's true plan all living things that are.
These are the things that have the deepest worth;
These are the most important things on earth.
MARY O'CONNOR

How often we place the thing of major importance upon the side track while the secondary consideration goes thundering through on the main line.

Let us not major on minor things.

It's nice to be important, but it's important to be nice.

Impossible

Only an all-powerful God can do the impossible with the impossible.
ELD

The difficult we do immediately, the impossible takes a little longer — this is a good motto for any business.

131

When God is going to do something wonderful He begins with a difficulty; if He is going to do something very wonderful, he begins with an impossibility!

———◆———

Impress, Impressions

"Don't write there," said one to a lad who was writing with a diamond pin on a pane of glass in the window of a hotel.

"Why?" the boy inquired.

"Because you can't rub it out."

Glass may be destroyed but the human soul is immortal. What about impressions made on the minds and hearts of boys and girls? They, too, are indelible.   *Sunday School Journal*

———◆———

Improve, Improvement

By improving yourself is the world made better.

———◆———

Americans seem to have an excess of everything except parking space and religion. Is this an improvement of things?

———◆———

The biggest room in the world is the room for improvement.

———◆———

If you are still breathing, you can improve.

———◆———

Where we cannot invent we can at least improve.

———◆———

Inaction, Inertia

Iron rusts from disuse; stagnant water loses its purity, and in cold weather becomes frozen; even so does inaction sap the vigors of the mind.

LEONARDO DA VINCI

———◆———

Indifference, Indifferent

The crude and physical agony of the Cross was nothing compared to the indifference of the crowd on Main Street as they "passed by."

ALLAN KNIGHT CHALMERS

When . . .

When parents use movies and television sets for baby sitters, regardless of the nature of pictures and programs . . .

When workers come to church meetings only if there is nothing else to do . . .

When people feel no responsibility for the welfare of others besides those in their own families . . .

When workers do not fill places of service at the church and do not explain their absence to leaders . . .

When parents leave little children in the care of others while they make money for luxuries . . .

When workers are unwilling to spend three hours a week preparing to teach Bible truths in the Sunday school . . .

When people use Sundays to mow lawns, fish, play baseball, and attend the movies . . .

When parents give much time to their own social life and little to good times with their children . . .

When workers do not keep their promises to boys and girls . . .

When people prefer to live where church people will not "bother them" . . .

Then . . . it must be time for a moral awakening in America!

The Sunday School Builder

———◆———

Even if you are on the right track you will get run over if you just sit there.   *Rays of Sunshine*

———◆———

How to Kill a Sunday School

Attend only when convenient;

Arrive late when you do go;

Grumble about having to go;

Criticize the officers and teachers before your family and friends;

Decline to take any office, do it grudgingly and neglect it often;

Avoid all meetings of officers and teachers;

Neglect your records and reports, considering them unnecessary;

Be disinterested and sleepy throughout the teaching period;

Appear relieved when the session is over;

Be icily dignified and distant toward strangers;

Let outsiders feel that you belong and they don't;

Show as little enthusiasm as possible with any new venture;

Never cooperate with new workers or their plans and methods;

If teaching, be impatient and distant with your scholars;

Don't let the children of your Sunday school get the idea you love them;

Regard the teachers of your children as upstarts or busybodies;

Be free to show your distrust or disapproval of them when they call;

Never introduce your pastor or Sunday school superintendent to your friends or neighbors;

Don't let it be known what Sunday school you attend; it might be humiliating to have them go, too.

On no account support it with your money;

Never make sacrifices to see it go;

Squelch every effort to beautify grounds or Sunday school rooms;

Grumble habitually because your Sunday school is dying out.

ALICE LYONS DYER *in*
The Sunday School Worker

———◆———

Influence

The only way in which one human being can properly attempt to influence another is by encouraging him to think for himself, instead of endeavoring to instill ready-made opinions into his head.   SIR LESLIE STEPHEN

———◆———

The serene, silent beauty of a holy life is the most powerful influence in the world, next to the might of God.

PASCAL

———◆———

In the footprints on the sands of time some people leave only the marks of a heel.

The rocking chair used by a hymn-singing mother has more power to rid the world of evil than the electric chair used by a justice meeting state.

C. EARL COOPER

———◆———

Plastic Clay

I took a piece of plastic clay,
And idly fashioned it one day,
And as my fingers pressed it still,
It bent and yielded to my will.

I came again when days were past;
The bit of clay was hard at last.
The form I gave it still it bore,
But I could change that form no more.

I took a piece of living clay
And gently formed it day by day
And molded it with power and art —
A young child's soft and yielded heart.

I came again when years were gone;
He was a man I looked upon.
The early imprint still he bore,
But I could change him then no more.

AUTHOR UNKNOWN

———◆———

My Influence

My life shall touch a dozen lives before this day is done,
    Leave countless marks for good or ill ere sets the evening sun,
This is the wish I always wish, the prayer I always pray;
Lord, may my life help other lives it touches by the way.   *Selected*

———◆———

The Things I Do

The things I do,
The things I say,
Will lead some person
Aright or astray.
So the things we do
Should be the best,
And the things we say
Should be to bless.

CAL STARGEL *in This Day*

———◆———

Inform

Seek information from the experienced.

CICERO

———◆———

Never awake me when you have good news to announce, because, with good news, nothing presses; but when you have bad news, arouse me immediately, for then there is not an instant to be lost. NAPOLEON

Ingenuity

A young mother was worried about her nine-year-old son. No matter how much she scolded, he kept running round with his shirt tails flapping. On the other hand, her neighbor had four boys, and each one of them always wore his shirt neatly tucked in. Finally the young mother asked her neighbor to tell her the secret.

"Oh, it's simple," she replied. "I just take all their shirts and sew an edging of lace around the bottom."

c. VICTORY in *The Evangel*

Inspiration

Sometimes the best inspiration is born of desperation.

Inspiration in presentation is perspiration in preparation.

Intellect, Intelligence

The intelligent person is one who has learned how to choose wisely and therefore has a sense of values, a purpose in life and a sense of direction.

J. MARTIN KLOTSCHE

Intentions

Good intentions never saved anyone.

The road to hell is paved with good intentions.

Unless one is a genius, it is best to aim at being intelligible. A. HOPE

The smallest deed is better than the grandest intention. *Sunday School Counselor*

Good intentions and good eggs soon spoil unless they soon hatch.

Interest

The whole secret of life is to be interested in one thing profoundly, and in a thousand things well.

HUGH WALPOLE

Interpretation

The great religions express the second great commandment, "Thou shalt love thy neighbor as thyself," thus:

Christianity: All things whatsoever ye would that men should do to you, do ye even so to them; for this is the law and the prophets.

Judaism: What is hateful to you, do not to your fellow men. That is the entire law; all the rest is commentary.

Buddhism: Hurt not others in ways that you yourself would find hurtful.

Islam: No one of you is a believer until he desires for his brother that which he desires for himself.

Brahmanism: This is the sum of duty: Do nought unto others which would cause you pain if done to you.

Confucianism: Is there one maxim which ought to be acted upon throughout one's whole life? Surely it is the maxim of loving-kindness: Do not unto others what you would not have them do unto you.

Taoism: Regard your neighbor's gain as your own gain, and your neighbor's loss as your own loss.

Zoroastrianism: That nature alone is good which refrains from doing unto others whatsoever is not good for itself.

Many young stage and screen hopefuls are under the impression that to become a star they have to stay out late at night.

At a missionary meeting some young people were discussing the text, "Ye are the salt of the earth." One suggestion after another was made as to the meaning of "salt" in this verse. "Salt imparts a desirable flavor," said one.

"Salt preserves from decay," another suggested.

Then at last a Chinese Christian girl spoke out of an experience none of the others had. "Salt creates thirst," she said, and there was a sudden hush in the room. Everyone was thinking, "Have I ever made anyone thirsty for the Lord Jesus Christ?"

——◆——

Intolerance

He that will have none but a perfect brother must resign himself to remain brotherless.   *Italian Proverb*

Invitation

God put a crook in your arm to hook into another fellow's and bring him to church.

——◆——

Come unto Me

(Matthew 11:28)
C - stands for Children
O - stands for Old People
M - stands for Middle-aged People
E - stands for Everybody.
The Christian Parent

——◆——

Irritation

Irritation in the heart of a believer is always an invitation to the devil to stand by.

J

Jealousy

Suspicion and jealousy never did help any man in any situation.
ABRAHAM LINCOLN

——◆——

Moral indignation is jealousy with a halo.   H. G. WELLS

——◆——

Stones and sticks are thrown only at fruit-bearing trees.   SAADI

——◆——

Jew

The Jew
Scattered by God's avenging hand,
  Afflicted and forlorn,
Sad wanderers from their pleasant land,
  Do Judah's children mourn;
And e'en in Christian countries, few
  Breathe thoughts of pity for the Jew.

Yet listen, Gentile, do you love
  The Bible's precious page?
Then let your heart with kindness move
  To Israel's heritage;
Who traced those lines of love for you?
  Each sacred writer was a Jew.

And then as years and ages passed,
  And nations rose and fell,
Though clouds and darkness oft were cast
  O'er captive Israel
The oracles of God for you
  Were kept in safety by the Jew.

And when the great Redeemer came
  For guilty man to bleed,
He did not take an angel's name;
  No, born of Abraham's seed,
Jesus, who gave His life for you —
  The gentle Saviour — was a Jew.

And though His own received Him not,
  And turned in pride away,
Whence is the Gentile's happier lot?
  Are you more just than they?
No! God in pity turned to you —
  Have you no pity for the Jew?

Go, then, and bend your knee to pray
  For Israel's ancient race;
Ask the dear Saviour every day
  To call them by His grace.
Go, for a debt of love is due
  From Christian Gentiles to the Jew.
AUTHOR UNKNOWN

135

Job

Do not pray for an easy task. Pray to be stronger.

————

Don't worry about the job you don't like — someone else will soon have it.

————

The best job insurance is work well done.

————

Nothing turns out right unless someone makes it his job to see that it does.

————

If you aspire to the assignment of big jobs, be faithful in the performance of little ones.

————

Times are always hard for those who seek soft jobs.

————

Looking for a soft job is the job of a soft man.

————

When you make your job important, it will return the favor.

————

Always ask, "Isn't there some better way to do it?"

————

You won't ever get started if you wait for all the conditions to be "just right."

————

If you paddle your own canoe, there's no one to rock the boat.

Joy

Joy shared is joy doubled.

————

Joy is multiplied as it is divided with others.

————

Mirth is never good without God.

————

So rejoice that you can rejoice over your rejoicing.

————

Joy is more divine than sorrow, for joy is bread and sorrow is medicine. H. W. BEECHER

————

Joys are our wings; sorrows our spurs. RICHTER

I Have Found Joy

I have found such joy in simple
    things —
A plain clean room, a nut-brown loaf
    of bread,
A cup of milk, a kettle as it sings,
And in a leaf-flecked square upon a
    floor,
Where yellow sunlight glimmers
    through a door.

I have found such joy in things that fill
My quiet days, — a curtain's blowing
    grace,
A growing-plant upon a window sill,
A rose fresh-cut and placed within a
    vase,
A table cleared, a lamp beside a chair,
And books I long have loved beside
    me there.

————

If life seems full of struggle, it is also full of joy. Trouble is temporary; happiness is eternal. CHARLES M. SHELDON

————

Grief can take care of itself, but to get the full value of joy, we must have somebody to divide it with. MARK TWAIN

————

Judge, Judgment, Justice
See also Accuse, Criticize

Judge not thy friend until thou standest in his place. RABBI HILLEL

————

The judgments of our fellow men serve as weights to hold us.

————

Judge not without knowledge, nor without necessity and never without charity. ————

'Tis with our judgments as our
    watches, none
Go just alike, yet each believes
    his own. ———— ALEXANDER POPE

In giving your judgment, give it boldly and with decision, but never give a reason for it; your judgment, nine times out of ten, will be right, because it is founded on experience; but your reason will probably be wrong, being only an afterthought.
GEORGE WHITEFIELD

Too often we judge ourselves by our motives; others by their actions.

———♦———

Do Not Judge Too Hard

Pray do not find fault with the man
    that limps —
  Or stumbles along the road, unless
    you have worn the shoes he
    wears —
  Or struggled beneath his load.
There may be tacks in his shoes that
    hurt, though hidden from view,
  Or the burdens he bears placed on
    your back —
  Might cause you to stumble, too.

Don't sneer at the man who is down
    today —
  Unless you have felt the blow that
    caused his fall,
  Or felt the pain that only the fallen
    know.

You may be strong, but still the blows
    that were his,
  If dealt to you in the selfsame way
    at the selfsame time —
  Might cause you to stagger, too.

Don't be too hard on the man who sins,
  Or pelt him with words or a stone,
    unless you are sure, doubly sure,
  That you have not sins of your own.

For you know perhaps if the tempter's
    voice
  Should whisper as soft to you as it
    did to him when he went astray,
  'Twould cause you to falter, too.
                 AUTHOR UNKNOWN

———♦———

Justice is truth in action.
                 JOSEPH JOUBERT

———♦———

My great concern is not whether God is on our side; my great concern is to be on God's side. ABRAHAM LINCOLN

K

Kindness

Kindness has converted more sinners than zeal, eloquence, or learning.
        DR. HENRIETTA C. MEARS

———♦———

Kindness gives birth to kindness.
                SOPHOCLES

———♦———

Don't expect to enjoy life if you keep your milk of human kindness all bottled up.

———♦———

Kindness is the golden chain by which society is bound together.
                GOETHE

———♦———

Forbearance should be cultivated till your heart yields a fine crop of it. Pray for a short memory as to all unkindness.   SPURGEON

———♦———

To give pleasure to a single heart by a single kind act is better than a thousand head-bowings in prayer.
                SAADI

So many gods, so many creeds,

———♦———

Seeds of Kindness

If you have a friend worth loving,
  Love him. Yes, and let him know
That you love him, ere life's evening
  Tinge his brow with sunset glow.
Why should good words ne'er be said
Of a friend — till he is dead?

If you hear a song that thrills you,
  Sung by any child of song,
Praise it. Do not let the singer
  Wait deserved praises long.
Why should one who thrills your heart
Lack the joy you may impart?

If you hear a prayer that moves you
  By its humble, pleading tone,
Join it. Do not let the seeker
  Bow before his God alone.
Why should not your brother share
The strength of "two or three" in
  prayer?

If you see the hot tears falling
  From a brother's weeping eyes
Share them. And by kindly sharing
  Own your kinship in the skies.
Why should anyone be glad
When another's heart is sad?
                    AUTHOR UNKNOWN

——————◆——————

One can pay back the loan of gold,
but one dies forever in debt to those
who are kind.   *Malayan Proverb*

——————◆——————

  Two things stand like stone:
  Kindness in another's troubles;
  Courage in one's own.   LORD DEWAR

——————◆——————

So many paths that wind and wind;
When just the art of being kind
Is all this sad world needs.
                    ELLA WHEELER WILCOX

——————◆——————

He who has conferred a kindness
should be silent; he who has received
one should speak of it.   SENECA

——————◆——————

There is no debt so heavy to a grateful mind as a debt of kindness unpaid.
                    STERNE

——————◆——————

Forget and Remember

Forget each kindness that you do
As soon as you have done it,
Forget the praise that falls on you
The moment you have won it;
Forget the slander that you hear
Before you can repeat it;
Forget each slight, each spite, each
  sneer,
Wherever you may meet it.
Remember every kindness done
To you, whate'er its measure;
Remember praise by others won
And pass it on with pleasure;
Remember those who lend you aid
And be a grateful debtor;
Remember every promise made
And keep it to the letter.   ANONYMOUS

——————◆——————

Knowledge

Knowledge is not what the pupil remembers but what he cannot forget.

What is meant by "knowledge of the
world" is simply an acquaintance with
the infirmities of men.   DICKENS

——————◆——————

Half knowledge is worse than ignorance.

——————◆——————

Knowledge and timber should not
be used until they are seasoned.
                    OLIVER WENDELL HOLMES

——————◆——————

Nice 'Twould Be

How nice 'twould be if knowledge
  grew
On bushes as the berries do;
Then we would plant our spelling seed
And gather all the words we need!
And sums from off the slates we'd
  wipe
And wait for figures to be ripe,
And go into the field and pick
Whole bushels of arithmetic!

Or, if we wished to learn Chinese
We'd just go out and shake the trees,
And grammar, then in all our towns
Would grow with proper verbs and
  nouns;
And in the garden there would be
Great bunches of geography,
And all the passersby would stop
And marvel at the knowledge crop.
                    AUTHOR UNKNOWN

——————◆——————

It is in knowledge as in swimming;
he who flounders and splashes on the
surface makes more noise and attracts
more attention than the pearl diver
who quietly dives in quest of treasures
at the bottom.   WASHINGTON IRVING

——————◆——————

Knowledge is power only if a man
knows what facts not to bother about.
                    ROBERT LYND

——————◆——————

Whoever requires a knowledge and
does not use it is like one who plows
but does not sow.   SAADI

——————◆——————

Knowledge humbleth the great man,
astonishes the common man, puffeth
up the little man.

He who knows, and knows he knows —
He is wise — follow him.
He who knows, and knows not he knows —
He is asleep — wake him.
He who knows not, and knows not he knows not —

He is a fool — shun him.
He who knows not, and knows he knows not —
He is a child — teach him.

Arabian Proverb

As for me, all I know is that I know nothing.

SOCRATES

L

Labor

The greatest labor saving device today is tomorrow.

———♦———

Labor disgraces no man: unfortunately man occasionally disgraces labor.

ULYSSES S. GRANT

———♦———

Set it down as a fact to which there are no exceptions, that we must labor for all that we have, and nothing is worth possessing or offering to others, which costs us nothing.

The Sunday School

———♦———

Language

The six sweetest phrases in the American language:

I love you.
Dinner is served.
All is forgiven.
Sleep until noon.
Keep the change.
Here's that five.

———♦———

The art of saying appropriate words in a kindly way is one that never goes out of fashion, never ceases to please and is within the reach of the humblest.

F. W. FABER

———♦———

The common faults of American language are an ambition of effect, a want of simplicity and a turgid abuse of terms.

JAMES FENIMORE COOPER

———♦———

Language, like linen, looks best when it is clean.

A lad in Boston, rather small for his age, worked in an office as an errand boy. One day his employers were chaffing him a little about being so small and said, "You will never amount to much; you are too small."

The lad looked at them and said, "Well, I can do something which none of you four men can do."

"What is it?" they asked.

"I don't know that I should tell you," he replied.

They were eager to know and urged him to tell them what he could do that none of them was able to do.

"I can keep from swearing," said the little fellow.

That ended the conversation.

The Sign

———♦———

If we put the word "but" after God, there is paralysis. When the word is put before God it is power.

———♦———

The story is told of Gordon Maxwell, missionary to India, that when he asked a Hindu scholar to teach him the language, the Hindu replied:

"No Sahib, I will not teach you my language. You would make me a Christian."

Gordon Maxwell replied, "You misunderstand me. I am simply asking you to teach me your language."

Again the Hindu responded, "No, Sahib, I will not teach you. No man can live with you and not become a Christian."

Selected

139

Kathy tripped over a block. "I always knowed that was going to happen," she remarked to her teacher.

"I always knew it was going to happen," the teacher corrected.

"Oh!" Kathy exclaimed in delighted surprise at the coincidence. "You always knowed it, too?"   *NEA Journal*

———◆———

The Funniest Language

We'll begin with box, the plural is boxes;
But the plural of ox should be oxen, not oxes;
One fowl is a goose, but two are called geese
But the plural of mouse should never be meese;
You may find a lone mouse or a whole nest of mice
But the plural of house is houses, not hice;
If the plural of man is always called men,
Why shouldn't the plural of pan be called pen?
The cows in the plural may be called cows, or kine;
But a bow, if repeated, is never called bine.
And the plural of vow is vows, never vine.
If I speak of a foot you show me two feet
And I give you a boot, would a pair be called beet?
If one is a tooth and a whole set are teeth
Why shouldn't the plural of booth be called beeth?
If the singular's this and the plural is these
Should the plural of a kiss ever be written keese?
And the one may be that, and the two may be those
Yet hat in the plural would never be hose.
And the plural of cat is cats and not cose.
We speak of brother and also of brethren
But the way we say mother, we never say methren.
Then the masculine pronouns are his, he and him,
But imagine the feminine, she, shis and shim!
So the English, I think you will agree
Is the funniest language you ever did see.   AUTHOR UNKNOWN

———◆———

Laugh, Laughter

Laugh

Build for yourself a strong box,
Fashion each part with care;
Fit it with hasp and padlock,
Put all your troubles there.
Hide therein all your failures,
And each bitter cup you quaff,
Lock all your heartaches within it
Then — sit on the lid and laugh!

Tell no one of its contents;
Never its secrets share;
Drop in your cares and worries,
Keep them forever there,
Hide them from sight so completely,
The world will never dream half.
Fasten the top down securely,
Then — sit on the lid and laugh!   ANONYMOUS

———◆———

Laugh and the world laughs with you, complain and you live alone.

———◆———

A woman without a laugh in her is the greatest bore in existence.   WILLIAM THACKERAY

———◆———

A laugh is worth a hundred groans in any market.   LAMB

———◆———

Whether laughter is healthful or not depends on the size of the fellow you're laughing at!

———◆———

Laughing is the sensation of feeling good all over, and showing it principally in one spot.   JOSH BILLINGS

———◆———

Laughter is wholesome. God is not so dull as some people make out. Did He not make the kitten to chase its tail?   HEINRICH HEINE

We never stop laughing because we are old. We grow old because we stop laughing.

———✦———

He who laughs last laughs best.

———✦———

I am persuaded that every time a man smiles, but much more when he laughs, it adds something to this fragment of life. STERNE

Law, Lawyer

The Law was broken in the people's hearts before it was broken by Moses' hand.

———✦———

There are 35 million laws and no improvement on the Ten Commandments.

———✦———

The laws of God are to be obeyed, not debated.

———✦———

The state that tolerates disrespect for any law breeds defiance to all law.

———✦———

Lawyer: "When I was a boy, my highest ambition was to be a pirate."
Client: "Congratulations."

———✦———

God works wonders now and then;
Behold! a lawyer, an honest man.
BENJAMIN FRANKLIN

———✦———

Layman

The Layman's Beatitudes

Blessed is the man whose calendar contains prayer meeting nights.

Blessed is the man who does not remain away from church because it rains.

Blessed is the man who can stay over an hour in a church service.

Blessed is the man who loves the Lord's work with his pocketbook as well as his heart.

Blessed is the man whose watch keeps church time as well as business time.

Blessed is the man who leaves the back pew for the late comers.

Blessed is the man who does not have a summer "lay-off" from his religion.
Sunday School Digest

It's the Layman

Leave it only to the pastors, and soon the church will die;
Leave it to the womenfolk, the young will pass it by.
For the church is all that lifts us from the coarse and selfish mob,
And the church that is to prosper needs the layman on the job.
Now a layman has his business, and a layman has his joys,
But he also has the training of all our girls and boys;
And I wonder how he'd like it if there were no churches here,
And he had to raise his children in a godless atmosphere.
It's the church's special function to uphold the finer things,
To teach that way of living from which all that's noble springs;
But the pastor can't do it singlehanded and alone,
For the laymen of the country are the church's buildingstones.
When you see a church that's empty, though its doors are open wide,
It's not the church that's dying — it's the laymen who have died.
It's not just by song or sermon that the church's work is done,
It's the laymen of the country who for God must carry on. EDGAR A. GUEST

———✦———

Laziness, Lazy

While some are standing on the promises, others just sit on the premises.

———✦———

A lazy man is good for two things: good for nothing and no good.

———✦———

Experience has taught us that laziness may get a man a good day's rest, but in time it will cost him dearly.
Church Management

———✦———

Doctor: "To be quite candid with you, your trouble is just laziness."
Patient: "Yes, doctor, I know, but what is a scientific name for it? I've got to report to my wife."

Father told his little son that he couldn't go to church because he was suffering from a severe case of voluntary inertia.

"I bet you aren't," the little boy answered, "I bet you're just lazy."

———◆———

Many want to learn the "tricks of the trade" without the trouble of learning the trade.

———◆———

There are lazy minds as well as lazy bodies.   BENJAMIN FRANKLIN

———◆———

We are as lazy as our circumstances permit us to be.

———◆———

An indolent man is just a dead one who can't be legally buried.

———◆———

Leader, Leadership

A Born Leader

I'm paid to be a foreman.
My job is leading men.
My boss thinks I'm a natural,
But if I am, why then,
I wish someone would tell me
Why snow-swept walks I clean,
When in the house sit two grown sons
Who made the football team.
                    AUTHOR UNKNOWN

———◆———

A leader is an ordinary person with extraordinary determination.
                    Southwestern Advocate

———◆———

The mob has many heads, but no brains.

———◆———

Followers will never go any further than their leader.

———◆———

Of a good leader,
When his task is finished, his goal
    achieved,
They will say,
"We did this ourselves."   LAO-TSE

———◆———

A leader is anyone who has two characteristics: First he is going someplace; second he is able to persuade other people to go with him.
                    W. H. COWLEY

Those who participate also contribute.

———◆———

Don't beg men to serve, stimulate them.

———◆———

He who leads without leading others to lead is no leader.

———◆———

Leaders are servers.

———◆———

Be an opener of doors for such as come after thee, and do not try to make the universe a blind alley.
                    RALPH WALDO EMERSON

———◆———

A man who wants to lead the orchestra must turn his back on the crowd.

———◆———

A leader sees three things: what ought to be done, what can be done, and how to do it.

———◆———

A good leader never does anything he can give someone else the privilege of doing.

———◆———

What America Needs

A leader like Moses, who refused to be called the son of Pharaoh's daughter, but was willing to go with God.

Army generals like Joshua, who knew God and could pray and shout things to pass rather than blow them to pieces with atomic energy.

A food administrator like Joseph, who knew God and had the answer to famine.

Preachers like Peter, who would not be afraid to look people in the eye and say, "Repent or perish," and denounce their personal as well as national sins.

Mothers like Hannah, who would pray for a child that she might give him to God, rather than women who are delinquent mothers of delinquent children.

Children like Samuel, who would talk to God in the night hours.

Physicians like Luke, who could care for physical needs and introduce their patients to Jesus Christ who is a specialist in spiritual trouble.

A God like Israel's, instead of the "dollar god," the "entertainment god," and the "auto god."

A Saviour like Jesus, who could and would save from the uttermost to the uttermost. *Quo Vadis, from UEA*

Christ the Leader

L - oving   Hebrews 2:10
Because He has made the way at such a cost.
E - ssential   Philippians 4:19
Cannot do without Him.
A - bsolute   John 21:22
Must let Him lead altogether.
D - ivine   John 14:6
He knows the way.
E - xcellent   Psalm 23:2, 3
Good company, and He cannot err.
R - eady   Isaiah 48:17
But only becomes ours when we accept Him.

Learn, Learning

To live is not to learn, but to apply.
LEGOUVE

If you would turn the best schoolmaster out of your life, fail to learn from your mistakes.

You can't learn much by listening to yourself all the time. *National Motorist*

We learn only what we accept for our living. DR. WM. HEARD KIRKPATRICK

Supposing is good, but finding out is better. MARK TWAIN

Learn from the mistakes of others — you can't live long enough to make them all yourself.

It's what you learn after you know it all that counts. WILLARD GRIFFIN

They can't call you an old dog as long as you're learning new tricks.

The great trouble with most men is that those who have been educated become uneducated just as soon as they stop inquiring and investigating life and its problems for themselves.
NEWTON D. BAKER

Yearn to learn.

And one student told the teacher that an adjective is a word, phrase, or clause that mortifies a noun or pronoun. *NEA Journal*

The wise man studies others so that he can learn from their mistakes and at their expense.

Anyone who stops learning is old, whether this happens at twenty or eighty. Anyone who keeps on learning not only remains young but becomes increasingly valuable. *Bible News Flashes*

Someone has figured out that the peak years of mental activity must be between the ages of four and eighteen.
At four we know all the questions.
At eighteen we know all the answers.

I can neither eat for you nor learn for you. RALPH W. HOUSE

Legal

It is easier to make certain things legal than to make them legitimate.
S. R. N. CHAMFORT

Leisure

Leisure is the time you spend on jobs you don't get paid for. *Changing Times*

Lesson

His Last Regrets

(With apologies to
Clement Clark Moore)

'Twas on Monday before Sunday and all through his head
Not an idea was stirring, not even a thread

LESSON — LIBERTY

Of thought for the Sunday school lesson to learn
To teach those ten boys with ambition to burn.

And Tuesday came on with a decided ambition
To study the lesson, his soul to condition.
And Wednesday slipped by with no preparation
And Thursday escaped with the same consternation.

Now Friday was here and still there was time
To get at his lesson by six fifty-nine.
But Amos 'n Andy his thoughts did envelope
And left him no time the lesson to develop.

But Saturday is free from manual care
To leave him full time his lesson to prepare.
No foolin', he'll get at his lesson tomorrow
And end the glad day with no inward sorrow.

But the day was too filled with un-thought-of-chores —
The flivver to polish and other such lures
That evening came on with no preparation
To teach those ten boys 'gainst worldly temptations.

He'll wait till that evening when all through the house
Not a creature'll be stirring, not even a mouse,
His mind will be clear from annoying confusion
And the lesson he'll learn with the Spirit's infusion.

The supper now ended, the day's labor past,
He'll get at his lesson to prepare it at last
As soon as he glances at the headlines all through
To end up with Dagwood and Palooka, too.

144

But the day was too strenuous, the supper too good:
He soon fell asleep with no likelihood
Of getting his lesson those "rascals" to teach
He'd try it tomorrow — his achievement to reach.

'Twas the hour before Sunday school when all through the house
Every creature was stirring, yes, even the mouse.
With full desperation he studied in vain
His thoughts to collect and the lesson to gain.

'Twas five minutes to ten and all through his heart
Condemnation was stirring in every part
The school now is over and all his week's flare
Ended up in confusion and perfect despair.

A. L. BROWN, in Sunday School Journal

———◆———

One college student to another: "Never let your lessons interfere with your education."

———◆———

Liberty

God grants liberty only to those who love it, and are always ready to guard and defend it.

DANIEL WEBSTER

———◆———

Your personal liberty ends where my nose begins.

———◆———

Liberty has never come from the government. . . . The history of liberty is the history of the limitations of governmental power, not the increase of it.

WOODROW WILSON

———◆———

They that can give up essential liberty to obtain a little temporary safety deserve neither liberty nor safety.

BENJAMIN FRANKLIN

———◆———

God grant that not only a love of liberty but a thorough knowledge of the rights of men may pervade all the nations of the earth, so that a philosopher may set his foot anywhere on its surface and say, "This is my country."

BENJAMIN FRANKLIN

Library

A man's library consists of all the books he has that no one wants to borrow.

———◆———

A sparrow sat on a window sill
And shook his head in doubt
He wondered where those book worms were
He'd heard so much about.

———◆———

Lie, Lying

One lie begets another.

———◆———

You can get to the ends of the earth by lying, but you'll never get back.

Russian Proverb

———◆———

Sin has many tools, but a lie is a handle that fits them all.

———◆———

Those who are given to white lies soon become color blind.

———◆———

No man has a good enough memory to be a successful liar.   LINCOLN

———◆———

It is easy to tell one lie, but hard to tell just one.

———◆———

A lie has no legs to support itself — it requires other lies.

———◆———

He who approves a white lie will find the shade growing darker.

———◆———

A lie stands on one leg, truth on two.

BENJAMIN FRANKLIN

———◆———

Mrs. Brown was shocked to learn that Junior had told a lie. Taking the youngster aside for a heart-to-heart talk, she graphically explained the consequences of falsehood:
"A tall black man with red fiery eyes and two sharp horns grabs little boys who tell lies and carries them off at night. He takes them to Mars where they have to work in a dark canyon for fifty years. Now," she concluded, satisfied, "you won't tell a lie again, will you, dear?"
"No, Mom," replied Junior gravely. "You tell better ones."   F. G. KERNAN

———◆———

Life

What Is Life?
Life is what we make it,
Sweet or bitter,
Hot or cold;
As water slaking thirst,
We take it;
Life is either ashes, or pure gold.
The Old Shoemaker

———◆———

It is such a comfort to drop the tangles of life into God's hands and leave them there.

———◆———

Jesus never taught men how to make a living. He taught men how to live.

DR. BOB JONES, SR.

———◆———

Life makes one demand on every living organism; namely, that it come to terms with the situation it confronts, realizing there are two ways to meet a situation. Sometimes you can change the situation; other times you must change yourself.

———◆———

If place I choose, or place I shun,
My soul is satisfied with none;
But when Thy will directs my way,
'Tis equal joy to go or stay.

———◆———

However mean your life is, meet it and live it, do not shun it and call it hard names. It is not so bad as you are. The faultfinder will find faults even in Paradise. Love your life, poor as it is.   HENRY DAVID THOREAU

———◆———

Life, like a mirror, never gives back more than we put into it.

———◆———

In the Orient, living is substituted for efficiency and a cup of tea for on-the-dot punctuality.

LIFE

Life bores only when it has no purpose.

———♦———

Three Anchors of Life —
1. I believe God.
2. I belong to God.
3. I serve God.

———♦———

Life is no looseleaf book; each page that is turned remains intact with all that we have penned, and when we've turned the last there is no refill.
FRED BECK

———♦———

Since life is so short, let's make it broader.

———♦———

When young men are beginning life, the most important period, it is often said, is that in which their habits are formed. That is a very important period. But the period in which the ideas of the young are formed and adopted is more important still. For the ideal with which you go forth determines the nature, so far as you are concerned, of everything you meet.
H. W. BEECHER

———♦———

What is put into the first of life is put into all of life.
J. M. PACE

———♦———

Life is a one-way street and we are not coming back.

———♦———

We do not need a new leaf to turn over but a new life to receive.

———♦———

If life is a grind, use it to sharpen your wits.

———♦———

Outline of Life

Tender Teens
  Teachable Twenties
    Tireless Thirties
      Fiery Forties
        Forceful Fifties
          Serious Sixties
            Sacred Seventies
              Aching Eighties
                . . . shortening breath.
              Death,
              Sod . . .
              God.

A handful of good life is worth a bushel of learning.
GEORGE HERBERT

———♦———

A useless life is only an early death.
GOETHE

———♦———

The great use of life is to spend it for something that will outlast it.
WILLIAM JAMES

———♦———

Let God have your life; He can do more with it than you can.
D. L. MOODY

———♦———

The Secret of a Happy Life

The secret of a happy life
Is an industrious hand,
Which gladness finds in earnest work
For noble purpose planned.
It leaves no time for idle fears,
Thoughts morbid or depressed,
But cheerfully it does its part
And leaves to Heaven the rest.

The secret of a happy life
Is in a loving heart
Whose good-will flows to all its kind,
To all would joy impart.
It shares in others' weal and woe;
Is not with self engrossed.
The richest and the happiest heart
Is his who loves the most.

The secret of a happy life
Is a believing soul
Serenely trusting in the power
Which animates the whole.
On earnest, upright, loving lives
Heavens' choicest blessings fall;
The Christ of God within the soul
The crowning joy of all.
CHARLES WENDTE

———♦———

Key Words to Life

1 - 20 years — learning
20 - 30 years — ladies
30 - 40 years — living
40 - 50 years — liberty
50 - 60 years — leisure
60 - 70 years — living

———♦———

There has never yet been a man in our history who led a life of ease whose name is worth remembering.
THEODORE ROOSEVELT

The first years of man's need make provision for the last. SAMUEL JOHNSON

———♦———

Do not take life too seriously; you will never get out of it alive. ELBERT HUBBARD

———♦———

Enjoy your life without comparing it with that of others. MARQUIS DE CONDORCET

———♦———

Calmly, see the mystic Weaver
  Throw His shuttle to and fro:
'Mid the noise and wild confusion,
  Well the Weaver seems to know
What each motion and commotion,
  What each fusion and confusion
In the grand result will show.

———♦———

Beware of the easy road — it always leads down.

———♦———

Life is not salvage to be saved out of the world, but an investment to be used in the world.

———♦———

Life — What Is It?

(James 4:14)

Life Is a Mystery.
  Life itself is thus. Our earthly life, likewise, is often mysterious.
Life Is a Gracious Gift from God.
  There is nothing we count more precious than life.
Life Is a Race.
  It involves preparation, struggle and reward.
Life Is a Journey.
  This speaks of observations, experiences and destination.
Life Is Uncertain.
  This is true as to its content, as well as its length.
Life Is Brief.
  It is like a vapor, the flower, the grass, etc.
Life Is Eternal.
  Death does not end all. ANONYMOUS

———♦———

It is not doing the thing we like, but liking the thing we have to do that makes life happy. GOETHE

Life is a story in volumes three,
    The Past
    The Present
    The Yet-to-be
The first is finished and laid away,
The second we're reading day by day,
The third and last of volume three
    Is locked from sight;
    God keeps the key!

———♦———

Take care of your life and the Lord will take care of your death. GEORGE WHITEFIELD

———♦———

Life is not a cup to be drained, but a measure to be filled.

———♦———

A Bible and a newspaper in every house, a good school in every district — all studied and appreciated as they merit — are the principal support of virtue, morality and civil liberty. BENJAMIN FRANKLIN

———♦———

Life with Christ is an endless hope; without Him a hopeless end.

———♦———

Only God can live a holy life in sinful flesh. GORDON

———♦———

The latter part of a wise man's life is taken up in curing all of the follies, prejudices and false opinions he had contracted in the former. JONATHAN SWIFT

———♦———

Do not despise your situation. In it you must act, suffer and conquer. From every point on earth we are equally near to heaven and the infinite. AMIEL

———♦———

In life, as in driving, there is nothing wrong with wanting to get ahead, but it's not considered good form to blow your horn while passing. *National Motorist*

———♦———

Certainly life expectancy is increasing. Nowadays you can expect anything.

———♦———

Life does not require us to make good; it asks only that we give our best on each new level of experience. HAROLD W. RUOPP

Things That Count

Not what we have, but what we use;
  Not what we see, but what we
    choose.
These are the things that mar or bless
  The sum of human happiness.

The things near by, not things afar;
  Not what we seem, but what we are.
These are the things that make or
    break
  That give the heart its joy or ache.

Not what seems fair, but what is true;
  Not what we dream, but the good
    we do,
These are the things that shine like
    gems,
  Like stars in fortune's diadems.

Not what we take, but what we give;
  Not as we pray, but as we live,
These are the things that make for
    peace,
  Both now and after time shall cease.

A Garden We All Can Plant

Four rows of peas:
  Patience,
  Perseverance,
  Promise to win others,
  Prayer.
Three rows of lettuce:
  Let us be unselfish,
  Let us love,
  Let us tithe.
One row of squash:
  Squash indifference.
Four rows of turnips:
  Turn up for church,
  Turn up regularly,
  Turn up to help,
  Turn up with determination.
                    AUTHOR UNKNOWN

A holy life will produce the deepest impression. Lighthouses blow no horns; they only shine.   D. L. MOODY

Life is a fragment, a moment between two eternities, influenced by all that has preceded, and to influence all that follows.   W. E. CHANNING

Life is too short to be little.   DISRAELI

Light

Harry Lauter once talked about the man in England who went around with a light on a long pole to light the gas lamps along the street. The man couldn't be seen at the end of the pole but he left a light in the darkness.

The Lord Jesus didn't say, "Let your light so twinkle" — but let it "shine!"

The light that shines the farthest shines brightest at home.

The class had been told about the prodigious rate at which light travels. "Just think," said the teacher, "of light coming to us from the sun at the rate of all those thousands of miles a second. Isn't it wonderful?"
"Not so very," said one lad. "It's downhill all the way!"

Liquor (Alcohol, Temperance)

See Who I Am

I am the greatest criminal in history.
I have killed more men than have fallen
  in all the wars of the world.
I have turned men into brutes.
I have made millions of homes unhappy.
I have transformed many ambitious
  youths into hopeless parasites.
I made smooth the downward path for
  countless millions.
I destroy the weak and weaken the
  strong.
I make the wise man a fool and trample the fool into his folly.
I ensnare the innocent.
The abandoned wife knows me, the
  hungry children know me.
The parents, whose child has bowed
  their gray heads in sorrow, know me.
I have ruined millions and shall try to
  ruin millions more.
I am alcohol.   H. W. GIBSON in Young Pilgrim

Statistics show that 10,000 people are killed by liquor where only one is killed by a mad dog; yet we shoot the dog and license the liquor. What sense is there to this?   *Bible Crusaders News*

The liquor traffic would destroy the church if it could, and the church could destroy the liquor traffic if it would.   *National Voice*

The last man hired, the first man fired — the man who drinks.
Poster of U. S. Steel Corp.

There are more old drunkards than old doctors.   BENJAMIN FRANKLIN

The most valued thing in the world is the human brain, and the worst enemy of the brain in modern society is beverage alcohol.   DR. GEORGE A. LITTLE

A hangover is something to occupy a head that wasn't used the night before.

Dignity can't be preserved in alcohol.

When wine enters, wisdom goes abroad.

To put alcohol in the human brain is like putting sand in the bearing of an engine.   THOMAS A. EDISON

He is a fool who puts into his mouth that which takes away his brains.

Booze builds business up — for the undertaker.

Drink is the mother of want and the nurse of crime.   LORD BROUGHMAN, 1830

First the man takes a drink,
Then the drink takes a drink,
Then the drink takes the man.
Japanese Proverb

The tavern keeper likes the drunkard, but he does not want him for a son-in-law.   *Greek Primer*

Drink does not drown care, but waters it, and makes it grow faster.
BENJAMIN FRANKLIN

Better shun the bait than struggle in the snare.   DRYDEN

William Penn was once advising a drunkard to give up his habit of drinking intoxicating liquors.
"Can you tell me how to do it?" the man asked.
"Yes, friend," Penn replied. "It is just as easy as to open thy hand."
"Convince me of that," the drunkard explained, "and I will promise upon my honor to do as you tell me."
"Well, my friend, when thou findest any vessel of intoxicating liquor in thy hand, open the hand that contains it before it reaches thy mouth, and thou wilt never be drunk again."
This plain advice so delighted the drunkard that he straightway proceeded to follow it.

Drunkenness, that worst of evils, makes some men fools, some beasts, some devils.   BENJAMIN FRANKLIN

The tavern keeper is the only business man who is ashamed of his customers.

Sir William Osler, the famed physician, was examining a patient who was a heavy drinker.
"You'll have to cut out alcohol," ordered Osler.
"But, doctor," protested the other, "I've heard it said that alcohol makes people do things better."
"Nonsense," said Osler, "it only makes them less ashamed of doing them poorly."   *Listen*

Said the glass of beer to the bottle of gin, "I'm not much of a mathematician, but I can
Add to a man's nervous troubles;
Subtract cash from his pocketbook;
Multiply his aches and pains;
Divide his property with liquor sellers, so that

149

Fractions only remain for him. More-
over, I
Take interest from his work, and
Discount his chances for health and
success."   AUTHOR UNKNOWN

———◆———

Listen

Listening is fifty per cent of our
education.

———◆———

A good listener is not only popular
everywhere, but after a while he knows
something.   WILSON MIZNER

———◆———

Always listen to the opinions of
others. It probably won't do you any
good but it will them.

———◆———

A pair of good ears will drink dry a
hundred tongues.   BENJAMIN FRANKLIN

———◆———

If you want your wife to listen, talk
to another woman.

———◆———

Little Things

Little Things

Only a little shriveled seed —
It might be a flower or grass or weed;
Only a box of earth on the edge
Of a narrow, dusty window-ledge;
Only a few scant summer showers;
Only a few clear, shining hours —
That was all. Yet God could make
Out of these for a sick child's sake,
A blossom-wonder as fair and sweet
As ever broke at an angel's feet
Only a life of barren pain,
Wet with sorrowful tears for rain;
Warmed sometimes by a wandering
    gleam
Of joy that seemed but a happy dream.
A life as common and brown and bare
As the box of earth in the window
    there;
Yet it bore at last the precious bloom
Of a perfect soul in a narrow room —
Pure as the snowy leaves that fold
Over the flower's heart of gold.
                   HENRY VAN DYKE

Little Things

Oh, it's just the little, homely things,
The unobtrusive, friendly things,
The "Won't-you-let-me-help-you" things
That make the pathway light.
And it's just the jolly, joking things,
The "Laugh-with-me-it's-funny" things,
The "Never-mind-the-trouble" things
That make our world seem bright.

For all the countless, famous things,
The wondrous, record-breaking things,
Those "Never-can-be-equalled" things
That all the papers cite,
Can't match the little, human things,
The "Just-because-I-like-you" things,
Those "Oh-it's-simply-nothing" things,
That make us happy, quite.

So here's to all the little things,
The every-day-encountered things,
The "Smile-and-face-your-trouble"
    things,
"Trust God to put it right,"
The "Done-and-then-forgotten" things,
The "Can't-you-see-I-love-you" things,
The hearty "I-am-with-you!" things
That make life worth the fight.
                   EVA M. HINCKLEY

———◆———

Live, Living

The world owes you a living only
when you have earned it.

———◆———

You can make a good living yet live
a poor life.

———◆———

If we teach a child nothing about
right living we have no reason to complain if he goes wrong. It is not his
fault, it is our neglect.

———◆———

Too much of our living is resolution-
ary and not revolutionary.

Live the Gospel first! Tell about it
afterwards!

———◆———

Free to know, free to do — this is
living!

———◆———

A living dog is better than a dead
lion.

Right living will keep you out of jail, but not out of hell; only Christ can do that.

———◆———

Too many persons live in imitation of Christ instead of in identification with Him.　　　　VANCE HAVNER

———◆———

Work determines what we get out of living; giving determines what we put into living.

———◆———

The Christian dies to live.　D. L. MOODY

———◆———

Jesus perfectly lived what he perfectly taught.　　HERMAN H. HORNE

———◆———

Live among men as if God beheld you; speak to God as if men were listening.　　　　SENECA

———◆———

I live every day as if this were the first day I had ever seen and the last I was going to see.　WILLIAM LYON PHELPS

———◆———

You have not lived a perfect day, even though you have earned your money, unless you have done something for someone who will never be able to repay you.　ANONYMOUS

———◆———

A Negro lady was testifying in court in behalf of her husband and admitted during the questioning that he never worked and she had to support him.

"Why do you live with such a trifling husband?" she was asked.

"Well, it am dis way, I makes de livin' and he makes de livin' worthwhile."

———◆———

Let us endeavor so to live that when we come to die even the undertaker will be sorry.　　MARK TWAIN

———◆———

He that would live in peace and ease
Must not speak all he knows nor judge all he sees.　　BENJAMIN FRANKLIN

———◆———

Life would be a perpetual flea hunt if a man were obliged to run down all the innuendos, inveracities, insinuations and misrepresentations which are uttered against him.　　H. W. BEECHER

He Truly Lives

Who has a work he can respect.
Who has found a cause he would die for.
Who has a faith that supports him in the days of difficulty.
Who has great causes to live for, regardless of what he has to live on.
Who has great ideas to keep him company in lonely hours.

———◆———

Your town will be a delightful place to live in if you are a delightful person to live beside.　*O'Brannons Between Calls*

———◆———

There are two things needed in these days: first, for rich men to find out how poor men live; and second, for poor men to know how rich men work.　　E. ATKINSON

———◆———

It is better to live for Christ than to wish you had.

———◆———

This country will not be a really good place for any of us to live in if it is not a really good place for all of us to live in.　THEODORE ROOSEVELT

———◆———

The philosopher says to live and learn but some people just live.

———◆———

According to doctors, you will live much longer if you give up everything that makes you want to.

———◆———

Live as if you expected to live a hundred years, but might die tomorrow.　　ANN LEE

———◆———

To live the resurrection life in Christ is to lead many to believe in Christ as the resurrection and the life.

———◆———

Part of the world is living on borrowed time while the rest of it is living on borrowed money.

———◆———

We will never have life taken in high seriousness by all people unless the best people repudiate shallow and superficial ways of living.

We can always live on less when we have more to live for.

S. STEPHEN MC KENNY

———◆———

Let all live as they would die.

GEORGE HERBERT

———◆———

A good description of modern living: "A senseless whirl which has been spelled in three words — hurry, worry, bury."

Moody Monthly

———◆———

When life seems just a dreary grind,
And things seem fated to annoy,
Say something nice to someone else
And watch the world light up with joy.

AUTHOR UNKNOWN

———◆———

The way you teach is very important, and what you teach is even more important, but how you live is most important.

———◆———

To live well in the quiet routine of life; to fill a little space because God wills it; to go on cheerfully with a petty round of little duties, little avocations; to smile for the joy of others when the heart is aching — who does this, his works will follow him. He may not be a hero to the world, but he is one of God's heroes.

AUTHOR UNKNOWN

———◆———

Livelihood

Don't believe the world owes you a living; the world owes nothing — it was here first.

ROBERT J. BURDETTE

———◆———

Loaf

A sign on the bus station window read, "If you have nothing to do, don't do it around this window."

———◆———

The Bible promises no loaves to the loafer.

———◆———

Father to son: "I can tell that you are going to become a baker by your loaf."

Loneliness, Lonely

Alone I sit
And sip my tea;
I dream of you
Eternally.

It's been so long
Since you were here . . .
Do you sip tea
Alone, my dear?

ELIZABETH WILDT

———◆———

If we spend our life building walls around our private preserves, what right have we to complain if we're lonely?

———◆———

Loneliness is not so much a matter of isolation as of insulation.

HAROLD W. RUOPP

———◆———

People are lonely because they build walls instead of bridges.

J. F. NEWTON

———◆———

It is better to be alone than in bad company.

———◆———

When alone, guard your thoughts; in the family, guard your temper; in company, guard your words.

———◆———

Last summer Jim spent his first week away from home at a summer camp. He was not much of a letter writer, but one day I did receive a card from him. All it said was:
"Dear Mom,
"There are 50 boys here this week but I sure wish there were only 49. Jim."

The Instructor

———◆———

Alone with a book by a fire — that's swell.
Alone on the dunes — there's a certain spell to that.
Or alone is a pleasant way to go for a walk on a stormy day.
It's thrilling alone, with the reins in hand
And to be alone, with some work is grand.
Alone in a mist, with a moon — that's magic.
Alone on a Saturday night — that's tragic.

MARGARET ENGLEMAN

Look

Some people never look up until they are flat on their back.

Seven Looks

LOOK BACK — Remember God's
goodness ....I Kings 8:56
LOOK UP — In praise....Psalm 103:1
LOOK DOWN — In humility;
in caution.......I Corinthians 10:12
LOOK FORWARD—In confidence;
in hope ....II Timothy 1:12
LOOK WITHIN — Daily,
thoroughly ....Psalm 19:14
LOOK AROUND —
Be vigilant ....Hebrews 12:15
LOOK UNTO JESUS ....Isaiah 45:22

Lord

If Christ is not Lord of all, He is not Lord at all.

Where the Lord Is

The Lord is *before* His people —
Micah 2:13; John 10:4
The Lord is *behind* His people —
Psalm 139:5
The Lord is *above* His people —
Deuteronomy 33:12; Psalm 63:7; 91:1
The Lord is *beneath* His people —
Deuteronomy 32:11;
Isaiah 40:11; 46:4
The Lord is *around* His people —
Psalm 125:2; 139:3
The Lord is *with* His people —
Numbers 23:21; Matthew 1:23; 28:20
The Lord is in the *midst* of His
people — Isaiah 12:6; Zephaniah 3:17

Lose, Loses

He who loses money loses much; he who loses a friend loses more; but he who loses his spirit loses all.

Love, Love of Christ, Lovers

Love is like the measles, worse if it comes late in life.

Love at first sight never happens before breakfast.

"Yes, Robert, amo is the Latin word meaning 'I love you.' Now what word suggests its opposite?"
"Reno," replied Robert.
The Watchman Examiner

Love is a funny thing,
It's just like a lizard.
It curls up round your heart
And jumps in your gizzard!

Love is like an onion
We taste it with delight
But when it's gone, we wonder
What ever made us bite.

The lasting love knot is tied with just one beau.

The magic of first love is our ignorance that it can ever end.   DISRAELI

It is hard to express love with a clenched fist.

Love is swell.
It's so enticing,
It's orange jell,
It's strawberry icing,
It's chocolate russe,
It's roasted goose,
It's ham on rye,
It's banana pie.
Love's all good things without a question,
In other words — it's indigestion!

To My Ever Present Temptation

I have tried to love you lightly
But without success;
To love you very little
And never to excess.
I have sought to love you wisely
But this I cannot do,
For all my vows are shattered
Each time I look at you.
AUTHOR UNKNOWN

They who love are but one step from heaven.
JAMES RUSSELL LOWELL

Remember, we were enjoined only to love our neighbor. We don't have to agree with all his silly ideas.

We love according to the way people treat us. EUGENIA PRICE

Love never asks how much must I do, but how much can I do. FREDERICK A. AGAR, *Royal Service*

There are more people who wish to be loved than there are willing to love. CHAMFORT

Interest will begin a hard work. Grit will continue it. But only love makes a man endure to the end.

God purposes that we should love Him — not just the things He gives us. *Eternity*

The cat and the love you give away always come back to you.

Lovers remember everything.

Love gives everything, but only to lovers. BALZAC

An old man used to go about selling little boxes of cement which could mend all family jars and even broken hearts.

Some only laughed at him, but those who purchased one of the little boxes for a cent or so found a small piece of paper inside. On it was written the word *Love*. What a sure cure for family jars and broken hearts.

Children need love, especially when they do not deserve it. HAROLD S. HULBERT

Love and a toothache have many cures, but none infallible, except possession and dispossession. BENJAMIN FRANKLIN

To love the whole world
For me is no chore;
My only real problem's
My neighbor next door. C. W. VANDERBERGH

So long as we love, we serve; so long as we are loved by others I would almost say that we are indispensable; and no man is useless while he has a friend. ROBERT LOUIS STEVENSON

We must love men ere they will seem worthy of our love. SHAKESPEARE

The love that unites Christians is stronger than the differences that divide them.

Human beings must be known to be loved; but divine things must be loved to be known. PASCAL

If there is a tug-of-war, let the rope be the love of God.

Love Is . . .
Slow to suspect — quick to trust,
Slow to condemn — quick to justify,
Slow to offend — quick to defend,
Slow to expose — quick to shield,
Slow to reprimand—quick to forbear,
Slow to belittle—quick to appreciate,
Slow to demand — quick to give,
Slow to provoke — quick to help,
Slow to resent — quick to forgive. AUTHOR UNKNOWN

God's love for us is not a love that always exempts us from trials, but rather, a love that sees us through trials.

God is the source of love.
Christ is the proof of love.
Service is the expression of love.
Boldness is the outcome of love.

Love is not getting, but giving; not a wild dream of pleasure and a madness of desire — oh, no — love is not that! It is goodness and honor, and peace and pure living — yes, love is that and is the best thing in the world, and the thing that lives longest. VAN DYKE

The fact that you have never experienced the love of God does not prove it doesn't exist. EVERT MORGAN

One's love for God is equal to the love one has for the man he loves least.

JOHN J. HUGO

When Hudson Taylor was staying in the home of a friend on one occasion, his host asked him, "But are you always conscious of abiding in Christ?"

"While sleeping last night," replied Mr. Taylor, "did I cease to abide in your home because I was unconscious of the fact? We should never be conscious of not abiding in Christ."

A little four-year-old boy didn't want to eat the peas his mother had put on his plate.

"If you don't eat these, Bobby, you will have to leave the table," his mother said.

Whereupon Bobby left the table. After a time mother went to look for him and found him in the bathroom.

He had climbed upon a stool and was looking into the mirror. Tears were streaming down his face but he was looking at himself and singing, "*Jesus Loves Me.*"

Walking down the street one day a lady noticed a little girl leaving the church by herself. When the child passed her, the lady inquired where she had been.

"In there," replied the little girl, pointing to the church.

"And what were you doing in there?" the woman asked.

"Praying," was the prompt reply.

Thinking the child was probably bothered with some problem the lady inquired, "What were you praying for, dear?"

"Nothing," the child replied. "I was just loving Jesus."

M

Magnanimous

Let us be excusers rather than accusers.

Write injuries in dust, benefits in marble.

BENJAMIN FRANKLIN

Don't look for the flaws as you go
    through life,
And even if you find them,
Be wise and kind and somewhat blind,
And look for the good behind them.

AUTHOR UNKNOWN

Any fool can find fault but it takes a man with a great heart to discover the good in others and speak of that good.

Have a deaf ear for unkind remarks about others, and a blind eye to the trivial faults of your brethren.

WALTER SCOTT

Seven Things You Never Regret

Showing kindness to an aged person.
Destroying a letter written in anger.
Offering the apology that saves a friendship.
Stopping a scandal that was wrecking a reputation.
Helping a boy find himself.
Taking time to show your mother consideration.
Accepting the judgment of God on any question.

ROY L. SMITH

Try

To be so young that nothing can disturb your peace of mind.

To talk health, happiness and prosperity to every person you meet.

To make all your friends feel that there is something in them.

To look on the sunny side of everything and make your optimism come true.

To think only of the best, to work only for the best and to expect only the best.

To be just as enthusiastic about success for others as you are about your own.

To forget the mistakes of the past and press onward to greater achievements in the future.

To wear a cheerful countenance at all times and to have a smile ready for every living creature you meet.

To give so much time to the improvement of yourself that you have no time to criticize others.

To be too large for worry, too noble for anger, too strong for fear and too happy to permit the presence of trouble. *The Rustler*

Maiden

A certain congregation had dwindled in size so much that when the minister said "Dearly Beloved," the maiden lady in the front row thought he was proposing.

———◆———

The maiden lady, chairman of a school organization, was outlining the program for the coming year. "Our basic need," she said, "is a man."

———◆———

Under the bunch of mistletoe,
The homely maiden stands,
And stands, and stands, and stands, and stands,
And stands, and stands, and stands.

———◆———

Manager

A manager is a "glue man" who can hold a good team together and give it leadership, direction and esprit de corps.

———◆———

Man, Manhood, Men

The man wears the pants in the family, but the woman provides the suspenders.

Many a man thinks he's being cultivated when he's only being trimmed.

———◆———

"There are two kinds of men who never amount to very much," Cyrus H. K. Curtis remarked one day to his associate, Edward Bok.

"And what kinds are those?" inquired Bok.

"Those who cannot do what they are told," replied the famous publisher, "and those who can do nothing else."
Sunday School Journal

———◆———

Unknown Man

Oh, unknown man, whose rib I am,
Why don't you come for me?
A lonely, homesick rib I am
That would with others be.
I want to wed — There, now, 'tis said!
(I won't deny and fib) —
I want my man to come at once
And claim his rib!

Some men have thought that I'd be theirs,
But only for a bit;
We found out soon it wouldn't do:
We didn't seem to fit.
There's just one place
The only space
I'll fit (I will not fib) —
I want that man to come at once
And claim his rib!

Oh, don't you sometimes feel a lack,
A new rib needed there?
It's I! Do come and get me soon
Before I have gray hair!
Come, get me, dear!
I'm homesick here!
I want (and I'll not fib) —
I want my man to come at once
And claim his rib. AUTHOR UNKNOWN

———◆———

The Noblest Man

The happiest man that you can know
Is one who daily lives above
The plane where sordidness can grow,
And breathes the atmosphere of love

When ill will bides within a heart,
  It brews a venom with a sting
More harmful than a poisoned dart,
  And not the least of good will bring.

Revenge and lust and greed are foes
  More deadly than the rapier's thrust,
And enmity brings naught but woes
  That wisest men cannot adjust.

The noblest man is one who will
  Not harbor evil in his breast,
But fits it for love's domicile
  That every joy may be his guest.

REV. WILLIAM JAMES ROBINSON

Measure of a Man

Not — how did he die?
  But — how did he live?
Not — what did he gain?
  But — what did he give?
These are the units
  To measure the worth
Of a man as a man
  Regardless of birth.

Not — what was his station?
  But — had he a heart?
And how did he play
  His God-given part?
Was he ever ready
  With a word of good cheer,
To bring back a smile,
  To banish a tear?

Not — what was his church?
  Nor — what was his creed?
But — had he befriended
  Those really in need?
Not — what did the sketch
  In the newspapers say?
But — how many were sorry
  When he passed away?

AUTHOR UNKNOWN

Men will always be what the women make them; if, therefore, you would have men great and virtuous, impress upon the minds of women what greatness and virtue are. ROUSSEAU

Some men depend entirely upon themselves. Others marry.

Man was made before woman, and perhaps the reason was to give him time to think up some answers to her first questions. *Glendale News Press*

Average man: one who has had unusual expenses every month of his life — but expects none next month.

It may be a man's world, but we'll give you odds that it's in his wife's name. *Glendale News Press*

Manners

The test of good manners is to be able to put up pleasantly with bad ones. WENDELL WILKIE

A bird in the hand is bad table manners. *National Motorist*

The society of woman is the foundation of good manners. GOETHE

Manners are the happy ways of doing things.

No amount of manner can make up for matter when making a speech.

Manners is the ability to say, "No, thank you," when you're still hungry.

Marriage

Slippery ice — very thin;
Pretty girl — tumbled in.
Saw a fellow on the bank;
Gave a shriek — then she sank.
Boy on hand — heard her shout;
Jumped right in — pulled her out.
Now he's hers — very nice,
But she had to break the ice.

Success in marriage consists not only in finding the right mate, but also in being the right mate.

A man and his wife were getting along just fine — until the other day when she decided to return home.

157

MARRIAGE

There'd be less fuss in married life
  If husbands would extend
The selfsame courtesy to a wife
  That they do to an average friend;
Or even a little less
  Would be o.k., I guess.
W. E. FARBSTEIN

————◆————

"Doctors say that married men live longer than bachelors," the young miss said to the bachelor.

"Well, I've heard that, too," he replied, "but my married friends claim that it only seems longer."

————◆————

The sum which two married people owe to one another defies calculation. It is an infinite debt, which can only be discharged through all eternity.
GOETHE

————◆————

It might be said that a wedding ring is a sort of tourniquet which is worn on a girl's left hand to stop her circulation.

————◆————

Usher, passing collection plate at church wedding: "Yes, ma'am, it is unusual, but the father of the bride requested it."

————◆————

When it comes to such activity as painting a room or pruning a tree, I've learned my wife's editorial "we" means ME!

————◆————

After man came woman and she has been after him ever since.

————◆————

When the late Mr. and Mrs. Henry Ford celebrated their golden wedding anniversary, a reporter asked them, "To what do you attribute your 50 years of successful married life?"

"The formula," said Ford, "is the same formula I have always used in making cars — just stick to one model."

————◆————

A man never realizes his insignificance until he gets married.
Town Journal

————◆————

Marriage begins when you sink in his arms and ends with your arms in the sink.

"How come you never married?"

"It was like this. I kept looking for an ideal woman."

"And you never found her?"

"Oh, sure, but just my luck — she was looking for the ideal man."

————◆————

Keep thy eyes wide open before marriage, and half shut afterwards.
BENJAMIN FRANKLIN

————◆————

The average wife remembers when and where she got married. What escapes her is why.

————◆————

A neighbor's four-year-old daughter confided to me one day: "When I grow up I'm going to marry Danny."

I asked her why she was going to marry the boy next door and she replied seriously: "I have to. I'm not allowed to cross the street where the other boys live."
The Instructor

————◆————

It seems that Rusty misunderstood what the preacher said at his uncle's wedding, because later he was overheard re-enacting it in play, "Rosemary, do you take this man for your awful wedded husband?"
Presbyterian Life

————◆————

"Where have you been the last three hours?" demanded the minister's wife, annoyed.

"I met Mrs. Jones on the street and asked how her married daughter was getting along," sighed the weary pastor, "so she told me."

————◆————

Muddle at home make husbands roam.

————◆————

Yawn: Nature's provision for letting married men open their mouths.

————◆————

Doing housework for ten dollars a week is domestic service — but doing it for nothing is matrimony.

————◆————

Marriage is like a cafeteria, you can look over all the dishes, then choose one and pay later.

The sea of matrimony is filled with hardships.

———♦———

It takes two to make a marriage — a single girl and an anxious mother.

———♦———

The way to fight a wife is with your hat — grab it and run.

———♦———

Jack: "Do you tell your wife everything?"

Jim: "No, what she doesn't know won't hurt me."

———♦———

A man always chases a woman until she catches him.

———♦———

Honeymoon: The period between "I do" and "You'd better."

———♦———

"We've been married a year and never quarreled. If a difference of opinion arises and I'm right, my husband gives in."

"And what if he's right?"

"That has never occurred."

———♦———

"John is two-thirds married," said his sister to a friend.

"How's that?"

"Well, he's willing and the preacher is willing."

———♦———

Mature, Maturity

Few Christians ever grow up. They merely change their play things.

———♦———

A Maturity I.Q. Check-up

1. A mature person does not take himself too seriously — his job, yes!
2. A mature person keeps himself alert in mind.
3. A mature person does not always "view with alarm" every adverse situation that arises.
4. A mature person is too big to be little.
5. A mature person has faith in himself which becomes stronger as it is fortified by his faith in God.
6. A mature person never feels too great to do the little things and never too proud to do the humble things.
7. A mature person never accepts either success or failure in themselves as permanent.
8. A mature person never accepts any one of his moods as permanent.
9. A mature person is one who is able to control his impulses.
10. A mature person is not afraid to make mistakes. LEONARD WEDEL

———♦———

So far in the history of the world, there have never been enough mature people in the right places. GEORGE CHISHOLM

———♦———

You are young only once, but you can stay immature indefinitely. *R & R Magazine*

———♦———

Maxims

Three things most difficult:
To keep a secret.
To forget an injury.
To make good use of leisure. CHILD

———♦———

Early to bed and early to rise,
Makes a man healthy, wealthy and wise. BENJAMIN FRANKLIN

———♦———

Modern version of the above:
Late to bed and early to rise
Makes a man baggy under the eyes.

———♦———

Four New England Maxims:
Eat it up.
Wear it out.
Make it do.
Do without. *Quoted by* CALVIN COOLIDGE

———♦———

Meditation

Meditation is mental mastication.

———♦———

Every factor of the Bible is meant to be a factor of life.

Meditation — thinking with a view of doing.

———◆———

A Moment with Him

We mutter and sputter,
We fume and we spurt;
We mumble and grumble,
Our feelings get hurt;
We can't understand things,
Our vision grows dim,
When all that we need is
A moment with Him.   *Selected*

———◆———

Meet, Meeting

The pastor noticed a man who came way down front for service.

Afterwards the pastor spoke to the man and asked, "How was it that you came and sat right in front, being a stranger here?"

"Oh," said the man, "I'm a bus driver and I just came to see how you get everyone to the rear of the building."

———◆———

A model meeting:
    Participated in by everybody;
    Monopolized by nobody;
    Where everybody is somebody.

———◆———

After a speaker had wearied the Sunday school assembly he asked, "What shall I say next?"

A small boy near the front answered promptly: "Say amen and sit down."

———◆———

Memory

Memory is the receptacle and sheath of all knowledge.   CICERO

———◆———

Memory is the sheath in which the sword of the Lord is kept.

———◆———

One of the best uses of memory is to remember to forget the unpleasant things.

———◆———

Don't worry if you start losing your memory. Just forget about it.

Many complain of their memory, few of their judgment.   BENJAMIN FRANKLIN

Memory alone is a poor substitute for thought.

———◆———

"Say the Bible words, 'God is Love,' after me," the kindergarten teacher asked her class.

And so, in unison they said, "God is love after me."

———◆———

Mental

Jumping at conclusions is not nearly as good a mental exercise as digging for facts.

———◆———

Fog is exceedingly dangerous to drive in, especially if it's mental.   *Presbyterian Life*

———◆———

Ten Rules for Mental Health

1. I will mind my own business and not gossip.
2. I will not wear my feelings on my sleeve or be so sensitive that I look for personal offenses or slights.
3. I will wear a smile. When I am gloomy, I will go away and hide rather than inflict myself on others.
4. I will be considerate of others.
5. I will not be headstrong.
6. I will play the game of life on the square.
7. I will hold my temper and each night ask God to forgive me as I have forgiven my neighbors.
8. I will face the world each morning with confidence, determined to be as happy and brave as I can.
9. I will move into battle for a worthy cause.
10. I will not be too egotistical to pray.
    Milwaukee Road Magazine

———◆———

Mercy

Blessed are the merciful for they shall obtain mercy.

———◆———

Teach me to feel another's woe
To hide the fault I see;
That mercy I to others show,
That mercy show to me.   *Selected*

God's wrath comes by measure; His mercy without measure.

———◆———

The quality of mercy is not strained;
It droppeth as the gentle rain from heaven
Upon the place beneath: it is twice blest;
It blesseth him that gives and him that takes:
'Tis mightiest in the mightiest; it becomes
The throned monarch better than his crown. SHAKESPEARE

———◆———

Methods

Be sure your method is modern but your message old-fashioned.

———◆———

An old-fashioned faith with modern methods makes your teaching effective.

———◆———

Mind

The human mind is the greatest tramp in the universe. Some of you are in China right now! WM. M. RUNYAN

———◆———

The neurotic builds castles in the sky. The psychotic lives in them. The psychiatrist collects the rent.

———◆———

The worth of the mind consisteth not in going high, but in marching orderly. MICHEL DE MONTAIGNE

———◆———

Some minds are like concrete — thoroughly mixed and permanently set.

———◆———

"Closed for Repairs" should be posted on a lot of open minds.

———◆———

In the scale of destinies, brawn will never weigh so much as brain.

———◆———

Minds are like parachutes — they only function when open. LORD DEWAR

———◆———

The easiest way to get a reputation for possessing a superior mind is to nod approval and let the other fellow do all the talking.

Cobwebs form in the unused human attic.

———◆———

The greatest undeveloped territory in the world lies under your hat.

———◆———

I have a photographic memory. My brain is just like a negative — all it needs is developing.

———◆———

One day a young man had an accident: He was struck with a thought.

———◆———

You can lead a horse to water but you can't make him think.

———◆———

Think, do not guess.

———◆———

There's nothing more useless than a train of thought which carries no freight. BILLY B. VAN

———◆———

The brain is no stronger than its weakest think.

———◆———

Give your mind to Christ that you may be guided by His wisdom. *Eternity*

———◆———

Sometimes when a person thinks his mind is getting broader, it is just his conscience stretching. *Tid-Bits*

———◆———

Keep God's love in your mind as well as your heart.

———◆———

The one thing worse than a vacant mind is one filled with spiteful thoughts.

———◆———

Many men boast of an open mind when it really is only a blank space.

———◆———

When the tongue is making 1200 revolutions a minute, the brain must be in neutral.

———◆———

It wouldn't be so bad to let one's mind go blank if one always remembered to turn off the sound.

———◆———

Man's mind, stretched to a new idea, never goes back to its original dimensions. OLIVER WENDELL HOLMES

People sometimes grow so broad-minded that their thinking gets shallow.

———◆———

Little minds are wounded too much by little things; great minds see all, and are not even hurt. LA ROCHEFOUCAULD

———◆———

A man cannot think constantly of himself without being discouraged.
DAVID GRAYSON

———◆———

It takes a strong mind to hold an unruly tongue.

———◆———

Quiet minds cannot be perplexed or frightened, but go on in fortune or misfortune at their own private pace, like a clock during a thunderstorm.
ROBERT LOUIS STEVENSON

———◆———

Vacant lots and vacant minds usually become dumping grounds for rubbish.

———◆———

The absent-minded professor called his biology class to order shortly after the lunch hour.

"Our special work this afternoon," he said, "will be cutting up and inspecting the inward workings of a frog. I have a dead frog here in my pocket to be used as a specimen."

He reached into his pocket and pulled out a paper sack, shook its contents on the table and out rolled a nice looking ham sandwich. The professor looked at it, perplexed, scratched his head and muttered:

"That's funny; I distinctly remember eating my lunch." *Selected*

———◆———

Minister

A burglar had entered a poor minister's house at midnight, but was disturbed by the awakening of the occupant of the room he was in.

Drawing his weapon, he said, "If you stir you are a dead man. I'm hunting for your money."

"Let me get up and turn on the light," said the minister, "and I'll hunt with you."

A strong and faithful pulpit is no mean safeguard to a nation's life.

———◆———

The former minister and his wife decided to attend the church social of his previous parish.

The new minister greeted his predecessor heartily. "I'm very pleased to see you," he said, "and this must be your most charming wife?"

"This," the other replied, "is my only wife."

———◆———

It may be that you don't like your minister. Then here is a tested prescription by which you can get rid of him:

1. Look him straight in the eye when he's preaching, and maybe say "amen" occasionally. The man will preach himself to death in a short time.

2. Start paying him whatever he is worth. Having been on starvation wages for years, he'll promptly eat himself to death.

3. Shake hands with him, tell him he's doing a good job. He'll work himself to death.

4. Rededicate your own life to God and ask the minister to give you some church work to do. Very likely he'll keel over with heart failure.

5. If all else fails, this one is certain to succeed — get your congregation to unite in prayer for him. He will soon be so effective that some larger church will take him off your hands.
Presbyterian Life

———◆———

The church elders in the little New Hampshire town had voted to keep their minister in spite of his radical tendencies. A visitor to the village, knowing their extremely narrow beliefs, commended one of the elders for having taken such a broad view.

"Broad view, nonsense!" retorted the elder. "We all know the dominie has dangerous ideas, but we'd rather have him here." The elder winked a shrewd eye. "If he wasn't here, he'd be somewhere else. *There* people might listen to him." *Coronet*

Johnny and the Ministry

My folks is Methodists, and so
When conference comes our way, you
    know,
Or some big meetin' is in town
That brings a lot of preachers 'round,
Why, Mother opens wide the door
And entertains a few — or more —
            Of preachers.

And don't I like to see 'em come?
I tell you what, we're goin' some
When we have chicken twice a day,
And fruit that Mother's put away
For winter — jam and preserves!
She sure gets reckless when she serves
            The preachers.

And I can't help a-thinkin' — well,
When I set there and hear 'em tell
About the boys *they* used to be,
Just little chaps like Joe and me,
And had to milk, and chop the wood —
That they must find it mighty good,
            Bein' preachers.

And then they sometimes want to know
If I don't think I'd like to go
To Afriky as soon's I can,
And help to save my fellowman;
But I don't 'spress no special haste,
'Cause cann'bals has an awful taste
            For preachers.

I'd whole lot ruther, when I'm grown,
Just be a preacher here at home.
There's drawbacks even then, of course,
Some things is better, and some worse,
But when they go a-visitin', why,
There's allus chicken and pumpkin pie
            For preachers.

                    FRANCES POINDEXTER

Miracles

A sixth grade girl's definition of a miracle: "Something extraordinary that happens without any strings attached."

Miracles

There are those who doubt the story
Of the fishes and the bread —
I have watched a daffodil lifting
From its cheerless winter bed.

There are those who say that Jesus
Never walked upon the sea —
I have learned to hear the willows
Whispering strange things to me.
"Lazarus," some wise folks tell me,
"Was not dead, when Jesus came!"
I have watched the spring returning
In a green and fragrant flame.

                    AUTHOR UNKNOWN

Misfortune

The greatest misfortune of all is not to be able to bear misfortune. *Bias*

Misquotes, Misconceptions

The Lord is my shepherd, I can do what I want.

"He anointeth my head with coal oil," said the little boy when quoting the twenty-third Psalm.

Three boys about four years of age were displaying a new toy. One boy said, "Let's see your gun."
The other said, "It's not a gun, it's a pistol!"
Our four-year-old daughter added, "I know what a pistol is! Our minister talks about one every Sunday."
                    Christian Parent

A junior high school student wrote about the "writ of hideous corpus" in an examination.
Another junior high student quoted thus from the Declaration of Independence: ". . . Every man should be divided equal." *NEA Journal*

Missionary, Missions

Visions without work is visionary; work without vision is mercenary; together they are missionary.

A true missionary is God's man in God's place, doing God's work in God's way for God's glory.

The one calling not overcrowded is the missionary calling.

The Missionary's Equipment

A life yielded to God and controlled by His Spirit.

A restful trust in God for the supply of all needs.

A sympathetic spirit and a willingness to take a lowly place.

Tact in dealing with men and adaptability toward circumstances.

Zeal in service and steadfastness in discouragement.

Love for communion with God and for the study of His Word.

Some experience and blessing in the Lord's work at home.

A healthy body and a vigorous mind.

HUDSON TAYLOR

———◆———

A worthy vicar in a rural parish waxed eloquent in the interest of foreign missions one Sunday, and was surprised on entering the village shop during the week to be greeted with marked coldness by the woman who kept it.

On asking the cause, the good woman produced a half crown from a drawer, and throwing it down before him, said:

"I marked that coin and put it in the plate last Sunday, and here it is back in my shop. I know well them poor Africans never got the money!"

———◆———

An African pastor asked missionaries leaving on furlough to "tell our friends in America that we do not have refrigerators and other modern contrivances. Tell them that we could even dispense with automobiles, but tell them we cannot do without the Gospel of the Son of God."

———◆———

The Lordship of Jesus Christ is the first step in missions.   J. ALLEN BLAIR

———◆———

The missionary enterprise is not the church's afterthought; it is Christ's forethought.   HENRY VAN DYKE

———◆———

A New Hebrides chieftain sat peacefully reading the Bible, when he was interrupted by a French trader.

"Bah," he said in French. "Why are you reading the Bible? I suppose the missionaries have got hold of you, you poor fool. Throw it away! The Bible never did anyone any good."

Replied the chieftain, calmly, "If it weren't for this Bible, you'd be in my kettle there by now!"   Selected

———◆———

Out of fifty who offer their lives for missionary service, only twelve do anything; four go to the field and only one returns a second time.

———◆———

The missionary can know that he has been sent, that he is safe and that he is supplied by God.   ALAN REDPATH

———◆———

Where there is one who does not know Jesus Christ there is a mission field.   Eternity

———◆———

What are the churches for but to make missionaries?

What is education for but to train them?

What is commerce for but to carry them?

What is money for but to send them?

What is life itself for but to fulfill the purpose
of Missions!
the enthroning of Jesus
in the hearts of men?

AUGUSTUS H. STRONG

———◆———

I Believe in Missions

Because the greatest mission ever known was when God sent His only begotten Son into the world to save it.

Because the world will never be brought to Christ until men bring Christ to the world.

Because Jesus Himself taught us that missions was the only way to make disciples.

Because I am a disobedient lover of Jesus if I do not obey His command when He said . . . "Go."

Because if salvation means everything

to me, I cannot be happy unless I share it with others.

Because a Christian who does not believe in missions always gets narrow and loses his world vision.

Because the missionary is the greatest hope of the world in its present historical crises. CHARLES M. SHELDON

Bessie's mother gave her a quarter just as the minister came to call.

"Ah, Bessie," the pastor said, "I see you have a shiny new coin. Why don't you give to the missions?"

"I thought about that," the girl answered, "But I think I'll buy a soda and let the druggist give it to the missions."
Together

Mistake, Mistakes

With mistakes, like a lot of other things, it isn't the initial cost — it's the upkeep.

To err is human, but if the eraser wears out before the pencil, you're overdoing it a bit. *National Motorist*

To err is human, to forgive is divine. POPE

He who never made a mistake never made anything.

Everyone is liable to make mistakes, but fools practice them.

To err is human, to repent divine; to persist devilish.

The man who never makes a mistake probably gets his salary from one who does. *Trailer Talk*

When a fellow makes the same mistake twice he's got to own up to carelessness or cussedness. G. H. LORIMER

Money

Riches may have wings all right, but all I ever see is the tail feathers.

That money talks I will agree.
It always says good-by to me.
ALAN DORSEY

A fool and his money are welcome everywhere.

The one person you have to watch if you're going to save money is yourself.

A man whom others called poor, but who had just enough fortune to support himself, went about the country in the simplest way, studying and enjoying the life and beauty of it.

He once talked with a great millionaire who was engaged in business, working at it daily, and getting richer each week. The poor man said to the millionaire, "I am a richer man than you are."

"How do you figure that?" asked the millionaire.

"Why," he replied, "I have as much money as I want, and you haven't."
Sunday School Chronicle

"How do you manage to get money from your husband?"

"It's easy. I just say I'm going back to mother and he hands me the fare."

Today, after you make money, you have to hire an accountant to explain how you did it.

Money is a good servant, but a poor master. BONHOURS

It is known that Lincoln had no great admiration for mere financial success. "Financial success," he once said, "is purely metallic. The man who gains it has four metallic attributes: gold in his palm, silver on his tongue, brass in his face, and iron in his heart!"
This Day

The proper use of money is the only advantage there is in having it.

Money is made round to slip through your fingers. EDWIN L. BROOKS

Spend less than you earn and you'll never be in debt. *Amish Proverb*

———◆———

A farmer once went to hear John Wesley preach. The great leader was dealing with the question of money, and was examining it under three divisions.

His first thought was. "Get all you can."

The farmer nudged his neighbor and said: "That man has got something in him; it is admirable preaching!"

Wesley reached his second thought. "Save all you can."

The farmer became quite excited. "Was there ever anything like this!" he said. The preacher denounced thriftlessness and waste, and the farmer rubbed his hand as he thought, *all this have I been taught from my youth up.* What with getting and with hoarding, it seemed to him that "salvation" had come to his house.

But Wesley went on to his third thought which was, "Give all you can."

"Oh, dear," exclaimed the farmer, "he's gone and spoiled it all!"

Getting without giving makes only stagnant pools of men and women.

———◆———

Take care of your pennies — and the dollars will take care of your heirs and their lawyers.

———◆———

A beggar will never be bankrupt.

———◆———

Not only will a man rob God, but he will take an income tax deduction on it.

———◆———

A fool and his money are soon parted.

———◆———

There are no pockets in a shroud. ELD

———◆———

If you want dough do what the word says, "Do."

———◆———

I have learned that money is not the measure of a man, but it is often the means of finding out how small he is. OSWALD J. SMITH

It is better to have your bank in heaven than to have your heaven in a bank.

———◆———

A six-year-old went into a bank and asked to see the president. A courteous clerk showed her into his private office. She explained that her girls' club was raising money for a new club house and would he please contribute?

The banker laid a dollar and a dime on the desk and said, "Take your choice, Miss."

She picked up the dime and said, "My mother always taught me to take the smallest piece." Picking up the dollar bill also, she added: "But so I won't lose this dime, I'll take this piece of paper to wrap it up in." *National Motorist*

———◆———

Dollars go farther when accompanied by sense.

———◆———

Mr. Average American spends only 5c a day for religious and welfare causes. In contrast to this nickel, each day he spends 9c for tobacco, 15c for alcoholic beverages, 22c for recreation, 58c for transportation including foreign travel, 59c for taxes, $1.12 for food and $2.30 for other household expenses such as rent, clothing, savings, medical and miscellaneous expense. *Southern Baptist Handbook*

———◆———

Money talks all right; but in these days a dollar doesn't have enough cents to say anything worthwhile.

———◆———

He who works only for money seldom gets far.

———◆———

A fool and his money are soon petted.

———◆———

When your outgo exceeds your income, your upkeep is your downfall. *Executive Digest*

———◆———

The Scotchman sent an indignant letter to the editor of the newspaper. He said that if any more stories about stingy Scotchmen appeared in the columns, he was going to stop borrowing the paper.

Hard work is the yeast that raises the dough.

———♦———

When it comes to money, enough is enough — no man can enjoy more.
ROBERT SOUTHEY

———♦———

One reason why it's hard to save money is that our neighbors are always buying something we can't afford.

———♦———

People are funny; they spend money they don't have, to buy things they don't need, to impress folks they don't like.

———♦———

A banker is a man who will loan you money if you prove to him you don't need it.

———♦———

If money is your only hope for independence, you will never have it. The only real security that a man can have in this world is a reserve of knowledge, experience and ability.
HENRY FORD

———♦———

Budget: a system of reminding yourself that you can't afford the kind of living you've grown accustomed to.
Changing Times

———♦———

A small boy came home from Sunday school and began emptying his pockets of money — pennies, nickels and dimes — while his parents gasped.
"Where did you get all that money?"
The youngster replied, "At Sunday school. They've got bowls of it."
San Antonio Express

———♦———

The younger generation will learn the value of money when it begins paying off our debts.

———♦———

$1.00 spent for lunch lasts five hours.
$1.00 spent for a necktie lasts five weeks.
$1.00 spent for a cap lasts five months.
$1.00 spent for an auto lasts five years.
$1.00 spent for a railroad lasts five decades.
$1.00 spent in God's service lasts for eternity.
ROGER W. BABSON

Some people are in debt because they spend all their neighbors think they make.

———♦———

In the old days a man who saved money was a miser; nowadays he's a wonder.
ANONYMOUS

———♦———

If you would lose a troublesome visitor, lend him money.
FRANKLIN

———♦———

A London paper offered a prize for the best definition of money. This was the winning answer:
Money is an instrument that can buy you everything but happiness and pay your fare to every place but heaven.

———♦———

How America Spends Her Dollars

Gambling	30 Billion Dollars
Crime	20 Billion Dollars
Alcoholic Beverages	9.05 Billion Dollars
Tobacco	5,373 Billion Dollars
Religious and Welfare	3,356 Billion Dollars
Dog Food	175 Million Dollars
Foreign Missions	130 Million Dollars

The Evangel

———♦———

Money is that which, having not, we want; having, want more; having more, want more still; and the more we get the less contented we are.

———♦———

Money in the Bible

A farthing would equal one and one-half cents.

A gerah would be worth about three cents.

A shekel of gold would equal eight dollars.

A shekel of silver would equal about fifty cents.

A mite would be less than a quarter of a cent.

A piece of silver or a penny would equal thirteen cents.

A talent of gold would equal thirteen hundred dollars.

Money, like flowing water, when it becomes stagnant, is less useful.

———◆———

Money isn't everything . . . but it's way ahead of whatever is in second place.

———◆———

Money and time are the heaviest burdens of life, and the unhappiest of all mortals are those who have more of either than they know how to use. JOHNSON

———◆———

Mother

God could not be everywhere, and so He made mothers. *Jewish Proverb*

———◆———

Heaven is at the feet of mothers. *Persian Proverb*

———◆———

An ounce of mother is worth a pound of clergy. *Spanish Proverb*

———◆———

Mother is the name for God in the lips and hearts of little children. WILLIAM MAKEPEACE THACKERAY

———◆———

He who takes the child by the hand takes mother by the heart. *Danish Proverb*

———◆———

I think it must somewhere be written, that the virtues of the mothers shall be visited on their children as well as the sins of the fathers. DICKENS

———◆———

The sweetest face in all the world to me,
Set in a frame of shining golden hair,
With eyes whose language is fidelity;
This is my mother. Is she not most fair? MAY RILEY SMITH

———◆———

An old-timer is one who can remember when a baby sitter was called mother.

———◆———

It is easy to pick out the children whose mothers are good housekeepers; they are usually found in other yards.

———◆———

I don't think there are enough devils in hell to take a young person from the arms of a godly mother. BILLY SUNDAY

Where there is a mother in the home, matters speed well. A. B. ALCOTT

———◆———

The mother's heart is the child's schoolroom. HENRY WARD BEECHER

———◆———

Men are what their mothers make them. EMERSON

———◆———

The sweetest sounds to mortals given
Are heard in mother, home and heaven. WILLIAM GOLDSMITH BROWN

———◆———

The future destiny of the child is always the work of the mother. NAPOLEON BONAPARTE

———◆———

All that I am or hope to be, I owe to my angel mother. ABRAHAM LINCOLN

———◆———

You may have tangible wealth untold;
Caskets of jewels and coffers of gold;
Richer than I you can never be —
I had a mother who read to me. STRICKLAND GILLILAN

———◆———

Oh, the comfort, the inexpressible comfort of feeling safe with a person, having neither to weigh thoughts nor measure words, but pour them all right out just as they are, chaff and grain together, knowing that a faithful hand will take and sift them, keep what is worth keeping and then with the breath of kindness blow the rest away. This is mother. *Selected*

———◆———

Most of all the other beautiful things in life come by twos and threes, by dozens and hundreds. Plenty of roses, stars, sunsets, rainbows, brothers, and sisters, aunts and cousins, but only one mother in the whole world. KATE DOUGLAS WIGGIN

———◆———

Men and women frequently forget each other, but everyone remembers mother. JEROME PAINE BATES

———◆———

Of all the men I have known, I cannot recall one whose mother did her level best for him when he was little, who did not turn out well when he grew up. FRANCES PARKINSON KEYES

She could not paint, nor write, nor rhyme
Her footprints on the sands of time,
As some distinguished women do;
Just simple things of life she knew —
Like tucking little folks in bed,
Or soothing someone's aching head.

She was no singer, neither blessed
With any special loveliness
To win applause and passing fame;
No headlines ever blazed her name.
But, oh, she was a shining light
To all her loved ones, day and night!

Her home her kingdom, she its queen;
Her reign was faithful, honest, clean,
Impartial, loving, just, to each
And every one she sought to teach.
Her name? Of course, there is no other
In all the world so sweet — just Mother!   MAY ALLREAD BAKER

A mother is the only person on earth who can divide her love among ten children and each child still have all her love.

Mother

The noblest thoughts my soul can claim,
The holiest words my tongue can frame,
Unworthy are to praise the name
More sacred than all other.
An infant, when her love first came —
A man, I find it just the same;
Reverently I breath her name,
The blessed name of mother.
                GEORGE GRIFFITH FETTER

To Mother — At Set of Sun

As once you stroked my thin and silver hair
So I stroke yours now at the set of sun.
I watch your tottering mind, its day's work done,
As once you watched with forward-looking care
My tottering feet. I love you as I should.

Stay with me; lean on me; I'll make no sign.
I was your child, and now time makes you mine.
Stay with me yet a while at home, and do me good.   AUTHOR UNKNOWN

Motive

Many a good thing is done with a wrong motive.

The noblest motive is the public good.

Music

A father had taken his small son to church. The boy sat and listened attentively without saying a word until the clergyman announced, "We will now sing hymn two hundred and twenty-two: 'Ten Thousand Times Ten Thousand,' two hundred and twenty-two."
The puzzled boy nudged his father. "Daddy, we don't have to work this out, do we?"

I must have lots of music in me as none of it ever came out.

A violinist is one who is up to his ear in music.

Music Lessons:
Sometimes B sharp
Never B flat
Always B natural

A little girl was standing between her parents during a hymn so they gave her an open hymnal. After looking it over carefully, she handed it back with this comment: "No pictures; all advertising."   *Together*

The leading soloist in the church cantata was unable to get a baby sitter. So she had to drag her reluctant young son to every practice session. Finally, completely bored with the reiterated musical expression, he rebelled and insisted on remaining at home.

169

MUSIC

The singer acknowledged his flowery introduction by saying: "I sing for my own amazement."

———♦———

"But, darling," the young mother remonstrated, "you should learn to enjoy church music. Why, the angels sing around God's throne all day long!"

"Well," said the child, "I just can't see how God can stand it."

Watchman Examiner

———♦———

The young pastor was quite long-winded one night talking to the young people. After nearly an hour he suddenly stopped, smiled and asked, "What hymn shall we sing?"

One boy called out, appropriately, "Revive Us Again."

———♦———

A child who went to Sunday school for the first time came home and told her father that she learned the train song — "Lead Us Not into Penn Station." Later her father learned that the children had sung a prayer hymn, "Lead Us Not into Temptation."

———♦———

A loyal minister's wife sang in the choir to bolster its membership. One Sunday the father of an eight-year-old in the congregation asked the child if he knew the minister's wife.

"Oh, yes," came the reply, "she's one of the chorus girls."

Together

———♦———

After the little girl returned from Sunday school where she had learned the song, "Jesus Wants Me for a Sunbeam," she sang the song to her mother and then, seriously, asked her: "Mother, why does Jesus need me for a mixmaster?"

———♦———

The fine symphony orchestra from the big city had played in a small New England town, the first experience of the kind for many of the inhabitants. Next day some of the old-timers gathered around the stove in the general store and expressed their opinions. The comment of one of the oldest inhabitants was: "All I got to say is — it was an awful long way to bring that big bass drum only to bang it once."

———♦———

"Has your husband a good ear for music?"

"I'm afraid not. He seems to think that everything he hears in church is a lullaby."

———♦———

The little girl was happily humming a hymn as she dusted the furniture to help her mother.

"Mommie, will I be dusting God's chair when I get to heaven, the way the hymn says?" she asked.

Mother looked up with surprise. "Which hymn, honey?"

"And dust around the throne," her little girl quoted. It took a while before the mother learned that she was quoting a line from the hymn "Marching to Zion," "and thus surround the throne."

Adapted

———♦———

Bill: "Since when did you stop singing in the choir?"

Charlie: "Since the Sunday I was absent, and everyone thought the organ had been tuned!"

———♦———

Confusion was created by a church bulletin which read: Text for today, "Thou Shalt Not Steal." The choir will sing, "Steal Away, Steal Away."

———♦———

A third-grade Sunday school teacher asked her students to list their favorite hymns. One little girl looked up in surprise, blushed, then scribbled, "Peter and Tom."

———♦———

A little five-year-old girl had been attending the church kindergarten. Each day before the children were dismissed, the teacher had them sing the Doxology, which the little five-year-old loved to sing, but in her own words: "Praise God from whom all blessings flow, Praise Him all creatures, here we go!"

Christian Parent

At a banquet in the Russian capital during World War II, United States Chamber of Commerce President Eric Johnston and Author William L. White listened to their hosts sing Russian songs. Then the Russians requested their guests to sing an American song.

Johnston and White consulted for a few moments and responded with the only song they both remembered — "Jesus Wants Me for a Sunbeam."

Sunday School Digest

There are many interesting versions of hymn titles, according to children who do not understand the words. Here are a few most interesting ones:

"The Cross-Eyed Bear" for "Jesus, I Thy Cross Would Bear."

"Bringing in the Sheets" for "Bringing in the Sheaves."

"He Carrots for You" for "He Careth for You."

N

Name

If your name is to live at all, it is much better to have it live in people's hearts than only in their brains.

HOLMES

Your name is something you have that everyone else uses more than you do.

If I had been named according to the life I have lived my first name would be "Ima" and my last name "Mess."

Some folks have trouble naming a new baby. Others have rich relatives.

Times, Thief River Falls, Minn.

Nation

National honor is national property of the highest value.

JAMES MONROE

The government is us; we are the government, you and I.

THEODORE ROOSEVELT

Nature

Nature's Message

There is a God, all nature cries,
I see it in the painted skies.
I see it in the flow'ring spring,
I hear it when the birdlings sing.

I see it in the flowing main,
I see it in the falling rain,
I see it stamped on hail and snow,
I see it when the streamlets flow.
I see it in the clouds that soar,
I hear it when the thunders roar.
I see it when the morning shines,
I see it when the day declines,
I see it in the morning height,
I see it in the smallest mite,
I see it everywhere abroad.
I feel — I know — there is a God.

AUTHOR UNKNOWN

Outdoors

I like to get out in the open,
    Outdoors, 'neath the blue of the sky
Away from the hustle,
    The turmoil and bustle —
And let all my worries go by!
    I like to lie down on a hillside
And loaf in the shade of the trees —
    Not planning and scheming,
    But dozing and dreaming,
Caressed by the fan of the breeze!

And soothing to me is the quiet,
    And restful is each gentle sound —
The chirp of the cricket,
    A bird in a thicket,
Or twigs falling down to the ground.
    I seem far away from my troubles,
As there I recline on the sod,
    Beneath the Great Ceiling —
And I have the feeling
    Outdoors, that I'm closer to God.

CHARLES S. KINNISON

171

Dogwood Is Barking

The crocuses are crowing
  The southern zephyrs blowing;
The nectarines are necking by the sea;
  The cat-tails cater-wauling;
The cauliflowers calling
  And spring is springing up along the
    lea.

The yellow cowslip's slipping;
  The catnip starts a nipping,
And the saps along the street begin to
    stir;
You know that spring is springing
When the bluebell's bells are ringing,
  And the pussywillow buds begin to
    purr.   JUDGE

———◆———

He who lives after nature shall never
be poor.

———◆———

Need

To know the need is to sow the seed.

———◆———

He looks most that longs most.

———◆———

The tragedy of our generation is that
there are untold millions still untold.

———◆———

God can't meet your need until you
feel your need.

———◆———

Place your needs up against His
riches and they will soon disappear.
                                   Eternity

———◆———

Neglect

Miss Meant-to has a comrade
And her name is Didn't-do.
Have you ever chanced to meet them,
Did they ever call on you?
These two girls now live together
In the house of Never-win,
And I'm told that it is haunted
By the ghost of Might-have-been.
                    The Sunday School Journal

———◆———

The Cost of Neglecting One Boy

Ex-governor Dickinson, of the state
of Michigan, told the following story.

A young lad, the son of a businessman, walked up to his busy father and
said, "Dad, if you do not send me off
to a state institution today, I am going
to commit suicide tonight." This was
startling to a father who had been
making money, looking after public interests, but neglecting his own offspring. The young lad went on to
relate that he was socially diseased.
And it is appalling when we learn
that millions of our American youth
are in the same condition today.

Mr. Dickinson said that the businessman's son was sent off to a state institution for treatment. In a year he came
back home thinking he was cured. But
God says that the sins of the fathers
are visited unto the children of the
third and fourth generation of them
that hate Him. Whatever a boy sows
in his early life, he shall reap in later
years.

This lad married a beautiful young
girl. Their first and only child was a
son. The mother died in childbirth.
The young diseased father went over
and looked at a half-blind idiotic baby.
He exclaimed, "It is more than I can
bear." He picked up a revolver, went
outside the bedroom and took his own
life.

The baby lived. In later years he
stood in a long line in Buffalo, New
York, to shake the hand of President
William McKinley. When his turn
came, he stretched out one hand to
the President, drew a revolver with
the other hand, and out went the life
of William McKinley.

It was not long until this young man
was brought to justice. He was sen-
tenced to die. And one of the saddest
sights on earth is to see a young man
awaiting his day of execution! What a
pity that the state has to take the
life of any young man or woman as
penalty for a crime.

The ex-governor said that five tragedies resulted from the failure of the
church and state to save one boy.

First, there was the premature death
of a young mother. She paid the pen-

alty of the sins of another by losing her life.

Second, there was the birth of a baby, born with inherited criminal tendencies.

Third, there was the suicide of the young father.

Fourth, there was the tragic death of President William McKinley, a Christian statesman.

Fifth, there was the execution of a young man who had been neglected in his formative years, and who knew nothing but a life of crime and degradation and shame.

It was costly business to fail to save Leon Czolgosz. Five tragedies came out of this one lad's sin. And it may be that the boy at your door, or just around the corner from your home or church, will commit a crime which will shock the state and nation if he is not won to the Sunday school and to Christ.   *Sunday School Digest*

———◆———

Neighbor

Love Thy Neighbor

Let me be a little kinder;
Let me be a little blinder
To the faults of those about me;
   Let me praise a little more.

Let me be, when I am weary,
Just a little bit more cheery;
Let me serve a little better
   Those whom I am striving for.

Let me be a little braver
When temptation bids me waver;
Let me strive a little harder
   To be all that I should be.

Let me be a little meeker,
With the brother who is weaker,
Let me think more of my neighbor
   And a little less of me.
                    AUTHOR UNKNOWN

———◆———

I love the path my neighbor made
   Across the grass up to my door;
My lawn that once was smoothly green,
   Is now much dearer than before.
                    WILLIAM A. WOFFORD

Talk About Your Neighbors

Let us talk about our neighbors;
Talk of them where'er we go;
Talk about our friend and brother,
And of everyone we know.
Let us talk about our kindred,
Spread the news both near and far,
Till the whole town hears the story
Of what splendid folks they are.

Let us talk about our neighbors;
Of the kindly deeds they do;
Of the little acts of kindness
Which they do for me — for you.
Tell about the hours of watching
Through the night with you in pain;
Of the words of cheer and courage
When your struggles all seem vain.

Let us talk about our neighbors,
In the home or at our work,
Where the conversation's cheerful
Or where germs of envy lurk.
Let us talk about our neighbors,
But let's be as neighbors should —
Let's not talk about their failures —
Let us tell of something good.
                    AUTHOR UNKNOWN

———◆———

Every man's neighbor is his mirror.

———◆———

Love your neighbor, yet don't pull down your hedge. BENJAMIN FRANKLIN

———◆———

New Year

Happy New Year

H - ear God's Word.......Isaiah 55:3
A - nswer God's Call..Matthew 11:28
P - ardon Receive.....Nehemiah 9:17
P - eace Possess ....Romans 15:33
Y - ield to God..........Romans 6:13

N - o Condemnation ......Romans 8:1
E - ternal Life Is a Gift...Romans 6:23
W - alk Uprightly ......Ephesians 5:2

Y - outh Is the Time for
   Service ....Ecclesiastes 12:1
E - arly Seek God........Psalm 63:1
A - ttend to God's
   Word.............Numbers 12:6a
R - ejoice in the Lord..Philippians 4:4

173

Another year is but another call from God
To do some deed undone and duty we forgot;
To think some wider thought of man and good.
To see and love with kindlier eyes and warmer heart.
Until acquainted more with Him and keener-eyed to sense the need of man
We serve with larger sacrifice and readier hand our kind.

————◆————

This Year Is Yours

God built and launched this year for you,
Upon the bridge you stand;
It's your ship, your own ship,
And you are in command.
Just what the twelve months' trip will do
Rests wholly, solely, friend with you,
Your log book kept from day to day —
My friend, what will it show?
The log will tell, like guiding star
The sort of captain that you are.
For weal or woe, this year is yours;
Your ship is on life's sea, your acts
As captain must decide
Which ever it will be.
So now, in starting on your trip,
We ask God to help you sail your ship.

EMMA MARTINDALE

————◆————

Another Year

Another year! The future path lies hidden;
And shadows seem to fall across the way.
Press on! a light before thee shineth
Yet more and more unto the perfect day.

Another year! The days are growing evil,
And Satan's threat'nings dark forebodings send.
Fear not! thy Lord hath surely spoken,
"Lo I am with you . . . even to the end."

Another year! the land is parched and thirsty;
Our souls are faint — low droops the precious grain.
Plead on! Elijah's God will answer,
And pour, in mighty floods, the latter rain.

Another year! we wait with eager longing;
The hour is late — midnight comes on apace.
Look up! Redemption's day is dawning;
Perhaps this year we'll see the Bridegroom's face.

MARGARET ARMSTRONG

————◆————

Good-by, Old Year!

Good-by, Old Year! Before you go
Into oblivion's starless night —
With recording book — of wrong and right,
With broken vows and words of hate;
Kind deeds, forgot — until too late —
Bless and forgive me, e'er you go.

New Year, with gladness you arrive —
And with radiant torch new trails you blaze —
To fresh endeavor and better days.
Weak faith make strong, with strength to win —
Amid temptations, nor with sin.
New Year, oh, keep that faith alive.

M.R.W. in Southern Churchman

————◆————

The New Year

A flower unblown; a book unread;
A tree with fruit unharvested;
A path untrod; a house whose rooms
Lack yet the heart's divine perfumes;
A landscape whose wide border lies
In silent shade 'neath silent skies;
A wondrous fountain yet unsealed;
A casket with its gifts concealed—
This is the year that for you waits
Beyond tomorrow's mystic gates.

HORATIO NELSON POWERS

————◆————

The path into the New Year is aglow with opportunity to work for Christ.

174

Facing the New Year

We pledge ourselves
  To follow through the coming year
The light which God gives us;
  The light of Truth, wherever it may
    lead;
The light of Freedom, revealing new
  opportunities for individual devel-
  opment and social service:
The light of Faith, opening new visions
  of the better world to be;
  The light of Love, daily binding
    brother to brother and man to
    God in ever closer bonds of friend-
    ship and affection.
Guided by this light,
  We shall go forward to the work of
  another year with steadfastness
  and confidence.   AUTHOR UNKNOWN

———◆———

No one ever regarded the first of
January with indifference.   CHARLES LAMB

———◆———

The New Year!

The New Year like a book lies before
  me;
  On its cover two words, "My Life,"
    I see.
I open the covers and look between —
  Each page is empty, no words can
    be seen,
For I am a writer, I hold the pen
  That'll fill these pages to be read by
    men.
Just what kind of book will my book
  be,
  My life written there for others to
    see,
Each day a page written, one by one —

Will it be worthwhile when finished
  and done?
Lord, help me keep these pages clean
  and fair
By living the life I'd have written
  there.   GERTRUDE LAURA GAST

———◆———

The first thing that's broken after
Christmas is a New Year's resolution.

———◆———

Noise

"Breaking through the sound barrier"
is an expression that applies to avia-
tion, and not to a man trying to make
himself heard on the telephone while
Cub Pack No. 21 meets in the next
room.

———◆———

Now

Just Now

Never mind about tomorrow —
  It always is today;
Yesterday has vanished.
  Wherever, none can say.
Each minute must be guarded —
  Make worth the while somehow;
There are no other moments;
  It's always, Just Now.

Just now is the hour that's golden,
  The moment to defend.
Just now is without beginning;
  Just now can never end.
Then never mind tomorrow —
  'Tis today you must enjoy
With all that's true and noble;
  And the time for this is —
Now!   AUTHOR UNKNOWN

O

Obedience, Obey

It is a great deal easier to do that
which God gives us to do, no matter
how hard it is, than to face the responsibilities of not doing it.   DR. J. R. MILLER

Obedience is the fruit of faith; patience the bloom on the fruit.
   CHRISTINA ROSSETTI

———◆———

Obedience to law is the largest
liberty.

175

Let thy child's first lesson be obedience, and the second will be what thou wilt. BENJAMIN FRANKLIN

A child has to learn obedience in the home or he will never learn obedience to the Heavenly Father. DR. BOB SMITH

He that cannot obey, cannot command. BENJAMIN FRANKLIN

Resistance to tyrants is obedience to God. JEFFERSON

Offend

When anyone has offended me, I try to raise my soul so high that the offense cannot reach me.

Omnipotence

A Sunday school teacher was examining her pupils after a series of lessons on God's omnipotence. She asked, "Is there anything God can't do?"

There was silence. Finally, one lad held up his hand. The teacher, disappointed that the lesson's point had been missed, asked resignedly, "Well, just what is it that God can't do?"

"Well," replied the boy, "He can't please everybody." *Together*

Opinion

What young America thinks of Christ today determines our nation's tomorrow.

People who are so sure they know where the younger generation is going should try to remember where it came from.

Often the fellow who hits the nail right on the head is driving it in the wrong direction.

Many people think they are broadminded just because they are too lazy to form an opinion.

Opinion is free, facts are scarce.

Everyone all over the world takes a wife's estimate into account in forming an opinion of a man. BALZAC

In a discussion, the difficulty lies, not in being able to defend your opinion, but to know it. ANDRE MAUROIS

Opinions are a luxury.

The man who never alters his opinion is like standing water, and breeds reptiles of the mind. BLAKE

My idea of an agreeable person is a person who agrees with me. DISRAELI

Man is a creature who has to argue down another man's opinion before he can believe in his own.

God cares nothing about public opinion. The voice of the people is rarely, if ever, the voice of God. W. W. AYER

"Public opinion" is what some people think most people are thinking.

Public opinion is just private opinion that makes enough noise to attract attention.

A well-informed person is one who has opinions just like yours.

Opportunity

The measure of your responsibility is the measure of your opportunity. DR. BOB JONES, SR.

Opportunities like millstones may drown you or grind your corn.

God's best gift to us is not things, but opportunities.

The doors of opportunity are marked "push."

We don't need more opportunities, we should take advantage of the opportunities we have.

I have known God to use people who never had a chance, but I have never known God to use a person who has had a chance and will not take it.
DR. BOB JONES, SR.

Greater opportunity is the reward of past accomplishment.

If you want to open the door of opportunity, push.

Don't wait for opportunity to come; it's already here.

Sometimes opportunity drops into a lap, but the lap must be where opportunity is.

Opportunity sometimes comes dressed in overalls.

Opportunity is often lost by deliberation.

With every opportunity comes the weight of responsibility.

People are so anxious to talk about closed doors that they forget the open doors.
CHR. CHRISTIANSEN

A closed door is not a call to inactivity, but a leading into a new field of service.
CHR. CHRISTIANSEN

When you dismiss an opportunity you miss success.

High privileges prompt us to high living.

A Dutch farmer in South Africa used to sit on a stone ridge that crossed his farm and mourn over the sterility of his land. He was only too happy to sell it for $25,000. But the man who bought the farm opened a gold mine right under the rocky ridge where the farmer used to sit and pity himself.

Striking while the iron is hot is all right but don't strike while the head is hot.

Opportunity never knocks at the door of a knocker.

My Opportunity

My opportunity! Dear Lord, I do not ask
That Thou shouldst give me some high work of Thine.
Some noble calling, or some wondrous task —
Give me a little hand to hold in mine.

I do not ask that I should ever stand
Among the wise, the worthy, or the great;
I only ask that softly, hand in hand,
A child and I may enter at the gate.

Give me a little child to point the way
Over the strange, sweet path that leads to Thee;
Give me a little voice to teach to pray;
Give me two shining eyes Thy face to see.

The only crown I ask, dear Lord, to wear,
Is this: that I may teach a little child
How beautiful, oh, how divinely fair,
Is Thy dear face, so loving, sweet and mild!

I do not ask for more than this,
My opportunity! 'Tis standing at my door;
What sorrow if this blessing I should miss!
A little child! What should I ask for more?
MARION C. CRAIG

There is no security on this earth. There is only opportunity.
DOUGLAS MAC ARTHUR

The stairs of opportunity
Are sometimes hard to climb;
And that can only be well done
By one step at a time.
But he who would go to the top
Ne'er sits down and despairs;
Instead of staring up the steps
He just steps up the stairs.
AUTHOR UNKNOWN

Opposition

Hardship and opposition are the native soil of manhood and self-reliance.
NEAL

Optimism, Optimist

Optimism is what the teakettle has — up to its neck in hot water, it keeps on singing.

An optimist is a man who thinks he can find some big strawberries in the bottom of the box.

Optimism is the content of small men in high places.   F. SCOTT FITZGERALD

Opportunity does not batter a door off its hinges when it knocks.

There is a new definition of an optimist and a pessimist. The optimist says, "A year from now we will all be begging."
The pessimist asks, "From whom?"

An optimist sees windows as something to let light shine through; a pessimist sees them as something that gets dirty.

The optimist is wrong as often as the pessimist is, but he has a lot more fun.

Two frogs fell into a deep cream bowl,
One was an optimistic soul,
But the other took the gloomy view,
"We shall drown," he cried without more ado!
So with a last despairing cry,
He flung up his legs and he said, "Good-by!"
Quoth the other frog with a merry grin,
"I can't get out, but I won't give in,
I'll just swim around till my strength is spent,
Then will I die the more content!"
Bravely he swam till it would seem,
His struggles began to churn the cream!
On the top of the butter at last he stopped,
And out of the bowl he gaily hopped!
What is the moral? 'Tis easily found:
If you can't hop out, keep swimming round!   AUTHOR UNKNOWN

Organization, Organize

If effort is organized, accomplishment follows.

A boy can usually find as many reasons for harboring a stray dog as a man can find for keeping up his membership in some useless organizations.

Original, Originality

The merit of originality is not novelty, it is sincerity. The believing man is the original man; he believes for himself, not for another.   CARLYLE

The more originality you have in yourself, the more you see in others.
PASCAL

Others

If you are looking for Christ in folks you will not be dwelling on their faults.   CHARLES E. FULLER

There is no loving others without living for others.

Others

Lord, help me to live from day to day
In such a self-forgetful way
That even when I kneel to pray
My prayer shall be for — others.

Help me in all the work I do
To ever be sincere and true
And know that all I'd do for you
Must needs be done for — others.

Let "Self" be crucified and slain
And buried deep; and all in vain
May efforts be to rise again
Unless to live for — others.

And when my work on earth is done
And my new work in heaven's begun
May I forget the crown I've won
While thinking still of — *others.*

Others, Lord, yes, others
Let this my motto be,
Help me to live for others
That I may live like Thee.

C. D. MEIGS

To keep in the middle of the road
one must be able to see both sides.

Outlook

To look around is to be distressed.
To look within is to be depressed.
To look to God is to be blessed.

AUTHOR UNKNOWN

Look at self and be disappointed.
Look at others and be discouraged.
Look at Christ and be satisfied.

P

Paraphrases

If

If you can trust when everyone about
  you
  Is doubting Him, proclaiming Him
  untrue,
If you can hope in Christ though all
  forsake you
  And say 'tis not the thing for you to
  do;
If you can wait on God, nor wish to
  hurry,
  Or, being greatly used, keep humble
  still,
Or if you're tested, cater not to worry
  And yet remain within His sovereign
  will;
If you can say 'tis well when sorrow
  greets you
  And death has taken those you hold
  most dear,
If you can smile when adverse trials
  meet you
  And be content e'en though your
  lot be drear;
If you can be reviled and never murmur,
  Or being tempted not give way to
  sin;
If you can fight for right and stand
  the firmer,
  Or lose the battle when you ought
  to win;

If you can really long for His appear-
  ing,
  And therefore set your heart on
  things above;
If you can speak for Christ in spite
  of sneering,
  Or to the most unlovely one show
  love;
If you hear, hear the call of God to
  labor,
  And answer "yes," in yieldingness
  and trust,
And go to tell the story of the Saviour
  To the souls in darkness o'er the
  desert's dust;
If you can pray when Satan's darts are
  strongest
  And take the road of faith instead
  of sight,
Or walk with God, e'en though His
  way be longest,
  And swerve not to the left or to the
  right;
If you desire Himself alone to fill you,
For Him alone you care to live and
  be;
Then 'tis not you, but Christ that
  dwelleth in you,
  And that, O child of God, is Victory.

GRACE REYNOLDS

The Seaman's Psalm

The Lord is my Pilot; I shall not
drift. He lighteth me across the dark

waters; He steereth me in the deep channels; He keepeth my log.

He guideth me by the star of holiness for His name's sake. Yea, though I sail 'mid the thunders and the tempests of life, I shall dread no danger; for Thou art near me; Thy love and Thy care, they shelter me.

Thou preparest a harbor before me in the homeland of eternity; Thou anointest the waters with oil; my ship rideth calmly.

Surely sunlight and starlight shall favor me on the voyage I take, and I will rest in the port of my God forever.

CAPTAIN J. ROGERS

———◆———

Modernistic Version of Psalm 23

(Suggested after reading much of the present-day jargon of life and morals, by those who have forsaken God as their Good Shepherd, and now darken counsel by words without knowledge.)

The unseen Infinite is the source of my motivation, and I shall not want personality. He maketh me to experience true self-expression and to attempt new projects in the psychology of adolescence. He restoreth the right complex to my introvert soul. He leadeth me into a preface to morals for goodness' sake! Yea, though I peregrinate through the present depression, exuberant health gives me a stiff upper lip. I grin and bear my fate. Good luck is always with me. Its creative impulse and the pep of my *élan vital* comfort me. Surely normal behaviorism and carefully controlled altruism will follow me until the jig is up, and then (properly cremated) I shall dwell in a marble urn forever. DR. SAMUEL M. ZWEMER

———◆———

The Teacher's Psalm

The Lord is my helper, I shall not fear in guiding these pupils.

He leadeth me into the Holy of Holies before I prepare this lesson.

He leadeth me to the heart of the truth and prepareth the minds of the pupils for the truth.

He giveth me a vision of the immortality of these lives.

He leadeth me to see the sacredness of teaching His Book.

Yea, tho' I become discouraged and despair at times, yet shall I lift up my head, for His promises cannot fail me.

His Word will not return to Him void, and my faith undimmed shall burn through all the coming years.

Thou walketh before me that the seed planted shall grow.

Thou shalt stand by my side on Sunday and speak through these lips so that these pupils feel the nearness of God.

Thou shalt cause each broken effort to gather sheaves through unnumbered years. My joy is full when I know that every effort in Thy Name shall abide forever.

Surely Thy love and watch care shall be with me every day of my life and someday I shall live with those who turn many to righteousness forever and ever. ROSALEE MILES APPLEBY

———◆———

Understanding

A Paraphrase of I Corinthians 13

Though I teach with the skill of the finest teachers (leaders), and have not understanding,

I am become only a clever speaker and a charming entertainer,

And though I understand all techniques and all methods,

And though I have much training,

So that I feel quite competent

But have no understanding of the way my pupils think,

It is not enough.

And if I spend many hours in lesson preparation,

And become tense and nervous with the strain,

But have no understanding of the personal problems of my pupils,

It is still not enough.

The understanding teacher is very patient, very kind;
Is not shocked when young people bring him their confidences;
  does not gossip;
  is not easily discouraged;
  does not behave himself in ways that are unworthy;
But is at all times a living example to his students of the good way of life of which he speaks.

Understanding never fails.
But whether there be materials,
  they shall become obsolete;
Whether there be methods,
  they shall be outmoded;
Whether there be techniques,
  they shall be abandoned;
For we know only a little
  and can pass on to our children
  only a little.

But when we have understanding,
  then all our efforts will become creative
And our influence will live forever in the lives of our pupils.
When I was a child
  I spoke with immaturity,
  My emotions were uncontrolled
  And I behaved childishly
But now that I am an adult,
  I must face life as it is,
  With courage and understanding.

And now abideth
  skill,
    devotion,
      understanding,
        these three,
and the greatest of these is understanding.
                              ELOUISE RIVINIUS

-----◆-----

Blessed Is the Church

Blessed is the church which has a concern for the children of the community, for it will find a way to minister to them and to their homes.
Blessed is the church which provides a comfortable, attractive place for children, for it is the most evident sign that the church counts them important.
Blessed is the church that has teachers who respect children, and have warm, friendly ways, for children want to do and be their best in their presence.
Blessed is the church that provides the best teaching materials for its children, for good work is more easily done with good tools.
Blessed is the church that helps its teachers improve their skill in teaching, for the effectiveness of their work shall surely show in the lives of children.
Blessed is the church whose teachers are wise and genuinely Christian, for children will try to be like them.
Blessed is the church that, when all manner of needs and difficulties press in upon it, still provides an adequate program for children, for they shall love this church, and determine to be a part of its fellowship all of their lives.   *The Messenger*

-----◆-----

Parents

To Parents

"I'll lend you for a little time
  A child of mine," He said,
"For you to love the while she lives
  And mourn for when she's dead.
I cannot promise she will stay,
  Since all from life return,
But there are lessons taught down there
  I want this child to learn.
I've looked the wide world over
  In my search for teachers true,
And from the throngs that crowd life's lanes
  I have selected you.
Now, will you give her all your love,
  Nor think the labor vain,
Nor hate me when I come to call
  To take her back again?"
                              AUTHOR UNKNOWN

181

PARENTS

The parent's life is the child's copy-book.

———◆———

One father said, "When it comes to being a godly Christian counselor to my boy, I either skid or skidoo."

———◆———

The influence of the parent surpasses the influence of the pastor, the superintendent, the Sunday school teacher, the public school teacher or any other person.

———◆———

If, for Parents

If you can stay the spanking hand
And truly say you understand;
If you can keep your savoir-faire
When your offspring's in your hair;
If you can quietly listen to
The cute things others' children do;
And when the neighbors' kids are naughty
And their parents cold and haughty
Blame your little "innocence,"
If you do not take offence;
And if you find you're in position
To keep a sunny disposition
When Junior's friends daub him with paint
— You're no parent — you're a saint!
ALICE DUCH

———◆———

Parents wonder why the streams are bitter when they themselves have poisoned the fountain. JOHN LOCKE

———◆———

Ye parents hear what Jesus taught
When little ones to Him were brought;
Forbid them not, but heed My plea
And suffer them to come to Me.

Obey your Lord and let His truth
Be taught your children in their youth
That they in church and school may dwell
And learn their Saviour's praise to tell.

For if you love Him as you ought,
To Christ your children will be brought.
If thus you place them in His care,
You and your household well shall fare.
LUDWIG HELMBOLD, 1596

A parent is no sooner through worrying about the scratches children put on the furniture than he has to begin worrying about the ones they put on the car. ANONYMOUS

———◆———

A Mother's Prayer

I wash the dirt from little feet,
And as I wash I pray,
"Lord, keep them ever pure and true
To walk the narrow way."
I wash the dirt from little hands,
And earnestly I ask,
"Lord, may they ever yielded be
To do the humblest task."
I wash the dirt from little knees,
And pray, "Lord, may they be
The place where victories are won,
And orders sought from Thee."
I scrub the clothes that soil so soon,
And pray, "Lord, may her dress
Throughout eternal ages be
Thy robe of righteousness."

E'er many hours shall pass, I know
I'll wash these hands again;
And there'll be dirt upon her dress
Before the day shall end,
But as she journeys on through life
And learns of want and pain,
Lord, keep her precious little heart
Cleansed from all sin and stain;
For soap and water cannot reach
Where Thou alone canst see
Her hands and feet, these I can wash—
I trust her heart to Thee. B. RYBERG

———◆———

For Parents Only

THINKING that three hours of any movie are harmless for the child, but that two hours of Church and Sunday school are too much for his nervous system is just bad thinking.

GIVING him a nickel for the collection and fifty cents for the movie not only shows a parent's sense of value, but is also not likely to produce a giver.

LETTING him watch and listen to several hours of TV thrillers a day with no time for one short prayer and a few Bible verses is criminal unbalance.

BEING careful that Junior has his weekday lessons, and caring not that he knows not his Sunday school lesson makes for spiritual illiteracy.

SAYING that a child must make his own decisions as to whether or not he should go to church, or as to what church, is shirking parental responsibility.

WHEN FATHER spends Sunday morning in mowing the lawn, cleaning the garden, or playing golf, his sons are left to walk alone.

WHEN PARENTS idle away Sunday morning in reading the paper or listening to the radio or TV while brother and sister are sent by themselves to church, something happens to the children's evaluation of church attendance.   *Selected*

———◆———

C — Cheerful, courageous, a churchgoer, converts others.

H — Hopeful, honest, helpful, hospitable, humble.

R — Reverent, responsible, righteous, reliable.

I — Industrious, informed, inspiring.

S — Sincere, slow to anger, shares with others, serene.

T — Tolerant, temperate, thankful, trustworthy.

I — Instrument for good, increasing in grace.

A — Alert, appreciative.

N — Neighborly, never coveting or gossiping.

P — Patient, practical, participates in children's activities.

A — Appreciative, affectionate, approachable,

R — Religious, reasonable, relaxed.

E — Enthusiastic, even-tempered.

N — Neighborly, never breaks a promise.

T — Tolerant, tactful, temperate in all things.   *Selected*

Hands

My hand is large and his is small,
And there is nothing on earth at all
More important than the task
That lies ahead of me. I ask
For wisdom, Lord, that I may lead
This child aright; his every need
Depends on me. Be Thou my guide
That I, in walking by his side,
May choose the right paths for his feet.
The days are swift, the years are fleet,
Make me alert in deed and word
As we go forward, blessed Lord:
His precious clinging hand in mine,
With always, Lord, my hand in Thine.
GRACE NOLL CROWELL

———◆———

Past

We live in the present
We dream of the future,
But we learn eternal truths from the past.   MADAME CHIANG KAI-SHEK

———◆———

Patience, Patient

Patience is like a mosquito sitting on the bed of an anemic person who is waiting for a blood transfusion.

———◆———

Be patient! God always uses the yielded life — but in His own way.

———◆———

To hold one's ground calmly and steadfastly often requires more courage than to attack.

———◆———

We must be a patient people
        With children,
        With parents,
        With administrators,
        With ourselves.
Watching with a quiet, anxious breath,
Listening with a still, magnetic ear,
Living with a slow, emerging self.
Guided by the values we hold dear,
While following a planned and charted course,
To find the time in every day "to do the right,
As God would have us see the right" to do.   JANET EATON

Try Him Once More

Some years ago in a manufacturing town of Scotland a young lady applied to the superintendent of a Sunday school for a class. At his suggestion she gathered a class of poor boys. The superintendent told them to come to his house during the week and he would get them each a new suit of clothes. They came, and each was nicely fitted out.

The worst and most unpromising boy in the class was a lad named Bob. After two or three Sundays he was missing and the teacher went out to hunt him up. She found that his new clothes were torn and dirty, but she invited him back to the school, and he came. The superintendent gave him a second new suit, but, after attending once or twice, Bob was again absent. Once again she sought him out, only to find that the second suit had gone the way of the first.

"I am utterly discouraged with Bob," she said, when she reported the case to the superintendent, "and I must give him up."

"Please don't do that," the superintendent replied. "I can't but hope there is something good in Bob. Try him once more. I'll give him a third suit if he'll promise to attend regularly."

Bob did promise, and received his third new suit. He attended regularly after that, and became interested in the school. He became an earnest and persevering seeker after Jesus, and found Him. He joined the church. He was made a teacher. He studied for the ministry. The end of the story is that this discouraging boy—forlorn, ragged, runaway Bob—became Robert Morrison, the great missionary to China who translated the Bible into the Chinese language, and by so doing, opened the kingdom of heaven to the teeming millions of that vast country.   *Selected*

The most useful virtue is patience.
JOHN DEWEY

Patience is a plaster for all sores.

Whoever is out of patience is out of possession of his soul. Men must not turn bees and kill themselves in stinging others.

After several hours of fishing the little girl suddenly threw down her pole and cried, "I quit!"
"What's the matter?" her father asked her.
"Nothing," said the child, "except I can't seem to get waited on."

Patience is a virtue,
Possess it if you can,
Seldom in a woman,
Never in a man!

He that can have patience can have what he will.   BENJAMIN FRANKLIN

Patriotic, Patriotism

Patriotic men do not shrink from danger when conscience points the path.

Peace

Where there is no peace, there is no feast.

From prudence peace; from peace abundance.

Peace is not made at the council tables, or by treaties, but in the hearts of men.   HERBERT HOOVER

We lose the peace of years when we hunt after the rapture of moments.
BULWER

Peace comes only from loving, from mutual self-sacrifice and self-forgetfulness. Few today have humility or wisdom enough to know the world's deep need of love. We are too much possessed by national and racial and cultural pride.   HORACE W. B. DONEGAN, D.D.

He that would live in peace and at ease, must not speak all he knows, nor judge all he sees.   BENJAMIN FRANKLIN

Peace rules the day when Christ rules the mind.

———◆———

The peace of God passeth all understanding and misunderstanding.

Eternity

———◆———

No one is fool enough to choose war instead of peace. For in peace sons bury fathers, but in war fathers bury sons.   HERODOTUS

———◆———

Hidden Treasures

There is a calm the poor in spirit know,
That softens sorrow, and that sweetens woe;
There is a peace that dwells within the breast,
When all without is stormy and distressed:
There is light that gilds the darkest hour.
When dangers thicken and when tempests lower,
That calm, to faith and hope and love is given,
That peace remains when all beside is riven.
That light shines down to man direct from heaven.   *From the Latin*

———◆———

Lord, make me an instrument of thy peace!
Where there is hatred . . . let me sow love.
Where there is injury . . . pardon.
Where there is doubt . . . faith.
Where there is despair . . . hope.
Where there is darkness . . . light.
Where there is sadness . . . joy.
O Divine Master, grant that I may not so much seek
To be consoled . . . as to console,
To be understood . . . as to understand,
To be loved . . . as to love.
For,
It is in giving . . . that we receive,
It is in pardoning . . . that we are pardoned,
It is in dying . . . that we are born to eternal life.   SAINT FRANCIS OF ASSISI

Rest is not a hallowed feeling that comes over us in church; it is the repose of a heart set deep in God.   HENRY DRUMMOND

———◆———

Peace dwells only in the soul.

———◆———

Pentecost

Pentecost was only a few drops of the coming shower.

———◆———

People

Some folks we click with, some folks we cross with. Love is manifested when we love those who cross us.   TED KUMMERFELD

———◆———

Of course it takes all kinds of people to make a world. But a lot of them won't help.

———◆———

People respond to you like you treat them.

———◆———

People are funny; they spend money they don't have, to buy things they don't need, to impress people they don't like.

———◆———

We do not love people so much for the good they have done us, as for the good we have done them.   TOLSTOY

———◆———

Whatever you may be sure of, be sure of this, that you are dreadfully like other people.   OLIVER WENDELL HOLMES

———◆———

We get from people what we give;
We find in them what we bring;
We discover that the changes in them are really changes in ourselves.

———◆———

There are three kinds of people in the world:

the wills,
the won'ts,
the can'ts.

The first accomplish everything;
The second approve everything;
The third fail in everything.

Electric Magazine

185

Which Are You?

The bones in the body are two hun-
    dred or more,
But in sorting out people, we need only
    four:

Wishbone People

They hope for, they long for, they wish
    for and sigh;
They want things to come, but aren't
    willing to try.

Funnybone People

They laugh, grin and giggle, smile,
    twinkle the eye;
If work is a joke, sure, they'll give it
    a try.

Jawbone People

They scold, jaw and sputter, they
    froth, rave and cry,
They're long on the talk, but they're
    short on the try.

Backbone People

They strike from the shoulder, they
    never say die;
They're winners in life — for they know
    how to try.   *First Free Footnotes*

Persecute, Persecution

People aren't persecuted for doing
wrong but for doing right.

Perseverance, Persevere, Persist, Persistence

School Teacher: "Johnny, can you
tell me the difference between perseverance and obstinacy?"

Johnny: "One is a strong will and
the other is a strong won't."

The best place to find a helpin' hand
is at the end of your own arm.

Everyone has his superstitions. One
of mine has always been when I started
to go anywhere, or to do anything,
never to turn back or to stop until the
thing intended was accomplished.
    ULYSSES S. GRANT

Don't wait to see what happens —
take hold and make it happen.

Teacher (lecturing on perseverance):
"He drove straight to his goal. He
looked neither to the right nor to the
left, but pressed forward, moved by
a definite purpose. Neither friend nor
foe could delay him, nor turn him from
his course. All who crossed his path
did so at their own peril. What would
you call such a man?"

Graduate: "A truck driver!"

If you are not afraid to face the
music, you may someday lead the
band.   *Spuk Tidings*

It is better to stumble toward a better life than not to take any steps at
all.   *Church Management*

Even if you are on the right track,
you will get run over if you just sit
there.   *The Journeyman Barker*

There is always water if you bore
deep enough.

Faint heart never won fair lady, nor
escaped one either.

The line between failure and success
is so fine that we scarcely know when
we pass it — so fine that we are often
on the line and we do not know it.

The only way to make a "come back"
is to go on.

Nothing in the world, including talent, genius and education, can take
the place of persistence.

The man who removed the mountain
began by carrying away small stones.
    Chinese Proverb

It's the daily grind which gives you
the edge.

Don't Quit

When things go wrong, as they some-
    times will,
When the road you're trudging seems
    all up hill,

When the funds are low and the debts
   are high,
And you want to smile, but you have
   to sigh,
When care is pressing you down a bit,
Rest, if you must — but don't you quit.

Life is queer with its twists and turns,
As every one of us sometimes learns,
And many a failure turns about
When he might have won had he
   stuck it out;
Don't give up, though the pace seems
   slow —
You might succeed with another blow.

Often the goal is nearer than
It seems to a faint and faltering man,
Often the struggler has given up
When he might have captured the
   victor's cup,
And he learned too late, when the
   night slipped down,
How close he was to the golden crown.

Success is failure turned inside out —
The silver tint of the clouds of doubt —
And you never can tell how close you
   are,
It may be near when it seems afar;
So stick to the fight when you're hard-
   est hit —
It's when things seem worst that you
   mustn't quit.　　AUTHOR UNKNOWN

Don't Give Up!

I've taught a class for many years;
Borne many burdens — toiled through
   tears
But folks don't notice me a bit;
I'm so discouraged — I'll just quit.

Sometime ago I joined the choir
That many folks I might inspire;
But folks don't seem moved a bit
And I won't stand it. I'll just quit.

I've led young people day and night
And sacrificed to lead them right.
But folks won't help me out a bit,
And I'm so tired, I think I'll quit.

Christ's cause is hindered everywhere
And folks are dying in despair.
The reason why? Just think a bit;
The Church is full of folks who quit.
　　AUTHOR UNKNOWN

Personality

The personality should give wings to
thoughts.

Why be difficult when with a little
more effort you could be impossible?

The contact of every human personality is for a divine purpose.

On his second trip to see the doctor
about an illness, the doctor asked Mose,
"How do you feel?"

"Exuberatin'," Mose said. "I took all
dat subscription you give me and it
went through my whol' personality."

Personality has the power to open
many doors but character must keep
them open.　　*Megiddo Message*

The power to purpose in the heart
is the spinal column of personality and
the measure of manhood.

Blessed is the man who has a skin
of the right thickness. He can work
happily in spite of enemies and friends.
　　HENRY T. BAILEY

Perspective

Write it on your heart that every day
is the best day of the year.
　　RALPH WALDO EMERSON

A father reading his paper came
across a map of the world. He clipped
it out, cut it into pieces, and told his
small son to put the world together.
After a while the boy called, "I've done
it!"

His father marveled, "As quick as
this? How did you do it?"

The son said, "I turned it over and
on the back was a picture of a man. I
put the man together — and the world
was right!"　　AUTHOR UNKNOWN

187

The blue of heaven is larger than the cloud.   E. B. BROWNING

———◆———

To be honest, to be kind, to earn a little
   and to spend a little less;
To make, upon the whole, a family
   happier for his presence;
To renounce when that shall be necessary and not be embittered;
To keep a few friends but these without capitulation — above all, on the
   same condition to keep friends with
   himself —
There is a task for all that a man has
   of fortitude and delicacy.
                    ROBERT LOUIS STEVENSON

———◆———

Persuade, Persuasion

Few are open to conviction, but the
majority of men are open to persua-
sion.   GOETHE

———◆———

Would you persuade, speak of interest, not of reason.   BENJAMIN FRANKLIN

———◆———

Pessimism, Pessimist

A pessimist is a person who suffers
seasickness during the entire journey
of life.

———◆———

A pessimist is a person who blows
out the candle to see how dark it is.

———◆———

A fellow who says it can't be done
is likely to be interrupted by someone
doing it.

———◆———

The pessimist says, "If I don't try,
I can't fail." The optimist says, "If I
don't try, I can't win."

———◆———

A pessimist says: "I don't think it
can be done."
   An optimist says: "I'm sure there is
a way."
   A peptimist says: "I just did it."

———◆———

'Twixt optimist and pessimist
The difference is droll:
The optimist sees the doughnut,
While the pessimist sees the hole.

A farmer was watching the men fire
a locomotive. "They'll never make her
go," he said.
   But they did. As he watched it
move, the farmer said, "They'll never
make her stop."

———◆———

A pessimist is a man who financed
an optimist.

———◆———

The Pessimist's Creed

What's the use of sunshine? Only
   blinds your eyes.
What's the use of knowledge? Only
   makes you wise.
What's the use of smiling? Wrinkles
   up your face.
What's the use of flowers? Clutter up
   the place.
What's the use of eating? Nothing —
   only taste.
What's the use of hustling? Haste is
   only waste.
What's the use of music? Just a lot of
   noise.
What's the use of loving? Only for the
   joys.
What's the use of singing? Only makes
   you glad.
What's the use of goodness when the
   whole world's bad?
What's the use of health? You might
   as well be sick.
What's the use of doing anything but
   kick?   AUTHOR UNKNOWN

———◆———

Petty

Do not make a business of the trivial:
to convert petty annoyances into matters of importance is to become seriously involved over nothing.

———◆———

Philosophy

A philosopher says we are not what
we think we are; we are what we
think. Well, then, if we are what we
think, what we think we are, we are,
are we not — or are we?
                    AUTHOR UNKNOWN

Philosophy is a study which enables a man to be unhappy more intelligently.

———◆———

Philosophy: a system of thinking about things which enables one to be quite happy, or hopping mad, about the whole mess.

———◆———

Plagues

The four greatest scourges of mankind have been drink, war, pestilence and famine—and strong drink has been more destructive than war, pestilence and famine combined. WM. E. GLADSTONE

———◆———

Plan, Planning

Plan your work! Work your plan!

———◆———

Plan in marble if you would work in stone.

———◆———

If God is your partner, make your plans large.

———◆———

Nothing of importance is ever done without a plan.

———◆———

I try to have no plans the failure of which would greatly annoy me. Half the unhappiness in the world is due to the failure of plans which were never reasonable, and often impossible. EDGAR WATSON HOWE

———◆———

Plan for today as well as for tomorrow.

———◆———

He Has a Plan for Me

I to Christ my life have given,
  Ever His alone to be;
Oh, what peace and blest assurance,
  That He has a plan for me!

Now I know that He is leading
  In His love so full and free;
I can rest in Him securely,
  For He has a plan for me.

As I walk along life's pathway,
  Though the way I cannot see
I shall follow in His footsteps,
  For He has a plan for me.

So I look to Him for guidance,
  Saviour, Lord and King is He;
I can trust Him — aye, forever,
  Since He has a plan for me!

Trusting Him in full assurance,
  This would be my only plea —
Reveal, Oh Lord, just step by step
  Thine own perfect plan for me!
ROSELLA THIESEN

———◆———

Please

Please God and you will please good men.

———◆———

Please God in all you do and be pleased with all God does.

———◆———

When you do what you please, do you do what pleases God?

———◆———

No man has a right to do as he pleases unless he pleases to do right.

———◆———

Pleasure

Not what we have, but what we enjoy constitutes our abundance.

———◆———

That man is richest whose pleasures are cheapest. HENRY D. THOREAU

———◆———

Many a man thinks he is buying pleasure when he is really selling himself a slave to it. BENJAMIN FRANKLIN

———◆———

Poise

A politician was speaking with his accustomed eloquence and poise. There were thousands of bugs flying around the bright light overhead. Some bugs zoomed around him like jets, but he remained calm and devoted to his speech. Every time he inhaled the people thought sure he would suck in a bug. Finally the inevitable happened — he did! "What will he do?" they questioned. When he got his breath, the politician said, "Served the bug right, he should have watched where he was going!"

189

When asked to define the word poise, the Dutchman said, "That's what girls go out with."

———♦———

Poise is the art of raising the eyebrows instead of the roof.

———♦———

Nonchalance is the ability to look like an owl when you have behaved like an ass.

Polite

Politeness is an inexpensive way of making friends.

———♦———

Politeness is to do and say the kindest things in the kindest way.

———♦———

The lady gave Tommy an orange. "What do you say to the lady, Tommy?" asked his mother.
"Peel it," said Tommy.

———♦———

A small boy was told that when visitors came to the house it was his duty to pay them some attention.
Shortly afterward a Mrs. Daniel called, and the small boy shook hands with her politely and exclaimed in his best drawing-room manner:
"How do you do, Mrs. Daniel? I've just been reading about your husband in the den of lions."

———♦———

Politics

A politician is a gent who works up his gums before election and gums up the works afterward. *Presbyterian Life*

———♦———

We are not so much interested in where a politician "stands" as we are in which direction he's moving—if any.

———♦———

Nothing is politically right which is morally wrong. LINCOLN

———♦———

Crooked politicians get into office because honest men fail to do their duty.

Popular, Popularity

One of the easiest ways to become popular is to remember the nice things folks say about a person, and repeat them to him.

———♦———

Possess, Possessions

If we don't have the things we want, let's want the things we have.

———♦———

Don't let your possessions possess you. M. R. SIEMENS

———♦———

Our children are the only earthly possessions we can take with us to glory.

———♦———

The only difference between the man who has one million dollars and six children and the man who has one million dollars, is that the man with one million dollars wants more.

———♦———

Poverty

Poverty in the way of duty is to be chosen rather than plenty in the way of sin.

———♦———

Bein' poor is a problem, but bein' rich ain't the answer. C. GRANT

———♦———

Power

The power to purpose in the heart is the spinal column of personality and the measure of manhood.

———♦———

Horsepower was much safer when only horses had it.

———♦———

If the heartbeats for a single day were concentrated into one huge throb of vital power, it might be sufficient to to throw a ton of iron 120 feet into the air. AUBREY J. CARPENTER

———♦———

The power of God is given to enable us to do a spiritual thing in a spiritual way in an unspiritual world.
MALCOLM CRONK

Power cannot go from the rushing water to the high tension wire without going through the power house.

———◆———

Dynamite comes in small packages!

———◆———

Power

I ask not wealth, but power to take
And use the things I have aright;
Not years, but wisdom that shall make
My life a profit and delight.
PHOEBE CARY

———◆———

Praise

Try praising your wife, even if it does frighten her at first.   BILLY SUNDAY

———◆———

Self-praise is half scandal.

———◆———

The hardest thing any man can do is to fall down on the ice when it's slippery, and get up and praise the Lord.   JOSH BILLINGS

———◆———

If you would reap praise you must sow the seeds, gentle words and useful deeds.   BENJAMIN FRANKLIN

———◆———

If you think that praise is due him, now's the time to slip it to him, for he cannot read his tombstone when he's dead.   BERTON BRALEY

———◆———

The trouble with most of us is that we would rather be ruined by praise than saved with criticism.

———◆———

Prayer

Prayer is the key of the morning and the bolt of the night.

———◆———

It is good for us to keep some account of our prayers that we may not unsay them in our practice.

———◆———

A man may offer a prayer, beautiful in diction and perfect in the number of its petitions, but if it gives him gratification afterwards, that prayer cannot have been truly prayed.   G. C. MORGAN

A coffee break is good; a prayer break is better; a praise break is best!

———◆———

You cannot stumble if you are on your knees.

———◆———

No nation has better citizens than the parents who teach their children how to pray.

———◆———

Prayer takes the very highest energy of which the human is capable.
JOHN COLERIDGE

———◆———

What cannot be told to human ears can be poured into God's sympathetic ear.

———◆———

Fellowship with a holy God produces holiness among men.

———◆———

What the church needs today is not more machinery or better, nor new organizations or more and novel methods, but men whom the Holy Ghost can use — men of prayer, men mighty in prayer. The Holy Ghost does not flow through methods, but through men. He does not come on machinery, but on men. He does not anoint plans, but men — men of prayer.   E. M. BOUNDS

———◆———

If stress and strife of the times causes us to become weak-kneed, perhaps we should let them collapse entirely and while in that position do a little serious praying.

———◆———

The doorway into the secret place of the Most High is always open to the hand of need, and at the knocking of that hand only.

———◆———

Prayer is not an easy way of getting what we want, but the only way of becoming what God wants us to be.
STUDDERT KENNEDY

———◆———

The Christian on his knees sees more than the philosopher on tiptoe.
AUGUSTUS TOPLADY

———◆———

A short prayer will reach the throne — if you don't live too far away.

191

PRAYER

The history of the church's progress is the history of prayer.

If prayer does not drive sin out of your life, sin will drive prayer out.

He stands best who kneels most.

Prayer does not need proof; it needs practice.

Prayer is to ask not what we wish of God, but what God wishes of us.

Motto in a church: If you must whisper, whisper a prayer.

The Bible doesn't say we should preach all the time, but it does say we should pray all the time.   JOHN R. RICE

If the world is ever again to get on its feet, the church will have to get on its knees.

Prayer does not fit us for the greater works; prayer is the greater work. We think of prayer as a common sense exercise of our higher powers in order to prepare us for God's work. In the teaching of Jesus Christ prayer is the working of the miracle of redemption in others by the power of God.
OSWALD CHAMBERS

Prayer is the most important thing in my life. If I should neglect prayer for a single day, I should lose a great deal of the fire of faith.   MARTIN LUTHER

Kneeling in prayer keeps you in good standing.

Prayer is a serious thing. We may be taken at our words.   D. L. MOODY

When it is hardest to pray, we ought to pray hardest.

Prayer is releasing the energies of God. For prayer is asking God to do what we cannot do.   CHARLES TRUMBULL

We organize instead of agonize.

The secret of prayer is prayer in secret.

Nothing lies beyond the reach of prayer, except that which lies outside the will of God.

It isn't the words we say on bended knee that count, but rather it's the way we think and live out our prayers.

Prevailing prayer brings perpetual power.   *Sunday School Journal*

Prayer is not overcrowding God's reluctance, but taking hold of God's willingness.

The halting utterances of the consecrated pupil, earnest though inexperienced, are better than the mere fluency of long practice.

Daily prayer is the gymnasium of the soul.

Groanings which cannot be uttered are often prayers which cannot be refused.   C. H. SPURGEON

No praying man or woman accomplishes so much with so little expenditure of time as when he or she is praying.   C. E. COWMAN

Prayer is the first thing, the second thing, and the third thing necessary for a Christian worker. Pray, then, my dear brother, pray, pray and pray.
EDWARD PAYTON

The godly man's prayers are his best biography, his most exact portrait. People who do a lot of kneeling don't do much lying.   *Moody Church News*

If your knees knock, kneel on them.

The only place we can hide from God's presence is in His presence.

You can do more than pray *after* you have prayed, but you cannot do more than pray *until* you have prayed.

192

Prayer moves the arm that moves the world.   G. D. WATSON

Why not change the pattern of your prayers now and then? Wake up some morning and ask, "Dear Lord, is there anything I can do for You today?"
Presbyterian Life

It has been reckoned that out of 667 prayers for specific things in the Bible there are 454 traceable answers. We spend too much time studying how to pray whereas we ought rather to pray. The Bible is predominantly a book of prayer.

Finney says prayer is not to change God but to change us.

Anchor yourself to the throne of God, then shorten the rope.

The only way to do much for God is to ask much of God.

Prayer is being intimate with God.

It is not the arithmetic of our prayers, how many they are; nor the rhetoric of our prayers, how eloquent they be; nor the geometry of our prayers, how long they may be; nor the music of our prayers, how sweet our voice may be; nor the logic of our prayers, how argumentative they may be; nor the method of our prayers, how orderly they may be; or even the theology of our prayers, how good the doctrine — which God cares for. Fervency of spirit is that which availeth much.
Moody Monthly

Two men praying the same prayers anywhere on earth will raise a commotion in heaven.
Blasts from the Ram's Horn

How deeply rooted must unbelief be in our hearts when we are surprised to find our prayers answered.   HARE

Short prayers have the largest range and the surest aim.

The man who does all his praying on his knees does not pray enough.

Life gets scorched and lumpy when we forget to stir it up with prayer.

Satan trembles when he sees the weakest Christian on his knees.

All heaven listens when we send up a heartfelt prayer for an enemy's good.
Blasts from the Ram's Horn

I have so much to do that I must spend several hours in prayer before I am able to do it.   JOHN WESLEY

Teachers, to be prepared you must be pre-prayered.

If you are too busy to pray, you are busier than you ought to be.

Hem in the day with prayer and it will be less likely to ravel out before night.

A child once prayed, "O Lord, make the bad people good, and the good people nice."

The Christian should have an appetite for prayer. He should want to pray. One does not have to force food upon a healthy child. Exercise, good circulation, health and labor demand food for sustenance. So it is with those who are spiritually healthy. They have an appetite for the Word of God, and for prayer.

Sin breaks fellowship with God. A little girl committed a certain offense and when her mother discovered it she began to question her daughter. Immediately the child lost her smile and a cloud darkened her face as she said, "Mother, I don't feel like talking." So it is with us when our fellowship with God is broken by sin in our lives. We do not feel like talking to Him. If you do not feel like praying, it is probably a good indication that you should start praying immediately.   BILLY GRAHAM

193

When we pray for rain we must be willing to put up with some mud.

———◆———

Don't pray for tasks equal to your powers, but powers equal to your tasks.

———◆———

Abraham prayed and brought God down almost to his own terms.

Elijah prayed and called down fire from heaven.

Daniel prayed and was saved from the lions.

Paul prayed and the prison walls were shaken.

Luther prayed and the gates of Rome shook.

Knox prayed and Queen Mary trembled.

Wesley prayed and a great revival saved England.

Muller prayed and great orphanages were reared.

Roberts prayed and a Pentecost swept Wales. *Selected*

———◆———

A little girl was caught listening at the keyhole while her spinster aunt was saying her prayers. Her mother told her it was wrong to eavesdrop.

"But, Mommy," the child said, "Aunt Emma ended her prayer so funny."

"What did she say?" asked mother.

"Well, when she finished praying she said, 'World without men, ah me.'"

———◆———

The coed concluded her prayers with a modest appeal: "I'm not asking for myself, but please send my mother a son-in-law." *Glendale News Press*

———◆———

Here's the prayer of a child: "And, dear God, I hope You'll also take care of Yourself. If anything should happen to You, we'd be in an awful fix."

———◆———

One night a little two-and-one-half-year-old boy told his mother, "You can go now, Jesus can hear me without you here." But the mother listened at the door and heard her son say, "Jesus, will You help me to be a good boy? O.K. Amen." *Christian Parent*

Some folks are like the little boy who, when asked by his pastor if he prayed every day, replied, "No, not every day. Some days I don't want anything."

———◆———

One night little Susanne ended her prayers thus: "Good-by, dear Lord, we're moving to New York. It has been nice knowing You. Amen."

———◆———

Four-year-old Nancy's brother, Charles, had been tormenting her all afternoon by throwing stones. That night while praying, Nancy asked God to bless Charles and keep him from throwing stones. Then she remembered, after she had finished praying, that she had told God about this problem before so she added the following P.S.: "And by the way, dear God, I've mentioned this to You several times before."

———◆———

One day a mother noticed that her little girl was in her room a long, long time and she had said she was going in to pray to Jesus. Finally, when the little girl came out her mother asked her what she was doing in her room for such a long time when she had just gone in to pray.

"I was just telling Jesus that I love Him and He was telling me that He loves me. And we were just loving each other."

———◆———

When the searchers found a five-year-old boy who had been lost in the mountains for two days, they asked, "Were you afraid?"

"It was scary," the little boy answered, "but I prayed and God took good care of me."

———◆———

One day a Sunday school superintendent came to Sunday school with her arm in a cast because she had broken it. The children placed a marker in the Bible at the front of the room to mark the place where God promised to hear the prayers of His children. It was their custom to do this when they had a special prayer request and today it was a request to heal the superintendent's arm.

Several weeks went by. The superintendent had forgotten that the children kept the marker in the Bible as a reminder of their request for her. She mentioned to a teacher that the doctor was going to remove the cast that week and she hoped the arm would be all right, and not need to be reset.

One little girl had heard the superintendent mention this and so she quickly spoke up: "Oh, your arm will be all right. I prayed for you and marked the Bible where God gives His promise. Your arm will be okay." And, of course, it was.

———◆———

During the afternoon a mother had to paddle her four-year-old daughter because she deliberately disobeyed her. That evening when the little girl prayed she said, "Dear Lord, please help me to understand my mother. Amen."

———◆———

Little Raymond returned home from Sunday school in a joyous mood. "Oh, Mother," he exclaimed as he entered the house, "the superintendent said something awfully nice about me in his prayer today."

"Isn't that wonderful!" said the mother. "What did he say?"

"He said, 'Oh, Lord, we thank Thee for food and Raymond,'" replied the lad.

———◆———

Roger and his mother were visiting an aunt during deer season. They knew there were a lot of hunters out but were surprised toward evening to hear shooting right in the barnyard. They rushed from the house just in time to see a wounded deer enter the orchard and start up the canyon. The hunters who had wounded the deer turned back for easier game. Knowing the deer to be badly wounded, Roger's mother took a rifle and followed its trail while Roger stayed with his aunt.

Time went on and it grew quite dark. Roger worried and finally went to his aunt and said: "It's getting blacker and blacker, Aunty, and Mother isn't back. Don't you think we'd better pray a little and set God on her trail?"

———◆———

One evening six-year-old Bobby asked his father for a pet.

"Sorry, Son," his father said, "not now. But if you pray real hard for two months, perhaps God will send you a baby brother."

Bobby prayed faithfully for a month, but it seemed futile to pray longer so he gave up.

How surprised he was, when a month later, a little baby boy arrived at their home, or so Bobby thought when he saw a squirming bundle beside his mother. His proud father drew back the cover and Bobby saw another baby. Twins!

"Aren't you glad you prayed for a baby brother?" asked his father.

"I sure am," said the boy. "But aren't you glad I stopped praying when I did?"

Together

———◆———

President Eisenhower opened his second inaugural address with a plea for "the favor of almighty God" on the common labor of all Americans.

"And the hopes of our hearts fashion the deepest prayers of our people. May we pursue the right — without self-righteousness. May we know unity — without conformity. May we grow in strength — without pride of self. May we, in our dealings with all peoples of the earth, ever speak truth and serve justice."

———◆———

A British soldier one night was caught creeping stealthily back to his quarter from a near-by woods. He was immediately hauled before his commanding officer and charged with holding communications with the enemy. The man pleaded that he had gone into the woods to pray. That was his only defense.

"Have you been in the habit of

spending hours in private prayer?" growled the officer.

"Yes, sir."

"Then down on your knees and pray now!" he roared. "You never needed to so much."

Expecting immediate death, the soldier knelt and poured out his soul in prayer that for eloquence could have been inspired only by the power of the Holy Spirit.

"You may go," said the officer when he had finished. "I believe your story. If you hadn't drilled often, you couldn't have done so well at review."

Sunday School Promoter

The Power of Prayer

MOSES prayed, his prayer did save,
  A nation from death and from the grave.
JOSHUA prayed. The sun stood still
  His enemies fell in vale and hill.
HANNAH prayed, God gave her a son;
  A nation back to the Lord he won.
SOLOMON prayed for wisdom.
  Then God made him the wisest of mortal men.
ELIJAH prayed with great desire,
  God gave him rain, and sent the fire.
JONAH prayed, God heard his wail;
  He quickly delivered him from the whale.
Three HEBREWS prayed, through flames they trod;
  They had as a comrade the "Son of God."
ELISHA prayed with strong emotion;
  He got the mantle and a "double portion."
DANIEL prayed. The lion's claws
  Were held by the angel who locked their jaws.
Ten LEPERS prayed, to the priests were sent;
  Glory to God! they were healed as they went.
PETER prayed, and Dorcas arose
  To life again, from death's repose.
The THIEF who prayed — for mercy cried,
  He went with Christ to Paradise.

The CHURCH, she prayed, then got a shock;
  When Peter answered her prayer with a knock!
ABRAM stopped praying, cities fell,
  With all their sins, into hell!
The DISCIPLES kept praying, the Spirit came,
  With "cloven tongue," and revival flame!
Conviction filled the hearts of men;
  Three thousand souls were "born again!"
When CHRISTIANS pray, as they prayed of yore,
  With living faith, for souls implore,
In one accord, united stand —
  Revival fires shall sweep the land!
And SINNERS shall converted be,
  And all the world God's glory see!

My Gift

I cannot sway the multitudes
With words of grace sublime,
But I can pray for those who speak,
And God's anointing for them seek —
  This gift is mine!

I cannot go to lands afar
Engulfed in heathen night,
But I can give myself to prayer
For those who the glad tidings bear
  Of Christ, the light.

Yes, though I cannot preach or go,
Sin's strongholds I may sway
While on my knees before God's throne,
I intercede for all His own,
  For I can pray!   AVIS B. CHRISTIANSEN

Those Who Talk with God

How lovely are the faces
  Of those who talk with God,
Lit with an inner sureness
  Of the path their feet have trod.

Keen are the hands and feet—oh, yes!—
  Of those who wait His will;
And clear as crystal mirrors
  Are the hearts His love can fill.
    AUTHOR UNKNOWN

Keep on Praying

Just keep on praying "Till light breaks
   through!"
The Lord will answer, will answer you,
God keeps His promise, His Word is
   true —
Just keep on praying "Till light breaks
   through!"

————

The Importance of Prayer

Prayer is like . . .
   The porter — to watch the door of
   our lips.
   The guard — to keep the fort of our
   hearts.
   The hilt of the sword—to defend our
   hands.
   A *master workman* — who accomplishes things.
   A *barometer* — to show our spiritual
   condition.   *Selected*

————

I met a poor soul in the depths of despair,
Who climbed to the heights in answer
   to prayer.

————

A Sunday School Teacher's Prayer

Several souls
Will come to me today
To hear of Thee.
What I am,
What I say,
Will lead them to Thee,
Or drive them away.
Stand by, Lord, I pray.

————

Prayer

Prayer is so simple;
It is like quietly opening a door
And slipping into the very presence of
   God,
There in the stillness
To listen to His voice;
Perhaps to petition,
Or only to listen;
It matters not.
Just to be there
In His presence
Is prayer.   *Selected*

Pray

When the great seething mass
   of others' need
      overwhelms me,
      I will pray.

When the great scalding blow
   of others' wrath
      falls round me,
      I will pray.

When the blind indifference
   of this world
      dismays me,
      I will pray.

When selfish greed and lack
   of faith hold sway,
      appall me,
      I will pray.

When the loved beauty of
   our Father's world
      enchants me,
      I will pray.

When His great loving kindness
   fills my soul,
      delights me,
      I will pray.

When God's mercy, His pardon
   and His grace
      challenge me,
      I will pray.

This His good gift to us
   His children here —
      that we may pray.
          MARY C. RIDER

————

Prayer

If radio's slim fingers
Can pluck a melody
From night, and toss it over
A continent or sea —

If the petaled white notes
Of a violin
Are blown across a mountain
Or a city's din —

If songs, like crimson roses
Are culled from thin blue air,
Why should mortals wonder
If God hears prayer?
          EDITH ROMIG FULLER

197

The Christian's Prayer

Lord, make me free . . .
From fear of the future;
From anxiety of the morrow;
From bitterness toward anyone;
From cowardice in face of danger;
From failure before opportunity;
From laziness in face of work.
SOURCE UNKNOWN

Humble words and simple faith,
Trust in God, complete,
Eagerness to cast itself
At the Savior's feet.

So must you to find the way,
Mark the Savior's word;
As a humble, simple child,
Come unto the Lord.   RUDOLPH EVERS

A Child's Prayer

Angel of God, my guardian dear,
To whom His love commits me here,
Ever this day be at my side
To light and guard, to rule and guide.
Amen.

Bobbie's Prayer

Dear Father, there is this other boy
tonight
Who's praying to a god that's made
of wood:

He asks it to take care of him tonight
And love him — but it won't do any
good.

He is so far I cannot make him hear.
I'd call to him and tell him if I could

That You'd take care of him, that You
are near
And love him — but his god is made
of wood.

I know he'd ask You if he only knew,
I know he'd love to know You if he
could.

Dear God, take care of him and love
him, too,
The other boy whose god is made of
wood.   Selected

Evening Prayer

Thank You, God, for this nice day,
Thank You for my work and play
For Your care the whole day through.
Thank You, God, for all You do. Amen.

The Way

Have you ever watched a child
At the close of day —
Have you ever seen that child
Fold its hands and pray?

Not a thought of human pride,
Envy, doubt or care;
Not the love of earthly things
Can be reigning there.

The Difference

I got up early one morning
And rushed right into the day;
I had so much to accomplish
That I didn't take time to pray.

Problems just tumbling about me,
And heavier came each task;
"Why doesn't God help me?" I won-
dered.
He answered: "You didn't ask."

I wanted to see joy and beauty —
But the day toiled on, gray and bleak;
I wondered why God didn't show me,
He said: "But you didn't seek."

I tried to come into God's presence,
I used all my keys at the lock
God gently and lovingly chided:
"My child, you didn't knock."

I woke up early this morning
And paused before entering the day;
I had so much to accomplish
That I had to take time to pray.   Selected

Heavenly Father, hear our prayer,
Keep us in Thy loving care.
Guard us through the livelong day
In our work and in our play.
Keep us pure and sweet and true
In everything we say and do.
Amen.

Now I lay me down to sleep;
I pray the Lord my soul to keep.
If I should die before I wake,
I pray the Lord my soul to take.
ISAAC WATTS, 1732

———◆———

Morning Prayers

Father, we thank Thee for the night,
And for the pleasant morning light
For rest and food and loving care,
And all that makes the world so fair.

Help us to do the things we should,
To be to others kind and good,
In all we do in work and play
To grow more loving every day.
Amen.

———◆———

Childlike Trust

"Now I lay me" — say it, darling;
"Lay me," lisped the tiny lips
Of my daughter, kneeling, bending,
O'er her folded finger tips.

"Down to sleep" — "to sleep," she murmured,
And the curly head drooped low;
"I pray the Lord," I gently added,
"You can say it all, I know."

"Pray the Lord" — the words came faintly,
Fainter still — "My soul to keep,"
Then the tired head fairly nodded,
And the child was fast asleep.

But the dewy eyes half opened
When I clasped her to my breast,
And the dear voice softly whispered,
"Mamma, God knows all the rest."

Oh, the trusting, sweet confiding
Of the child-heart! Would that I
Thus might trust my Heavenly Father,
He who hears my feeblest cry.
COL. THOS. H. AYERS

———◆———

Table Graces

God is great and God is good;
Let us thank Him for our food.
By His hand we all are fed;
Thank You, God, for daily bread.
Amen.

Father in heaven, sustain our bodies
with this food, our hearts with true
friendship, and our souls with Thy
truth, For Jesus' sake. Amen.

Father, bless the food we take
And bless us all for Jesus' sake.
Amen.

Lord Jesus, be our holy Guest,
Our morning Joy, our evening Rest;
And with our daily bread impart
Thy love and peace to every heart.
Amen.

———◆———

The Teacher's Prayer

Lord, who am I to teach the way
To little children, day by day —
So prone myself to go astray?

I teach them knowledge — but I know
How faint they flicker and how low —
The candles of my knowledge glow.

I teach them power to will and do —
But only now to learn anew
My own great weakness through and
through.

I teach them love for all mankind
And all God's creatures — but I find
My love comes lagging still behind.

Lord, if their guide I still must be,
O let the little children see
The teacher leaning hard on Thee.
EDWARD A. ESTAPER

———◆———

The Secret

I met God in the morning
When the day was at its best,
And His presence came like sunrise,
Like a glory in my breast.
All day long the Presence lingered,
All day long He stayed with me
And we sailed in perfect calmness
O'er a very troubled sea.
Other ships were blown and battered
Other ships were sore distressed
But the winds that seemed to drive
them
Brought to us a peace and rest.
Then I thought of other mornings
With a keen remorse of mind

When I, too, had loosed the moorings
With the Presence left behind.
So I think I know the secret
Learned from many a troubled way
You must seek Him in the morning
If you want Him through the day.

AUTHOR UNKNOWN

———◆———

The Kitchen Prayer

Lord of all pots and pans and things,
  since I've not time to be
A saint by doing lovely things or
  watching late with Thee
Or dreaming in the dawn light or
  storming Heaven's gates,
Make me a saint by getting meals
  and washing up the plates.
Although I must have Martha's hands,
  I have a Mary mind
And when I black the boots and
  shoes, Thy sandals, Lord, I find.
I think of how they trod the earth,
  what time I scrub the floor
Accept this meditation Lord, I haven't
  time for more.
Warm all the kitchen with Thy love,
  and light it with Thy peace
Forgive me all my worrying and
  make my grumbling cease.
Thou who dids't love to give men food,
  in room or by the sea
Accept this service that I do, I do it
  unto Thee.   AUTHOR UNKNOWN

———◆———

Preach, Preacher, Preaching

The Preacher

If he's young, he lacks experience;
if his hair is gray he's too old.

If he has five or six children, he has
too many; if he has none, he isn't setting a good example.

If his wife sings in the choir, she's
being forward; if not, she's not interested in her husband's work.

If he speaks from notes, he has
canned sermons and is dry; if he is ex-
temporaneous, he's too deep.

If he spends too much time in his
study, he neglects his people; if he
visits he's a gadabout.

If he is attentive to the poor, he's
playing the grandstand; if to the
wealthy, he's trying to be an aristocrat.

If he suggests improvements, he's a
dictator; if he doesn't he's a figure-
head.

If he uses too many illustrations he
neglects the Bible; if not enough, he's
not clear.

If he condemns wrong, he is cranky;
if he doesn't he is a compromiser.

If he preaches an hour, he's windy;
if less, he's lazy.

If he preaches the truth, he's offen-
sive; if not, he's a hypocrite.

If he fails to please everyone, he's
hurting the church; if he does please
everyone, he has no convictions.

If he preaches tithing, he's a money
grabber; if he doesn't, he is failing to
develop his people.

If he receives a large salary he's mercenary; if a small salary it proves he's
not worth much.

If he preaches all the time, the people get tired of hearing one man; if
he invites guest preachers he's shirking
responsibility.

And some folks think the preacher
has an easy time.

AUTHOR UNKNOWN

———◆———

Qualifications of a Pastor

The strength of an ox.
The tenacity of a building.
The daring of a lion.
The patience of a donkey.
The industry of a beaver.
The versatility of a chameleon.
The vision of an eagle.
The melodies of a nightingale.
The meekness of a lamb.
The hide of a rhinoceros.
The disposition of an angel.
The resignation of an incurable.
The loyalty of an apostle.
The faithfulness of a prophet.
The tenderness of a shepherd.
The fervency of an evangelist.
The devotion of a mother.

Christian Beacon

———◆———

You can preach a better sermon with
your life than with your lips.

When I preach I regard neither doctors nor magistrates, of whom I have above forty in the congregation; I have all my eyes on the servant maids and on the children. And if the learned men are not well pleased with what they hear, well, the door is open.
MARTIN LUTHER

———◆———

As long as there are people in the world, so long must we preach the Gospel of Christ. CHR. CHRISTIANSEN

———◆———

Preaching without emotion is not preaching, but beware of the cheap substitute.

———◆———

The preacher who does not evangelize will fossilize.

———◆———

The sexton had been laying the new carpet on the pulpit platform and had left a number of tacks scattered on the floor. "See here, James," said the parson, "what do you suppose would happen if I stepped on one of those tacks right in the middle of my sermon?"
"Well, sir," replied the sexton, "I reckon there'd be one point you wouldn't linger on!"

———◆———

A preacher who was in the habit of writing his sermons out carefully found himself at church one Sunday morning without his manuscript. "As I have forgotten my notes," he began his sermon, "I will have to rely on the Lord for guidance. Tonight I shall come better prepared."

———◆———

For an hour and a half the pastor droned on with his fervent sermon. Finally he asked: "What more can I say?"
There was a pause. Then from the rear pew: "You might say amen."

———◆———

A preacher was disturbed by the snoring of the grandpa at the front. He stopped preaching and asked the little boy to awaken him.
He promptly answered, "You wake him up, you put him to sleep."

A zealous preacher with a sense of humor posted this on his office door: "If you have troubles, come in and tell me about them. If not, by all means come in and tell me how you avoid them." *Presbyterian Life*

———◆———

A preacher had succeeded in putting an elderly man asleep by his sermon. Preaching for a decision, in the midst of his sermon, he shouted, "Those who want to go to hell, *stand up.*" The old man heard the "Stand up" and did so.
He looked around, paused with a puzzled look on his face and said, "Preacher, I don't know what we're voting on, but it looks like you and I are the only ones for it."

———◆———

He who lives well is the best preacher. CERVANTES

———◆———

A preacher's diet consists of cold shoulder and spiced tongue.

———◆———

The parson should tell folks how to get on, not where to get off.
C. GRANT

———◆———

"In time of trial," the preacher droned after seventy minutes of droning, "what brings us the greatest joy?"
Some sinner in the back row answered, "An acquittal!" *Presbyterian Life*

———◆———

You can't tell how much a preacher is doing for the Lord by the size of his salary.

———◆———

Prejudice

When a prejudiced man thinks, he just rearranges his thoughts.

———◆———

People are usually down on what they are not up on.

———◆———

The tight skirts of prejudice shorten the steps of progress.

———◆———

We should never let our prejudices against certain people prejudice us against their ideas and their accomplishments.

There isn't a parallel of latitude but thinks it would have been the equator if it had had its rights.   MARK TWAIN

————♦————

A chip on the shoulder is the heaviest load you can carry.

————♦————

Prejudice has always been the greatest obstacle to progress.

————♦————

A prejudice is a vagrant opinion without visible means of support.   BIERCE

————♦————

Prepare, Prepared, Preparation

Before beginning, prepare carefully.
   CICERO

————♦————

Seventy-five per cent of the victory depends on preparation.
   DR. C. E. MATTHEWS

————♦————

The prepared man succeeds; the unprepared man fails.

————♦————

Press, Printing

The press is the foe of rhetoric, but the friend of reason.

————♦————

The Reformation was cradled in the printing press, and established by no other instrument.   AGNES STRICKLAND

————♦————

A drop of ink may make a million think.

————♦————

Four hundred years ago Martin Luther said, "We must throw the printer's inkpot at the devil."

————♦————

Pretender, Pretense

No Sense in Pretense

You tell what you are by the friends you seek,
By the manner in which you speak.
By the way you employ your leisure time,
By the use you make of dollar and dime.
You tell what you are by the things you wear,
By the spirit in which you burdens bear,
By the kind of thing at which you laugh,
By records you play on the phonograph.
You tell what you are by the way you walk,
By the things of which you delight to talk,
By the manner in which you bear defeat,
By so simple a thing as how you eat.
By the books you choose from the well-filled shelf;
In these ways and more, you tell on yourself.
So there's really no particle of sense
In any effort at pretense.
   AUTHOR UNKNOWN

————♦————

Children are quick to detect pretense and to shun the pretender. Only the genuine, the true man or woman, can hope to lead them long.   *Selected*

————♦————

Pride, Proud

Always hold your head up, but be careful to keep your nose at a friendly level.

————♦————

The remarkable thing about family pride is that so many people can be so proud of so little.

————♦————

Swallowing of pride seldom leads to indigestion.

————♦————

Don't let your pride get inflated — you may have to swallow it someday.

————♦————

The man who is not proud of his church seldom makes the church proud of him.   T. J. BACH

————♦————

The proud hate pride — in others.
   BENJAMIN FRANKLIN

————♦————

Problem, Problems

Problems are only opportunities in work clothes.   HENRY J. KAISER

Why can't life's problems hit us when we are 18 and know everything!

Glendale News Press

Show Us

Folks say we do a lot of things
We hadn't oughta had;
We never mean a bit of harm
Nor do them to be bad.

But when a chance just comes along
With fun a-peekin' through
We take it mostly just because
We've nothing else to do.

Kids are an awful problem
All the grownup people say
But honest all we really want
Is just a chance to play.

And all of us from country towns
And from the cities, too,
Will quit what you call mischief
If you show us what to do.

AUTHOR UNKNOWN

Procrastinate

You may delay, but time will not.

BENJAMIN FRANKLIN

Always put off until tomorrow the things you shouldn't do at all.

FRANCES RODMAN

Profane, Profanity

Someone has said that profanity is the effort of a feeble mind to express itself forcibly.

He knew not what to say, and so he swore.   LORD BYRON

Progress

It is a "little farther" that costs, but it is a "little farther" that counts.

You only go as far as you go on your knees.

Progress is the great law of life.

Progress has little to do with speed, but much with direction.

If you want to go higher, go deeper.

After Calvin Coolidge made known to the public that he "did not choose to run," he was besieged by newspaper reporters for a more elaborate statement. It seems that one was more persistent than the others.

"Exactly why don't you want to be president again?" he inquired.

"No chance for advancement," was the president's reply.   WALTER J. BARTAZEK

Progress, like running a locomotive, requires cooperation.
The crew must be organized.
Machinery must be well-oiled.
It must be fired up.
There must be steam.
Someone must be at the throttle.

Promise, Promises

There is no more perishable freight than a bulging crate of promises.

A fair promise makes a fool merry.

He who promises runs in debt.

Tarry at the promise till God meets you there. He always returns by way of His promises.

While some stand on the promises, others just sit on the premises.

He who is most slow in making a promise is usually the most faithful in the performance of it.   ROUSSEAU

Promises may get their friends, but non-performance will turn them into enemies.   BENJAMIN FRANKLIN

Promote, Promotion

Promotion is achieved by motion.

If you want to go up, get down to work.

Two-thirds of promotion consists of motion.

PROMPTNESS — PROVERBS

Promptness

During a busy life I have often been asked, "How did you manage to do it all?" The answer is simple: Because I did everything promptly.

SIR RICHARD TANGYE

Prosperity

Sobriety is the door of prosperity.

Few of us can stand prosperity. Another man's, I mean. MARK TWAIN

Proverbs

A good anvil is not afraid of the hammer.

There is nothing new except what hath been forgotten. *English Proverb*

From saying to doing is a long stretch. *French*

Fuel is not sold in the forest, nor fish on the shore of a lake. *Chinese*

One dog barks at something, and a hundred bark at the sound. *Chinese*

He who wants to know himself should offend two or three of his neighbors. *Chinese*

Well begun is half done.

Little boats should keep the shore.

An old fox is not caught in a trap.

One flower does not make a garland.

An eagle does not feed on flies.

A bow too much bent is easily broken.

The statelier the tower the heavier the crash.

Glasses and lasses are brittle ware.

There is no compassion like the penny.

Man is caught by his tongue, and an ox by his horns. *Russian*

To perfect diligence nothing is difficult. *Chinese*

It is easy to cut thongs from other men's leather. *Dutch*

Fashion is more powerful than any tyrant. *Latin*

The great calabash tree has a seed as its mother. *African*

He is great whose failings can be numbered. *Hebrew*

A guest sees more in an hour than the host in a year. *Polish*

The heron's a saint when there are no fish in sight. *Bengalese*

Hunger changes beans into almonds. *Italian*

Everyone can keep house better than her mother until she trieth. *English*

It is not easy to straighten in the oak the crook that grew in the sapling. *Gaelic*

A man without religion is like a horse without a bridle. *Latin*

Many mickles make a muckle.

He that is warm thinks all so.

One swallow does not make a summer.

The handsome flower is not the sweetest.

Rashness is the parent of misfortune.

A cracked plate may last as long as a sound one.

Little brooks make great rivers.

204

A thousand probabilities do not make one truth.

———◆———

Rough stones grow smooth from hand to hand.

———◆———

In an orderly house all is soon ready.

———◆———

Running hares need no spurs.

———◆———

He that lies down with dogs rises with fleas.   *English*

———◆———

We can never see the sun rise by looking into the west.   *Japanese*

———◆———

For a good dinner and a gentle wife you can afford to wait.   *Danish*

———◆———

He who plants trees loves others besides himself.   *English*

———◆———

Provide, Provision

Winter finds out what summer has laid up.

———◆———

God gives every bird food, but he does not throw it into the nest.
J. G. HOLLAND

Psychiatry, Psychology

Two psychologists met on the street one day. One said to the other, "You're fine today, how am I?"

———◆———

"Child psychology, as a rule," says a child psychologist, "always works better when it is applied like paint — with a brush."

———◆———

Psychiatrist: "Don't worry too much if your son likes to make mud pies, and even if he tries to eat them it is quite normal."
Mother: "Well I don't think so, and neither does his wife."

———◆———

Have you heard about the cannibal who went to a psychiatrist because he was fed up with people?

Do you know the difference between a neurotic, a psychotic and a psychiatrist?
A neurotic dreams about castles in the air.
A psychotic lives in castles in the air.
A psychiatrist collects the rent from those castles.

———◆———

"He's a psycho-ceramic."
"What's that?"
"A crackpot."

———◆———

Mother of small boy to child psychiatrist: Well, I don't know whether or not he feels insecure, but everyone else in the neighborhood certainly does.

———◆———

A psychiatrist is a guy who asks you a lot of expensive questions that your wife asks for nothing.

———◆———

A man went to a psychologist for help. "I have an inferiority complex," the man said.
"You don't have a complex," the psychologist said, "you are inferior."

———◆———

One young couple told their friends that they raised their first child according to "The Book" on child psychology. But they raised their second child on the covers of the book!

———◆———

Punctual, Punctuality

A teacher is late unless he's a half-hour early.

———◆———

Punctuality is the politeness of kings.

———◆———

Purity

Subdue your passion or it will subdue you.

———◆———

Purpose

The purposes of God are sometimes delayed, but never abandoned!

205

It is better to die for something than it is to live for nothing.

DR. BOB JONES, SR.

———◆———

A great purpose leads to great achievement.

———◆———

A teacher's purpose should be as great as the purpose of God.

———◆———

Poverty of purpose is worse than poverty of purse.

———◆———

A man without a purpose or goal is like a ship without a rudder, adrift on the foaming, trackless ocean.

———◆———

It is not the man with a motive but the man with a purpose who wins.

———◆———

The person with no purpose in life can never show progress.

The greatest thing in this world is not so much where we stand, as in what direction we are moving.

OLIVER W. HOLMES

———◆———

My Symphony

To live content with small means;
To seek elegance rather than luxury
  and refinement rather than fashion;
To be worthy, not respectable, and
  wealthy, not rich;
To listen to stars and birds, babes and
  sages with open heart;
To study hard;
To think quietly, act frankly, talk gent-
  ly, await occasions, hurry never;
In a word, to let the spiritual, un-
  bidden and unconscious, grow up
  through the common —
This is my symphony.

WILLIAM HENRY CHANNING

Q

Quality

Only a mediocre person is always at his best.   SOMERSET MAUGHAM

———◆———

God does not want us to do extraordinary things;
He wants us to do the ordinary things extraordinarily well.   BISHOP GORE

———◆———

Nothing comes out of a sack but what was put into it.

———◆———

All is not gold that glitters.

———◆———

Quarrel, Quarreling

Where one will not, two cannot quarrel.

———◆———

Quarrels would never last long if there were not faults on both sides.

LA ROCHEFOUCAULD

———◆———

A quarrelsome man has no good neighbors.   BENJAMIN FRANKLIN

Those who in quarrels interpose, must often wipe a bloody nose.

BENJAMIN FRANKLIN

———◆———

Questions, Quizzes

I can't understand why goods sent by ship are called cargo, while goods sent in a car are a shipment.

———◆———

We may not put a question mark where God puts a period.

———◆———

Who was a lady but was never a little girl? Eve.

———◆———

What man was never born? Adam.

———◆———

The Master's Question

Have ye looked for my sheep in the
  desert,
For those who have missed the way?
Have you been in the wild, waste
  places,

Where the lost and wandering stray?
Have ye trodden the lonely highway,
    The foul and the darksome street?
It may be ye'd see in the gloaming
    The print of My wounded feet.

Have ye folded home to your bosom
    The trembling, neglected lamb,
And taught to the little lost one
    The sound of the Shepherd's Name?
Have ye searched for the poor and
    needy
    With no clothing, no home, no
    bread?
The Son of Man was among them —
    He had nowhere to lay His head.

Have ye carried the living water
    To the parched and thirsty soul?
Have ye said to the sick and wounded,
    "Christ Jesus make thee whole"?
Have ye told My fainting children
    Of the strength of the Father's hand?
Have ye guided the tottering footsteps
    To the shore of the golden land?

Have ye stood by the sad and weary
    To soothe the pillow of death;
To comfort the sorrowful, stricken,
    And strengthen the feeble faith?
And have ye felt when the glory
    Has streamed through the open door,
And flitted across the shadows,
    That there I have been before?

Have ye wept with the broken-hearted
    In their agony of woe?
Ye might hear Me whispering beside
    you,
" 'Tis the pathway I often go!"
                        AUTHOR UNKNOWN

——————◆——————

Quiet

Quietness

"Be still and know that I am God,"
That I who made and gave thee life
Will lead thy faltering steps aright;
That I who see each sparrow's fall
Will hear and heed thy earnest call.
    I am thy God.

"Be still and know that I am God,"
When aching burdens crush thy heart.
Then know I formed thee for thy part
And purpose in the plan I hold.
Thou art the clay that I would mold.
    Trust thou in God.

"Be still and know that I am God,"
Who made the atom's tiny span
And set it moving to my plan,
That I who guide the stars above
Will guide and keep thee in my love.
    Be thou still.   AUTHOR UNKNOWN

——————◆——————

Beware of a silent dog and still
water.

——————◆——————

Quit

Don't Quit

When things get wrong, as they some-
    times will,
When the road you are trudging seems
    all up hill;
When the funds are low and the debts
    are high
And you want to smile, but you have
    to sigh;
When care is pressing you down a bit,
Rest if you must, but don't you quit.
Success is failure turned inside out;
The silver tint of the clouds of doubt.
And you can never tell how close you
    are
It may be near when it seems afar;
So stick to the fight when you're hard-
    est hit —
It's when things seem worst that you
    mustn't quit.   AUTHOR UNKNOWN

——————◆——————

Too many people have finishing
fever.

——————◆——————

Someone worse than a quitter is
someone who finishes something he
should never have started.

——————◆——————

Trying times are no time to quit
trying.

R

Read, Readings

Time to Read the Bible

It takes 70 hours and 40 minutes to read the Bible at pulpit rate.

It takes 52 hours and 20 minutes to read the Old Testament.

It takes 18 hours and 20 minutes to read the New Testament.

In the Old Testament the Psalms take the longest to read: 4 hours and 28 minutes.

In the New Testament the Gospel of Luke takes 2 hours and 43 minutes to read.

———◆———

Reading is of no value unless we translate what we read into life itself.

———◆———

The number of people who can read is small, and the number of those who can read to any purpose, much smaller, and the number of those who are too tired after a hard day's work to read — enormous. But all except the blind and deaf can see and hear.　GEORGE BERNARD SHAW

———◆———

The man who does not read good books has no advantage over the man who can't read them.

———◆———

Reading is to the mind what exercise is to the body.　JOSEPH ADDISON

———◆———

To acquire the habit of reading is to construct for yourself a refuge from almost all the miseries of life.　SOMERSET MAUGHAM

———◆———

Show me a family of readers, and I will show you the people who move the world.　NAPOLEON

———◆———

Resolve to edge in a little reading every day. If you gain but 15 minutes a day, it will make itself felt at the end of a year.　HORACE MANN

Sales-minded executives should cultivate faster, more effective reading. Reading should not be regarded as an isolated skill. Many jobs presuppose the ability to read well. Sales executives have to read for a variety of purposes and should not have to read everything the same way. To be a flexible reader requires fast, effective reading habits. Reading, vocabulary, comprehension and rate can be improved through definite and systematic training. Effective reading habits may mean the difference between lacking self-confidence and having it. Improved reading will result in improved effectiveness in your job and you will be a greater asset to your company.　ELIZABETH A. SIMPSON

———◆———

Primary-age children enjoy reading. One day six-year-old Johnny, who had just started public school, volunteered to read the twenty-third Psalm for the Scripture lesson in primary church. Carefully he picked up the Bible, opened it and read the verses, letter-perfect.

The teacher, knowing Johnny had just started school, was so surprised that she slipped up behind him to observe his reading. Sure enough, he read the passage right, line for line, word for word — but the Bible was upside down!

———◆———

The love of reading enables a man to exchange the wearisome hours of life which come to everyone for hours of delight.　MONTESQUIEU

———◆———

Real, Reality

What you would seem to be, be really.　BENJAMIN FRANKLIN

———◆———

A rainbow is as real as a derrick.　RICHARD LE GALLIENNE

Water changes its color while passing through rocks and swift currents: for a moment it is churned into white foam. Reality often looks unreal when passing through tests and opposition.

———♦———

Reason, Reasonings

To everything there is a reason.

———♦———

A man without reason is out of season.

———♦———

It has been said that there are two reasons for everything we do — a good reason and the real reason. We can give a good reason to others. But to God we have to give the real reason.

———♦———

He who will not reason is a bigot; he who cannot is a fool; he who dares not is a slave.   WALTER DRUMMOND

———♦———

Reason never shows itself so unreasonable as when it ceases to reason about things which are above reason.

———♦———

Hear reason or she'll make you feel her.   BENJAMIN FRANKLIN

———♦———

"Are you in pain, my little man?" asked the kind old gentleman.
"No," answered the boy, "the pain's in me."

———♦———

Teacher: "Which is more important to us — the moon or the sun?"
Johnny: "The moon."
Teacher: "Why?"
Johnny: "The moon gives us light at night when we need it. The sun gives us light only in the daytime when we don't need it."   Christian Herald

———♦———

The father played possum while his youngsters tried their best to rouse him from a Sunday afternoon nap to take them for a promised walk. Finally, his five-year-old daughter pried open one of his eyelids, peered carefully, then reported: "He's still in there."   Reville

Recitation, Recite

A Methodist missionary to the Spanish mission in Florida was giving a program for the children and had given them pieces to learn. One day he received a note from a mother: "Dear Pastor — I am sorry Carlos will not be able to recite on Friday. The goat ate his speech."   Together

———♦———

Albert was taking a part in a local concert. He was only seven years old, but recited so well that he was encored.
"Well, Albert, and how did you get on?" asked the proud father when he returned home.
"Why, I thought I did all right," replied the youngster, "but they made me do it again."

———♦———

Redemption

Redemption was not an afterthought with God.

———♦———

Refine, Refinement

The turning lathe that has the sharpest knives produces the finest work.

———♦———

Some people become so polished they cast reflections on everyone.

———♦———

Reform, Reformer

A reformer is one who insists upon his conscience being your guide.   Town Journal

———♦———

Reform only yourself; for in doing that you do everything.   MONTAIGNE

———♦———

A man who reforms himself has contributed his full share towards the reformation of his neighbor.   NORMAN DOUGLAS

———♦———

Refuge

Can I find refuge
          in Jesus? — Question
I find refuge in Jesus. — Affirmative
Find refuge in Jesus. — Exhortation

Refuge in Jesus. — Consolation
In Jesus. — Exaltation
Jesus. — Satisfaction

———◆———

Regret

Why cry over spilt milk when it is already four-fifths water?

———◆———

Seven Things You Never Regret
Feeling reverence for your Maker.
Showing kindness to an aged person.
Destroying a letter written in anger.
Offering the apology that saves a friendship.
Stopping a scandal that could wreck a reputation.
Taking time to show loved ones consideration.
Accepting the judgment of God on any question. ANONYMOUS

———◆———

Religion, Religious

The religions of the world say "do and live." The religion of the Bible says, "live and do." DR. BOB JONES, SR.

———◆———

Religion is the best armor that a man can have, but it is the worst cloak. JOHN BUNYAN

———◆———

It is natural to be religious; it is supernatural to be Christian. W. M. CRAIG

———◆———

If men are so wicked with religion, what would they be without it? BENJAMIN FRANKLIN

———◆———

It is a poor religion that is never strong except when the owner is sick.

———◆———

Sure religion costs — but irreligion's bill is bigger.

———◆———

The need of the hour is not more legislation. The need of the hour is more religion. ROGER BABSON

———◆———

"Are mosquitoes religious?"
"Yes. They first sing over you and then they prey on you."

Some people endure religion; others enjoy salvation.

———◆———

Some people never think of religion until they come in sight of a cemetery.

———◆———

A religion that never suffices to govern a man will never suffice to save him. That which does not distinguish him from a sinful world will never distinguish him from a perishing world. JOHN HOWE

———◆———

People are not interested in religion but in reality. DR. HENRIETTA C. MEARS

———◆———

Religion
Get religion like a Methodist,
Experience it like a Baptist,
Be sure of it like a Disciple,
Stick to it like a Lutheran,
Pay for it like a Presbyterian,
Conciliate it like a Congregationalist,
Glorify it like a Jew,
Be proud of it like an Episcopalian,
Practice it like a Christian Scientist,
Propagate it like a Roman Catholic,
Work for it like a Salvation Army lassie,
And enjoy it like a colored man. DR. EDGAR DE WITT JONES

———◆———

Religion without morality is a tree without fruits; morality without religion is a tree without roots. HAROLD W. RUOPP

———◆———

When asked why I was looking so healthy, I explained that I had taken up yogurt. My friend exclaimed, "It just shows that some of those funny foreign religions can really help a person!"

———◆———

Many have quarreled about religion that never practiced it. BENJAMIN FRANKLIN

———◆———

The religion that makes a man look sick certainly won't cure the world. PHILLIPS BROOKS

———◆———

The world does not need a definition of religion so much as it needs a demonstration.

Let your religion be not a goad but a goal.

———◆———

Still religion like still water freezes first.

———◆———

A religion that costs nothing does nothing.

———◆———

Remember, Recall

When We Were Kids

Some of us — but we'd hate to admit it — can remember when —
Nobody swatted the fly.
Nobody had appendicitis.
Nobody wore white shoes.
Cream was five cents a pint.
Cantaloupes were muskmelons.
Milk-shake was a favorite drink.
Advertisers were supposed to tell the truth.
You never heard of a gas wagon.
Doctors wanted to look at your tongue.
The hired girl received one-fifty a week.
And the hired man got ten dollars a month.
Farmers drove to town for their mail.
Nobody listened in on a telephone.
Nobody was bothered with static on the radio.
Nobody cared about the price of gasoline.
The butcher threw in a chunk of liver.
The clothing merchant threw in a pair of suspenders with a new suit.
Straw stacks were burned instead of baled. ANONYMOUS

Repent, Repentance

You cannot repent too soon, because you know not how soon it may be too late.

———◆———

Repentance is being so sorry for sin you quit sinning.

———◆———

Repentance is a change of heart, not an opinion. *Eternity*

Reputation

Every dissipation of youth must be paid for with a draft on old age.
DR. BOB JONES, SR.

———◆———

Honest confession is good for the soul but hard on the reputation.

———◆———

Do not be too concerned about what people think about you — chances are they seldom think about you at all.

———◆———

Reputation is to virtue what light is to a picture.

———◆———

Reputation is precious, but character is priceless. *Youth's Companion*

———◆———

The only reputation that matters is your reputation in heaven.

———◆———

Glass, china and reputation are easily cracked and never well mended.
BENJAMIN FRANKLIN

———◆———

Beware of him who regards not his reputation. *Proverb*

———◆———

It takes a lifetime to build a good reputation: It may be lost in a moment.

———◆———

A good reputation always proves to be good business capital.

———◆———

Your ideal—what you wish you were.
Your reputation — what people say you are.
Your character — what you are.

———◆———

An ill wound but not an ill name may be healed. BENJAMIN FRANKLIN

———◆———

The way to gain a good reputation is to endeavor to be what you desire to appear. SOCRATES

———◆———

Research

It takes a lot to teach a little.

———◆———

You never get anything you don't dig for.

211

We do not need many researchers today; what we need are searchers.

LOUIS N. KATZ, M.D. *in A.M.A. Journal*

Resist

Every moment of resistance to temptation is a victory.   FABER

Better shun the bait than struggle in the snare.   DRYDEN

"I can resist everything," said the young lady, "except temptation."

Resolutions

The first things broken each new year are resolutions.

Good resolutions are like babies crying in church: They should be carried out immediately!   CHARLES M. SHELDON

He that resolves to mend hereafter resolves not to mend now!

Resources, Resourceful

It is seldom that we find out how great are our resources until we are thrown upon them.   BOVEE

A father was taking his blonde toddler on a tour of the zoo and they had stopped outside the lion's cage.

"Daddy," the little tyke asked, "if the lion gets out and eats you up, what bus do I take to get home?"

Responsible, Responsibilities

We measure ourselves by the responsibility we shoulder successfully.

Some people grow under responsibility; others swell.

Weary is the head that wears the crown.

Not your responsibility, but your response to God's ability is what counts.

Regal honors have regal cares.

A youth answered an advertisement for a responsible boy. "What makes you think you're responsible?" asked the employer.

"On every job I have ever had so far," the young man answered, "whenever anything went wrong, the boss has always said to me, 'You're responsible!'"

Responsibility is our response to God's ability.

In the great ocean family the whale and herring at one time were inseparable. One day, however, they had a serious quarrel and separated, vowing never to speak again. The entire ocean family was sad. Finally, one day, a mackerel was sent to investigate the situation and see what could be done. He talked at length with the whale who he thought should be big and remedy the situation. But the whale got tired of listening to the mackerel and asked, "Say, am I my brother's kipper?"

If I am decent merely because the neighbors require it, my decency is not really decent. But when I am honest, not because business demands it, but because I demand it . . . when I am generous, not because my friends insist upon it, but because my heart insists upon it . . . when I am decent, not because the neighbors require it, but because I require it . . . *then* I have found the secret of responsibility.

COTTON

Rest

Rest

Rest is not quitting
    The busy career;
Rest is the fitting
    Of self to its sphere.
'Tis loving and serving
    The highest and best!
'Tis onward, unswerving,
    And that is true rest.

J. S. DWIGHT

There's no rest for the wicked and the righteous don't need it.

———

Resurrection

In resurrection stillness there is resurrection power.

———

Our Lord has written the promise of the resurrection, not in books alone, but in every leaf in springtime.

MARTIN LUTHER

———

Retribution, Revenge

In taking revenge a man is but equal to his enemy, but in passing it over he is his superior. BACON

———

'Tis more noble to forgive and more manly to despise, than to revenge an injury. BENJAMIN FRANKLIN

———

He who pelts every barking dog must pick up many stones.

———

Do not look for wrong and evil;
You will find them if you do:
As you measure for your neighbor,
He will measure back to you.

———

After a lengthy search through her purse, the lady who had just boarded a streetcar handed the conductor a twenty dollar bill.

"I'm sorry," she snapped, noting the conductor's disapproving glance, "but I don't have a nickel."

"Oh, don't worry lady," he reassured her. "You'll have three hundred and ninety-nine of them in a minute!"

———

The only people you should try to get even with are those who have helped you in some way.

Hoard's Dairyman

———

You can never get ahead of anyone as long as you are trying to get even with him.

———

Don't lay for your enemies nor lie for your friends.

Reverence

Reverence for the things of God must be taught as well as caught. H. C. GARNER

———

Reverence controls behavior, behavior does not control reverence.

———

Revival

When Will We Have Revival?

When Christians wear out more carpets around the family altar than around the dressing table;

When Christians wear out more rubber tires calling on needy homes than they wear out on pleasure trips.

When Christians stop bickering over little things, and have fellowship in the spirit of divine love;

When "My people, which are called by my name, shall humble themselves and pray and seek my face and turn from their wicked ways; then will I hear from heaven, and will forgive their sins, and will heal their land" — then the revival will come.

When dad stays home from the club and lodge.

When mother stays away from the amusement places and parties.

When the car is left in the garage long enough to cool off;

When the radio and TV are turned off long enough for the entire family to tune in on God; then we shall have revival.

When preachers preach the Word of God, rather than essays on philosophy and psychology and the opinions of men.

When churches quit trying to hold together by means of entertainment and picnics.

When the folks all get back in one accord, rather than discord; then shall we have revival.

In genuine humility and submission, let us seek God's face. We must save our homes, our churches, our country. BISHOP WM. F. ANDERSON

They tried to stamp out the fire of God in Jerusalem, but they scattered the embers all over the world.

HAROLD L. LUNDQUIST

———◆———

A revival spasm furnishes no permanent stimulation.

———◆———

Rich, Riches

A Child of the King

Poor? No, of course not! Why, how
  could I be,
When Christ, the King, is taking care
  of me?
Tired? Sometimes — yes, more than
  tired; but then,
I know a place where I can rest again!
Lonely? Ah, well I know the aching
  blight;
But now — I've Jesus with me day and
  night.
Burdens? I have them; oft they press
  me sore,
And then — I lean the harder, trust
  the more.
Worthy? Oh, no! The marvel of it is
That I should know such boundless
  love as His!
And so, I'm rich; with Christ I am
  "joint heir,"
Since He once stooped my poverty to
  share.

EDITH LILLIAN YOUNG

———◆———

It is not the fact that a man has riches which keeps him from the Kingdom of Heaven, but the fact that riches have him.

DAVID CAIRD

———◆———

The rich have plenty of relations.

———◆———

The rich are not always godly, but the godly are always rich.

———◆———

Riches exclude only one inconvenience, and that is poverty.

SAMUEL JOHNSON

———◆———

A man is rich in proportion to the number of things which he can afford to let alone.

THOREAU

Write it on your heart that every day is the best day in the year. He only is rich who owns the day, and no one owns the day who allows it to be invaded with worry, fret and anxiety. Finish every day and be done with it. You have done what you could.

RALPH WALDO EMERSON

———◆———

He who multiplies riches, multiplies cares.

BENJAMIN FRANKLIN

———◆———

Finances

When I think of the gold in the sunset,
  And the silver of stars bright at
    night;
The platinum glow of the moonbeams,
  And the pearls in a smile of delight,
    I wonder if I am poor.

When I figure the emeralds in tree-
  tops,
  And the turquoise of fresh bluebells,
The diamonds in sparkling dew,
  And the wealth of a baby's yells,
    I wonder if I am poor.

The gold and silver and platinum,
  The sunsets rich and fine;
The diamonds and the emeralds
  Are God's and God is mine.
    Why, I'm rich!

VERNE ARENDS

———◆———

Ridiculous

The ridiculous man is one who never changes.

———◆———

Right, Righteous, Righteousness

No man has a right to all of his rights.

PHILLIPS BROOKS

———◆———

Our country, right or wrong. When right, to be kept right; when wrong, to be put right.

CARL SCHURZ

———◆———

I prefer to do right and get no thanks rather than to do wrong and get no punishment.

MARCUS CATO

———◆———

It is never right to do wrong!

God never alters the robe of righteousness to fit man, but the man to fit the robe.

Rut

The only difference between a rut and a grave is length.

S

Saints

Brother Mose said there were two kinds of people in his church: The saints and the ain'ts.

———◆———

Great saints are only great receivers.

———◆———

Salvation

Born once, die twice; born twice, die once.

———◆———

Salvation may come quietly, but we cannot remain quiet about it.

———◆———

Salvation of a child is like a multiplication table, capacity to win others.

———◆———

The recognition of sin is the beginning of salvation.   LUTHER

———◆———

If Christ is the way, why waste time traveling some other way?

———◆———

You asked me how I gave my heart
    to Christ,
    I do not know;
There came a yearning for Him in my
    soul
    So long ago;
I found earth's flowers would fade and
    die,
I wept for something that would
    satisfy
And then, and then, somehow I seemed
    to dare
To lift my broken heart to God in
    prayer.
I do not know, I cannot tell you
    how;
I only know He is my Saviour now.
                    ANONYMOUS

Which?

Just see how short this candle is,
This candle that I hold.
It represents a man who found
The Lord when he was old.
And though his light is shining now
And bright beyond a doubt
He hasn't much to give because
His light will soon be out.

This candle that I have will
Burn much longer than the other.
I love its glowing light, don't you?
It represents a mother.
She found the Lord in middle age
Her children were all grown.
If only she had known the Lord
When they were still at home.

This candle is a larger one
It represents a youth
Who gave his heart to God
And walks the path of right and truth.
His light can shine out long and bright
With many trophies won;
With more to give because
He found the Lord when he was young.

Which candle do you want to be?
The short one or the tall?
The voice of Jesus calls to you
Come now! Give Christ your all.
                AUTHOR UNKNOWN

———◆———

It has been said that chances are 5,000 to 1 against getting decisions for Christ between the ages of 18 and 25; 25,000 to 1 between 25 and 35; 80,000 to 1 between 35 and 45; 1,000,-000 to 1 between 45 and 85.

———◆———

There is but one ladder to heaven — the cross.

SALVATION

Better never to have been born at all, than never to have been born again.

———◆———

A little girl in the kindergarten department hurried home one day from Sunday school and weighed herself.

"Why did you weigh yourself again today when you just weighed yourself yesterday?" the mother asked.

"Because," the little girl replied, "I gave my heart to Jesus this morning and I wanted to see how much I weighed without it. And, Mommy, I weigh just the same."

———◆———

Suppose that Paul had been converted at seventy instead of twenty-five. There would have been no Paul in history. There was a Matthew Henry because he was converted at eleven and not at seventy; a Dr. Watts because he was converted at nine and not at sixty; a Jonathan Edwards because he was converted at eight and not at eighty; a Richard Baxter because he was converted at six and not at sixty.

How much more a soul is worth that has a lifetime of opportunity before it than the soul which has nothing! Lambs are of more worth than sheep in the realm of souls as well as in the marketplace.   J. O. WILSON

———◆———

Too Little

Said a precious little laddie,
  To his father one bright day,
"May I give myself to Jesus,
  Let Him wash my sins away?"

"Oh, my son, but you're too little,
  Wait until you older grow,
Bigger folks, 'tis true, do need Him, but
  Little folks are safe, you know."

Said the father to his laddie
  As a storm was coming on,
"Are the sheep all safely sheltered,
  Safe within the fold, my son?"

"All the big ones are, my father,
  But the lambs, I let them go,
For I didn't think it mattered,
  Little ones are safe, you know."

Oh, my brother! Oh, my sister!
  Have you too made that mistake?
Little hearts that now are yielding
  May be hardened then — too late.

'Ere the evil days come nigh them,
  "Let the children come to Me,
And forbid them not," said Jesus,
  "For such shall My kingdom be."
                              AUTHOR UNKNOWN

———◆———

I'm a Christian

I am a Christian, though I'm small;
  Jesus does not care at all
If we're three years old, or four;
  Or if we are fifty more.

If we come to Him and say,
  "Jesus, wash my sins away,"
And His Word we then believe,
  He will gladly us receive.
                              AUTHOR UNKNOWN

———◆———

What Think Ye of Christ?

Youth: Too happy to think — time yet.

Manhood: Too busy to think — more gold.

Prime: Too anxious to think — worry.

Declining Years: Too aged to think — old hearts harder to get.

Dying Bed: Too ill to think — weak, suffering alone.

Death: Too late to think — the spirit has flown.

Eternity: Forever to think — God's mercy past. Into hell I am righteously cast, forever to weep my doom.
                              AUTHOR UNKNOWN

———◆———

The A B C of Salvation

All have sinned, and come short of the glory of God. Romans 3:23

Behold the Lamb of God, which taketh away the sin of the world. John 1:29

Come now, and let us reason together, saith the Lord: though your sins be as scarlet, they shall be as white as snow; though they be red like crimson, they shall be as wool. Isaiah 1:18

"Dear Mother," said the little maid,
  "Please whisper it to me —
Before I am a Christian
  How old ought I to be?"

"How old ought you to be, dear child,
  Before you can love me?"
"I always loved you, Mommy dear,
  Since I was tiny, wee."

"I love you now, and always will,"
  The little daughter said,
And on her mother's shoulder hid
  Her golden curly head.

"How old, my girlie, must you be
  Before you trust my care?"
"Oh, Mother dear, I do, I do,
  I trust you everywhere."

"How old ought you to be my child,
  To do the things I say?"
The little girl looked up and said,
  "I can do that today."

"Then you can be a Christian, too,
  Don't wait 'til you are grown.
Tell Jesus, now, you come to Him
  To be His very own."

And so the little maid knelt down,
  And said, "Lord, if I may,
I'd like to be a Christian now,"
  He answered, "Yes; today."
                              AUTHOR UNKNOWN

Satisfaction

If you are satisfied with little in yourself, how can you demand much from others?

When you have got a thing where you want it, it is a good thing to leave it where it is.   WINSTON CHURCHILL

Scholarship

The riches of scholarship, the benignities of literature, defy fortune and outline calamity. They are beyond the reach of thief or moth or rust. As they cannot be inherited, so they cannot be alienated.   LOWELL

School

On the first day of school the little boy was telling his teacher about his dog.
Teacher: "What kind is it?"
Boy: "Oh, he's a mixed-up kind — sort of a cocker scandal!"

The most difficult school is the school of hard knocks. One never graduates.

Schools

There is a little school called home,
  Where childhood's heart must learn
To meet aright the years to come,
  Their hidden truth discern.

There is a larger school called books,
  Where further facts are taught.
It is a tower that brightly looks
  Across the world of thought.

There is a mighty school called life,
  Where we must all make good
Courses conditioned in the strife
  Of earlier studenthood.

The school of life will try the wit,
  Nor are its courses free.
The less one waits to learn from it
  The better it will be.
                              CLARENCE E. FLYNN

School houses are the republican line of fortifications.   HORACE MANN

School is not preparation for life, but school is life.   JOHN DEWEY

After Tommy's first day at school, his mother asked him what happened during the day.
"Oh, nothin'," said Tommy. "A woman wanted to know how to spell 'cat,' and I told 'er."   *Florida School Journal*

Scripture

It's not a matter of Scripture being hard to understand, but of our unwillingness to yield to it.   M. D. CHRISTENSEN

Different Rendering of Psalm 23:5

My cup runneth over. *Authorized Version*

My cup is teemin' fu'. *Broad Scotch*

My happiness cup fills to overflowing. *Chinese*

My cup He fills till it runs over. *Indian*

My drinking cup bubbles over. *Zulu*

Thou dost fill my cup to running over. *Tibetan*

Thou pourest out fullness to me. *German*

My cup runs over. Yes, happen what may, happiness and grace will accompany me. *French* Now

———◆———

Sea

The Set of the Sail

I stood on the shore beside the sea;
  The wind from the west blew fresh
    and free,
While past the rocks at the harbor's
    mouth
  The ships went north and the ships
    went south.
And some sailed out on an unknown
    quest,
  And some sailed into the harbor's
    rest;
Yet ever the wind blew out of the west.

I said to one who had sailed the sea
  That this was a marvel unto me;
For how can the ships go safely forth,
  Some to the south and some to the
    north,
Far out to sea on their golden quest,
  Or into the harbor's calm and rest,
And ever the wind blow out of the
    west?

The sailor smiled as he answered me,
  "Go where you will when you're on
    the sea,
Though head winds baffle and flaw a
    delay,
  You can keep the course by night
    and day;
Drive with the breeze or against the
    gale;
  It will not matter what winds prevail,
For all depends upon the set of the
    sail."

Voyager soul on the sea of life,
  O'er waves of sorrow and sin and
    strife,
When fogs bewilder and foes betray,
  Steer straight on your course from
    day to day;
Though unseen currents run deep and
    swift,
  Where rocks are hidden and sandbars shift,
All helpless and aimless, you need not
    drift.

Oh, set your sail to the heavenly gale,
  And then, no matter what winds
    prevail,
No reef shall wreck you, no calm delay,
  No mist shall hinder, no storm shall
    stay;
Though far you wander and long you
    roam,
  Through salt sea-spray and o'er white
    sea foam,
No wind that can blow but shall speed
    you home. AUTHOR UNKNOWN

———◆———

Seasons

Autumn Time

With rustling rows of cornstalks,
  Gay pumpkins heaped in mounds,
And hubbard squash in hummocks,
  The countryside abounds.

In garb of gold and crimson,
  The forest is arrayed,
The woodland wears a mantle
  Of beauty on parade.

The summer sun retreating
  Leaves tonic in the air,
And in the dawn there glistens
  A frosty carpet fair.

It is a season teeming
  With charm and festive cheer,
And life unfolds new treasures
  When autumn days are here. B. L. BRUCE

———◆———

Scarlet Ribbon

A country road is jubilant
  When April runs its length
To find a fragile crocus cupped
  Against a gray hill's strength;

And there is hushed tranquility
Upon the moonlit track,
Half-drifted-in, when snow lies deep
Where a country road runs back.

But when the frosted wayside vines
Hang crimson, and the curled
Bronze leaves drift underneath
Proud plumes the sumacs have un-
furled,
A country road goes up the hills
And down through autumn weather,
A gallant scarlet ribbon which
Ties farm and farm together.
RAMONA VERNON

Secrecy, Secret

When you part from your friend,
both should lock up their secrets and
exchange keys.

———♦———

Don't have more secrets than you
can carry yourself.

———♦———

The secret of life is not to do what
one likes, but to try to like what one
has to do. DINAH MULOCH CRAIK

———♦———

Women can keep a secret as well as
men can, but it takes more of them to
do it.

———♦———

Don't expect other people to keep
your secrets if you don't do it yourself!

———♦———

If you would keep your secret from
an enemy, tell it not to a friend.
BENJAMIN FRANKLIN

———♦———

It is wise not to seek a secret and
honest not to reveal it.
BENJAMIN FRANKLIN

———♦———

Three can keep a secret if two of
them are dead. BENJAMIN FRANKLIN

———♦———

Secretary

Dictated, But Not Read

"Now look here, I fired three girls
for revising my letters, see?" said the
boss to his new secretary.
"Yes, Sir."

"All right; now take a letter and take
it the way I tell you."

And the next morning Mr. C. J.
Squizz of the Squizz Soap Co., received
the following letter:

Mr. O., or A. J. or something, look
it up, Squizz, what a name, Soap
Company, Detroit, that's in Michigan, isn't it? Dear Mr. Squizz, hmmm.
The last shipment of soap you sent
us was of inferior quality and I want
you to understand — no, scratch that
out. I want you to understand —
hmmm — unless you can ship — furnish, ship, no, furnish us with your
regular soap you needn't ship us no
more, period, or whatever the grammar is.

Where was I? Paragraph. Your
soap wasn't what you said — I should
say it wasn't. Them bums tried to
put over a lot of hooey on us.
Whadda you want to paint your faces
up like Indians on the warpath?
We're sending back your last shipment tomorrow. Sure, we're gonna
send it back, I'd like to feed it to 'em
with a spoon and make 'em eat it,
the bums. Now read the letter over
—no, don't read it over, we've wasted
enough time on them crooks, fix it
up and sign my name. What do you
say we go out to lunch?

———♦———

My typist has gone on hir holiday
My typist has gohn on a spree,
My typish hap gone oh hyr haliduy,
O gring bacq mu hypist to me.
Bling bac% oK Sring back
O bynk b4ck my tipishth to me, tu
mo,
Btung gicq ocsling Beck
Oh blynck ba'k mg t1/2pys? to mi.
No credit necessary

———♦———

Security

At all times in history there have
been many who sought escape into
"security" from self-reliance.
HERBERT HOOVER

———♦———

You cannot establish security on borrowed money. ABRAHAM LINCOLN

Self, Selfish, Selfishness

A man's Sunday-self and his week-self are like two halves of a round-trip ticket; not good if detached.
Link

We can suffer from the paralysis of self-analysis. EUGENIA PRICE

Self is the only prison that can bind the soul. HENRY VAN DYKE

To have a respect for ourselves guides our morals; and to have a deference for others governs our manners. LAURENCE STERNE

Memo to Me:
"Others live here, too."

Yourself

You know the model of your car,
You know just what its powers are,
You treat it with a deal of care,
Nor tax it more than it will bear,
But as to self — that's different!
Your mechanism may be bent,
Your carburetor gone to grass,
Your engine just a rusty mass,
Your wheels may wobble, and your cogs
Be handed over to the dogs.
And then you skip and skid and slide
Without a thought of things inside.
What fools indeed we mortals are
To lavish care upon a car,
With ne'er a bit of time to see
About our own machinery!
JOHN KENDRICK BANGS

We have to make peace with our limitations. DR. HAROLD LINDSELL

A man can stand a lot as long as he can stand himself. AXEL MUNTHE

Self control is more often called for than self-expression. WILLIAM W. COMFORT

The seed of strife is in selfish seeking for glory. T. C. HORTON

You Tell on Yourself

You tell on yourself by the friends you seek,
By the very manner in which you speak,
By the way you employ your leisure time,
By the use you make of dollar and dime.
You tell what you are by the things you wear
By the spirit in which you your burdens bear.
By the kind of things at which you laugh.
By the records you play on the phonograph.
You tell what you are by the way you walk,
By the things of which you delight to talk,
By the manner in which you bear defeat,
By so simple a thing as how you eat.
By the books you choose from the well-filled shelf;
By these ways and more, you tell on yourself;
So there's really no particle of sense
In an effort to keep up false pretense.
Selected

Whenever you are too selfishly looking out for your own interest, you have only one person working for you — yourself. When you help a dozen other people with their problems, you have a dozen people working with you.
WILLIAM B. GIVEN, JR.

The greatest difficulty with the world is not its inability to produce, but its unwillingness to share. ROY L. SMITH

No one is fooled when you try to make him think that you have more than you have, know more than you know, are more than you are. This is one of the most pitiful gestures a young person can make. Avoid it. Be yourself. Someone is sure to like you for what you really are, and everyone will respect your lack of pretense.
S. S. Informer

Myself

I have to live with myself, and so,
I want to be fit for myself to know;
I want to be able as days go by
Always to look myself in the eye.

I don't want to stand with the setting
    sun
And hate myself for the things I've
    done.
I want to go out with my head erect;
I want to deserve all men's respect.

But here, in the struggle for fame and
    wealth
I want to be able to like myself.
I don't want to look at myself and
    know
That I'm a bluster, and bluff, and
    empty show.

I can never hide myself from me
I see what others may never see;
I know what others may never know:
I can never fool myself and so
Whatever happens, I want to be
Self respecting, and conscience free.
Selected

Make it thy business to know thyself,
which is the most difficult lesson in the
world.   CERVANTES

Master selfishness or it will master
you.

He who lives to benefit himself con-
fers on the world a benefit when he
dies.   TERTULLIAN

Far too frequently in this life we
are interested in only three persons:
Me, Myself and I.

To some, "mine" is better than "ours."

Mother: "Why Bobby, you ate all
that cake without thinking of your
little sister."
Bobby: "I was thinking of her all
the time. I was afraid she would come
before I finished it."

It is dangerous to be self-satisfied.

Edith was a little country bounded
on the north, south, east and west by
Edith.   *Reader's Digest*

A Tea Party

I had a little tea party
This afternoon at three.
'Twas very small —
Three guests in all —
Just I, Myself and Me.

Myself ate all the sandwiches,
While I drank up the tea;
'Twas also I who ate the pie
And passed the cake to me.
AUTHOR UNKNOWN

Sell, Selling

Tips on Selling

1. Look competent, well groomed,
   businesslike.
2. Create a pleasant buying atmosphere. Avoid pressure.
3. Be courteous, patient and helpful.
4. If you see that your customer is in
   a hurry, be quick. Indifference and
   slowness are irritating and explain
   many lost sales.
5. If you see that your customer is
   slow, wants to linger and look, adjust your speed to his. Be patient,
   be slow.
6. Do not make any criticism or comparison of any competitive merchan-
   dise to gain a sale.
7. Stress what is new, unusual or ex-
   clusive in the product.
8. Seem cooperative, sincere and convinced yourself.
9. Know the product you are selling.
   Selected

The salesgirl at the perfume counter
leaned toward her young customer and
whispered: "If I may, let me give you
a word of advice — please don't use
this if you are bluffing."

He who has a thing to sell
And goes and whispers in a well,
Is not so apt to get the dollars
As he who climbs a tree and hollers.

Don't Sell Me "Things"

Don't sell me clothes. Sell me neat appearance . . . style . . . attractiveness.

Don't sell me shoes. Sell me foot comfort and the pleasure of walking in the open air.

Don't sell me candy. Sell me happiness and the pleasure of taste.

Don't sell me furniture. Sell me a home that has comfort, cleanliness, contentment.

Don't sell me books. Sell me pleasant hours and the profits of knowledge.

Don't sell me toys. Sell me playthings to make my children happy.

Don't sell me tools. Sell me the pleasure and profit of making fine things.

Don't sell me refrigerators. Sell me the health and better flavor of fresh kept food.

Don't sell me tires. Sell me freedom from worry and low-cost-per-mile.

Don't sell me plows. Sell me green fields of waving wheat.

Don't sell me things. Sell me ideals . . . feelings . . . self-respect . . . home life . . . happiness.

Please don't sell me things!

Your Customer
*Adventures in Salesmanship,
Sears Roebuck & Co.*

———◆———

Sense

The average man has five senses: touch, taste, sight, smell and hearing. The successful man has two more: horse sense and common sense.

———◆———

The sermon is the house; the illustrations are the windows that let in the light.   SPURGEON

———◆———

The most powerful part of a sermon is the man behind it.   PHILLIPS BROOKS

———◆———

A good sermon consists in saying all that is necessary and nothing that is unnecessary.   *Church Management*

Sermons

The Living Sermon

I'd rather see a sermon than hear one any day,
I'd rather one would walk with me than merely tell the way,
The eye's a better pupil and more willing than the ear;
Fine counsel is confusing, but example's always clear.
The best of all the preachers are the men who live their creeds.
For to see good put in action is what everybody needs.

I soon can learn to do it if you'll let me see it done,
I can watch your hands in action, but your tongue too fast may run;
The lectures you deliver may be very wise and true,
But I'd rather get my lessons by observing what you do.
I may not understand the high advice that you may give
But there's no misunderstanding how you act and how you live!
ANONYMOUS

———◆———

Sermonettes are just fine for Christian-ettes.

———◆———

You can preach a better sermon with your life than with your lips.
OLIVER GOLDSMITH

———◆———

When Donald came out of church earlier than usual, his surprised friend Sandy asked in dismay, "What, Donald, is the sermon all done?"
"No," replied Donald. "It is all said, but it's not even started to be done."
Sunday School Journal

———◆———

Ignoring a mouse can be difficult. A seminarian, pinch-hitting in a pulpit, tried for ten minutes to ignore the mouse that climbed his chancel flowers and cavorted while his congregation giggled. Finally he reacted with a logical fervor — rolled his sermon manuscript into a club and got rid of the intruder. Must have been some good solid material in that message!
Presbyterian Life

The Alphabetical Test of a Message

It's Not The:	It's The:
Ability	Aim
Beauty	Book
Contention	Cross
Delivery	Decisions
Eloquence	Effect
Fragments	Fruit
Gloominess	Gladness
Hate	Harvest
Imagination	Instruction
Jesting	Justice
Knowledge	Kindness
Language	Love
Method	Message
Noise	New Birth
Offense	Object
Presentation	Power
Quantity	Quality
Reformation	Regeneration
Strength of Man	Spirit of God
Tradition	Truth
Understanding	Unction
Volume	Vision
Wisdom of Man	Word of God
eXcerpts	eXample
Yearns	Yieldedness
Zip	Zeal!

EDDIE WAGNER

———————————

A famous clergyman told his congregation, "Every blade of grass is a sermon."

A few days later a parishioner saw him mowing his lawn. "That's right, Reverend," the man said, "cut your sermons short."

———————————

Serve, Service

What we can do for Christ is the test of service. What we can suffer for Him is the test of love.

———————————

Service can put a new coat on a man. The grace of God alone can put a new man in the coat.

———————————

The great violinist, Nicolò Paganini, willed his marvelous violin to the City of Genoa, on condition that it must never be played upon.

No service without separation from the world.

———————————

Wood, while used and handled, wears but slightly. Discarded, it begins to decay. The lovely-toned violin has become worm-eaten and useless except as a relic. It is only a reminder that a life withdrawn from service to others becomes quite useless. *Selected*

———————————

Three things the Master asks of us,
And we who serve Him here below
And long to see His Kingdom come
May pray or give or go.
He needs them all — the open hand,
The willing feet, the praying heart,
To work together and to weave
A threefold cord that shall not part.

AUTHOR UNKNOWN

———————————

*I'll Go Where You Want Me to Go —
Maybe*

I'll go where you want me to go, dear
  Lord,
Real service is what I desire.
I'll sing a solo any time, dear Lord.
But don't ask me to sing in the choir.

I'll do what you want me to do, dear
  Lord,
I like to see things come to pass.
But don't ask me to teach boys and
  girls, O Lord.
I'd rather just stay in my class.

I'll do what you want me to do, dear
  Lord,
I yearn for thy kingdom to thrive.
I'll give you my nickels and dimes, dear
  Lord.
But please don't ask me to tithe.

I'll go where you want to me go, dear
  Lord.
I'll say what you want me to say.
I'm busy just now with myself, dear
  Lord
So I'll help you some other day.

Bible Crusader News

———————————

The service that counts is the service that costs.

———————————

Service is love in working clothes.

223

Service can never become slavery to one who loves. J. L. MASSEE

If we are devoted to the cause of humanity, we shall soon be crushed and brokenhearted, for we shall often meet more ingratitude from men than we would from a dog; but if our motive is love for God, no ingratitude can hinder us from serving our fellow men. OSWALD CHAMBERS

Only a burdened heart can lead to fruitful service. ALAN REDPATH

You do not do God a favor by serving Him. He honors you by allowing you to serve Him. VICTOR NYQUIST

To be of real service you must give something which cannot be bought or measured with money, and that is sincerity and integrity.

Service is the rent we pay for the space we occupy in this world.

You can measure what you would do for the Lord by what you do. T. C. HORTON

We are saved to serve, not to be served.

Share, Sharing

One child said to another, "If one of us would get off this tricycle, I could ride it much better." DR. HENRIETTA C. MEARS

Homily

Share your laughter every day;
Shun folks when you weep;
For joy was made to give away,
Sorrow made to keep. M. E. USCHOLD

Two children at a Sunday school picnic found a third who had no lunch. Remembering the lesson on the loaves and fishes in the Bible, Ronny said to his friend Timmy: "We are going to share our lunch with our new friend, aren't you, Timmy?"

The way to share much is to share a little each day. ELD

Don't share your troubles; people are already over-supplied.

Shine, Shining

There is no shining without burning.

Silence, Silent

Silence is the most satisfactory substitute for wisdom.

A man is wise until he opens his mouth.

Six young housewives living in the same apartment building in Canada fell into a dispute of such magnitude that it resulted in their being haled into court. When the case was called, they all made a concerted rush for the bench and, reaching it, all broke into bitter complaints at the same moment.

The judge sat momentarily stunned, as charges and countercharges filled the air. Suddenly he rapped for order. When quiet had been restored, the patient magistrate said gently, "Now, I'll hear the oldest first."

That closed the case.

It often shows a fine command of language to say nothing. ANONYMOUS

Luigi Tarisio was found dead one morning with scarce a comfort in his home, but with two hundred and forty-six fiddles, which he had been collecting all his life, crammed into an attic, the best in the bottom drawer of an old rickety bureau. In very devotion to the violin he had robbed the world of all that music all the time he treasured them; others before him had done the same, so that when the greatest Stradivarius was first played it had had one hundred and forty-seven speechless years. W. Y. FULLERTON

To sin by silence, when they should protest, makes cowards of men.
ABRAHAM LINCOLN

Simple, Simplicity

Simplicity is truth's most becoming garb.
DR. BOB JONES, SR.

Simplicity, of all things, is the hardest to be copied.
STEELE

Sin, Sinners

Sin in a Christian's life makes a coward of him.

There is no degree of sin in the sight of God.

God's children are made to smart when they yield to sin. But woe to the man who sins without pain; he feels no correction and sinneth again.

Sin is not hurtful
Because it is forbidden
But it is forbidden
Because it is hurtful.
BENJAMIN FRANKLIN

The sin that robs God of your soul will rob your soul of God.

There is more evil in a drop of sin than in a sea of affliction.

Sin can keep you from the Bible and the Bible can keep you from sin.

The wages of sin is death — thank God I quit before pay day.
REAMER LOOMIS

Sin, a moment of gratification; an eternity of remorse.

The best way to show that a stick is crooked is not to argue about it or to spend time denouncing it, but to lay a straight stick alongside it.
D. L. MOODY

Sin is the greatest of all detectives; be sure it will find you out.

The only people on the face of the earth for whom Christ can do anything are sinners.

Whether a man is an up-and-out or down-and-out sinner it is only when he recognizes that he is "out" that he is able to get "in."

The trouble with a little sin is that it won't stay little.

The biggest trouble with sin is the I in the middle of it.
ELD

Christ hates sin but loves the sinner.

The easiest thing to confess is a neighbor's sin.

Sin is a clenched fist and its object is the face of God.

When sin pays, the corn is not enjoyed for long.

Sin has a medium of exchange that trades in sorrows, disillusionment and death.

A preacher recently announced there were 726 sins. He is now being beseiged by requests for the list by people who think they are missing something.

He that hath slight thoughts of sin never had great thoughts of God.
OWEN

The Seven Modern Sins

Politics without principles.
Pleasures without conscience.
Wealth without work.
Knowledge without character.
Industry without morality.
Science without humanity.
Worship without sacrifice.
CANON FREDERIC DONALDSON

Sincere, Sincerity

Earnestness is the solemn realization of the soberness of your errand.

Earnestness is the salt of eloquence.
VICTOR HUGO

———◆———

Be sincere — you cannot sell anything you don't believe in.

———◆———

"Now we come to sincerity," declared the how-to-win friends expert. "Always be sincere, whether you mean it or not."

———◆———

Sing, Singing

They who wish to sing always find a song.

———◆———

You don't have to know how to sing, it's feeling as though you want to that makes the day successful.

———◆———

A former choir member was asked when he had stopped singing in the choir, and he gave an honest answer — "Since that Sunday I was absent, and everyone thought the organ had been tuned!"

———◆———

"What new thing did you learn in Sunday school today?" her mother asked Susan.
"For one thing," the little girl said, "we learned a song about carrots. It goes like this, 'He carrots for you, He carrots . . .'"

———◆———

When the teacher asked the children what song they wanted to sing one little boy said, "The Laundry Song."
"Tell us how it goes," the teacher said, not recognizing she had taught such a song.
"You know," the boy said. "Bringing in the sheets, bringing in the sheets; We shall come rejoicing, bringing in the sheets."

———◆———

A little girl kept singing seemingly strange words to the old familiar song, "Jesus died for all the children." Upon listening closely her mother heard these words: "Jesus diapered all the children."

The child came home happy from Sunday school and said, "Mommy, we learned the bear song today."
"Sing it to me, dear," said mother.
And so the child sang, "Jesus eyed the cross-eyed bear. . . ."

———◆———

Sleep, Sleepy, Sleepyhead

He that rises late must trot all day.
BENJAMIN FRANKLIN

———◆———

Early to bed, early to rise makes a man baggy under the eyes.

———◆———

Laugh and the world laughs with you, snore and you sleep alone.

———◆———

Some people count sheep and some people talk to the Shepherd!

———◆———

Oversleeping keeps a lot of dreams from coming true. CHARLEY GRANT

———◆———

"I tried counting sheep, as you advised me," a clothing manufacturer told his partner, "but I couldn't get to sleep. I counted thousands of sheep. Then, before I realized what I was doing I sheared them, combed the wool, spun it into cloth and made the cloth into suits. But I lost twenty dollars on each suit — and for the rest of the night I lay awake worrying."

———◆———

Kind Sleep

How good the pillow feels at night to him
Who kept a silent tongue when evil thought
Was on his lips! The heart fills to the brim
With satisfaction that his soul has bought.
How restless he may lie upon his bed
Who carried some choice gossip to a friend,
Which may have been much better left unsaid.
Quick spoken words are often hard to mend!

Kind sleep oft gently soothes the weary brow
Of him whose soul has found a battle won,
While wakefulness will very often plow
A deeper furrow, at some evil done.
The man who wears a bridle on his tongue
May surely keep the heart forever young. CHRISTINE GRANT CURLESS

Sorrow

Remorse is the echo of a lost virtue.
BULWER-LYTTON

Only the soul that knows the mighty grief can know the mighty rapture. Sorrows come to stretch out spaces in the heart of joy. EDWIN MARKHAM

It sweetens every sorrow to know what can come of it.

The true way to mourn the dead is to take care of the living who belong to them. EDMUND BURKE

The young man who has not wept is a savage, and the old man who will not laugh is a fool. GEORGE SANTAYANA

God washes the eyes by tears until they can behold the invisible land where tears shall come no more.

Soul, Soul Winning

Christ's last act was winning a soul.
His last command was to win a soul.
His last prayer was forgiveness to a soul.

A man cannot touch his neighbor's heart with anything less than his own.

Personal Work

All can do it.
It can be done anywhere.
It can be done any time.
It reaches all classes.
It hits the mark.
It provides large results.
R. A. TORREY

If we work upon marble,
It will perish;
If we work upon brass,
Time will efface it;
If we rear temples,
They will crumble into dust;
But, if we work upon immortal souls,
If we imbue them with principles,
With the just fear of God
And the love of fellow man,
We engrave on those tablets
Something which will brighten all eternity. DANIEL WEBSTER

We are not supposed to spend time making fishing tackle but to tackle fish.

He was an old man, tottering to the grave. After a class session in Ohio where he was visiting, he arose and said:
"I am an old man, but the greatest work I have ever done was to teach a Sunday school class. I arrived in an Ohio town a total stranger. The first Sunday morning I went to Sunday school and asked for a class but they didn't have one to give me.
"'If you want a class,' said the pastor, 'go out and get one.'
"I went and found four boys playing marbles in the street. I asked them to be my Sunday school class and they consented. I had the greatest time of my life with them. I stayed with them and they stayed with me. They write me every year on my birthday."
Who were they?
The old man went on to tell his story. "A few years have passed but here are three of those marble-playing boys:
"One is Charles Conway, a missionary to India. One became secretary to the President of the United States and one became President of the United States — Warren G. Harding."
That old man's name is lost. Who he was, the teacher of that Ohio class where the story was told, did not know, but the results of his teaching are unforgettable. *The Sunday School*

If we would win some we must be winsome.

———◆———

The seventy who went out did not hire a hall to preach Christ, they used their soles to go after souls.

———◆———

A Sunday School Teacher's Prayer

Several souls
Will come to me today
To hear of Thee —
What I am,
What I say,
Will lead them to Thee,
Or drive them away —
Stand by, Lord, I pray.

———◆———

If You Will

If God can make an ugly seed,
  With a bit of earth and air,
And dew and rain, sunshine and
  shade —
A flower so wondrous fair;
What can He make of a soul like you,
  With the Bible and faith and prayer,
And the Holy Spirit, if you do His will
And trust His love and care!

A. D. BURKETT

———◆———

A pastor was passing a large department store and followed a sudden impression to speak to the proprietor.

He said, "I've talked carpets and beds but never my business with you. Will you give me a few minutes?"

Being led to the private office, the pastor took out his Testament and directed his attention to passage after passage, and urged him to become a Christian. Finally the tears began to roll down the man's cheeks.

"I'm seventy years old, I was born in this city and more than a hundred ministers and five hundred officers of the various churches have known me in a business way. You are the only man who has ever talked to me about my soul."   Service

———◆———

Speak, Speakers, Speeches

I was cut out to be a speaker all right, but I got sewed up all wrong.

Three essentials for a good speaker to remember:
1. Stand up.
2. Speak up.
3. Shut up.

———◆———

If the speaker cannot strike oil in the first twenty minutes there is no need to keep boring.

———◆———

Joe: "They really enjoyed my speech. After I finished they kept yelling, 'Fine! Fine!' "

Moe: "If you'd talked another ten minutes they'd have been yelling imprisonment!"   National Motorist

———◆———

On his return home from a meeting, the fond wife asked her husband, "How was your talk tonight?"

"Which one," he asked, "the one I was going to give, the one I did give, or the one I delivered so brilliantly to myself on the way home in the car?"

Watchman Examiner

———◆———

Charles Lamb was giving a talk at a mixed gathering and someone in the crowd hissed. A stunned silence followed. Finally Lamb calmly said, "There are only three things that hiss — a goose, a snake and a fool. Come forth and be identified."

———◆———

Toastmaster to guest speaker: "Shall we let the folks enjoy themselves a little longer, or do you think you'd better begin your speech now?"

———◆———

Toastmaster: "I cannot do justice to the speaker in the way of an introduction so I'll just let you listen to him and draw your own conclusions."

———◆———

Speaker's prayer: "Lord, fill my mouth with proper stuff, and nudge me when I've said enough."

———◆———

Speaker's lament: "I feel like an Egyptian mummy — pressed for time."

———◆———

Toastmaster: One who uses a few appropriated words.   ANONYMOUS

SPEAK

Chairman, introducing speaker: "There are two types of speakers — one needs no introduction; the other deserves none."

Many good speakers have a head of steam and a fine train of thought but no terminal facilities.

A man isn't a finished speaker until he sits down.

Every speaker should remember to
Be good.
Be brief.
Be seated.

A man walked out of a hall where a speaker was addressing a meeting. Someone in the corridor asked if the speaker had finished his speech. "Yes," was the reply, "but he hasn't stopped talking."

A fashionable speech: long enough to cover the subject and short enough to be interesting.

After the banquet speaker sat down from delivering a lengthy dissertation, profuse with unfamiliar words on the value of education, the toastmaster arose and commented, "Now we are all confused on a higher level."

Commented one after-dinner speaker: "The trouble with us speakers is that after we eat the blood rushes from the head to the stomach and leaves us light-headed."

A new minister was asked to speak at a civic banquet and was quite nervous about it. When he arose to speak he said, "Before I came there were two who knew what I was going to say, the Lord and I. Now only the Lord knows."

Speech making, like a Texas long-horned steer, has a point here and there and a lot of bull in between.

It's all right to have a train of thought as long as you have a terminal in mind.

If a thing goes without saying, let it go.

A speaker ought to be the first person to know when he's through.

A distraught speaker who had been left only a very few moments following lengthy preliminaries arose and said, "I have a very good address. It is at 123 Main Street. I am going there now, gentlemen. Good-by." And with that, he left.

Someone has said that the writer of Psalm Ninety-one must have been speaking at a luncheon club when he wrote about "The Destruction that wasteth at noon day." Perhaps he referred to banquets when he spoke of "The Pestilence that walketh in darkness."

CHARLES F. BANNING in Church Management

A long-winded speaker was continuing to deliver his dry and lengthy address. He was running long over time. The master of ceremonies tried to get him to stop, but couldn't attract his attention. Finally, in desperation, he picked up the gavel, aimed and fired, but missed the speaker and hit a man in the first row. The man slumped down, then groaned, "Hit me again, I can still hear him."

In discussing dangerous weapons, one over-clubbed and over-banqueted gentleman said, "In my opinion, the most dangerous weapon is the jawbone of an ass."

A colonel was speaking at a dinner given in his honor before embarking for Africa.
"I thank you," he concluded, "for your kind wishes regarding my welfare, and I want you to know that when I am far away, surrounded by ugly, grinning savages, I shall always think of you."

229

SPEAK

A speaker was telling his audience why he always used notes. A lady in the back remarked to a friend, "If he can't remember what he's saying, how does he expect us to?"

———♦———

A speaker was encouraging contributions to a worthy community fund. "All who will give $5.00 stand up," he said. But aside, to the orchestra leader he whispered, "Play the 'Star Spangled Banner.'"

———♦———

What grandpa used to say about getting water is true of speakers: "When you're through pumping, bud, let go the handle."

———♦———

Five crows were sitting on a pump handle. The farmer's wife opened the door and threw out some prunes.

One crow flew off the handle and ate some prunes. Soon he died. That left four crows. A second flew down and ate some prunes and soon he died. Three crows were left. After a time a third crow flew down and ate some prunes. Yes, he rolled over and died, too. That left only two crows. Finally a fourth crow was tempted by the prunes and he flew down and ate some. Of course he didn't live long. One crow remained. For a time he debated about the prunes and decided to try them. Well, it wasn't long until he was in crow heaven.

The moral of the story? Don't fly off the handle when you are full of prunes.

———♦———

An old man found his way to the speaker after the meeting and said, "It was a good talk, son, but you talked too long."

The man continued complimenting the speaker, then said, "And you talked too fast." He paused and added, "You didn't say anything either."

The speaker was at a loss for words but a friend tried to console him and said, "Don't worry, my friend, that poor old fellow isn't quite all there and he only repeats what he hears."

Some speakers talk so long they need a calendar instead of a clock to keep track of time.   ELD

———♦———

Better to be quiet and be thought a fool than to speak and remove all doubt.

———♦———

Most of us know how to say nothing; few of us know when.

———♦———

You earn the right to speak by listening.

———♦———

Learn to speak deliberately, so that the hearer will remember what he should never forget.

———♦———

The most important thing is not being prepared with a message, but for a message.   MILLIE STAMM

———♦———

"Mrs. Jones was outspoken at the knitting circle today, John."

"I can't believe it. Who outspoke her?"

———♦———

The Duke of Windsor tells about his first attempts at public speaking after he became the Prince of Wales:

"The more appearances I had to make, the more I came to respect the really first-class speech as one of the highest human accomplishments. No one I knew seemed to possess that rare and envied gift of speaking well in so high a degree as Mr. Winston Churchill, who was a sympathetic witness of some of my earliest attempts. 'If you have an important point to make,' he advised, 'don't try to be subtle and clever about it. Use the pile driver. Hit the point once, and then come back and hit it again, and then hit it the third time, a tremendous whack!'"

———♦———

If you think twice before you speak, you'll speak the better for it.

———♦———

I do not agree with a word you say, but I will defend to the death your right to say it.   VOLTAIRE

Love simple speech as much as you hate shallow thinking.

———◆———

Be careful to say nothing to embarrass new scholars or hurt the feelings of old ones.

———◆———

A young preacher was candidating in a rural area and was being entertained at the home of one of the faithful, godly women of the church. When Sunday evening supper was served the young preacher refused, saying: "I always speak better if I don't eat supper."

After the service was over, on the way home the anxious young man asked his hostess what she thought of his preaching.

"Young man," she said, "you might as well have 'et!'"

———◆———

Don't say things. What you are stands over you the while, and thunders so that I cannot hear what you say to the contrary.

EMERSON

———◆———

Kind words don't wear out the tongue.

Danish Proverb

———◆———

Orville Wright, guest at a dinner, was reproached by a friend for not taking up the challenge of some that it was Professor Langley, and not the Wright brothers, who flew first.

"Your trouble," said the friend, "is that you're too taciturn. You don't assert yourself enough. You should press-agentize more. Talk man, talk!"

"My friend," replied Mr. Wright, "the best talker and the worst flier among the birds is the parrot!"

———◆———

Speech belongs half to the speaker, half to the listener.

MONTAIGNE

———◆———

Spirit, Spiritual

There are two world powers, the sword and the spirit, but the spirit has always vanquished the sword.

NAPOLEON

Let the Spirit in, in order that you may be emptied.

D. L. MOODY

———◆———

Empty yourself for the Spirit to come in.

A. J. GORDON

———◆———

In newspaper English, Galatians 5: 22, 23 would read something like this: "The fruit of the Spirit is an affectionate, lovable, disposition, a radiant spirit and a cheerful temper, a tranquil mind and a quiet manner, a forbearing patience, in provoking circumstances and with trying people, a sympathetic insight and tactful helpfulness, generous judgment and a big-souled charity, loyalty and reliableness under all circumstances, humility that forgets self in the joy of others, in all things self-mastered and self-controlled, which is the final mark of perfecting."

SAMUEL CHADWICK

———◆———

The Spirit of God can dwell with many people when the rest of us cannot.

———◆———

To solve one's spiritual problems one must remain spiritually solvent.

———◆———

Great men are they who see that spiritual force is stronger than any material force; that thoughts rule the world.

EMERSON

———◆———

God develops spiritual power in our lives through pressure of hard places.

———◆———

If nine-tenths of you were as weak physically as you are spiritually, you couldn't walk.

BILLY SUNDAY

———◆———

State, Statesmanship

True statesmanship is the art of changing a nation from what it is into what it ought to be.

W. R. ALGER

———◆———

Statesmanship and diplomacy have failed and the only remedy is Jesus Christ — it is either Christ or chaos.

DAVID LLOYD GEORGE

Statistics

Startling Statistics

Of every 100 church members in an average church:
5 cannot be found
20 never pray
25 never read the Bible
30 never attend worship service
40 never give to the church budget
50 never go to Sunday school
60 never go to church at night
65 are not in worship on a given Sunday
75 never give to missions
75 never do any church work
85 do not have family worship of any kind
90 never go to prayer services
95 do not tithe
95 never win another person to Christ

————◆————

The following notice appeared in a hotel room:

"This hotel is fully equipped with automatic sprinklers. Statistics show that loss of life has never occurred in a sprinklered building. In case of fire, you may get wet, but not burned."

After reading the notice a witty guest composed the following prayer to fit the circumstances:

Now I lay me down to sleep,
Statistics guard my slumber deep;
If I should die I'm not concerned,
I may get wet, but I won't get burned. *Church Management*

————◆————

Americans own:
71 per cent of the world's automobiles;
80 per cent of the hospital beds;
82 per cent of the bathtubs;
52 per cent of the high school enrollment;
48 per cent of the radio, telephone and telegraph facilities;
60 per cent of the life insurance policies;
34 per cent of the meat;
approximately 33⅓ per cent of the railroads.

You work, if an average worker:
4½ minutes to buy a pound of sugar, 9 minutes in England, 141½ in Russia;
32¼ minutes to buy a pound of butter, 33½ in England, 544 in Russia;
9½ minutes to buy a quart of milk, 29 in England, 59½ in Russia;
7 hours, 10 minutes to buy a pair of women's shoes, 15 hours in England, 98 in Russia.

You can earn $20 in real wages in:
8 hours in the United States, 19 hours in England, 81 in Russia.

You have:
140 doctors per 1,000,000 population, 114 in England, 103 in New Zealand, 75 in France, 4 in China.

You have:
6 per cent of the world's land and 7 per cent of the population, but you have created 45 per cent of the world's wealth. *The Weekly Messenger*

————◆————

Statistics can be used to support anything — especially statisticians.

————◆————

Stomach

A Boy's Remarks to His Stomach
(The Morning After)

What's the matter with you — ain't I always been your friend?
Ain't I been a pardner to you? All my pennies don't I spend
In getting nice things for you? Don't I give you lots of cake?
Say, stummick, what's the matter, that you had to go and ache?
Why, I loaded you with good things yesterday — I gave you more
Potatoes, squash and turkey than you'd ever had before.
I gave you nuts and candy, pumpkin pies and chocolate cake.
And last night when I got to bed you had to go and ache!

Say, what's the matter with you? Ain't
you satisfied at all?
I gave you all you wanted; you was
hard just like a ball;
And you couldn't hold another bit of
puddin', yet last night
You ached most awful, stummick; that
ain't treatin' me just right!
I've been a friend to you, I have; why
ain't you a friend of mine?
They gave me castor oil last night be-
cause you made me whine.
I'm awful sick this mornin' and I'm
feelin' mighty blue,
Because you don't appreciate the things
I do for you. *Hubbard's Silent Salesman*

———◆———

Story, Storytelling

Too many people want to tell a story
instead of having a story to tell.

———◆———

A story with a hidden lesson is like
an operation under an anesthetic — the
work is being done while the patient
is unconscious of what is really happening.

———◆———

Storytelling

See it —
  Feel it —
    Shorten it —
      Expand it —
        Master it —
          Repeat it.

———◆———

Strong, Strength

Be Strong

Be strong!
We are not here to play, to dream, to
drift;
We have had work to do, and loads to
lift;
Shun not the struggle — face it; 'tis
God's gift.

Be strong!
Say not, "The days are evil. Who's to
blame?"
And fold the hands and acquiesce —
oh, shame!
Stand up, speak out, and bravely, in
God's name.

Be strong!
It matters not how deep entrenched
the wrong,
How hard the battle goes, the day how
long;
Faint not — fight on! Tomorrow comes
the song. MALTBIE DAVENPORT BABCOCK

———◆———

There are two ways of exerting one's
strength; one is pushing down, the
other is pulling up. BOOKER T. WASHINGTON

———◆———

Nothing makes one feel so strong as
a call for help. GEORGE MACDONALD

———◆———

Who is strong? He that can conquer
his bad habits. BENJAMIN FRANKLIN

———◆———

Study

The more we study the more we discover our ignorance.

———◆———

Apply thyself wholly to the Scriptures and the Scriptures wholly to
thyself.

———◆———

By studying diligently from eighteen to eighty a person can learn about
half as much as he thought he knew
at eighteen.

———◆———

It is the glory of God to conceal a
thing but the honor of kings is to search
out a matter. Proverbs 25:2

———◆———

Philosophy of college students: "Don't
let your studies interfere with your
education."

———◆———

It is the studying that you do after
your school days that really counts.
Otherwise you know only that which
everyone else knows. HENRY L. DOHERTY

———◆———

Style

Style is a man's own; it is a part of
his nature. BUFFON

———◆———

Success, Successful

Success is a wonderful thing. You
meet such interesting relatives.

233

Teacher: "Be diligent and you will succeed. Remember my telling you of the great difficulty George Washington had to contend with?"

Little Jimmy: "Yes, ma'am, he couldn't tell a lie."

————◆————

The profit of life is life, not money.

CAMPBELL

————◆————

Make chariot wheels out of your difficulties and ride to success.

DR. BOB JONES, SR.

————◆————

What a wonderful world this would be if we all did as well today as we expect to do tomorrow.

————◆————

The secret of success for every man who is, or has ever been successful, lies in the fact that he has formed the habit of doing things that failures don't like to do.

————◆————

You cannot attain eminence by climbing on the fence.

————◆————

The man owns the world who remains its master.

————◆————

The fellow who wins success is the one who makes hay from the grass that grows under the other fellow's feet, and who doesn't restrict his efforts to the hours when the sun shines.

Reader's Digest

————◆————

Success lies not in achieving what you aim at but in aiming at what you ought to achieve.

————◆————

Ninety-nine per cent of success is built on former failure.

KETTERING of General Motors

————◆————

The door to the room of success swings on the hinges of opposition.

DR. BOB JONES, SR.

————◆————

Four things a man must learn to do
If he would make his record true:
To think without confusion, clearly,
To love his fellowmen sincerely;
To act from honest motives purely;
To trust in God and heaven securely.

HENRY VAN DYKE

The secret of success is constancy of purpose.

————◆————

To be able to carry money without spending it;
To be able to bear an injustice without retaliating;
To be able to do one's duty even when one is not watched;
To be able to keep at the job until it is finished;
To be able to accept criticism without letting it whip you;
This is success.

AUTHOR UNKNOWN

————◆————

Seven Steps to Success

1. Commencement by starting: "Ye must be born again." John 3:7
2. Confession of Christ by speaking: "Confess with thy mouth." Romans 10:9
3. Concentration by study: "Search the scriptures." John 5:39
4. Communion by seeking: "Pray without ceasing." I Thessalonians 5:17
5. Communication by serving: "Workers together with him." II Corinthians 6:1
6. Contribution by supplying: "Lay by him in store, as God hath prospered him." I Corinthians 16:2
7. Continuance by being satisfied: "Be thou faithful unto death." Revelation 2:10

————◆————

A man can't make a place for himself in the sun if he keeps taking refuge under the family tree.

————◆————

The successful man lengthens his stride when he discovers the signpost has deceived him; the failure looks for a place to sit down.

JOHN RUSKIN

————◆————

The man of the hour spent many days and nights getting there.

————◆————

Success is your birthright.

GREENVILLE KLEISER

————◆————

Most of us get what we deserve, but only the successful will admit it.

ANONYMOUS

We rise by the things we put under our feet.

———◆———

Every man owes it to himself to be a success. He also owes it to the collector of internal revenue.
Presbyterian Life

———◆———

One of the worst tragedies that can befall a man is to have ulcers and still not be a success.

———◆———

Behind every successful man there's a woman — constantly telling him he's not so hot.

———◆———

Behind every successful man can usually be found three people: his wife, and Mr. and Mrs. Jones.
National Motorist

———◆———

Success is not measured by the heights one attains, but by the obstacles one overcomes in their attainment.
BOOKER T. WASHINGTON

———◆———

Fortune smiles upon the person who can laugh at himself.   BRENDAN FRANCIS

———◆———

Achieving success is more a matter of waking up than climbing up.

———◆———

God doesn't call us to be successful. He calls us to be faithful.

———◆———

For success, try aspiration, inspiration and perspiration.

———◆———

No rule of success will work if you don't.

———◆———

To get to the top, get to the bottom of things.

———◆———

Man can climb to the highest summits, but he cannot dwell there long.
GEORGE BERNARD SHAW

———◆———

Successful is the man who goes straight forward — with an aim on only what is right.

———◆———

Some men think they have made a success of life when all they have made is money.

Success consists of getting up just one more time than you fell down.

———◆———

You are not obligated to succeed. You are obligated only to do your best.

———◆———

Our aim should be service, not success.

———◆———

Success comes from mastering defeat.

———◆———

Success gives us certain assurance at first but in the end you are never really sure.   FRANCOISE SAGAN

———◆———

How to succeed: Start at the bottom and wake up.

———◆———

The difference between success and failure is decided by little things, when you are least aware of it. MARTIN VANBEE

———◆———

Success is not the reverse of failure; it is the scorn of failure. Always dare to fail; never fail to dare.
STEPHEN S. WISE

———◆———

A Ladder of Success

100%	I did
90%	I will
80%	I can
70%	I think I can
60%	I might
50%	I think I might
40%	What is it?
30%	I wish I could
20%	I don't know how
10%	I can't
0%	I won't

———◆———

A Moravian missionary named George Smith went to Africa. He had been there only a short time and had only one convert, a poor woman, when he was driven from the country. He died shortly after, on his knees, praying for Africa. He was considered a failure.

But a company of men stumbled onto the place where he had prayed and found a copy of the Scriptures he had left. Presently they met the one poor woman who was his convert.

A hundred years later his mission counted more than 13,000 living converts who had sprung from the ministry of George Smith.   A. J. GORDON

In 1923 a group of the world's most successful financiers met at a Chicago hotel. Present were:

The president of the largest independent steel company.

The president of the largest utility company.

The greatest wheat speculator.

The president of the New York Stock Exchange.

A member of the President's cabinet.

The president of the Bank of International Settlements.

The head of the world's greatest monopoly.

Collectively, these tycoons controlled more wealth than there was in the United States Treasury, and for years newspapers and magazines had been printing their success stories and urging the youth of the nation to follow their examples. Twenty-five years later, let's see what happened to them.

The president of the largest independent steel company — Charles Schwab — lived on borrowed money the last five years of his life, and died penniless.

The greatest wheat speculator — Arthur Cutten — died abroad in poverty.

The president of the New York Stock Exchange — Richard Whitney — was recently released from Sing Sing.

The member of the President's Cabinet — Albert Fall — was pardoned from prison so he could die at home.

The president of the Bank of International Settlement — Leon Fraser — committed suicide.

The head of the world's greatest monopoly — Ivar Kreuger — committed suicide.

All of these men had learned how to make money, but not one of them had learned how to live.
United Evangelical Action

Suffer, Suffering

The school of suffering graduates rare scholars.

God will not look you over for medals, degrees or diplomas, but for scars.

Suffering is sin's index finger pointing out something wrong.

To have suffered much is like knowing many languages: It gives the sufferer access to many more people.

Most people are quite happy to suffer in silence, if they are sure everyone knows they're doing it.

Summer

Summer: The season when children slam the doors they left open all winter.

There's nothing wrong with summer that a little less heat, a little more lemonade, a little less humidity, and a little more swimming, a little less work, and a little more homemade ice cream wouldn't correct.   *Presbyterian Life*

Sunday

A world without a Sabbath would be like a summer without flowers.
HENRY WARD BEECHER

The Sabbath is the golden clasp that binds together the volume of the week.
MACAULEY

A man submerged in business all week had better come up for air on Sunday.   J. A. HOLMES

Some people seem to think that Sunday is Funday.

No Sabbath, no worship;
No worship, no religion;
No religion, no morals;
No morals, then — what?
CRAWFORD JOHNSON

The Lord's Day is the shadow of Christ on the hot highway of time.

R. E. SPIER

Recipe for a Useless Sunday

Stay in bed until ten;
Read Sunday papers until one;
Feed your face until three;
Lop around until nine;
Nothing doing; nothing done;
Good Night!

ANONYMOUS

Add It Up!

Every seventh day is a Sunday, therefore:
Every seven years one has lived a full year of Sundays.
A person 21 years old has had 3 years of Sundays for his spiritual improvement,
One of thirty-five has had five years,
One of seventy has had ten.
This is great addition if the Sundays are spent in church.

Sunday School (General)

Speak well of your Sunday school — you are a part of it.

You can have a Sunday school without a church, but you cannot have a church without a Sunday school.

The Sunday school that refuses to go is the goner.

The test of Sunday school courage comes when we are in the minority; the test of tolerance comes when we are in the majority.

Always keep in mind the fact that you run the school for the scholar and hence you must build on his interests and desires.

Someone asked John Wanamaker, "How do you get time to run a Sunday school with four thousand scholars in addition to the business of your stores and your work as Postmaster General?"

Instantly Mr. Wanamaker replied, "Why, the Sunday school is my business! All other things are just things. Forty-five years ago I decided that God's promise was sure, 'Seek ye first the Kingdom of God and His righteousness; and all these things shall be added unto you.'" *Sunday School Journal*

Weak Sunday Schools

A non-missionary Sunday school.
A minister with no program.
A gossiping, fault-finding group.
Pessimistic officials.
A Sunday school run by some one person with a "rule or ruin" disposition.
A Sunday school in which everything is done by the same two or three people.
A Sunday school that pays little, talks a lot, and does nothing worth-while.
A Sunday school that gets in the rut and stays there, afraid to try anything new.
None of the members tithe.
Poor music and no leader.
The Sunday school always started late.
Nothing in a social way for the members.
Strangers are ignored, while friends visit together.
Members are content, have no craving for souls and are spiritually dead.
Dirt and dust everywhere; no paint, poor light, and not much fire.

ANONYMOUS

In solving Sunday school problems, teachers should not substitute prejudices for good judgment.

No Sunday school worker is ever used in a large way who cannot be trusted in a small emergency.

Would You?

Would you go to Sunday school if you had to sit on chairs so high that your feet dangled in mid-air?
Would you go to Sunday school if you had to be in a dingy basement?
Would you go to Sunday school if

the teacher read the lesson to you every Sunday?

Would you go to Sunday school if you didn't like and understand the songs?

Would you go to Sunday school if you thought the teacher considered her work a bore?

Would you go to Sunday school if you were told to keep still every time you talked?

No, you wouldn't. But this is just what the children in so many schools endure every week.

MARY ELIZABETH BREWBAKER

Seven Reasons for Going to Sunday School

1. *The best book is studied* and taught, and I want to know it and follow it in my everyday life.

2. *The best day is utilized* and observed, and I wish to keep holy the holy day.

3. *The best people are assembled* and enlisted, and I desire the blessing of their fellowship and friendship.

4. *The best institution is awake* and at work for the Master, and I ought to invest myself where I will do my utmost for Christ and the Church.

5. *The best work is being done,* and I must not fail to do my part for the enlightenment, evangelization and upbuilding of my fellowmen.

6. *The best development is assured* and attained, and I yearn to grow mentally, morally and spiritually.

7. *The best equipment is supplied,* adopted and inspired, and I want to be thoroughly furnished unto all good works.

Exchange

How to Kill, Embalm and Bury Your Sunday School

1. Don't go.
2. If you do go, be late.
3. If it is too wet, or too dry, or too hot, or too cold to go, publicize the fact.
4. When you go, be sure to find fault.

5. Refuse every invitation to help, then tell how forward and overbearing those are who do help.
6. Never encourage the other officers; criticize them and tell others how you would do the job.
7. Never take part in the service.
8. Point out all the mistakes you can to the workers and teachers and condemn them for making such mistakes.
9. Never put more than three cents in the offering. If you had no pennies with you last Sunday, don't give twice as much this Sunday.
10. Believe everything you hear about the Sunday school without any investigation.
11. Wear a sour face to show your disapproval of everything that's going on.
12. Stalk out of church as soon as Sunday school is over. Don't speak to anyone. *Our Sunday School Counsellor*

Purpose of the Sunday School Class

To bring in the unreached.
To win them for Christ and the Church.
To train for effective Christian service.
To support the program of the Church.

The Sunday School Bees

Have you ever heard of the
  Sunday school bees
Which buzz in your ears short
  phrases like these?

O girls and boys, just hear what
  we hum:
On Sunday morning, to Sunday
  school come.

Be regular; every week in your place
Be cheerful, keeping a smile on your
  face;
Be punctual, every Sunday on time,
In your seat when the calling bell
  ceases to chime.
Be glad, lifting up your voices in song,
That the chorus of praise may be full
  and strong.

Be reverent, quietly bowing in prayer;
To those who are speaking, listen with
care.
Then everyone who your happy school
sees,
Will praise your swarm of Sunday
school bees.　　　MARY STARCK KERR

Ten Beatitudes for Sunday School Leaders

BLESSED is the leader who has not sought the high places, but who has been drafted into service because of his ability and willingness to serve.

BLESSED is the leader who knows where he is going, why he is going and how to get there.

BLESSED is the leader who knows no discouragement, who presents no alibi.

BLESSED is the leader who knows how to lead without being dictatorial; true leaders are humble.

BLESSED is the leader who seeks the best for those he serves.

BLESSED is the leader who leads for the good of the most concerned, and not for the personal gratification of his own ideas.

BLESSED is the leader who develops leaders while leading.

BLESSED is the leader who marches with the group, interprets correctly the signs on the pathway that leads to success.

BLESSED is the leader who has his head in the clouds but his feet on the ground.

BLESSED is the leader who considers leadership an opportunity for service.　　　S. S. Memo

"Say, Dad, did you go to Sunday school when you were a boy?"

"Yes, Son, regularly."

"Well, then, I don't guess it will do me any good either."　　　Together

Sunday School Training Pays

Max Jukes lived in the state of New York. He did not believe in Christian training. He married a girl of like character. From this union they have 1,026 descendants. Three hundred of them died prematurely. One hundred were sent to the penitentiary for an average of thirteen years each. One hundred and ninety were public prostitutes. There were one hundred drunkards and the family cost the state $1,200,000. They made no contribution to society.

But . . .

Jonathan Edwards lived in the same state. He believed in Christian training. He married a girl of like character. From this union they have 729 descendants. Out of this family have come three hundred preachers, sixty-five college professors, thirteen university presidents, sixty authors of good books, three United States congressmen and one vice-president of the United States, and except for Aaron Burr, a grandson of Edwards who married a questionable character, the family has not cost the state a single dollar. The difference in the two families: Christian training in youth and heart conversions.　　　A Good News folder

Thirteen Sunday School Beatitudes

BLESSED is the Sunday School that is striving for spirituality, evangelism and growth, in that order.

BLESSED is the Sunday school whose teachers do not rely on word pictures alone but who prepare visual aids.

BLESSED is the Sunday school which has officers who are providing the best possible equipment and materials for its teachers. Good lighting and ventilation, clean classrooms and auditoriums, sand tables, visual

239

aid boards, blackboards, maps and charts are necessary provisions.

Blessed is the Sunday school which operates in an evangelistic spirit.

Blessed is the Sunday school whose teachers and officers pool their ideas through the means of the Workers' Conference.

Blessed is the Sunday school whose workers are provided a Workers' Training class so that they may be better qualified to teach.

Blessed is the Sunday school which has good records.

Blessed is the Sunday school which has a definite visitation program.

Blessed is the Sunday school whose superintendent plans and conducts interesting opening services.

Blessed is the Sunday school whose teachers love to teach and are happy in their jobs.

Blessed is the Sunday school whose workers are prompt and faithful to Sunday school and all services of the church.

Blessed is the Sunday school whose workers set a living example of the principles they teach.

Blessed is the Sunday school for verily it will grow and win souls for the kingdom of God.

AUTHOR UNKNOWN

———◆———

A pastor once said, "Do away with the Sunday schools for 15 years and the church will be cut half in its membership."

A. S. LONDON

———◆———

Judge Fawcett, of Brooklyn, New York, said that out of 2,700 boys brought before his court, not one of them was a Sunday school pupil.

A. S. LONDON

Sunday School (Departments)

The following interesting stories are recorded according to ages of children as they are grouped in Sunday school departments. Other stories, ascribed to these ages, are given throughout the book: see the index.

———◆———

Nursery: (Two and Three Years)

After a little two-year-old child returned from her first visit to the nursery department of the Sunday school, her mother asked her what she learned. Without hesitation the tot replied, "Jesus loves me."

———◆———

Dickie often went with his daddy over a toll bridge. "Why do you always shake hands with the man on the bridge?" the tot asked.

Daddy had to explain he was paying toll, not shaking hands.

The Christian Parent

———◆———

Three-year-old to younger child: Come, Freddie, sit on the floor. Your chair fits me better than it fits you.

———◆———

Kindergarten: (Four and Five Years)

The little girl was lying in bed, her teeth chattering and her feet sticking out beneath the covers.

"Gracious!" exclaimed her mother. "Put your feet under the covers."

"Uh-uh," protested the child. "I'm not putting those cold things in bed with me." *The Instructor*

———◆———

For many weeks mother and daddy had cautioned little Al to "Please be still," during the church service — and their training was paying off, at least everyone thought so until one Sunday morning . . . at which time Al was thoroughly frustrated. The minister led the congregation in the singing of a hymn and the little boy turned to his parents and asked, "Why is everyone telling me to 'please be still'?" Quietly his mother comforted the lad by telling him the song they were singing was "Peace Be Still."

When the neighbor lady gave Tommy a piece of cake he politely said, "Thank you."

"Now I like to hear little boys say 'thank you,'" the kind neighbor said.

"If you want to hear me say it again," Tommy said, "you can put some ice cream on the cake."

———◆———

A little girl who went to Sunday school for the first time was telling her mother all about it. "Did you know," she asked mother, "that the teacher is baby Jesus' grandmother?"

"That's interesting," her mother replied. "And how do you know?"

"Because," the little girl said, "she talks about him all the time."

———◆———

Primary: (Six, Seven and Eight Years)

Little Diana had put through a very miserable day. Everything seemed to go wrong. Finally, her mother asked, "Diana, child, what in the world is wrong with you today?"

"Oh, Mummie," she sobbed wretchedly in her mother's arms, "I just can't seem to manage my aggravations."

Christian Home

———◆———

One day the teacher took her pupils on a trip to the Natural History Museum. Telling about it at home, little Jimmy said, "Our teacher took us to a dead circus today." *The Instructor*

———◆———

A first-grader, instructed to color the shirt blue on the sketch of a man, walked to the teacher's desk and asked for a white crayon.

"We're going to make the shirt blue, dear," said the teacher. "We don't need a white crayon."

"Maybe you won't," replied the youngster, "but he will. I wanna put white underwear on him first."

NEA Journal

———◆———

One version of why Adam and Eve were expelled from the Garden of Eden was contributed by a child as follows:

"One day Cain and Abel were talking to their father, Adam, and asked him just why it was they couldn't go back to the beautiful home God had given them. After thinking for a moment Adam said, 'Well boys, it's like this, one day your mother decided to eat us out of house and home.'"

———◆———

A Sunday school teacher had been telling a class of little boys about crowns of glory and heavenly rewards for good people.

"Now tell me," she said at the close of the lesson, "who will get the biggest crown?"

There was silence for a while then Johnnie replied, "Him wots got the biggest head." *Watchman Examiner*

———◆———

The teacher had carefully prepared a flannelgraph visual aid to use with the Bible story of Jesus ascending to heaven. She prepared the figure of Jesus so she could move it up and off the board. Of course the children were delighted with the story and listened breathlessly when the teacher told it.

When Terry got home he was so overwhelmed with the story that he insisted on his mother and dad sitting down and hearing him tell it. He got to the part where the disciples were with Jesus on the hill and he asked, "What do you think happened, then?"

"What?" asked the parents together.

"Well, then God used Scotch tape and string and took Jesus up to heaven!"

———◆———

A junior high school youth told his teacher not to be discouraged and quoted, "Blessed are they that go round in circles for they shall become big wheels."

———◆———

"I'm going to hurry and get married," the thirteen-year-old girl told her favorite teacher.

"Why are you going to do that?" her teacher asked.

"I want to have my children know you and learn from you, too," the girl told her teacher.

241

John came home from Sunday school one day and said:

"I'm afraid of my superintendent."

"Why, Johnny," said Mother, "why are you afraid of the superintendent? He seems like a nice Christian man to me, who loves Jesus."

"Maybe he loves Jesus but he said he would put us in a big furnace if we didn't come to Sunday school regular."

"Are you sure he said that?"

Johnny's mother was disturbed, so she paid a special visit to the superintendent who protested that he was innocent. Finally he said:

"I understand now . . . I did say once, 'Those who don't come regularly, we must finally drop from the register.'"

Christian Parent

————◆————

Junior: (Ages Nine, Ten, Eleven)

Last year, the first in our new school building, I was explaining the word EXIT over each door. One youngster said, "But all the doors say EXIT. Which one am I supposed to enter?"

The Instructor

————◆————

"What is the difference between results and consequences?" a teacher asked her class.

Little Billie answered: "Results are what you expect. Consequences are what you get."

————◆————

Youth: (Junior and Senior High)

When I was sixteen my father was an ignoramus; but when I was twenty-one I was amazed at how much progress the old man had made.

MARK TWAIN

————◆————

Superintendent

A superintendent is a person with *super*vision. How is your vision?

————◆————

The work of the Sunday school superintendent is comparable to an iceberg, that is, only a small percentage of it is visible above the surface. His public appearances represent only a fractional part of his work.

Christian Monitor

Mr. Superintendent

1. Wear a smile that won't rub off on a rainy day.
2. Common interest on week days may mean compound interest on Sunday.
3. The superintendent who never makes a mistake never makes progress.
4. Two things to observe with care: thyself and thy programs to prepare.
5. A book a month will keep the blues and blunders away.
6. A stitch in time may save nine boys and girls to the Sunday school; usually that stitch is a well-chosen teacher.
7. An efficient school is its own best advertisement.
8. No school has a right to sweep in new pupils until it does justice to the ones it already has.
9. Trained teachers mean bigger enrollment and better building.
10. Cease to learn, cease to lead.

Pittsburgh Conference Herald

————◆————

Some superintendents, like boats, toot loudest in the fog.

————◆————

Ten Commandments for Church School Superintendents

I. Thou shalt challenge thy teachers to grow continuously in personality, training and technique.

II. Thou shalt plan and hold regular Workers' Conferences for thy teachers; for verily, it is thy responsibility to keep them challenged, informed, inspired and interested.

III. Thou shalt select teachers wisely; for verily, they are the strength of the church school.

IV. Thou shalt not expect thy pastor to do thy work.

V. Thou shalt be a conscientious student of the Bible, a reader of religious books, a subscriber to thy church publications, and so "study to show thyself approved unto God, a workman that needeth not to be ashamed. . . ."

VI. Thou shalt see that accurate records are kept throughout the church school — for verily, the Lord's business demands utmost efficiency.

VII. Thou shalt encourage thy department superintendents and teachers to follow up absentees, and thy attendance will surely rise.

VIII. Thou shalt keep thy entire church informed of the work of the church school — its program, its plans and its needs.

IX. Thou shalt set an example of promptness for thy teachers on Sunday mornings.

X. Thou shalt challenge thy teachers to prepare their lessons well, to teach the Bible and its message, to continuously stress the meaning of stewardship, and to lead individuals to Christ and Christian maturity.

WILLIAM A. WARD *in The Church School*

———♦———

God never uses a superintendent in a large way who cannot be trusted in a personal emergency.

Sunday School Digest

———♦———

A superintendent is only as busy as the things about which he busies himself.

———♦———

The main idea in Sunday school teaching is to drive home the point, not the audience.

———♦———

Blessed Is the Superintendent

WHO does not think he knows it all, but recognizes there are a few things yet to learn.

WHO does not work by the tick of the clock, but by the beat of the heart.

WHO does not make announcements twice in exactly the same way, but cultivates variety and surprise.

WHO does not surrender to a chance visitor the precious closing moments of the school.

WHO does not ride hobbies, but who seeks to develop the school symmetrically.

WHO does not resign when his toes are stepped on.

WHO never expects to be satisfied with attainment.

WHO does not blame others for going to sleep because he is not awake.

Selected

———♦———

Superlatives

Superlative Words

The greatest word is God.
The deepest word is soul.
The longest word is eternity.
The swiftest word is time.
The nearest word is now.
The darkest word is sin.
The meanest word is hypocrisy.
The broadest word is truth.
The strongest word is right.
The tenderest word is love.
The sweetest word is heaven.
The dearest word is Jesus.

Selected

———♦———

Christ

Absolutely necessary.
Exclusively sufficient.
Instantaneously accessible.
Perennially satisfying.

ANONYMOUS

———♦———

Suspicion

Most of our suspicions of others are aroused by what we know of ourselves.

ANONYMOUS

———♦———

Sympathy

Sympathy is what one woman gives another in exchange for all the details.

———♦———

The people who least live their creeds are not seldom the people who shout loudest about them. The paralysis which affects the arms does not, in these cases, interfere with the tongue. . . .

The homely illustration of the very tender sympathy which gushes inwards, and does nothing to clothe naked backs or fill empty stomachs, perhaps has a sting in it. . . . Sympathy, like every other emotion is meant to influence action. If it does not, what is the use of it? What is the good of getting up fire in the furnace, and making a mighty roaring of steam, if it all escapes at the waste-pipe, and drives no wheels? And what is the good of a "faith" which only rushes out at the escape-pipe of talk? It is "dead in itself."

ALEXANDER MACLAREN

T

Tact

Tact is the knack of making a point without making an enemy.

HOWARD W. NEWTON

Tact is the best oil to use to keep the church machinery running smoothly.

Tact is a remarkable human quality that allows you to know just how far to go too far.

Many people are so tactful that they never make contact with people.

Tact formula: Be brief, politely; be aggressive, smilingly; be emphatic, pleasantly; be positive, diplomatically; be right, graciously.

ANONYMOUS

If you want to be popular, you must endure being taught many things that you already know.

Abraham Lincoln was once asked to give his definition of diplomacy. "Well," he mused, "I guess you might say that it's the knack of letting the other fellow have your way."

Talent

Too many people make cemeteries of their lives by burying their talents.

The real tragedy of life is not in being limited to one talent, but in the failure to use the one talent.

EDGAR W. WORK

Talent is the capacity of doing anything that depends on application and industry; it is voluntary power, while genius is involuntary.

HAZLETT

Nature has concealed at the bottom of our minds talents and abilities of which we are not aware.

LA ROCHEFOUCAULD

Use what talents you have. The woods would be very silent if no birds sang there except those which sang the best.

Sunday School Journal

If every man stuck to his talent, the cows would be well tended.

J. F. DE FLORIAN

Talent that is used is multiplied.

Talk, Talking

Most of us know how to say nothing. Few of us know when.

Have more than thou showest; speak less than thou knowest.

SHAKESPEARE

An ounce of illustration is worth a ton of talk.

What is in the well of your heart will show up in the bucket of your speech.

You are often sorry for saying a harsh word, but you never regret saying a kind one.

BERT ESTABROOK

People who talk much say nothing.

———◆———

Some people talk like the watch which ticks away the minutes but never strikes the hour. SAMUEL JOHNSON

———◆———

"What did you say?"
"Nothing."
"Of course. But how did you express it this time?" *National Motorist*

———◆———

We know a bird by its song and a man by his words.

———◆———

Do more than talk, say something.

———◆———

It takes a baby about two years to learn to talk, and some sixty or seventy years to learn to keep his mouth shut.

———◆———

The only way to save face is to keep the lower end of it closed.

———◆———

You may talk too much on the best of subjects. BENJAMIN FRANKLIN

———◆———

Don't ever prophesy — unless you know. J. R. LOWELL

———◆———

I have never been hurt by anything I didn't say. CALVIN COOLIDGE

———◆———

Great talkers should be cropped for they have no need of ears. BENJAMIN FRANKLIN

———◆———

Some people have a line long enough to hang their clothes on.

———◆———

It's when he doesn't keep his mouth shut that the fish gets caught.

———◆———

Some people don't have much to say. The only trouble is you have to wait so long to find out. *Town Journal*

———◆———

The three main kinds of communication are: telephone, telegraph, tell a woman.

———◆———

Polysyllables are not the signs of profanity. Often they are the cloak of poverty and bought at a jumble sale.

Never talk down to your audience; they are not there!

———◆———

Great talkers, little doers. BENJAMIN FRANKLIN

———◆———

As a man grows older and wiser, he talks less and says more.

———◆———

A lot of people are like buttons — always popping off at the wrong time.

———◆———

To talk and arrive nowhere is the same as climbing a tree to catch a fish.

———◆———

The man who says nothing at the right time is a good talker.

———◆———

The best rule for talking is the one carpenters use: measure twice, saw once.

———◆———

There is nothing wrong with having nothing to say unless you say it aloud.

———◆———

When in doubt about what to say, take a chance on getting by with the truth.

———◆———

Some say very little . . . and yet talk all the time.

———◆———

After all is said and done, more is said than done.

———◆———

To be successful in conversing, try to be more interested than interesting.

———◆———

Don't throw a stone into a well from which you have drunk.

———◆———

It's often the blunt man who makes the most cutting remarks.

———◆———

To know a man . . . listen carefully when he mentions his dislikes.

———◆———

Two good tips: Always say less than you think, and remember that how you say it often means more than what you say.

TALK, TASK — TEACH

As a rule anything that is either shouted or whispered isn't worth listening to. FREDERICK LANGBRIDGE

———♦———

Discretion of speech is more than eloquence; and to speak agreeably to him with whom we deal is more than to speak in good words. BACON

———♦———

The average man thinks about what he has said; the above average about what he is going to say.

———♦———

Task

Rate the task above the prize. CONFUCIUS

———♦———

Every man's task is his life preserver. *The Sunday School*

———♦———

Taxation, Taxes

The income tax division of our government should be mighty glad the taxpayers have what it takes.

———♦———

Whatever the government spends, its citizens must give up through taxation. EARL BUNTING

———♦———

A taxpayer is one who has the government on his payroll.

———♦———

Two things the country can always be sure of: taxes and children.

———♦———

The person who remembers when the only kind of tax was carpet tacks is really an old-timer.

———♦———

Teach, Teacher, Teaching

First I learned to love my teacher, then I learned to love my teacher's Bible, then I learned to love my teacher's Saviour. MARION LAWRENCE

———♦———

He who teaches the Bible is never a scholar; he is always a student.

———♦———

Many teachers who are not having great visions are dreaming troubled dreams.

A teacher should know more than he teaches, and if he knows more than he teaches, he will teach more than he knows.

———♦———

Good teachers are not born so; they are made by conscientious labor.

———♦———

All teachers are born; all teachers are *not* born made.

———♦———

The teacher is the hinge on which the Sunday school swings.

———♦———

The best teacher follows his own instruction.

———♦———

It takes a lot of preparation to teach just a little.

———♦———

Those who teach must be teachable.

———♦———

The things which hurt, instruct. BENJAMIN FRANKLIN

———♦———

If you want to succeed in the trade of teaching, you must be willing to learn the tricks of the trade.

———♦———

A teacher teaches by —
what he says —
what he does —
what he is!

———♦———

If you don't live it, don't teach it.

———♦———

If you feel you have to teach, don't.

———♦———

We can never teach more children than we can reach.

———♦———

Take your decisions to class with you.

———♦———

Much time is spent teaching young people how to make a living, yet few know how to make a life. DR. HENRIETTA C. MEARS

———♦———

If you cannot control self, you cannot control your class.

———♦———

Good teaching requires only one message but many dynamic techniques.

Children learn many things we have not planned to teach, such as coming in late, being absent, coming to class with lesson unprepared. You would be surprised, children learn from all that the Sunday school teacher *is* or *does!*

————◆————

To know how to suggest is the art of teaching. HENRI F. AMIEL

————◆————

To effect an act, apply the fact.

————◆————

If one member of the teaching team fumbles the ball the whole team loses ground.

————◆————

If you listen while you teach you will learn a little.

————◆————

A poor teacher has to teach something; a good teacher has something to teach.

————◆————

Sunday school teachers must be:
Saved —
Sound —
Separated —
Stable in Character —
Spirit-filled —
Sanctified —
Soul-burdened!

————◆————

Those teachers who try to memorize the Sunday school quarterlies are described thus: a Sunday school quarterly wired for sound.

————◆————

The teacher who is attempting to teach without inspiring the pupil with a desire to learn is hammering on cold iron. HORACE MANN

————◆————

Measured by the best standards of pedagogy, Jesus was the greatest teacher in the world:
He knew His subject;
He knew His pupils;
He lived what He taught.
DR. BOB JONES, SR.

————◆————

Good tools do not make an excellent teacher but an excellent teacher makes good use of tools.

There are three powers in the mastery of teaching:
1. The power of understanding.
2. The power of sympathy.
3. The power to communicate.
Education Summary

————◆————

The object of teaching a child is to enable him to get along without his teacher. ELBERT HUBBARD

————◆————

Many teachers are like rocking chairs — always in motion but getting no place.

————◆————

All teachers fall into some mould, but some are a little mouldier than others.

————◆————

You can lead a horse to water but you can't make him think.

————◆————

First student: "Why is teaching like a Model T Ford?"
Second student: "Why?"
First student: "A room full of nuts and a crank up front."

————◆————

A Sunday school teacher is a person whose job is to welcome a lot of live wires and see that they are well-grounded.

————◆————

Some teachers merely help the pupils to transfer information from the teacher's notebook to the pupil's notebook without going through the mind or heart of either.

————◆————

As all roads lead to Rome, all teaching should point to Christ.

————◆————

Teachers must be
Producers
Reproducers
Reproducers of producers
Reproducers of reproducers.
BILL GWINN

————◆————

Kindling of interest is the great function of the teacher. People sometimes say, "I should like to teach if only pupils cared to learn." But then, there would be little need of teaching.
GEORGE HERBERT PALMER

247

Good teachers cost more, but poor teachers cost most.
Delta Kappa Gamma Bulletin

———◆———

The question mark is the teacher's badge. HERMAN H. HORNE

———◆———

The way you teach is important, and what you teach is more important, but how you live is most important.

———◆———

To teach something you don't know is like coming back from somewhere you haven't been. VANCE HAVNER

———◆———

The teacher, under God, is the master key to every Sunday school problem. *Sunday School Journal*

———◆———

A good teacher may overcome poor physical equipment, but the most modern schoolroom and the brightest pupils cannot function without a teacher. No mechanical device can replace the teacher. Thus far no substitute has been found for the impact of mind upon mind, personality upon personality. Teachers may overcome limitations in environment, but they themselves are absolutely essential.

———◆———

The teacher is like the candle, which lights others in consuming itself. *Italian Proverb*

———◆———

The authority of those who teach is often an obstacle to those who wish to learn. CICERO

———◆———

Learn of the skillful: He that teaches himself hath a fool for his master. BENJAMIN FRANKLIN

———◆———

Would you write your name among the stars?
Then write it large upon
The hearts of children.
They will remember!
Have you visions of a nobler, happier world?
Tell the children!
They will build it for you. CLARA TREE MAJOR

Experience may be the best teacher, but even the best teachers need pupils smart enough to learn.

———◆———

A Successful Teacher Needs
The education of a college president
The executive ability of a financier
The humility of a deacon
The adaptation of a chameleon
The hope of an optimist
The courage of a hero
The wisdom of a serpent
The gentleness of a dove
The patience of Job, and
The grace of God. AUTHOR UNKNOWN

———◆———

What the Teacher Builds
Where teachers are building temples
With loving and infinite care,
Planning each arch with patience,
Laying each stone with prayer,
The temple the teacher is building
Will last while the ages roll:
For that beautiful unseen temple
Is a child's immortal soul. *Selected*

———◆———

England's great and good Queen Victoria was being honored by a great celebration while visiting a city. On a corner of one street a large stand was built where a great company of children was assembled to sing for her.

That night after all the excitement was over, the mayor received a telegram. Perhaps he thought it was a compliment about the celebration.

But the message was a simple one straight from a motherly heart: "The Queen wants to know whether all the children got home safely."

Is not this the concern of our Heavenly King regarding the children in our classes? ETHEL M. PATTERSON, *The Sunday School Times*

———◆———

The Average Teacher

Surveys have been taken of a cross section of teachers without regard to size or kind of church. There are said to be 2,741,929 Sunday school teachers in the United States. The results of the survey picture the average teacher:

4 out of 5 teachers are women;

she is about 45 years of age;

she is the mother of two children;

her formal education is high school and one year of college;

she had no teaching experience except that gained in her own church's Sunday school;

she began teaching in her teens;

she spends less than one hour a week preparing her Sunday school lesson for teaching;

lesson preparation is usually done on Saturday night;

she relies entirely upon her Bible and quarterly;

she usually arrives at Sunday school late;

10 Sundays out of the year she is absent;

although many improvements have been made in materials and teaching methods, she makes little use of them;

in spite of the above evidence, the "average teacher" feels that her work as a teacher has been successful;

she attributes her success to her "thorough and regular" preparation. DR. GUY P. LEAVITT

Some Don'ts for Teachers

Don't take a class just to have something to do.

Don't expect to take the wiggles and giggles out of boys and girls with philosophical lectures.

Don't spend your time a-scoldin' and a-fussin' when you ought to be ringing the religious bell in the class.

Don't wait for absentees to die before you visit them.

Don't expect to do your winning of boys and girls on Sundays only.

Don't expect the pastor and the superintendent to carry all the Sunday school load.

Don't forget the place of God . . . prayer . . . souls . . . the church in your work. *Sunday School Digest*

Teachers May Be Classified in Three Divisions

1. Opportunity Makers—such teachers, if the way does not present itself, will make a way to serve and glorify God.

2. Opportunity Takers — These teachers may not go out of their way to find means of serving God and of glorifying Him, but if a way does present itself they will not turn it down.

3. Opportunity Breakers — chance after chance comes to promote the work of the Kingdom — to bear fruit for God—but the opportunity breakers disregard them. They kill their own opportunities.

Are you making and taking every opportunity you can to acknowledge God and to work for Him? *Sunday School Counsellor*

A Teacher Is Succeeding —

If his pupils are becoming his closest friends rather than Sunday morning acquaintances.

If he is able to instill into them high ideals for Christian living.

If the teacher and class mutually desire each other's companionship throughout the week.

If he can look his boys straight in the eye and know there is nothing hidden which would cause him to blush if his boys should know.

If he definitely knows he is giving God first place in his life.

If he sets aside a portion of each day for spiritual growth through communion with God (reading His Word and talking with Him).

If he takes advantage of every opportunity offered for improvement. (Teachers' training books, con-

TEACH

ventions, conferences and teachers' meetings.)

If he is unwilling for a single pupil to remain in his class unsaved.

If he becomes so dissatisfied when his entire class has been won to Christ that he is constrained to go forth and bring in others that he might teach and win them to a "saving knowledge of Jesus Christ." *Moody Church News*

The Unknown Teacher

I sing of the unknown teacher. Great generals win campaigns, but it is the unknown soldier who wins the war. It is the unknown teacher who delivers and guides the young. She lives in obscurity and contends with hardship. For her no trumpets blare, no chariots wait, no golden decorations are decreed. She keeps the watch along the borders of darkness and makes the attack on the trenches of ignorance and folly. She awakens sleeping spirits. She quickens the indolent, the unstable. She communicates her own joy in learning and shares with boys and girls the very best treasures of her mind. She lights many candles which, in later years will shine back to cheer her. This is her reward. HENRY VAN DYKE

The Consecrated Teacher

The glory of life is brightest
  When the glory of life is dim,
And she has most compelled me
  Who most has pointed to Him.
She has held me, stirred me, swayed me,
  I have hung on her every word,
'Till I fain would rise and follow
  Not her, not her, but her Lord.

The manager of a factory inquired whether a new man was progressing with his work. The foreman, who had not gotten along very well with the man in question exclaimed: "Progressing! I have taught him everything I know, and he is still a perfect idiot."

The Teacher's Prayer

Lord, who am I to teach the way
To little children, day by day —
So prone myself to go astray?

I teach them knowledge — but I know
How faint they flicker and how low
The candles of my knowledge glow.

I teach them power to will and do —
But only now to learn anew
My own great weakness through and
  through.

I teach them love for all mankind
And all God's creatures — but I find
My love comes lagging still behind.

Lord, if their guide I still must be,
O let the little children see
The teacher leaning hard on Thee.
EDWARD A. ESTAPHER

A seventh grader's quote from the Declaration of Independence: ". . . Every man should be divided equal." *NEA Journal*

Pupil's Valentine to His Teacher

The bees do the work
  And the bees get the honey,
But we do the work
  And you get the money.

A Teacher's Prayer

Lord, in another hour I stand
Before a wide-eyed, wond'ring band
Of little ones — and mine to teach —
My little school! What longings lie
Behind this moment now so nigh?
Now, ere from out my room I fare,
Hear Thou, O Lord, a teacher's prayer.

Great Teacher — God, oh, make Thou me
The teacher that I long to be —
Who sees beyond the smiles and tears
Of schoolroom life to coming years,
Who touches children now, that then
His impress may be seen on men,
Who labors not for fame, or fee,
Who teaches e'en as unto Thee.

Help me, O Lord, as comes each morn
And with it countless cares are born —
The little things that mean so much
To every childish heart I touch.
Help me to laugh, and tho' tired and
    sad,
Help me to make my children glad,
Help me, O Lord, when things go
    wrong,
To carry on with cheery song.

Keep Thou each day my lips, dear
    Lord,
From sharp or harsh or hasty word,
Would patience yield to weary nerve,
Help me to remember Whom I serve.
I go to face this waiting band —
Oh, make me wise to understand
Each little heart within my care —
Grant Thou, O Lord, a teacher's prayer.

E. MARGARET CLARKSON

———◆———

One small boy in school always came
in dirty clothing, and it was quite no-
ticeable from his odor and appearance
that he had little contact with water.
The teacher sent home a note after a
week or two which read: "Please give
Johnny a bath so he will smell nice
and clean."

Imagine the teacher's surprise when
Johnny appeared as before, bearing a
reply to the note which read, "It ain't
your business to smell him, it's your
business to learn him."

———◆———

A teacher is one who, in his youth,
admired teachers.   H. L. MENCKEN

———◆———

Those who can, do; those who can't,
teach; and those who can't do anything
at all, teach the teachers.

———◆———

The Teacher

A teacher
    is a complex creature.
A saint
    she ain't.
Nor could she be ...
Nor should she be ...
For she's human, just as
    you and me,

But if she would charm her principal
    she should be a gal
With these characteristics:
(Strictly conjecture — not statistics)
The Patience of a bird dog at point ...
The Adaptability of a chameleon on
    a crazy quilt ...
A sense of Humor that enables her
    to laugh even at herself ...
The Self-control of a sphinx ...
A Personality that glows like a candle
    in a dark place ...
The Objectivity of a research
    chemist ...
The Sincerity of a five-year-old telling
    mother he loves her ...
A professional Attitude rivaling that of
    the surgeon ...
The Promptness of a seventeen-year-old
    calling on his first date ...
The Wisdom of the prophets ...
A Love of children that knows only
    infinity as its bounds ...
Superhuman? Impossible? I agree ...
But should you find her
    bind her
And send her to me!

HARRY A. HENDERSHOT, school principal

———◆———

A civics teacher reports on a ninth
grader's written answer in a test. The
student wrote of the "writ of hideous
corpus."   NEA Journal

———◆———

Soliloquy While Waiting for
the Bell to Ring

To teach or not to teach: — that is the
    question;
Whether 'tis nobler in the mind to
    suffer
The slams and curses of outrageous
    youth,
Or to take arms against the group of
    brats,
And by opposing, end them.
To expel — to flunk — and more;
And by a flunk to say we end
The headaches and the thousand nerv-
    ous shocks
That faculty is heir to — 'tis a position
Devoutly to be feared.
To expel — to flunk —

TEACH

To flunk. Perchance he may come
back!
Ay, there's the rub.
For in that ensuing year what troubles
may come
As to rob us of mind and reason
And make us old! There's the thing
That makes teaching of so long life;
For who could bear the scorns and
jeers of youth,
The oppressor's wrong, the professor's
contempt,
The pangs of disturbing conscience, the
law's delay,
The impudence of office force and the
sneers
That patient teachers of the unworthy
take
When they themselves might quietus
make
With a forty-five. Who would these
burdens bear
To grunt and sweat under such a life,
But that the dread of an empty pay
envelope,
A catastrophe in itself, puzzles the will
And makes us rather bear those ills
we have
Than fly to those we know not of?
Thus teaching does make cowards of
us all
And thus the lovely color of one's
complexion
Is sicklied o'er with the pale cast of
fear,
And faculty members of great frame
and stature,
After teaching a month, their sunny
smiles melt away
And they lose the name of humans.

PATRICIA MADDEN

———◆———

The names of Sunday school teachers are written on God's honor roll although few people in this world ever
hear of teachers. Usually the pupils
are the ones who are known and remembered as is D. L. Moody. Who
was the Sunday school teacher who
talked with him about Christ in the
back room of his uncle's shoe store?
It was Edward Kimball.

Advice to Sunday School Teachers

Don't argue.
Don't pull or use force.
Don't scathe or be mean.
Don't be too urgent with strangers.
Don't criticize their church.
Don't speak to the same person each
church service.
Don't return to those who resent
your coming.
Don't go to those with whom you
may have had difficulty.
Don't embarrass a soul by keeping
him standing while others are seated.
Don't put off until tomorrow that
which you should do today.
Don't get discouraged because you
do not see results.

JOHN HALL, Sunday School Digest

———◆———

A pastor was trying to persuade a
woman to teach a class in the church
school. She was well-qualified and had
time for it. She declined, saying over
and over, "I don't want to be tied
down to things." Finally, the pastor
had all of that he could take. He looked
her in the eye and said, in a kindly
voice, "You know we serve a Master
who was willing to be *nailed* down to
things. He was nailed to the Cross."

Christian Herald

———◆———

The Sunday school teacher was reviewing a lesson. "Who led the children of Israel out of Egypt?" There
was no answer, so she pointed to a
boy at the back of the room and repeated her question.
"It wasn't me," he said timidly. "We
just moved here from Tulsa."

Together

———◆———

The Sunday school teacher had been
telling her young class about the Christians who were thrown to the lions.
Then she showed them a picture of
the scene. One little boy looked so
stricken that the teacher asked what
was the matter. He pointed to the picture and wailed, "That poor lion didn't
get any Christian!"

Together

A Teacher's Code

To come before my class each Sunday with a prepared lesson, prepared heart and a prepared attitude.

To make every effort to grow in grace and in the knowledge of the Lord Jesus Christ, and to lead my pupils to do the same.

To contact absentees promptly, personally and persistently.

To set an example in faithfulness, regular attendance, punctuality and stewardship.

To make my instruction personal and practical, adapting the lesson to the individual needs.

To make a conscientious effort to win every pupil to Christ and to help him live a Christian life.

To be loyal to my church and Sunday school.

To cooperate gladly with my pastor, superintendent, and other officers.

To investigate and appropriate every possible means of improving my teaching ministry.

To esteem Christ first, others second and self last.   C. V. EGEMEIER

———◆———

The Sunday school teacher told his eager-beaver class that "we are here to help others."

One bright lad asked, "Well, what are the others here for?"

Presbyterian Life

———◆———

The story is told of a woodsman in northern Minnesota who was tormented day and night by gnats and mosquitoes. When, with patience worn thin, he had almost reached the limit of endurance, he cried out in desperation, "Lord, deliver us from these pesky gnats and mosquitoes; we will take care of the bears, ourselves."

Sunday school teachers, likewise, often find that more grace is needed for the constant, annoying trifles than for the really big problems, but he who intelligently and masterfully overcomes the gnats and mosquitoes will be well prepared to face the big black bear when he stalks out of the woods.

Sunday School Journal

My Sunday School Teacher

A Sunday school teacher
I don't know his name,
A wonderful preacher
Who never found fame.
So faithful, so earnest
When I was a boy —
He stuck to his task
Though I tried to annoy.
He never was missing
In cold or in heat,
A smile his face lighted
The moment we'd meet.
He taught by example
As well as by word,
This splendid old teacher
Who honored his Lord,
He helped my young life
More than ever he knew
Later years I remembered
And tried to be true.
I suppose he has gone now
To join heaven's ranks
May it be my good fortune
Someday to say, thanks.
                    WILL H. HOUGHTON

———◆———

The Teacher's Psalm

The Lord is my helper, I shall not fear in guiding these pupils.

He leadeth me to the heart of the truth, and prepareth the minds of the pupils for the truth.

He giveth me a vision of the immortality of these lives.

He leadeth me to see the sacredness of teaching His Book.

Yea, though I become discouraged and despair at times, yet shall I lift my head, for His promises cannot fail me.

His Word will not return to Him void, and my faith undimmed shall burn through all the coming years.

Thou walketh before me that the seed planted shall grow.

Thou shalt stand by my side on Sunday, and speak through these lips so that these pupils feel the nearness of God.

Thou shalt cause each broken effort to gather sheaves through unnumbered years. My joy is full when I know that every effort in Thy name shall abide forever.

Surely Thy love and watchcare shall be with me every day of my life, and someday I shall live with those who turn many to righteousness for ever and ever.   ROSALEE MILLS APPLEBY

———◆———

A *Teacher's Prayer*

My Lord, I do not ask to stand
As king or prince of high degree;
I only pray that hand in hand
A child and I may come to Thee.

To teach a tender voice to pray,
Two childish eyes Thy face to see,
Two feet to guide in Thy straight way —
This fervently I ask of Thee.

O grant Thy patience to impart
Thy holy law, Thy words of truth;
Give, Lord, Thy grace, that my whole heart
May overflow with love for youth.

As step by step we tread the way,
Trusting, and confident, and free —
A child and I, day by day,
Find sweet companionship with Thee.
The Sunday School World

———◆———

Parable of the Prodigal Teacher

A certain teacher had a Sunday school class; and one of his pupils said to this teacher, "Teacher, give us the portion of thyself and thy care and thy friendship and thy counsel which faileth us."

And he divided unto them his time in that he was present at Sunday school when it did not interfere with any of his own plans; he tried to visit each home, although somehow he never quite succeeded and he just never had time to attend the through-the-week activities of his class. Yet he continually told himself that he was doing everything for his class that could be expected of him.

And not many days after, the teacher gathered all his desires and plans and

ambitions and took his journey into a far country, into a land of selfishness and complacency and good intentions and other things which do not help a Sunday school pupil and there he wasted his precious opportunity of being a chum to his own pupils.

And when he had spent the very best of his time and had gained material things but had failed to meet the needs in the lives of those he taught, there arose a mighty famine in his heart; and he began to be in want of the sense of satisfaction which comes to those in real service for their Lord whom they love wholeheartedly.

But he went and joined himself to one of the organizations of the comunity; and they elected him chairman of one committee after another and kept him busy doing many things. And he would fain have satisfied himself with the husks that other men did eat, but over and over again came the still small Voice saying, "I have called thee to teach and thou art neglecting thy class."

And when he came to himself, he said, "How many teachers of my acquaintance have pupils whom they understand and who understand them — pupils who look to their teachers for advice and counsel — who associate with their pupils and seem perfectly happy in their comradeship and I perish with a sense of guilt because one of my pupils has gone astray. I will arise and go to that one and will say unto him, 'Son, I have sinned against Heaven and against thee; I am no more worthy to be called thy teacher; make me as one of thy friends and let me help thee now in thy need.'"

And he arose and came to his wayward pupil, but while he was yet afar off, his pupil saw him and was moved with amazement. Instead of running and greeting his teacher, however, he drew back and was ill at ease.

And the teacher said unto the pupil, "Son, I have sinned against Heaven and against thee; I am no more worthy to be called thy teacher. Forgive me now and let me be thy friend and help thee in thy need."

But the pupil said, "Not so, I wish it were possible but it is too late now. There was a time when I needed you, when I wanted your friendship and I received counsel; but I got the wrong kind and now, alas, I am wrecked in soul and body and there is nothing you can do for me. It's too late, too late, too late!"

NELS M. ANDERSON *in Christian Action*

———◆———

Traits of an Ideal Teacher

Tact
Earnestness
Adaptability
Character
Humility
Endurance
Reliability

———◆———

Hints for Sunday School Teachers

I will teach you the good and the right way (I Samuel 12:23).

When the hour is come (Luke 22:14), do not fail to be
*I*n your place; thus show a good example to your scholars.
Let some minutes, indeed, *before* school be occupied in
Loving, homely chats with them on their home life.

Take kindly notice of, as well as a keen interest in
Every scholar who enters the class. And, by all means,
Avoid favoritism among them. Be sure and see that each
Child is perfectly still as soon as the superintendent
*H*as rung the bell for the opening of the school.

You should also make sure that every scholar is possessed
Of a Bible and hymnbook and that these have their
Undivided attention while reading and singing are on.

The scholars, too, must be taught always to show the
*H*ighest reverence during prayer time; and see that
Every eye is closed, and every tongue quite still.

Give the children to understand it is imperative that
Order must be maintained in the class, and
On no account give any the full number of marks unless
Deserving of them. "Be just before you're generous."

Always try to arrange the scholars in such a way that
None can escape your attention, the best position, and most
Desirable, being in the form of a circle or square.

The illustrations used (if any) should have point in them,
Helping to lodge the truth. As the feather to the arrow,
Even so, should the illustration be to the subject.

Regular attendance on the teacher's part is of as much
Importance as that of the scholars; and notice should be
Given to the superintendent always in the event of one's
Having to be absent on a Sunday, in order
That a suitable substitute may be provided.

Whatsoever ye do, do it as to the Lord (Col. 3:23).
And let each and every scholar in your class see that
Your one desire is their eternal soul's salvation.

W. T. R.

———◆———

"If" for Sunday School Teachers

If you can trust when all your pupils scorn you
And make a mockery of all you do;
If you can teach the truth, though few will hear you

And all who are concerned are blaming you;
If you can rest in God nor fret nor waver,
But quietly remain within His will;
Or, being snubbed, you do not curry favor;
When you are greatly wronged, keep silence still;

If you can stay calm when giggles interrupt you,
And boredom blunts the point you've toiled to make;
If you can pray when anger might disrupt you,
Meet jealousy and spite for Jesus' sake;
If, often criticized, you do not murmur,
Accept nor give sly flattery to win;
If you can fight for truth, then stand the firmer;
When tempted, do not yield to secret sin;

If you can pray and work for their conversion
And therefore set your heart on things above;
Uphold the cross in spite of their aversion
And to the most contentious child show love;
If you can hear the call to worldly pleasure,
And yet refuse because you want to be with Him;
Let Christ be joy to you beyond all measure,
Nor let your service be a slave to whim;

If you can smile when criticism's rudest, too,
And take the road of tact instead of might;
Yield humbly when your way seems right to you
To do the thing the elders think is right;
To saturate yourself in prayer that always
Your Lord can live His life through you each day;

Then He, not you, will teach that class on Sundays
And, which is more, He'll win them, too — His way.

FLORENCE H. PLUMSTEAD

—————◆—————

And There Were TEN TEACHERS

Then shall the average Sunday school be likened unto ten teachers which took their quarterlies on a Sunday morning and went forth to meet their Sunday school pupils. And five of them were wise, and five were foolish.

They that were foolish took only their quarterlies, and took no center of interest with them. But the wise took many types of interest centers with their quarterlies and Bibles.

While the worship service was conducted, they all sang and listened. And at 10:15 there was the announcement made, "It is time for classes, you are dismissed." Then all those teachers arose, and gathered their pupils together.

And the wise teachers preceded their pupils to the classroom and verily, the boys and girls were quiet before they entered the room. Each pupil went to his own seat which was cleverly marked and behold, Jimmy was not next to Johnny for much had been their fighting in past days.

And as the wise teachers had been studying the lesson for a week, they knew the story of Achan and his sin so they closed their quarterlies.

One wise teacher had for her center of interest some magazine pictures of animals who hide, and behold the boys and girls knew much information they could tell, too. Soon the wise teacher told of Achan hiding his sin.

Verily, another wise teacher brought a newspaper headline that mentioned the Middle East with her and the pupils looked at maps until they found where Achan abode.

And likewise, the third wise teacher made a white sugar cube turn black and many boys and girls said unto her, "Sin is awful."

And before the fourth wise teacher sat many pupils watching her take the chalk and draw exceedingly great things with circles and lines. They knew it was Jericho and the tents and Achan hiding his sin.

And unto her class the fifth wise teacher was showing feltograms of important little things and many were guessing — David's stones, the widow's mite, the boy's basket and then the important little thing in Achan's life.

Behold, the centers of interest were many for one story and all these children said, "We will come back and bring others with us."

And when classes were over the five foolish teachers arose and said unto the wise, "Give us of your ideas; for our attendance has gone down." And the wise answered saying, "It is so, the center of interest is easy to have. Let us sit down and talk with one another and share some different interest centers." And while they were discussing, the Sunday school superintendent and pastor came by and they agreed that there must be the center of interest.

Afterward, not many weeks hence, came the ten teachers saying, "Pastor, pastor, what will we do? Our rooms are small and our attendance is great."

But he answered and said, "Verily I say unto you, as our attendance increases, so will our rooms."

JOYCE DODGE

————◆————

A True Teacher

When the last diploma's granted
  And the race takes its degree,
And the worth-while things are graven
  In the Hall of History;
When the world's great benefactors
  Gather at the Master's call,
There will be one more deserving,
  One more worthy than them all.

When the deeds of men are measured
  And their services are weighed,
And the Master of all masters
  Hands to each his final grade,

Then the warrior, merchant, banker,
  Each shall take his separate place
'Round about a central figure,
  The most honored of our race.

Then the ones who fought for power
  And the ones who strove for pelf
Will discover that the greatest
  Was the one who offered self;
Then the teacher, true and faithful,
  Will be greeted from the Throne
By the greatest of all Teachers;
  "Ye shall reap as ye have sown!"

RILEY SCOTT

————◆————

A Teacher's Meditation

Behold, there was a teacher who had taught for many years.

And, as she sat down to prepare for the new church year she saw in her mind's eye the many experiences of the past.

And in her imagination each experience did appear as a stone, all cut and ready for use.

And that teacher did examine each stone.

Then carefully she placed stone beside stone and stone upon stone until she had builded close around herself a high wall of stone.

Then she said within herself, "This is good, I will stay here safe and secure within this enclosure;

For I have taught these many years; I need not worry any more.

I now know all of the procedures well, and as for the new ways of teaching, I do not approve of those

I will not journey further."

And behold there was a second teacher who also had taught for many years.

And, as she sat down to prepare for the new church year she saw in her mind's eye the many experiences of the past.

And in her imagination each experience did appear as a stone, all cut and ready for use.

And this teacher did examine each stone.

Then carefully she placed stone beside

stone and stone upon stone until she had builded before herself a steep but sturdy flight of stairs.

Then eagerly she climbed the stairs and gazed out across the vistas of the future.

Then she said within herself, "This is good, but I must not stay here. I must keep on building.

For lo, I have taught these many years, but there is still so much to learn.

New and challenging opportunities lie ahead.

I must yet journey farther."

And behold, there was a third teacher; and she was brand new in this field of teaching.

And, as she sat down to prepare for the new church year it was given to her the privilege to see the innermost thoughts of her two fellow workers.

And as she viewed the high forbidding wall, and as she saw the steep but sturdy stairs —

She wrestled within herself saying, "The decision lies before me; the choice is for me to make.

What kind of teacher will I become?"

ELIZABETH SUITER

Feed My Lambs

I meant to study all the week,
  And very carefully prepare;
I meant to kneel — yes, every day,
  And bear each pupil up in prayer.
But I was busy, and I found
  So many things that I must do,
Important things, that could not wait —
  The week was gone before I knew.
I meant to visit several homes,
  And mail some cards to absentees,
To let them know that they were missed,
  For such a word is sure to please
And often brings them quickly back;
  But somehow every day went by
And not a single card I sent.
  And now I ask, "Why didn't I?"
And so this morning when I rose
  I tried to study while I ate;

I briefly read my quarterly
  And hurried out, five minutes late.
I found them singing, and I dropped,
  Breathless, ashamed, into my seat —
For I intended to be there
  That I the earliest child might greet.
Time for the lesson, and a group
  Of eager voices beg their turn
To quote by heart the memory verse
  Which I, alas, forgot to learn!
And so I stumbled through the hour,
  And built with stubble, hay, and wood
Instead of gold and precious stones,
  And silver, as His servants should.
"Go feed my lambs," was His command;
  And shall I hope for them to live
On little morsels such as this,
  When mighty feasts are mine to give?
Forgive me, Lord, that I should treat
  Thy Word in such a shameful way,
And may I never stand again,
  Defeated, as I've done today.

BARBARA COMER RYBERG

The Schoolmaster's Prayer

My God, first of all, let me learn of Thee, and to teach them under my charge as Thou teachest all Thy creatures.

That is, let me lead them to be just because I am just, wise because I am wise, great because I am great.

And, if their keen eyes see that I do fall short in these qualities, let them also perceive that I recognize my shortcomings, that I pretend not to virtues I do not possess and that I honestly strive to improve.

My God, let me study Thy methods and imitate them.

As Thou dost bring all life to its possible perfection by growth, so let me duly value the element of time in my pupils and endeavor rather to guide them to maturity than to force them to perfection.

Teach me Thy noble disdain of force and Thy shrewd indirection; that I may always induce and never resort to the weakness of compulsion.

Let me be a gardener of souls and not a mere merchant of facts.

Imbue me with Thy patience that I may thoroughly learn the supreme art of teaching, which is to wait.

Let me see every pupil of mine as a candle of the Lord and know that my business is to light him.

May I stimulate curiosity and feed it.

Show me how to handle fear and turn it into courage, to make the weak will strong, to cure indifference and transform it into ambition, to shame self-pity into self-confidence.

Give me the love of my pupils, for without love there is no teachableness.

Give me strength and that gentleness which is the garment of strength; and preserve me from weakness, and from petulance and tyranny, which are the signs of weakness.

Give me so mature a mind that I shall have a sense of values, that I may distinguish between essentials and non-essentials, and that I may not magnify little things.

Give me a wise blindness to the faults of exuberance and a wise evaluation of enthusiasm.

Make me sympathetic with youth, that I may not criticize as evil what is nothing but immaturity.

Teach me never to resort to the folly of reward and punishment, but to recognize that every human being wants to learn, wants to be strong and wants to be right; and show me how to uncover and how to develop these wants.

Let me never forget the profits of my calling, and that the greatest wealth one can gain in this world is the property right he clears in souls.

Invest me with the true dignity of my office, that I may always have a proper pride in knowing that mine is the highest of all callings, and that no man's business is nobler than his whose calling it is to guide and mold the unfolding mind.

Keep me humble that I may continue to learn while I teach.

May I strive not so much to be called master, as to be a master, not to show authority so much as to have authority.

And give me that joy in my work, the exaltation in my privilege and that satisfaction in my service that comes from the knowledge that, of all human occupations, that of teaching is most like the business of God Himself.

DR. FRANK CRANE

————◆————

Tears

Nothing dries sooner than a tear.

BENJAMIN FRANKLIN

————◆————

Water works: nothing but tears.

————◆————

Telephone

Did you hear about the preacher who called another preacher on the long distance telephone? It was a parson-to-parson call.

————◆————

Bad is he who breaks your slumber to mutter rudely, "Wrong number!" Worse is he who risks your wrath by phoning when you're in your bath. But worst of all is the pest who hisses in disguised voice, "Bet-you-can't-guess-who-this-is?"

————◆————

Television

Television has undoubtedly improved conversation. There's so much less of it.

————◆————

A poll was taken to find out how many people see television in taverns. The returns were staggering.

————◆————

A TV repairman was trying to locate the trouble in a friend's set. A six-year-old watching the operation said, "If you'd clean out all the old dead cowboys from the bottom of the set it might work again."

Corydon, Indiana, Democrat

259

Nowadays a husband and his wife have to have minds that run in the same channels . . . or else two television sets.

———◆———

The geography teacher asked Bobby a question about the English channel. "I don't know about that one," answered Bobby. "There's no such channel on our television set."

———◆———

First neighbor: "How do you like your new TV set?"
Second neighbor: "Fine, except for the jaberdizing."

———◆———

Temper, Temperamental

Every time you lose your temper you advertise yourself.

———◆———

A man's temper improves the more he doesn't use it.

———◆———

Temperament is temper that is too old to spank.   CHARLOTTE GREENWOOD

———◆———

Temperamental: Easy glum; easy glow.

———◆———

Temperamental: Ninety per cent temper, ten per cent mental.

———◆———

Temperance

We must plant the seed from which will grow the will to abstain!

———◆———

The drinking man commits suicide on the installment plan.

———◆———

We still want to meet the Christian who will tell us that Christ approved of drinking.

———◆———

Intemperance is one of the greatest — if not the greatest — of all evils known to mankind.   ABRAHAM LINCOLN

———◆———

Many a man has dug his grave with his teeth.

———◆———

Alcohol kills the living and preserves the dead.

Temptation

Of all essences, the devil likes acquiescence the best.

———◆———

Every temptation is an opportunity of our getting nearer to God.   J. Q. ADAMS

———◆———

Find out what your temptations are, and you will find out largely what you are yourself.   HENRY WARD BEECHER

———◆———

Why comes temptation but for man
  to meet
And master and make crouch beneath
  his feet,
And so be pedestaled in triumph?   BROWNING

———◆———

One young lady to another: "I can resist everything but temptation."

———◆———

To realize God's presence is the one sovereign remedy against temptation.   FENELON

———◆———

Some temptations come to the industrious, but all temptations attack the idle.   SPURGEON

———◆———

It is one thing to be tempted, another thing to fall.   SHAKESPEARE

———◆———

To pray against temptations, and yet to rush into occasions, is to thrust your fingers into the fire, and then pray they might not be burnt.   SECKER

———◆———

Following the path of least resistance makes both rivers and men crooked.

———◆———

People cannot be judged by what others say about them, but they can be judged by what they say about others.

———◆———

No one can honestly or hopefully be delivered from temptation unless he has himself honestly and firmly determined to do the best he can to keep out of it.   RUSKIN

———◆———

Keeping away from the mire is better than washing it off.

Our greatest temptations come to us when we are off duty. How and where we spend our spare time will react upon our Christian experience.

———◆———

Temptation is the tempter looking through the keyhole into the room where you are living; sin is your drawing back the bolt and making it possible for him to enter.

J. WILBUR CHAPMAN

———◆———

Temptation rarely comes in working hours. It is in their leisure time that men are made or marred. W. T. TAYLOR

———◆———

Some people feel that the only way to handle temptation successfully is to yield to it.

———◆———

Teacher: "How do you resist temptation, Jerry?"

Jerry: "I always have a little talk with the devil. I just say, 'Get thee behind me, Satan, and don't you dare push.'"

———◆———

Bring up a Child

'Twas a dangerous cliff as they freely confessed
Though to walk near its crest was so pleasant
But over its terrible edge there had slipped
A Duke and full many a peasant.

So the people said something would have to be done
But their project did not at all tally
Some said, "Put a fence 'round the edge of the cliff."
Some, "An ambulance down in the valley."

But the cry for an ambulance carried the day,
For it spread to a neighboring city.
A fence may be useful or not it is true
But each heart became brim full of pity.

For those who slipped over the terrible cliff
And the dwellers in highway and alley

Gave pounds or gave pence, not to put up a fence
But an ambulance down in the valley.

"For the cliff is all right if you're careful," they said,
"And if folks ever slip and are dropping
It isn't the slipping that hurts them so much
As the shock down below when they're stopping."

So day after day, as the mishaps occurred
Quick forth would rescuers sally
To pick up the victims
Who fell from the cliff
With an ambulance down in the valley.

Better guard well the young than reclaim them when old,
For the voice of true wisdom is calling
To rescue the fallen is good, but 'tis best
To prevent other people from falling.

Better close up the source of temptation and crime
Than deliver from dungeon and galley
Better build a strong fence 'round the top of the cliff
Than an ambulance down in the valley!

AUTHOR UNKNOWN

———◆———

Three ten-year-old boys were discussing how they could obtain three toys by paying for just one.

"Go in and buy the airplane," one lad suggested to one of the others, "and be sure to get the sales slip. When you bring the package out, take out the toy and give the bag and sales slip to me. I'll go in the store, get a toy and put it in the bag. The clerk won't know the difference because I'll have the toy in the bag and will be able to show the sales slip for it. After I come out I'll give the bag and sales slip to Joe. See? We'll all have a plane — three for the price of one."

"I won't do it," Joe said, remembering the lesson his Sunday school teacher had taught the previous Sunday.

"Why, Joe?" the first lad asked.

"Because," said Joe simply but confidently, "I know Jesus wouldn't like for us to do this. It is wrong."

What happened? The boys did not get the toys.

———✦———

Test, Testing

Testing proves real worth.

———✦———

Thank, Thankful

Giving thanks is a course from which we never graduate.

———✦———

Thanksgiving is good, thanksliving is better.

———✦———

Be careful for nothing;
Be prayerful for everything;
Be thankful for anything.
D. L. MOODY

———✦———

Gratitude is a duty which ought to be paid, but which none have a right to expect.   ROUSSEAU

———✦———

Christian gratitude keeps life from sagging because there is something underneath life.

———✦———

Unfailing gratitude makes a human magnet out of a common personality.

———✦———

A grateful mind is a great mind.

———✦———

He who thanks but with the lips
Thanks but in part;
The full, the true Thanksgiving
Comes from the heart.

———✦———

When I find a great deal of gratitude in a poor man, I take it for granted there would be as much generosity if he were rich.   POPE

———✦———

The debts which gold can't pay
Would stand for aye,
If we should never have Thanksgiving
    Day.   FRED BECK

———✦———

Gratitude is not only the memory, but the homage of the heart — rendered to God for His goodness.   N. P. WILLIS

Say So

Does a neighbor help a little,
    As along the way you go —
Help to make your burden lighter?
    Then why not tell him so!

Does a handclasp seem to lift you
    From the depth of grief and woe,
When an old friend shares your sorrow?
    Then why not tell him so!

Does your Heavenly Father give you
    Many blessings here below?
Then on bended knee before Him
    Frankly, gladly, tell Him so!
                GERALDINE SEARFOSS

———✦———

Gratitude is the memory of the heart.

———✦———

If you have nothing to be thankful for, make up your mind that there is something wrong with you.

———✦———

When the Sunday school teacher asked her class what they were thankful for, one little fellow replied, "My glasses."

He explained, "They keep the boys from fighting me and the girls from kissing me."   *Together*

———✦———

Father asked little Kathy if she didn't want to thank God for sending her such a fine new baby brother. Imagine his surprise when he heard this prayer: "Thank you, dear God, for Jimmy. I'm especially thankful that Jimmy wasn't twins like I heard the doctor say he might be."

———✦———

Think, Thinking, Thought, Thoughtful

There are two kinds of people:
    Those who stop to think and
    Those who stop thinking.

———✦———

It is the amount of thinking done with an ordinary amount of brains that gets an extraordinary amount accomplished, whether it be in religion or elsewhere.   *Carillonic Peals*

It is well to think well and it is divine to act well. HORACE MANN

————◆————

We think we are thinking when in reality we are only rearranging our thinking. C. T. JOHNSON

————◆————

No man has made any gain who only listens to the thing he already believes. The only man who is really thinking is the one who is waking up his mind.
K. V. P. Philosopher

————◆————

An engineer on the Twentieth Century Limited was asked by an interviewer what he thought about as he sat in his cab rushing along at seventy miles an hour.
"I am thinking about a half mile ahead," was the engineer's reply.
Sunday school wrecks as well as train wrecks may be avoided by thinking ahead. When teachers and leaders keep their thoughts speeding far ahead, into the future, they clear the track for continued success. Adapted

————◆————

When everyone thinks alike, few are doing much thinking. Nashua Cavalier

————◆————

There's nothing either good or bad but thinking makes it so. SHAKESPEARE

————◆————

"I think" is the most overworked and exaggerated expression in the English language.

————◆————

As the gardener, by severe pruning, forces the sap of the tree into one or two vigorous limbs, so should you stop off your miscellaneous activity and concentrate your force on one or a few points. EMERSON

————◆————

The brain is as strong as its weakest think.

————◆————

What you think means more than anything else in your life: More than what you earn, more than where you live, more than your social position, and more than what anyone else may think about you. GEORGE MATTHEW ADAMS

Thinking, not growth, makes manhood. Accustom yourself, therefore, to thinking. Set yourself to understand whatever you see or read. To join thinking with reading is one of the first maxims, and one of the easiest operations. ISAAC TAYLOR

————◆————

Why can't somebody give us a list of things that everybody thinks and nobody says, and another list of things that everybody says and nobody thinks?
OLIVER WENDELL HOLMES

————◆————

The Record Book

If all the things you ever said,
Were written in a book:
And all your thoughts were on display,
So all could take a look:
I guess there's not a living soul,
Who wouldn't hang his head:
And feel ashamed before the Lord
And wish that he were dead.

There is a record book I'm told
With every deed and word;
It even keeps the records of
Our thoughts that can't be heard;
The good, the bad and every sin
For nothing has been missed:
It really makes me feel ashamed,
To think what's on my list.

————◆————

We are what we think.

————◆————

Do more than think, *act.*

————◆————

And yet the pages of my past,
Shall never condemn me;
For Jesus nailed them to His cross,
One day at Calvary:
And now I stand in Him complete,
Redeemed from sin and strife.
And with His blood He wrote my name
Down in the book of life.
WALT HUNTLEY

————◆————

Broad-mindedness is the result of flattening high-mindedness out.
GEORGE SANTAYANA

————◆————

Many a man fails because his train of thought is only a local.

THINK

The man who thinks he knows it all has merely stopped thinking.

———◆———

Watch Your Thoughts

Watch your thoughts,
Keep them STRONG;
High resolve
Thinks no wrong.
Watch your thoughts,
Keep them CLEAR;
Perfect love
Casts out fear.
Watch your thoughts,
Keep them RIGHT;
Faith and wisdom
Give you light.
Watch your thoughts,
Keep them TRUE;
Look to God
He'll govern you.

GRENVILLE KLEISER

———◆———

What a person thinks greatly determines what he becomes.

———◆———

One day a young man had an accident: He was struck with a thought.

———◆———

A great many people think they are thinking when they are merely rearranging their prejudices.   WILLIAM JONES

———◆———

It is easy to decide without thinking; it is easy to think and not decide; but it is hard to think fairly and decide courageously.   *Youth's Companion*

———◆———

To him whose elastic and vigorous thought keeps pace with the sun, the day is a perpetual morning.

HENRY D. THOREAU

———◆———

You can drive a child to reading but you can't make him think.

———◆———

You have powers that you never dreamed of. You can do things you never thought you could do. There are no limitations in what you can do except the limitations in your own mind as to what you cannot do. Don't think you cannot. Think you can.

DARWIN P. KINGSLEY

According to the American Medical Association, sitting up in bed increases your energy requirements ten per cent; standing nearly doubles it; chopping wood causes your needs to shoot up nearly eight times. Now here's a blow for you: Heavy thinking requires hardly any energy at all . . . something to think about!

———◆———

Think all you speak but speak not all you think.   PATRICK DELANEY

———◆———

Think! It may be a new experience.

———◆———

Thinking is not knowing.
Portuguese Proverb

———◆———

Most folks have presence of mind. The trouble is absence of thought.

HOWARD W. NEWTON

———◆———

If I can give a man a thought, I've helped him, but if I can make him think, I've done him a service.

ELBERT HUBBARD

———◆———

Forethought spares afterthought.

———◆———

Consideration for the rights of others is the strongest link in the chain of human friendship.

———◆———

Remember a Shut-In

Let's remember a shut-in on this day.
Remember one in some little way:
Send him a card, pay a visit or two;
It will cheer him when he's feeling
    blue.

Take him some books, or send him
    flowers,
It will ease the pain in the lonely hours.
A friendly smile, and a cheery hello
Means more to him than you'll ever
    know.

God will reward you someday I'm sure;
A visit from a friend can be the best
    known cure.
I know we all have a moment to spare
So please, visit a shut-in and show him
    you care.   HELEN SULEY

Associate reverently, and as much as you can, with your own loftiest thoughts.

THOREAU

Time

You have time to kill? How about working it to death?

———♦———

Everything comes to him who waits — except the precious time lost waiting.

PAUL STEINER

Take Time

Take time to work — it is the price of success.
Take time to think — it is the source of power.
Take time to play — it is the secret of perpetual youth.
Take time to read — it is the foundation of wisdom.
Take time to worship — it is the highway to reverence.
Take time to be friendly—it is the road to happiness.
Take time to dream — it is hitching one's wagon to a star.
Take time to love and be loved — it is the privilege of the gods.
Take time to live — it is one secret of success.
Take time for friendship—it is a source of happiness.
Take time to laugh — it helps lift life's load.
Take time to worship — it is the highway of reverence.
Take time to pray — it helps to bring Christ near, and washes the dust of earth from our eyes.
Take time to be holy — for without holiness no man shall see the Lord.
Take time for God — it is life's only lasting investment.

Hawkinsville Dispatch News

———♦———

The Lord wants our precious time, not our spare time.

———♦———

Footprints in the sands of time were not made sitting down.

Americans have more time-saving devices and less time than any other people in the world.

———♦———

Waste of time is the most extravagant and costly of all expenses.

———♦———

Use time for the things that outlast time.

———♦———

He who kills time commits suicide.

FRED BECK

———♦———

You should take time before time takes you.

———♦———

Some people spend their time as recklessly as if it were just so much money.

A. C. LEE

Now

The time is now!
 It is not too soon,
For now it is late
 In the afternoon:
And our day is fading
 Without so seeming,
And into the sunset
 we go dreaming.
Awake, O nation —
 The Christ avow!
For God's salvation
 The time is now!

B. PHILIP MARTIN

———♦———

Time deals gently with those who take it gently.

ANATOLE FRANCE

———♦———

It takes less time to do a thing right than it does to explain why you did it wrong.

H. W. LONGFELLOW

———♦———

The Clock of Life

The clock of life is wound but once
And no man has the power
To tell just when the hand will stop —
At late or early hour.

Now is the only time you own!
Live, love, toil with will;
Place not faith in "tomorrow" for
The clock may then be still.

AUTHOR UNKNOWN

265

TIME

Time once lost is gone forever.

———◆———

One today is worth a dozen tomorrows.

———◆———

Time wasted is existence; used, life.

YOUNG

———◆———

Four things that never return:
> The spoken word,
> The sped arrow,
> The past life,
> The neglected opportunity.

ANONYMOUS

Just a Minute
I have only just a minute
Just sixty seconds in it;
Forced upon me — can't refuse it,
Didn't seek it, didn't choose it.
I must suffer if I lose it,
Give account if I abuse it;
Just a tiny little minute
But eternity is in it.

AUTHOR UNKNOWN

———◆———

Time works wonders. So would most people if they worked twenty-four hours a day as time does.

———◆———

The man who makes the best use of his time has most to spare.

———◆———

If you have time, don't wait for time.

BENJAMIN FRANKLIN

———◆———

Perfect Timing

God's help is always sure
His methods seldom guessed;
Delay will make our pleasure pure,
Surprise will give it zest.
His wisdom is sublime,
His heart profoundly kind;
God never is before His time,
And never is behind.

ANONYMOUS

———◆———

Little drops of water
  Little grains of sand,
Make the mighty ocean
  And the pleasant land.
So the little moments,
  Humble though they be,
Make the mighty ages
  Of eternity.

AUTHOR UNKNOWN

One always has time enough if one will apply it.

GOETHE

———◆———

Time is an herb that cures all diseases.

BENJAMIN FRANKLIN

———◆———

A Minute
It's the time it takes to smile, or to give a warm "hello."
It's the time it takes to say, "Well done."
It's the time it takes to sympathize —
Or avoid calling someone what he "should be called."
It's the time it takes to cheer someone or make things better.
How much is a minute worth? It's priceless or worthless—depending on how you use it.

AUTHOR UNKNOWN

———◆———

Time is infinitely long and each day is a vessel into which a great deal may be poured, if one will actually fill it up.

GOETHE

———◆———

He who neglects the present moment throws away all he has.

SCHILLER

———◆———

Better than counting your years is to make your years count.

———◆———

This Age
This is the age
Of the half-read page,
And the quick hash
And the mad dash,
And the bright night
With the nerves tight,
The plane hop
And the brief stop,
The lamp tan
In a short span,
The big shot
And a good spot,
And the brain strain
And the heart pain,
And the cat naps
Till the spring snaps —
And the fun's done
And then comes taps.

VIRGINIA BRASIER

Since you are not sure of a minute throw not away an hour.

BENJAMIN FRANKLIN

———◆———

Secretary's definition of time: The stuff between paydays.

———◆———

One of the illusions of life is that the present hour is not the critical, decisive hour. Write it on your heart that every day is the best day of the year. He only is rich who owns the day, and no one owns the day who allows it to be invaded with worry, fret and anxiety. Finish every day, and be done with it. You have done what you could.

EMERSON

———◆———

Tithe, Tithing

Not only will a man rob God, but he will take an income tax deduction on it.

———◆———

God's Tenth

Nine parts for thee and one for me.
  Nine for earth, and one for heaven;
The nine are thine, and one is mine,
  But, oh, how slowly given!
In gospel land thy life is spanned,
  With all Christ's blessings o'er thee,
While o'er the earth without new birth,
  Lost millions sink before thee.
They sink to hell, while you could tell
  The glorious gospel story;
Far from the gold which thou dost hold,
  My tithe could bring them glory.
Ten parts for thee and none for me;
  All for earth, and none for heaven!
Far from my gold which thou dost hold,
  My tithe thou hast not given.
No souls for thee, no souls for me,
  All for hell, and none for heaven!
For from my gold which thou dost hold,
  My tithe thou hast not given.

Selected

———◆———

Some pay their dues when due;
Some when overdue;
Some never do;
How do you do?

AUTHOR UNKNOWN

John D. Rockefeller is said to have once made the following statement concerning the habit of tithing: "I never would have been able to tithe the first million dollars I ever made if I had not tithed my first salary, which was $1.50 a week."

———◆———

Titles

It is not titles that reflect honor on men, but men on their titles.

MACHIAVELLI

———◆———

Toastmaster

Three reasons for the title, "Toastmaster":
  Always popping up.
  Always getting burned.
  The wrong plug won't work!

———◆———

The master of ceremonies said, "You are very fortunate to have me here. There are many lousy speakers but in me you have a double feature: I'm good and lousy."

———◆———

Three hints on speech-making:
  Be sincere,
  Be brief,
  Be seated.

———◆———

A speaker had informed the toastmaster that his address would be entitled "Shadrach, Meshach and Abednego." In preparing for the banquet, the toastmaster found he had trouble remembering the names and since he did not want to use notes, he was trying to find a way to help him remember these troublesome names. Finally a friend suggested that he write the three names on a slip of paper and pin it inside his coat. Then, when he was about to introduce the speaker he could enthusiastically gesture and open his coat and sneak a quick look at the names. And, that's just what he did — gestured and sneaked a quick look and said, "Our speaker's topic is Hart, Schaffner and Marx."

A machine has been invented that will unwrinkle raisins and blow up foods to as much as thirty times their true size. It must have been invented by the men who introduces public speakers. ZULA B. GREEN *in Capper's Weekly*

———◆———

A toastmaster is one who introduces others with a few appropriated words.

———◆———

Three-B formula for toastmasters:
Be alert.
Be specific.
Be seated.

———◆———

Toastmaster to audience: "I neglected to tell you before our speaker's address that he was not feeling well; I hasten to do so now."

———◆———

Today

Today

Fill it with gladness
With courage, and love, and trust.
Treat it not lightly,
For it is a part of life
That, when spent, can never return.

———◆———

Today is the day in which to express your noblest qualities of mind and heart, to do at least one worthy thing which you have long postponed.
GRENVILLE KLEISER

———◆———

Today is the tomorrow we worried about yesterday.

———◆———

Begin Today

Dream not too much of what you'll do
tomorrow,
How well you'll work another year;
Tomorrow's chance you do not need
to borrow —
Today is here.

Boast not too much of mountains you
will master
The while you linger in the vale below,
To dream is well, but plodding brings
us faster
To where we go.

Talk not too much about some new
endeavor
You mean to make a little later on.
Who idles now will idle on forever
Till life is gone.

Swear not some day to break some
habit's fetter,
When this old year is dead and passed
away;
If you have need of living, wiser, better
Begin today! ANONYMOUS

———◆———

A Bit of Heaven

There's a "little bit of heaven" in each
new passing day,
If you'll take the time to find it and
not hurry on your way.
The smile of a loved one, when you are
feeling blue,
Can banish all your cares away and
make you start anew.

The handclasp of a true friend is worth
far more than gold;
It is a priceless treasure that cannot
be bought or sold.
There's a "little bit of heaven" when
bright sunbeams entwine;
Also in a shaft of moonlight pouring
silver on the vine.

In the laughter of a child you can hear
the angels sing,
And a tiny, chubby hand in yours
makes you richer than a king.
The crimson splash of sunset on a
purple evening sky
Will paint your heart a memory that
cannot, ever, die.

There's a "little bit of heaven" in the
simple things of earth.
If you can only see them, your soul
will find new birth.
Take time to look around you, beneath
God's sky of blue —
And you'll find a "bit of heaven" right
here on earth with you.
LA VERNE P. LARSON

Tombstone

Even a tombstone will say good things about a fellow when he's down.

———◆———

The most upright thing about a dead criminal is his tombstone.

———◆———

The tombstone always sticks up for a man when he's down under.

———◆———

Tomorrow

Every tomorrow has two handles; we can take hold by the handle of anxiety or by the handle of faith.

HENRY WARD BEECHER

———◆———

Sometimes it helps a little, when the skies are overcast,
To remember that tomorrow, this day's troubles will be past;
And tomorrow always brings new strength, new courage too, some way,
For each dawn's a bright beginning, and each day's a brand new day.

AUTHOR UNKNOWN

———◆———

It was Anthony's first ride on a railroad. The train rounded a slight bend and plunged into a tunnel. There were gasps of surprise from the corner where Anthony was sitting. Suddenly the train rushed into broad daylight again, and a small voice was lifted in wonder. "It's tomorrow!" exclaimed the small boy.

———◆———

Yesterday is a cancelled check. Tomorrow is a promissory note. Today is ready cash. Use it wisely.

———◆———

Never put off 'til tomorrow what you can do today.

———◆———

A thing done right means less trouble tomorrow.

———◆———

I do not fear tomorrow, for I remember yesterday and I love today.

WILLIAM ALLEN WHITE

———◆———

Do it tomorrow—you've made enough mistakes today.

Tomorrow

He was going to be all that a mortal should be
Tomorrow.
No one should be kinder or braver than he
Tomorrow.
A friend who was troubled and weary he knew,
Who'd be glad of a lift and who needed it, too;
On him he would call and see what he could do
Tomorrow.

Each morning he stacked up the letters he'd write
Tomorrow
And thought of the folks he would fill with delight
Tomorrow.
It was too bad, indeed, he was busy today,
And hadn't a minute to stop on his way;
More time he would have to give to others, he'd say,
Tomorrow.

The greatest of workers this man would have been
Tomorrow
The world would have known him, had he ever seen
Tomorrow.
But the fact is he died and he faded from view,
And all that he left here when living was through
Was a mountain of things he intended to do
Tomorrow.

EDGAR A. GUEST

———◆———

Tongue

Let not your tongue cut your throat.

———◆———

Confine your tongue lest it confine you.

———◆———

If you keep your shoes tied tight your tongue won't wag.

———◆———

A still tongue makes a wise head.

TONGUE

A sharp tongue is the only edge tool that grows harder with constant use.
WASHINGTON IRVING

———◆———

Kind Sleep

How good the pillow feels at night to
   him
Who kept a silent tongue when evil
   thought
Was on his lips! The heart fills to the
   brim
With satisfaction that his soul has
   bought.
How restless he may lie upon his bed
Who carried some choice gossip to a
   friend,
Which may have been much better left
   unsaid.
Quick spoken words are often hard to
   mend!
Kind sleep oft gently soothes the weary
   brow
Of him whose soul has found a battle
   won
While wakefulness will very often plow
A deeper furrow, at some evil done.
The man who wears a bridle on his
   tongue,
May surely keep the heart forever
   young.
CHRISTINE GRANT CURLESS

———◆———

The Tongue

"The boneless tongue so small and
   weak
Can crush and kill," declared the
   Greek;
"The tongue destroys a greater horde,"
The Turk asserts, "than does the
   sword."

The Persian proverb wisely saith,
"A lengthy tongue — an early death,"
Or sometimes takes this form instead,
"Don't let your tongue cut off your
   head."

"The tongue can speak a word, whose
   speed,"
Says the Chinese, "outstrips the steed,"
While Arab sages this impart:
"The tongue's great storehouse is the
   heart."

From Hebrew with the maxim sprung;
"Though feet may slip, ne'er let the
   tongue,"
The sacred writer crowns the whole;
"Who keeps his tongue, doth keep his
   soul."
Selected

———◆———

It takes a strong mind to hold an unruly tongue.

———◆———

The heart of the fool is in his mouth, but the mouth of the wise man is in his heart.
BENJAMIN FRANKLIN

———◆———

By examining the tongue of a patient physicians find out the diseases of the body, and philosophers the diseases of the mind.
JUSTIN

———◆———

Don't let your tongue cut off your head.
Persian Proverb

———◆———

A bit of love is the only bit that will bridle the tongue.
FRED BECK

———◆———

Usually the first screw that gets loose in a person's head is the one that controls the tongue.

———◆———

Nothing is so opened more by mistake than the mouth.

———◆———

The part of the body some people talk with is generally too big for the part they think with.

———◆———

Man's tongue is soft,
   And bone doth lack;
Yet a stroke therewith
   May break a man's back.
BENJAMIN FRANKLIN

———◆———

The most untameable thing in the world has its den just back of the teeth.

———◆———

Teach your child to hold his tongue, he'll learn fast enough to speak.
BENJAMIN FRANKLIN

———◆———

A slip of the foot you may soon recover, but a slip of the tongue you may never get over.
BENJAMIN FRANKLIN

The Tattler

I met an ardent tattler,
Of prominent renown;
Her form was tall and slender
Her coat was long and brown.
I knew her by her swagger,
When first I saw her walk;
And in my mind I settled it
That she was much to talk.

She had a polished manner,
About her person spread;
And though she was deceitful,
She seemed to be well bred.
She was so very friendly
With those who knew her not;
Unwittingly she trapped them
With gossip and with rot.

She seemed quite bent on mischief,
And labored hard and long
To cover up the works of right,
And drag out what was wrong;
Of tales and scandals on the folks,
She loved much to relate;
When love and peace were given out,
She always came in late.

She whispered on the preacher,
And talked about the folk;
Her fellow members in the church
She loved to slur and joke.
Her neighbors on the right of her
Were filthy, low and base;
And those upon the other side,
She said were in disgrace.

Train, Training

Small boy, in hospital, to visiting parents: "Do they train the trained nurses in cages like they train animals?"

It is noble to train a child in the way he should go. Still better is to walk that way yourself.

Acknowledging an introduction, a lecturer declared that he received his moral training at the knee of a devout mother and across the knee of a determined father. It takes both knees for successful rearing. *Link*

Transform, Transformed

The man who —
Knows that God is the central fact of life,
Feels the daily nearness of God,
Sees the constant evidence of God's love,
Offers himself in gratitude to God,
Is a transformed man!

If you want to set the world right, start with yourself.

If you would reform the world from its errors and vices, begin by enlisting the mothers. CHARLES SIMMONS

Travel

It isn't the travel that broadens one — it's all that rich foreign food.

Flying is against my religion. I'm a devout coward.

Many individuals are going too fast morally, too slow spiritually, too recklessly domestically for their eternal safety. MARK F. SMITH

If you want to travel fast, travel light — take off all your jealousies, prejudices, selfishness and fears. GLENN CLARK

In America there are two classes of travel — first class and with children. ROBERT BENCHLEY

A tourist is a fellow who travels many hundreds of miles in order to get a snapshot of himself standing by his automobile. *National Motorist*

Two vacationing old maids were back from the Holy Land, and their pastor asked them if they had visited Tyre and Sidon.

"Why, no," they answered, looking astonished. "Are they places? Always thought they were man and wife, like Sodom and Gomorrah."

God may not plan for us an easy journey but he plans a safe one.

———◆———

Treasures

Treasures in heaven are laid up only as treasures on earth are laid down.

———◆———

Trouble

When we think about people
  Trouble grows;
When we think about God
  Trouble goes.   AUTHOR UNKNOWN

———◆———

Troubles that you borrow soon become your own.

———◆———

Be careful how you sidestep trouble; you might miss duty.   C. A. LEE

———◆———

The most trouble is produced by those who don't produce anything else.

———◆———

The people we have the most trouble with is ourselves.

———◆———

Trouble may drive you to prayer, but prayer will drive away trouble.

———◆———

When we run from the Lord we run into trouble.

———◆———

They who have nothing to trouble them will be troubled at nothing.
    BENJAMIN FRANKLIN

———◆———

Better never trouble trouble
  Until trouble troubles you;
For you only make your trouble
  Double-trouble when you do;
And the trouble, like a bubble,
  That you're troubling about,
May be nothing but a cipher
  With its rim rubbed out.
    DAVID KEPPEL

———◆———

The shadow of a trouble is mostly blacker than the trouble itself.

———◆———

Borrowing trouble's as easy as pie, but the carrying charges run pretty high.

Troubles, like babies, grow larger by nursing.

———◆———

In the presence of trouble, some people grow wings; others buy crutches.
    HAROLD W. RUOPP

———◆———

The best way to look at trouble is through the wrong end of a telescope.

———◆———

The brook would lose its song if you removed the rocks.   FRED BECK

———◆———

This world would be a better place in which to live if in these troubled times we turned to God and lived by His teachings.   J. EDGAR HOOVER

———◆———

Never attempt to bear more than one kind of trouble at once. Some people bear three kinds: all they had, all they have now, and all they expect to have.
    EDWARD EVERETT HALE

———◆———

If you brood over your troubles, you will have a perfect hatch.   J. HOPKINS

———◆———

If you can laugh at your troubles, you will never run out of something to laugh at.   The Christian Parent

———◆———

Of all our troubles great or small, the greatest are those that don't happen at all.

———◆———

Whatever trouble Adam had,
  No man in days of yore
Could say, when Adam cracked a joke,
  I've heard that one before.
    AUTHOR UNKNOWN

———◆———

Never go out to meet trouble. If you will just sit still, nine times out of ten someone will intercept it before it reaches you.   CALVIN COOLIDGE

———◆———

Trust

Trust

How often we trust each other,
  And only doubt our Lord.
We take the word of mortals,
  And yet distrust His word;

But, oh, what light and glory
Would shine o'er all our days,
If we always would remember
God means just what He says.

A. B. SIMPSON

———◆———

He that sells upon trust loses many
friends, and always wants money.

BENJAMIN FRANKLIN

———◆———

If you worry you do not trust. If you
trust you do not worry.   G. H. LUNN

———◆———

Let me no more my comfort draw
From my frail grasp of Thee;
In this alone rejoice with awe —
Thy mighty grasp of me.

Selected

———◆———

Trust before you try; repent before
you die.

———◆———

Trust in yourself, and you are
doomed to disappointment; trust in
your friends, and they will die and
leave you; trust in money, and you may
have it taken from you; trust in reputation and some slanderous tongue
may blast it; but trust in God, and you
are never to be confounded in time
or eternity.   D. L. MOODY

———◆———

Trust thyself and another shall not
betray thee.   BENJAMIN FRANKLIN

———◆———

The passengers on the train were uneasy as they sped along through the
dark, stormy night. The lightning was
flashing, black clouds were rolling and
the train was traveling fast. The fear
and tension among the passengers was
evident.

One little fellow, however, sitting all
by himself, seemed utterly unaware of
the storm or the speed of the train.
He was amusing himself with a few
toys.

One of the passengers spoke to him.
"Sonny, I see you are alone on the
train. Aren't you afraid to travel alone
on such a stormy night?"

The lad looked up with a smile and
answered, "No ma'am, I ain't afraid.
My daddy's the engineer."

Brethren Quarterly

Fret not — He loves thee.   John 13:1
Faint not—He holds thee. Psalm 139:10
Fear not — He keeps thee. Psalm 121:5

———◆———

I have held many things in my hands,
and I have lost them all; but whatever I have placed in God's hands, that
I still possess.   MARTIN LUTHER

———◆———

He that on earthly things doth trust
Dependeth upon smoke and dust.

———◆———

The family was enjoying a camping
trip and one evening after tucking four-
year-old Bobby in bed, they were sitting about the campfire.

After a time Bobby called out saying, "I'm not afraid, Mommy. I'm not
afraid, Daddy. God is watching over
me."

"You're a big boy," his mother replied. "I know you are not afraid."

But soon again Bobby called out asking his mother to come into the tent.

"I just wanted to tell you why I'm
not afraid," Bobby said. "You see all
those bright stars up in the sky?
They're the reason I'm not afraid. I
know that they must be God's peep-
holes. He can look through them and
watch over me."

———◆———

Truth

Truth is what God says about a
thing.

———◆———

"Ye shall know the truth, and the
truth shall make you free."

JOHN 8:32

———◆———

Who speaks the truth stabs falsehood to the heart.   JAMES RUSSELL LOWELL

———◆———

Know thou the truth thyself, if you
the truth wouldst teach.

———◆———

Five Truths

All Sin.	Romans 3:23
All Loved.	John 3:16, Romans 5:8
All Raised.	John 5:28, 29
All Judged.	Romans 14:10
All Bow.	Philippians 2:10

Beware of a half-truth; you may get hold of the wrong half.

———◆———

There is no fit search after truth which does not, first of all, begin to live the truth it knows.

———◆———

The greatest homage we can pay to truth is to use it.   EMERSON

———◆———

Seven years of silent inquiry are needful for a man to learn the truth, but fourteen in order to learn how to make it known to his fellow men.
                                                    PLATO

———◆———

The sting of a reproach is the truth of it.   BENJAMIN FRANKLIN

———◆———

Naturalness and simple truth will always find their opportunity and pass current in any age. The freedom of speech of a man who acts without any self-interest attracts little suspicion.
                                                    MONTAIGNE

———◆———

Nothing is more harmful to a new truth than an old error.   GOETHE

———◆———

The best method of eradication of error is to publish and practice truth.

———◆———

Truth is like the sun — all that hides it is a passing cloud.

———◆———

Any time you find that truth stands in your way, you may be sure that you are headed in the wrong direction.

———◆———

If the world goes against truth, then Athanasius goes against the world.
                                                    ATHANASIUS

———◆———

The terrible thing about the quest for truth is that you find it.
                                            ROMY DE GOURMONT

———◆———

The man who moves humbly in the direction of truth comes closer to it than the partisan who claims to have the truth assembled within the framework of some streamlined ideology.
                                            OSCAR OSTLUND

———◆———

Old truths are always new to us, if they come with the smell of heaven upon them.   JOHN BUNYAN

Truth not translated into life is dead truth.

———◆———

The greatest and noblest pleasure which men can have in this world is to discover new truths; and the next is to shake off old prejudices.
                                    FREDERICK THE GREAT

———◆———

Truth never fell dead in the streets. It has such affinity for the souls of men that seed, however broadcast, will catch somewhere and produce its fruit.
                                            THEODORE PARKER

———◆———

Truth wears a different face to everybody, and it would be too tedious to wait till all the world were agreed. She is said to lie at the bottom of a well, for the very reason, perhaps, that whoever looks down in search of her sees his own image at the bottom, and is persuaded not only that he has seen the goddess, but that she is far better-looking than he had imagined.
                                    JAMES RUSSELL LOWELL

———◆———

In quarreling the truth is always lost.

———◆———

Everyone wishes to have the truth on his side, but it is not everyone that wishes to be on the side of truth.

———◆———

Error is none the better for being common, nor truth the worse for having lain neglected.   JOHN LOCKE

———◆———

Error addresses the passions and prejudices; truth the conscience and understanding.

———◆———

Truth is the most robust and indestructible and formidable thing in the world.   WOODROW WILSON

———◆———

We must never throw away a bushel of truth because it happens to contain a few grains of chaff.   DEAN STANLEY

———◆———

Nothing ruins the truth like stretching it.

———◆———

Seek not greatness, but seek truth and you will find both.   HORACE MANN

Some people do not know what to do with truth when it is offered to them.   CHARLES LAMB

Truth crushed to earth shall rise again;
The eternal years of God are hers;
But error, wounded, writhes with pain,
And dies among his worshippers.
   WILLIAM CULLEN BRYANT

Father: "I want an explanation and I want the truth."
Son: "Make up your mind, Dad, you can't have both."

There are three sides to every story: your side, my side, the truth.

Teacher: "Johnny, can you tell us what happens if you tell a lie?"
Johnny: "Sometimes I ride for half fare and sometimes I see a ball game for half price."

Try

In trying times, too many people stop trying.

u

Understand, Understanding

Many people are troubled about the Scriptures which are mysterious and hard to understand. I am most troubled about those which I can understand.   MARK TWAIN

It is nothing to worry about if you are misunderstood. But you had better get all steamed up if you don't understand.

The man who understands one woman is qualified to understand well everything.   JOHN BUTLER YEATS

Understanding others changes us.

It is better to understand a little than to misunderstand a lot.   ANATOLE FRANCE

Unhappiness, Unhappy

Unhappiness invents no tools — discontent writes no song.

The discontented man finds no easy chair.   BENJAMIN FRANKLIN

Is there anything men take more pains about than to make themselves unhappy?   BENJAMIN FRANKLIN

How to Be Perfectly Miserable

1. Think about yourself.
2. Talk about yourself.
3. Use "I" as often as possible.
4. Mirror yourself continually in the opinion of others.
5. Listen greedily to what people say about you.
6. Expect to be appreciated.
7. Be suspicious.
8. Be jealous and envious.
9. Be sensitive to slights.
10. Never forgive a criticism.
11. Trust no one but yourself.
12. Insist on consideration and respect.
13. Demand agreement with your own views on everything.
14. Sulk if people are not grateful to you for favors shown them.
15. Never forget a service you may have rendered.
16. Be on the lookout for a good time for yourself.
17. Shirk your duties if you can.
18. Do as little as possible for others.
19. Love yourself supremely.
20. Be selfish.

This recipe is guaranteed to be infallible.   *Gospel Herald*

275

The quickest way to make yourself miserable is to start wondering whether you're as happy as you could be.

———◆———

Unkind, Unkindness

Pray for a poor memory when people seem unkind.

———◆———

Unselfish, Unselfishness

Teaching children ethics and morals presents difficulties. Take the woman who had been lecturing her small son on the benefits of unselfishness. She concluded with: "We are in this world to help others."

After due consideration, he asked her: "Well then, what are the others here for?"

———◆———

Urgency, Urgent

Expedients are for the hour; principles for the ages.   HENRY WARD BEECHER

Never lose your sense of urgency.
II Timothy 4:2, Phillips Translation

———◆———

Use, Useful, Usefulness

Everyone is of some use, even if nothing more than to serve as a horrible example.

———◆———

To be of use in the world is the only way to be happy.

———◆———

Egypt must be out of Moses as well as Moses out of Egypt before God can use him.   WILLIAM POWELL

———◆———

Shamgar had an oxgoad,
David had a sling,
Samson had a jawbone,
Rahab had a string,
Mary had some ointment,
Aaron had a rod,
Dorcas had a needle,
All were used for God.
Harvester Mission

V

Vacations

Vacations for mothers are when boys go to summer camps.

———◆———

A vacation puts you in the pink but leaves you in the red.

———◆———

Vacations are simpler now. A man has a wife to tell him where to go, and a boss to tell him when. All he needs is someone to tell him how.

———◆———

Value

The price is what you pay, the value is what you receive.

———◆———

True values are proved under stress. It is the ability to withstand the shocks and strains and overload that proves character.

Values Compared

Longfellow could take a worthless sheet of paper, write a poem on it and make it worth $6,000—that's genius.

Rockefeller could sign his name to a piece of paper and make it worth a million — that is capital.

Uncle Sam can take silver, stamp an emblem on it, and make it worth a dollar — that's money.

A mechanic can take metal that is worth only $5.00 and make it worth $50.00 — that's skill.

An artist can take a 50 cent piece of canvas, paint a picture on it and make it worth $1,000 — that's art.

But . . . *God* can take a worthless sinful life, wash it in the blood of Christ, put His spirit in it, and make it blessing to humanity — that's salvation.
The Compass

Not long ago the worth of a man was reckoned at $1.50 — based on the value of the chemical content of his body. Now, with atomic power in view, all this is changed.

Some smart fellow has figured out that the atoms in the human body will produce 11,400,000 kilowatts of power per pound. If they could be harnessed, that is. At $570.00 for that amount of power, a man who weighs in at 150 pounds is worth $85,500. All too often these days the boss can't get enough energy out of a man to make him worth a day's wages. *Convoys News Roundup*

Victory

There are no victories without conflicts, no rainbow without a cloud and a storm.

———◆———

The hardest victory is the victory over self. ARISTOTLE

Vigilance

Eternal vigilance is the price of victory. THOMAS JEFFERSON

———◆———

Observe all men, thyself most. BENJAMIN FRANKLIN

Virtue

Virtue is as good as a thousand shields.

———◆———

You may be more happy than princes if you will be more virtuous. BENJAMIN FRANKLIN

———◆———

There was never yet any truly great man that was not at the same time truly virtuous. BENJAMIN FRANKLIN

———◆———

Few men have virtue to withstand the highest bidder. GEORGE WASHINGTON

———◆———

He is ill clothed that is bare of virtue. BENJAMIN FRANKLIN

———◆———

The whole of virtue consists in its practice. CICERO

Virtue and happiness are mother and daughter. BENJAMIN FRANKLIN

———◆———

Sell not virtue to purchase wealth nor liberty to purchase power. BENJAMIN FRANKLIN

Vision

A superintendent is a person with *super* vision. How is your vision?

———◆———

The man who has vision and no task is a dreamer. The man who has a task and no vision is a drudge. The man who has a task and vision is a hero.

If you don't build castles in the air you won't build anything on the ground.

———◆———

Men have sight; women insight. VICTOR HUGO

———◆———

A task without vision is drudgery. A vision without a task is a dream. A task with a vision is victory.

———◆———

"I keep seeing spots in front of my eyes . . . red spots, black spots, all kinds of spots."
"Have you seen an oculist?"
"No, just spots." *Glendale News Press*

———◆———

The sorriest man in town is the one who has caught up with his vision. PAUL ELLIOTT

———◆———

The little present must not be allowed wholly to elbow the great past out of view. ANDREW LANG

———◆———

It is always wise to look ahead, but difficult to look further than you can see. WINSTON CHURCHILL

———◆———

You must scale the mountains if you would view the plain. CHINESE PHILOSOPHER

———◆———

One day Michelangelo saw a block of marble which the owner said was of no value.
"It is valuable to me," said Michelangelo. "There is an angel imprisoned in it and I must set it free."

Visit, Visitation

The church needs a little more foot-shaking as well as some good hand-shaking. DR. HENRIETTA C. MEARS

————♦————

One visit is worth a basket full of letters.

————♦————

The best way to know the home of your pupils is to go there.

————♦————

The young minister said, in welcoming visitors, "We thank God for those who are not regularly with us today."

————♦————

There is no substitute for consecrated shoe leather. GEORGE A. BUTTERICK

————♦————

Rules for Visiting

1. Pray as you go.
2. Look your best, but don't overdress.
3. Introduce yourself, your department, and your church at once.
4. Create a feeling of sincere interest.
5. Win confidence and approval of pupils as well as parents.
6. Stay long enough to accomplish the purpose of your call. But don't stay too long.
7. Be sure the advice you give is good. Take Christian literature with you that will meet their needs.
8. Don't discuss child's problems.
9. Remember you are visiting your pupil.
10. Don't let your first call be the last one.
11. Don't be irregular with your visits. INEZ SPENCE

————♦————

Visit

Christ needs you.
The church needs you.
Your pupils need you.
Your Sunday school department expects it.
Your ministers appreciate it.
You have promised to do it.
So, visit.

The non-church goer cannot be reached by the non-going church.

————♦————

Souls cost soles.

————♦————

Fish and visitors stink after three days. BENJAMIN FRANKLIN

————♦————

Visitation

V - italizes the work of the Sunday school.
I - ncreases the enrollment.
S - ecures home cooperation.
I - nspires regularity and punctuality in attendance.
T - ies the home closer to the church.
A - ids in the solving of problems.
T - ypifies the loving interest of the great Teacher.
I - nsures growth in grace on the part of the one who visits.
O - pens the doors of homes to the Lord Jesus Christ.
N - urtures friendliness and good will. *Baptist Outlook*

————♦————

V - erily, verily
I
S - ay unto thee,
I - f the Sunday school
T - eacher will visit
A - s he should,
T - he wonderful results
I - n his class will
O - vercome the absentee problem
N - ow facing him.

————♦————

To Visit or Not to Visit

(Paraphrase of Hebrews 12:1-17)

Therefore seeing we are compassed about with so great a crowd of unsaved people, let us lay aside all excuses and the hindrances which do so easily betray us, and let us walk with patience from door to door.

Looking unto Jesus, the author of personal evangelism, who for the joy of telling people of salvation, endured the problems, despising the reproach, and is now ready to go along with you.

For consider the salesman that endured such sales resistance against his products, lest ye be wearied and lose your courage.

Ye have not yet persisted unto blisters pushing doorbells.

And ye have forgotten the exhortation which speaketh unto you as Christians. Despise not thou the work of visitation evangelism, nor faint when thou art called upon to do some:

For whom the pastor respects, he calls, and keeps busy every member whom he receiveth.

If ye endure visitation, ye work then as good Christians; for what member is he who is not expected to do visitation.

But if ye be without any responsibility to personal visitation, whereof all needs must be, then are ye poor representatives of the Gospel of Christ and not good church members.

Furthermore, we have secular organizations which make similar demands of us and we respect them. Shall we not much rather be cooperative in this great crusade for souls, and live?

For they make unimportant demands reflecting their own interests, but this for our profit, that we might be participants in spreading the experience of heart holiness.

For no visitation at the moment will seem especially joyous, but rather strenuous: nevertheless, it yieldeth the glorious fruit of precious souls being brought into the Gospel of Jesus Christ.

Wherefore lift up the hands which hang down, and strengthen the feeble knees;

And make straight paths for your feet, lest those which are lazy fail to pound the pavement: rather, let them be revived.

Follow peace with all men and do personal evangelism, without which no church shall experience a real revival:

Looking diligently lest a man shirk responsibility, lest a flimsy excuse spring up to delay you, and thereby many be sidetracked;

Lest there be any fornicator, or profane person, as John Doe, who for a radio or television program, or as a visitor at your home, kept you from personal evangelism.

For you know that afterward, on Sunday, when he would have the church full, there were only a very few present, and he found no way of remedying his slothfulness at that time, though he prayed loudly and with tears in his eyes.

REV. DEWEY M. YALE, *Adapted in Sunday School Journal*

———◆———

V - ital

I - nterest

S - ends us

I - nto

T - he home.

———◆———

The A-B-C's of a Successful Visit

A - cquaint yourself with the family beforehand.

B - e prepared spiritually, mentally, physically.

C - all at the right time.

D - on't intrude if they are busy.

E - nter properly, introduce yourself.

F - ind a point of contact.

G - ive them a chance to talk.

H - ave things ready to talk about.

I - ntroduce them to the Saviour.

J - oin in with their interests.

K - eep from gossiping.

L - ead the conversation to spiritual things.

M - ake use of the Bible.

N - ever argue.

O - perate through the Holy Spirit.

P - ray as you visit.

Q - uiet their fears and misapprehensions.

R - adiate the love of Christ.

S - peak well of your church and pastor.

T - alk enthusiastically of your Sunday school.

U - nderstand and be patient with their needs.

V - ital personal witness to Christ is your best weapon.

W - atch the clock — don't stay too long.

X - pect unpleasant responses sometimes.

Y - ou may be Christ's only witness to them — press for decision.

Z - eal for God will always have a reward.

Wait, Waiting, Waits

He who waits obtains what he wishes.

———◆———

Waiting on God often brings us to our journey's end quicker than our feet.

———◆———

All things come to him who waits. But remember they come much more quickly to him who goes out to see what's the matter.   FRANK PIXLEY

———◆———

Don't wait for something to turn up, get a spade and dig for it.   T. JONES

———◆———

There is no time lost in waiting if you are waiting on the Lord.   *Eternity*

———◆———

Everything comes to him who hustles while he waits.   THOMAS A. EDISON

———◆———

A man would do nothing if he waited until he could do it so well that one could find no fault with what he has done.

———◆———

Walk

Don't let your talk exceed your walk.

———◆———

War

The war that will end war will not be fought with guns.

———◆———

Wars should be operated like street cars — pay as you enter. Then everyone would see what they're getting into, how much it will cost and where it will take them.

A battle is a terrible conjugation of the verb to kill: I kill, thou killest, he kills, we kill, they kill, all kill.   CARLYLE

———◆———

Waste

Willful waste makes woeful want.

———◆———

Wealth

A good wife and health are a man's best wealth.

———◆———

The wealth of a man is the number of things he loves and blesses, which he is loved and blessed by.   THOMAS CARLYLE

———◆———

It is not what you have in your pocket that makes you thankful but what you have in your heart.

———◆———

Wealth is of the heart, not of the hand.   MILTON

———◆———

Wealth: Any income that is at least one hundred dollars more a year than the income of one's wife's sister's husband.   H. L. MENCKEN

———◆———

Wealth is not his that has it, but his that enjoys it.   BENJAMIN FRANKLIN

———◆———

Riches are not an end of life, but an instrument of life.   HENRY WARD BEECHER

———◆———

Jonathan Brown

I will tell you the story of Jonathan Brown

The wealthiest man in Vanastorbiltown.

He had lands, he had houses, and fac-
tories and stocks,
Good gilt-edged investments, as solid
as rocks.
"Everything that I have," he so frequently said,
"Shall belong to the Lord just as soon
as I'm dead."
So he made out his will, with particular care,
A few hundred here, and a few thousand there.

For the little home church in the village
close by
He planned a new building with spire
great and high,
And chimes to be heard for miles upon
miles,
And deep crimson carpet all down its
long aisles.
For his pastor, a new home, with rooms
large and nice;
For the village library, a generous slice.
And then he remembered a college,
Where young folks were taught the
essentials of knowledge.
The promising son of his very best
friend
To prepare for the ministry he planned
to send.
He'd pay for his board and his room
and tuition,
Expecting the lad to fulfill a great
mission.

His pastor, in old shoes, and shabbiest
raiment,
Suggested the Lord might enjoy a
down payment.
And said it weren't smart to do business that way.
"I'd end in the poorhouse for certain,"
he said,
"If I give up my money before I am
dead."
He grumbled because the good
preacher'd been rash,
And sat down again to figure his cash.

Now Satan stood by with a devilish
grin,
Saw all that old Jonathan had to put
in;

"Ahem," said the devil, concealing a
smile,
"I'll see that this old fellow lives a long
while."
So Satan chased off every menacing
germ,
And sprayed with helseptic each
threatening worm,
Until not a disease could get near
Brother Brown,
And his excellent health was the talk
of the town.
He survived epidemics of flu and of
measles,
Of smallpox, diphtheria, Bavarian
teasles;
He escaped the distress of acute 'pendi-
citis,
He couldn't so much as have old tonsil-
litis.
At sixty he still was quite hearty and
hale,
At seventy he hadn't started to fail,
At eighty his step was still youthful and
spry,
At ninety his nieces said, "Why don't
he die?"

But the day after he was a hundred
and two,
And Satan weren't looking, a germ
wriggled through
And laid Brother Jonathan low in his
grave,
And his relatives gathered in solemn
conclave.
Lawyer Jones read the will in a voice
deep and round,
But there wasn't a legatee that could
be found.
The little home church he had loved
in his youth
Had long since closed its doors and
ceased spreading the truth.
His pastor had died poor a long time
before
And the village library existed no more,
The college, they found when they
wrote,
Was long ago sold on account of a
note,
And the boy that he planned to send
off to school

Had grown up in ignorance, almost a
    fool,
And had seven sons, each one worse
    than the rest,
And eleven grandchildren, the whole
    tribe a pest.

So his ungodly relatives each took a
    slice,
And his lawyers forgot and paid them-
    selves twice,
And there wasn't a friend and there
    wasn't a mourner,
Not even the paper boy down at the
    corner.
And Satan still smiled, turned to tasks
    fresh and new,
Muttered, "Brother, let this be a les-
    son to you,"
Wagged his fingers and spat as the
    casket went down.
Thus ended the story of Jonathan
    Brown.   *Herald of Holiness, adapted*

Weather

During last summer's heat-wave, a
church in the Midwest put this on its
bulletin board: "You think it's hot
here?"   *Reville*

Forecast for Mexico: chile today and
hot tamale.

Wedding

A four-year-old lad went to a church
wedding with his parents. He sat quietly, taking in every detail. Presently
there was a hush as the organist began to play and the minister, bridegroom, and four attendants came from
the side room to the altar. As they
filed out, the boy whispered, "Mom,
does she get to take her pick?"
    Together

Weight

I always watch my waistline — I've
got it out in front where I can keep
my eye on it.

She's all right in her way, but she
weighs too much.

A sure cure weight-reducing exercise
is to push yourself away from the table
three times a day.

The best reducing exercise is to move
the head slowly from side to side
when offered a second helping.

In a physiology class the teacher
said, "Joey, can you give a familiar example of the human body as it adapts
itself to changed conditions?"
"Yes, ma'am," answered Joey, "my
aunt gained 50 pounds last year, and
her skin never cracked."

Wicked

To swear is wicked because it is
taking God's name in vain. To murmur
is likewise wicked for it takes God's
promises in vain.

There is no rest for the wicked and
the righteous don't need it.

Wife

Of all home remedies, a good wife
is the best.   ABE MARTIN

When a wife has a good husband it
is easily seen in her face.   GOETHE

Mose: "Who introduced you to your
wife?"
Jose: "We just happened to meet. I
don't blame nobody."

May: "How did you meet your husband?"
June: "At a travel bureau. I was
looking for a vacation and he was the
last resort."

Will, God's Will

To know God's will is man's greatest treasure; to do His will is life's
greatest privilege.

Every hour comes with some little fagot of God's will fastened upon its back.

———◆———

Out of the will of God there is no such thing as success; in the will of God there cannot be any failure.

The Christian Chronicle

———◆———

God will not change your will against your will.

———◆———

God has given us a will with which to choose His will.

———◆———

A will of your own is more likely to help you succeed than the will of a rich relative.

Indianapolis Times

———◆———

Win, Winners, Winning

The cheerful loser is a sort of winner.

WILLIAM HOWARD TAFT

———◆———

A winner never quits and a quitter never wins.

———◆———

If we would win some, we must be winsome.

———◆———

Wisdom

Wisdom is the ability to use knowledge so as to meet successfully the emergencies of life. Men may acquire knowledge, but wisdom is a gift direct from God.

DR. BOB JONES, SR.

———◆———

There is this difference between happiness and wisdom: He that thinks himself the happiest man, really is so; but he that thinks himself the wisest is generally the greatest fool.

COLTON

———◆———

Common sense, in an uncommon degree, is what the world calls wisdom.

COLERIDGE

———◆———

The height of wisdom is to take things as they are, and look upon the rest with confidence.

MONTAIGNE

———◆———

He is truly wise who gains wisdom from another's mistakes.

No one ever asks a wasp to sit down when it comes to see him.

———◆———

Wisdom is the right use of knowledge.

SPURGEON

———◆———

Wisdom is knowing what to do;
Skill is knowing how to do it;
Virtue is doing it.

DAVID STARR JORDAN

———◆———

A wise man will not only bow at the manger but also at the cross.

———◆———

To have a low opinion of our own merits, and to think highly of others, is an evidence of wisdom. All men are frail, but thou shouldst reckon none as frail as thyself.

THOMAS A' KEMPIS

———◆———

The superior man measures his wisdom by watching people who have none.

———◆———

A fool tells what he will do; a boaster what he has done; the wise man does it and says nothing.

———◆———

There are four kinds of people:
Those who know not, and know not that they know not.
These are foolish.
Those who know not, and know they know not.
These are the simple, and should be instructed.
Those who know, and know not that they know.
These are asleep, wake them.
Those who know and know they know.
These are the wise, listen to them.

ARAB PHILOSOPHER

———◆———

A wise man will make more opportunities than he finds.

BACON

———◆———

He's a fool that cannot conceal his wisdom.

BENJAMIN FRANKLIN

———◆———

He who learns the rules of wisdom without conforming to them in his life is like a man who labored in his fields, but did not sow.

SAADI

Culture

My music is the patter
Of happy little feet,
Exploring house and attic
And scampering down the street.

My art is crayon scribbling
On table, door and wall
In classic style and modern —
I treasure one and all.

My literature comprises
The books my children know
And old tales I remember
From childhood long ago.

The kind of culture I acquire
No colleges impart,
Yet wisdom only life can teach
I cherish in my heart.
KATHERINE KELLY WOODLEY

The doorstep to the temple of wisdom is a knowledge of your own ignorance. BENJAMIN FRANKLIN

Wit

Wit is the salt of conversation, not the food. WILLIAM HAZLITT

There's many witty men whose brains can't fill their bellies.
BENJAMIN FRANKLIN

It is said that an Englishman gets three laughs from a joke: the first when it is told, the second when it is explained to him and the third when he catches on!

Half wits talk much but say little.
BENJAMIN FRANKLIN

The person who lacks wit is not necessarily a half wit.

There are no fools so troublesome as those who have wit. BENJAMIN FRANKLIN

Witness, Witnessing

Instead of being question marks for Christ, we need to be exclamation points.

Too many teachers and preachers think that they are called to be lawyers for Christ instead of witnesses for Him. Just testify concerning the things you know about Him!

Some Christians are like arctic rivers — frozen at the mouth.

The true disciple is a witness to the fact that the Lord gives us His presence.

Be not simply a reflector of Christ; be a radiator. *Christian Digest*

Speak Out for Jesus

You talk about your business,
Your bonds and stocks and gold;
And in all worldly matters
You are so brave and bold.
But why are you so silent
About salvation's plan?
Why don't you speak for Jesus,
And speak out like a man?

You talk about the weather,
And the crops of corn and wheat;
You speak of friends and neighbors
That pass along the street;
You call yourself a Christian,
And like the gospel plan —
Then why not speak for Jesus,
And speak out like a man?

Are you ashamed of Jesus
And the story of the cross,
That you lower His pure banner
And let it suffer loss?
Have you forgot His suffering?
Did He die for you in vain?
If not, then live and speak for Jesus,
And speak out like a man.

I'd like to tell the story sweet
Of Jesus, wouldn't you?
To help some other folks to meet
Their Saviour, wouldn't you?
I'd like to travel all the way
To where I'd hear my Jesus say:
"You've helped my work along today."
I'd like that. Wouldn't you?
AUTHOR UNKNOWN

Every time you walk a mile to church and carry a Bible with you, you preach a sermon a mile long.   D. L. MOODY

———◆———

If God could speak through Balaam's ass, He could speak through you.

———◆———

We do not stand in the world bearing witness to Christ, but stand in Christ and bear witness to the world.   GORDON

———◆———

A little girl was playing with some lettered blocks one day. Her mother showed her how to spell the word, "good," and explained how important it was for little girls to be good and do good. After a while, as her mother was working in the kitchen, the little girl ran to her and said, "Come and see the two nice words I made out of the word good." When her mother looked she saw the words, "go" and "do."

———◆———

Woman, Women

A Woman in It

They talk about a woman's sphere
As though it had a limit;
There's not a task to mankind given,
There's not a blessing or a woe,
There's not a whispered "yes" or "no,"
There's not a life, there's not a birth
That has a feather's weight of worth
     Without a woman in it.

———◆———

Women's faults are many,
Men have only two:
Everything they say,
And everything they do.

———◆———

There's only one way to handle a woman. The trouble is nobody knows what it is.   *Glendale News Press*

———◆———

There is in every true woman's heart a spark of heavenly fire, which lies dormant in the broad daylight of prosperity; but which kindles up, and beams and blazes in the dark hour of adversity.   WASHINGTON IRVING

Three women can keep a secret if two of them are dead.

———◆———

A sufficient measure of civilization is the influence of good women.   EMERSON

———◆———

A good woman inspires a man,
A brilliant woman interests him,
A beautiful woman fascinates him—
The sympathetic woman gets him.   HELEN ROWLAND

———◆———

To be happy in this life a woman needs the optimism of a child, the chic of a mannequin, the diplomacy of a prime minister, the nerves of a cold potato, the wisdom of Solomon and the complacency of a prize cat.

———◆———

A perfectly honest woman, a woman who never flatters, who never manages, who never conceals, who never uses her eyes, who never speculates on the effect which she produces — what a monster, I say, would such a female be!   THACKERAY

———◆———

When women live longer than men, it's often between birthdays.

———◆———

You can always tell a woman, but you cannot tell her much.

———◆———

Women have a wonderful instinct about things. They can discover everything except the obvious.   OSCAR WILDE

———◆———

When you find a great man playing a big part on life's stage you'll find in sight, or just around the corner, a great woman. Read history! A man alone is only half a man; it takes the two to make the whole.   ELBERT HUBBARD

———◆———

Nothing shall be impossible to the woman who knows how to cry in the right way, in front of the right man.   WINIFRED V. KNOCKER

———◆———

Woman was made from Adam's side that she might walk beside him, not from his foot that he should step on her.   DR. HAROLD LINDSELL

285

Being a woman is a terribly difficult trade, since it consists principally of dealing with men. JOSEPH CONRAD

———◆———

Intuition is suspicion in skirts.

———◆———

If you want to change a woman's mind, agree with her.

———◆———

Women have:
   A smile for every joy,
   A tear for every sorrow,
   A consolation for every grief,
   An excuse for every fault,
   A prayer for every misfortune,
   Encouragement for every hope.
                              SAINT-FOIX

———◆———

Woman

She's an angel in truth, a demon in fiction,
A woman's the greatest in all contradiction;
She's afraid of a cockroach, she'll scream at a mouse,
But she'll tackle a husband as big as a house.

She'll take him for better, she'll take him for worse,
She'll split his head open and then be his nurse.
And when he is well and can get out of bed,
She'll pick up a teapot and throw at his head.

She's faithful, deceitful, keen-sighted and blind;
She's crafty, she's simple, she's cruel, she's kind.
She'll lift a man up, she'll cast a man down,
She'll take him apart and make him a clown.

You fancy she's this, but you'll find she is that,
For she'll play like a kitten and bite like a cat.
In the morning she will, at evening she won't,
And you're always expecting she does, but she don't! AUTHOR UNKNOWN

Generally when a man climbs to success, a woman is holding the ladder.

———◆———

Women's styles may change, but their designs remain the same. OSCAR WILDE

———◆———

God created women beautiful and foolish: beautiful so that men would love them, foolish so that they would love the men.

———◆———

Woman — A New Chemical Element

Symbol — woe
Atomic — 120 pounds, approximately.
         Occurrence
1. Can be found wherever man exists.
2. Seldom in the free or natural state.
         Physical Properties
1. All sizes and colors.
2. Always appears in disguised conditions.
3. Boils at nothing and may freeze at any point.
4. Melts when properly heated.
5. Very bitter if not used correctly.
         Chemical Properties
1. Extremely active.
2. Great affinity for gold, silver, platinum, precious stones.
3. Able to absorb expensive food at any time.
4. Undissolved in liquids, but activity is greatly increased when saturated with spirit solution.
5. Sometimes yields to pressure.
6. Turns green when placed next to a better specimen.
7. Ages rapidly. The fresh variety has greater attraction.
8. Highly dangerous and explosive in inexperienced hands.

———◆———

Words

Kind words do not cost much. They never blister the tongue or lips. Though they do not cost much, they accomplish much. They make other people good-natured. They also produce their own image in other men's souls, and a beautiful image it is. PASCAL

Words

Words that are softly spoken,
Can build a world of charm.
Words of tender passion,
Can rescue a soul from harm.

Words of wondrous beauty,
Like silver imbedded in gold,
Can lift the brokenhearted
To heavenly joys untold.

Words of love and comfort,
Can calm a stormy sea.
Words of courage and wisdom,
Bring wonderful peace to me.

Words of hope like sunshine
Fill the heart and soul.
Wonderful words — how precious,
Are worth a future of gold.
CLAUDE COX

———◆———

Colors fade, temples crumble, empires fall, but wise words endure.
THORNDIKE

———◆———

Seest thou a man that is hasty in his words?
There is more hope of a fool than of him. SOLOMON

———◆———

One thing you can give and still keep is your word.

———◆———

The knowledge of words is the gate of scholarship. WILSON

———◆———

Words break no bones; hearts though sometimes. ROBERT BROWNING

———◆———

Don't use a gallon of words to express a spoonful of thought.

———◆———

There are two new words that have appeared in recent years that suggest the new tempo in business. The first of these is *pre-search* . . . it means preparing in advance, testing, planning, long before the time of need. The other word is *imagineering*, which is the wedding of imagination and engineering . . . and these two were meant for each other. It means hooking up vision and inspiration with technical knowledge. It pays to think ahead!
Selected

As we must account for every idle word, so we must for every idle silence.
BENJAMIN FRANKLIN

———◆———

Words

Calm words in any stress
Of pride or ire,
Are like slow falling rain
Upon a fire.
LALIA MITCHELL THORNTON

———◆———

Beware of the man who does not translate his words into deeds.
THEODORE ROOSEVELT

———◆———

Words

A careless word may kindle strife.
A cruel word may wreck a life.
A brutal word may smite and kill.
A gracious word may smooth the way.
A joyous word may light the day.
A timely word may lessen stress.
A loving word may heal and bless.
WALTER

———◆———

Words are like leaves, and where they most abound,
Much fruit of sense beneath is rarely found. ALEXANDER POPE

———◆———

Work

If a task is once begun
Never leave it till it's done.
Be the labor great or small,
Do it well or not at all.
ANONYMOUS

———◆———

To work at the things you love, or for those you love, is to turn work into play and duty into privilege.
PARLETTE

———◆———

When we are in the wrong place, the right place is empty.

———◆———

Each morning sees some task begun,
Each evening sees its close;
Something attempted, something done,
Has earned a night's repose.
LONGFELLOW, *The Village Blacksmith*

———◆———

The great thing with work is to be on top of it, not constantly chasing after it. DOROTHY THOMPSON

Do your work and you shall reinforce yourself. EMERSON

———◆———

A willing heart lightens work.

———◆———

Work!
Thank God for the swing of it,
For the clamoring hammering ring of it . . .
Oh, what is so fierce as the flame of it?
And what is so huge as the aim of it?
Thundering on through dearth and doubt
Calling the plan of the Master out.
ANGELA MORGAN, *Work*

———◆———

There aren't any rules for success that work unless you do. ANITA BELMONT

———◆———

An efficiency expert is smart enough to tell you how to run your business and too smart to start one of his own.
The Businessman's Book of Quotations

———◆———

Blessed are they that go 'round and 'round for they shall become big wheels.

———◆———

It is easier to do a job right than to explain why you did it.

———◆———

We are all good manufacturers — either making good or making trouble.

———◆———

No one ever kicks a dead dog.

———◆———

Few things come to him who wishes; all things come to him who works.

———◆———

I will go anywhere provided it is forward. LIVINGSTON

———◆———

Men do less than they ought, unless they do all that they can. CARLYLE

———◆———

The smartest person is not the one who is quickest to see through a thing, but it is the one who is quickest to see a thing through. *Selected*

———◆———

Work as if you were to live 100 years, pray as if you were to die tomorrow. BENJAMIN FRANKLIN

Too frequently we have a Samaria vision but only a Jerusalem zeal.

———◆———

Every man is as lazy as his circumstances permit him to be.

———◆———

Too many churches are full of willing workers: some are willing to work and the rest are willing to let them work.

———◆———

No one knows what he can do until he tries.

———◆———

I'd like to compliment you on your work — when will you start?

———◆———

Employer to new employee: "Young man, we have a record for doing the impossible in this place."
Young man: "Yes sir, I'll remember. I'll be as impossible as I can."

———◆———

You can do anything you ought to do. DR. BOB JONES, SR.

———◆———

It takes vision and courage to create — it takes faith and courage to prove. OWEN D. YOUNG

———◆———

Have plenty of time for work, none to waste.

———◆———

It is no disgrace to fail. It is a disgrace to do less than your best to keep from failing. DR. BOB JONES, SR.

———◆———

The world is blessed most by men who do things, and not by those who merely talk about them. JAMES OLIVER

———◆———

Anyone can do any amount of work as long as it isn't the work he is supposed to be doing. ROBERT BENCHLEY

———◆———

Do More
Do more than exist, live.
Do more than touch, feel.
Do more than look, observe.
Do more than hear, listen.
Do more than listen, understand.
Do more than think, ponder.
Do more than talk, say something.
Baptist Bulletin

Make stepping stones out of your stumbling stones. DR. BOB JONES, SR.

———◆———

No work is too trifling to be well done.

———◆———

There is only one way to improve one's work — love it. PHILLIP BROOKS

———◆———

The following formula is credited to Carnegie as the way to manage any kind of business:
1. Organize — which means to have the right man in the right place.
2. Deputize — which is to give the man full authority to do the job you hired him for.
3. Supervise — which means to keep after the whole gang to see that they do what they are supposed to do. Advertisers' Digest

———◆———

A Christian worker should be like a good watch:
Open face,
Busy hands,
Pure gold,
Well regulated,
Full of good works. Matthew 5:16

———◆———

A servant works; a king speaks.

———◆———

It doesn't make any difference what brand of polish you use; you have to mix elbow grease with it to make it shine the shoes.

———◆———

When you know you are doing a job perfectly, look for ways to improve it, or someone else will. MARTIN VANBEE

———◆———

Work and study as though all depended upon you, but pray and trust as though all depended upon God.

———◆———

Some people are so busy learning the tricks of the trade that they don't learn the trade.

———◆———

People who take pains never to do any more than they get paid for, never get paid for any more than they do. ELBERT HUBBARD

When your work speaks for itself, don't interrupt it. HENRY J. KAISER

———◆———

Keep thy shop, and thy shop will keep thee. BENJAMIN FRANKLIN

———◆———

Only horses work, and they turn their backs on it. ANONYMOUS

———◆———

In the ordinary business of life, industry can do anything which genius can do, and very many things which it cannot. HENRY WARD BEECHER

———◆———

Most footprints on the sands of time were left by work shoes. Town Journal

———◆———

It is better to wear out than to rust out.

———◆———

"I have saved myself a great deal of trouble," a friend once told me, "by always following this precept: When you have anything to do, do it." SIR JOHN LUBBOCK

———◆———

I am not worried about the amount of work I have to do, it's the condition of the shovel that concerns me.

———◆———

Raise your hat to the past and take off your coat to the future.

———◆———

A worker who does only what he has to do, is a slave. One who willingly does more than is required of him, is truly a free man.

———◆———

No one can do his work well who does not think it of importance.

———◆———

The best jobs haven't been started. The best work hasn't been done. BERTON BRALEY

———◆———

Approach the easy as though it were difficult and the difficult as though it were easy; the first, lest overconfidence make you careless, and the second, lest faint-heartedness make you afraid.

———◆———

It isn't the number of hours a man puts in, it's what a man puts in the hours that really counts.

WORK

Don't drift along. Any dead fish can float downstream.

———

A jockey always whispered this to his horse so he would win:
Roses are red, violets are blue,
Horses that lose are made into glue.

———

A man who needed a job saw an ad in the paper for a position open at the zoo. He accepted the job and was to dress up as a monkey and perform in one of the cages. All went well for several days and then, as he was going from limb to limb he fell.
"Help, help," he cried.
"Shut up," said the lion in the next cage, "or we'll both lose our jobs."

———

Don't always fret about your work
And rewards that are small and few,
Remember that the mighty oak
Was once a nut like you.

———

Nothing is really work unless you would rather be doing something else.
SIR JAMES BARRIE

———

There are four kinds of church workers:
Jaw-bone,
Wish-bone,
Back-bone,
Knee-bone.

Work for Christ

1. The *field* is large. Matthew 13:38
2. The *need* is great. John 4:35
3. The *time* is now. Galatians 1:10
4. The *call* is urgent. Matthew 20:6
5. The *work* is varied. I Corinthians 12:12
6. The *partner* is almighty. II Corinthians 6:1
7. The *means* are provided. Luke 19:15

———

I do not work my soul to save —
That my Lord hath done;
But I will work like any slave
For love of God's dear Son.

———

Do not let work divorce itself from imagination.

The things nearest are best . . .
breath in your nostrils,
light in your eyes,
flowers at your feet,
duties at your hand,
the path of right just before you.
Then do not grasp at the stars, but do life's plain, common work as it comes, certain that daily duties and daily bread are the sweetest things of life.
ROBERT LOUIS STEVENSON

———

Workers with Him

Little is much when God is in it;
Man's busiest day's not worth God's minute,
Much is little everywhere,
If God the labor does not share;
So work with God and nothing's lost,
Who works with Him does best and most:
Work on! Work on!
A. A. REES

———

The church needs to be a place full of wide-awake workers and not a dormitory of sleepyheads.

———

John Wesley traveled two hundred and fifty thousand miles on horseback, averaging twenty miles a day for forty years; preached forty thousand sermons; produced four hundred books; knew ten languages. At eighty-three he was annoyed that he could not write more than fifteen hours a day without hurting his eyes, and at eighty-six he was ashamed he could not preach more than twice a day. He complained in his diary that there was an increasing tendency to lie in bed until 5:30 in the morning.
The Arkansas Baptist

———

Work wrought out in activities which bless others produces joy in the heart of the one who does it.

———

Now I get me up to work,
I pray the Lord I may not shirk.
If I should die before tonight,
I pray the Lord my work's all right.
ANONYMOUS

A thing done right means less trouble tomorrow.

———◆———

The man who watches the clock never becomes the "Man of the Hour."

———◆———

Work is the best narcotic.

MAURICE MOLNAR

What the country needs is dirtier fingernails and cleaner minds.

WILL ROGERS

———◆———

A new employee had been caught coming in late for work three times and the fourth morning the foreman decided to read the riot act.

"Look here," he snapped, "don't you know what time we start work around here?"

"No, sir," said the man, "they're always working when I get here."

———◆———

Your Field of Labor

If you cannot on the ocean
 Sail among the swiftest fleet,
Rocking on the highest billows,
 Laughing at the storms you meet,
You can stand among the sailors
 Anchored yet within the bay;
You can lend a hand to help them,
 As they launch their boats away.

If you are too weak to journey
 Up the mountain steep and high,
You can stand within the valley
 While the multitudes go by;
You can chant in happy measure
 As they slowly pass along,
Though they may forget the singer,
 They will not forget the song.

Do not, then, stand idly waiting
 For some greater work to do;
Fortune is a lazy goddess,
 She will never come to you;
Go, and toil in any vineyard,
 Do not fear to do or dare;
If you want a field of labor,
 You can find it anywhere.

ELLEN H. COTES

World

We can only change the world by changing men.

CHARLES WELLS

———◆———

We cannot have a better world without first having better men.

Newsweek

———◆———

A ship is safe in the ocean as long as the ocean is not in the ship, and a Christian is safe in the world so long as the world is not in the Christian.

———◆———

The earth is a swinging cemetery of the dead.

———◆———

This World

This world is not so bad a world
 As some would like to make it;
Though whether good or whether bad,
 Depends on how we take it.
For if we scold and fret all day
 From dewy morn till even,
This world will ne'er afford to man
 A foretaste here of heaven.

This world in truth's as good a world
 As e'er was known to any
Who have not seen another world,
 And these are very many;
And if the men, and women, too,
 Have plenty of employment,
Those surely must be hard to please
 Who cannot find enjoyment.

This world is quite a clever world
 In rain or pleasant weather,
If people would but learn to live
 In harmony together;
Nor seek to burst the kindly bond
 By love and peace cemented,
And learn the best of lessons, yet
 To always be contented.

AUTHOR UNKNOWN

———◆———

He who would have no trouble in this world must not be born in it.

Italian Proverb

———◆———

The world is a globe that revolves on its taxes.

———◆———

When you deplore the condition of the world, ask yourself, "Am I part of the problem or part of the solution?"

MURRAY D. LINCOLN

Worry

Worry is interest paid on trouble before it is due. DEAN INGE

———◆———

Worrying takes up just as much time as work, but work pays better dividends.

———◆———

Our worst misfortunes never happen, and most miseries lie in anticipation.

———◆———

Worry, like a rocking chair, will give you something to do, but it won't get you anywhere.

———◆———

Those who live in a worry invite death in a hurry. ANONYMOUS

———◆———

The eagle that soars in the upper air does not worry itself as to how it is to cross rivers. Selected

———◆———

There are two days we should not worry over — yesterday and tomorrow.

———◆———

There is a great difference between worry and concern.
A worried person sees a problem, and the concerned person solves a problem. J. HAROLD STEPHENS

———◆———

Worry can cast a big shadow behind a small thing.

———◆———

In days of stress and strife, it is well to remember that worry is no one's friend, but everyone's enemy.
There are 773,692 words in the Bible but one will search in vain for a single occurrence of the word "worry" among them!
"Worry" is not in God's vocabulary and should not be in ours.

———◆———

Worry kills more people than work because more people worry than work.

———◆———

I never met a healthy person who worried much about his health, or a really good person who worried much about his soul. JOHN BURTON S. HALDANE

Said the robin to the sparrow,
  I should really like to know
Why these anxious human beings
Rush about and worry so.

Said the sparrow to the robin,
  I think that it must be
They have no Heavenly Father
Such as cares for you and me.
  The Prairie Pastor

———◆———

Nobody's Friend

I'm old man Worry, and I'm nobody's friend,
Though I'm called in many a home.
When trouble comes, for me they will send,
And it matters not where they roam.

For me they will lay awake many a night,
And I pay them in shattered nerves.
But they hold me and cuddle me tight —
I'm an old man whom many a one serves.

The rich and the poor invite me in,
And I go wherever they ask.
But they should know I hurt like sin,
And unfit them for any task.

I rob them of friends, as well as health,
And things that are held most dear.
And it matters not if they have wealth,
They are not happy when I am near.

But there are two smart ones where I can't abide —
They are Faith and Hope, I declare!
Wherever they go I stay outside —
No room to crowd in there.
  H. J. ANDREWS

———◆———

Worry affects the circulation, the heart, the glands, the whole nervous system, and profoundly affects the health. I have never known a man who died from overwork, but many who died from doubt. DR. CHARLES MAYO

———◆———

Worship

Satan doesn't care what we worship, as long as we don't worship God.
  D. L. MOODY

The man who bows the lowest in the presence of God stands the straightest in the presence of sin.

———◆———

Worship is fellowship with God.

———◆———

Gold has more worshipers than God.

———◆———

Worship is written upon the heart of man by the hand of God.

———◆———

Worship is the first step to wisdom.

———◆———

You can worship God in the woods . . . but you don't!
You can worship God on the lakes . . . but you don't!
You can worship God in your auto . . . but you don't!
You can worship God in a different church each Sunday . . . but you don't!
You can worship God by sending the children to Sunday school . . . but you don't!
The best place to worship God on Sunday is at your church!

———◆———

Ten Commandments for Worshipers

I. Thou shalt not come to service late
Nor for the amen refuse to wait.
II. When speaks the organ's sweet refrain
Thy noisy tongue thou shalt restrain.
III. But when the hymns are sounded out
Thou shalt lift up thy voice and shout.
IV. And when the anthem thou shalt hear
Thy sticky throat thou shalt not clear.
V. The endmost seat thou shalt leave free
For more must share the pew with thee.
VI. The offering plate thou shalt not fear
But give thine uttermost with cheer.
VII. Thou shalt the minister give heed
Nor blame him when thou art disagreed.
VIII. Unto thy neighbor thou shalt bend
And if a stranger, make a friend.
IX. Thou shalt in every way be kind,
Compassionate, and of tender mind.
X. And so, by all thy spirit's grace,
Thou shalt show God within this place. ANONYMOUS

———◆———

Write, Writing

Writing requires an application of a coat of glue to the seat of the chair.

———◆———

Scholars' pens carry farther and give a louder report than thunder. SIR THOMAS BROWNE

———◆———

Say it with flowers,
Say it with mink,
But never, oh, never
Say it with ink.

———◆———

Though authors use the same words, some do seem to string 'em together better.

———◆———

An author is never successful until he has learned to make his words smaller than his ideas. R. W. EMERSON

———◆———

He that composes himself is wiser than he that composes books. BENJAMIN FRANKLIN

———◆———

Dedication in a scientific book: "To my wife, without whose absence this book could not have been written."

———◆———

Editor: "You wish a position as a proofreader?"
Applicant: "Yes, sir."
Editor: "Do you understand the requirements of that responsible position?"
Applicant: "Perfectly. Whenever you make any mistakes in the magazine, just blame 'em on me, and I'll never say a word."

WRITE

Asked to paraphrase the sentence, "He had a literary bent," a city scholar gave this version:
"He was very round shouldered through excessive writing."

———◆———

The learned fool writes his nonsense in better language than the unlearned, but still 'tis nonsense.

———◆———

The teacher had asked the pupils to write a short composition on the subject, "Water."
One boy wrote: "Water is a white wet liquid which turns black when you wash in it."

———◆———

A student-made distinction: "The difference between prose and poetry is that prose is written all the way across the page, and poetry is written only half way across." LAURA GLOVER

———◆———

If you would not be forgotten, as soon as you are dead and rotten, either write things worth reading or do things worth the writing. BENJAMIN FRANKLIN

———◆———

Do right and fear no man; don't write and fear no woman.

———◆———

Reading makes a full man; conversation a ready man, writing an exact man.

———◆———

"The nose," wrote little Susie in her school paper, "is that part of the body which shines, snubs, snoops and sneezes." *Presbyterian Life*

———◆———

Newspaper editor to hopeful young writer: "Do you write for pay or do you write free verse?"

———◆———

Four men died on the same day. One was a struggling author; he left his family only $5. The second was a bookseller; he left $50. The third was a publisher; he left $500. The fourth was a dealer in waste paper. He left $50,000!

To Our Contributors

If you have a thing to say,
  Cut it down!
Something you must write today,
  Cut it down!
Let your words be short and few,
Aim to make them clear and true,
Monosyllables will do,
  Cut it down!

If you're writing to the press,
  Cut it down!
Make it half or even less,
  Cut it down!
Editors like pithy prose,
Lengthy letters are their foes,
Take a hint from "one who knows,"
  Cut it down!

Have to make a speech tonight?
  Cut it down!
Wish to have it take all right?
  Cut it down!
Do not be a talking bore,
Better far to listen more,
Don't monopolize the floor,
  Cut it down! GRENVILLE KLEISER

———◆———

Typographical Error

The typographical error
  Is a slippery thing and sly
You can hunt till you are dizzy,
  But it somehow will get by.
Till the forms are off the presses,
  It is strange how still it keeps
It shrinks down into a corner
  And it never stirs or peeps,
That typographical error,
  Too small for human eyes!

Till the ink is on the paper
  When it grows to mountain size,
The boss he stares with horror,
  Then he grabs his hair and groans.
The copy reader drops his head
  Upon his hands and moans —
The remainder of the issues
  May be clean as clean can be,
But that typographical error
  Is the only thing you see.
  AUTHOR UNKNOWN

The Poet's Truest Friend

The kindest friend the poet has,
 (Though poets least suspect it)
Is the editor who'll scan his verse,
Then mercifully reject it.

Like battercakes, on griddle hot,
 Ambitious poems sizzle,
But, were they baked on slower fire,
 They'd not be such a fizzle!

When the editor returns my verse
 I think him very hateful,
Yet, when I read that poem through,
 I'm really, deeply grateful.

'Twould never do to let it go,
 Just as I firstly wrote it;
For, till I've made it over new,
 No one would ever quote it.

'Tis best, you see, when writing verse,
 To polish and to shine it.
Or else, some brilliant editor,
 Will instantly decline it!
                              News and Courier

———◆———

The Editor's Request

If you have a tale to tell,
 Boil it down!
Write it out and write it well,
Being careful how you spell;
Send the kernel, keep the shell;
 Boil it down! Boil it down!

If you want the world to know,
 Boil it down!
If you have good cause to crow
If you'd tell how churches grow,
Whence you came or where you go,
 Boil it down! Boil it down!

Then, when all the job is done,
 Boil it down!
If you want to share our fun,
Know just how a paper's run,
Day by day from sun to sun,
 Boil it down! Boil it down!

When there's not a word to spare,
 Boil it down!
Heave a sigh and lift a prayer,
Stamp your foot and tear your hair,
Then begin again with care —
 Boil it down! Boil it down!

When all done, you send it in,
 We'll boil it down.
Where you end, there we begin;
This is our besetting sin;
With a scowl or with a grin,
 We'll boil it down; boil it down.
                    The Presbyterian Advance

Boil It Down

If you've got a thought that's happy,
 Boil it down;
Make it short and crisp and snappy,
 Boil it down;
When your brain its coin has minted
Down the page your pen has sprinted—
 Boil it down.

Take out every useless letter,
 Boil it down;
Fewer syllables the better;
 Boil it down;
Make it plain, express it
So we'll know, not merely guess it;
Then, my friend, ere you address it,
 Boil it down.

Boil out all the useless trimmings,
 Boil it down;
Skim it well, then skim the skimmings,
 Boil it down;
When you're sure 'twould be a sin to
Cut another sentence into,
Send it on and we'll begin to
 Boil it down.   JOE LINCOLN

———◆———

I would I were beside the sea,
 Or sailing in a boat,
With all the things I've got to write —
 wrote.

I would I were away from town
 As far as I could get,
With all the bills, I've got to meet —
 met.

I would I were out on a farm,
 A-basking in the sun,
With all the things I've got to do —
 done.   AUTHOR UNKNOWN

———◆———

It is hard to meet a deadline for a
man who likes to change things and
says, "That's fine, just what I want,
let's make these few changes, but finish
it today."

Wrong

Nothing is politically right which is morally wrong.   DANIEL O'CONNELL

——◆——

If you think the world is all wrong, remember that it contains people like you.   GANDHI

——◆——

Fear to do ill and you need fear nothing else.   BENJAMIN FRANKLIN

——◆——

To avoid doing wrong is not necessarily doing good.

——◆——

A man should never be ashamed to own he has been in the wrong, which is but saying that he is wiser today than he was yesterday.   ALEXANDER POPE

If you are willing to admit you are all wrong when you are all wrong, you are all right!

——◆——

To always be "consistent" is to be frequently wrong.

——◆——

If a thing is not *all* right it is *all* wrong.   ELD

——◆——

You may sometimes be much in the wrong, in owning your being in the right.   BENJAMIN FRANKLIN

——◆——

And now among the fading embers,
These in the main are my regrets;
When I am right, no one remembers;
When I am wrong, no one forgets.

Yesterday

The weak days are yesterday and tomorrow. Watch your step!

——◆——

Yield

Some people say "Let God go" instead of "Let go and let God."

——◆——

Youth

Youth to father: "Dad, could you go to a private P.T.A. meeting tonight with me and the principal?"

——◆——

Teenagers are too old to be children and too young to be adults. They subsist on hot dogs, noise, potato chips, giggles, food, telephone talk, emotional outbursts, and ice cream sodas. Their normal habitats are the schoolroom, the hot rod, the drive-in theater, and the swimming pool. They are not readily domesticated, but can be trained to do astonishing tricks if rewarded frequently with increased praise and/or an increased allowance. Their principal

enemies are parents, but teachers also frequently prey upon them. Some authorities — who do not have to live intimately with them — rank them as our nation's most valuable wild life.
                              Presbyterian Life

——◆——

An adolescent is an it turning into a he or a she.

——◆——

Growing up is the period spent in learning that bad manners are tolerated only in grownups.   *Changing Times*

——◆——

Adolescence is that period when children feel their parents should be told the facts of life.

——◆——

Adolescence is that period of life when a boy refuses to believe that someday he will be as dumb as his father.

——◆——

Seminary student's definition of "epistle": The wife of an apostle.

——◆——

Until a boy is sixteen he's a boy scout, after that he's a girl scout.

Ninety per cent of most youth problems is adult. DR. LOUIS H. EVANS

"If" for Youth

If you can live as youth today are living
And keep your feet at such a dizzy
pace;
If you can greet life's subtleties with
candor
And turn toward all its care a smiling
face;
If you can feel the pulse of youthful
vigor
Beat in your veins and yourself subdue;
If you can see untruth knee-deep about
you
And still to God and self and home be
true;
If you can cross the brimming flood of
folly,
And not dip from the stream to quench
your thirst;
If you can note life's changing scales
of values;
And still in your own life keep first
things first;
If you can feel the urge of disobedi-
ence,
Yet yield yourself to conscience rigid
rule;
If you can leave untouched the fruit
forbidden,
And daily learn in virtue's humble
school;
If you can play the game of life with
honor,
And losing, be inspired to strive the
more;
If you can teach men how to live life
better,
The world will beat a pathway to your
door. *Alberta Temperance Review*

Youth prefers to learn the hard way,
and some people never seem to grow
old.

A youth is a person who is going to
carry on what you have started. He is
going to sit right where you are sitting,
and, when you are gone, attend to
those things which you think are important. You may adopt all the policies
you please, but how they will be carried out depends on him.

He will assume control of your cities,
states and nations. He is going to move
and take over your churches, schools,
universities and corporations.

All your books are going to be
judged, praised or condemned by him.
The fate of humanity is in his hands.

So it might be well to pay him some
attention! *War Cry*

Love them, work them, feed them —
and you'll have them. DR. HENRIETTA C. MEARS

At four they know all the questions;
at fourteen they know all the answers.

If the world seems to beat a path to
your door, you probably have a pretty
teen-age daughter.

Youth is that time of life when boys
have the open-mouth disease. DR. HENRIETTA C. MEARS

The trouble with the younger generation is that so many of us don't
belong to it any more. *Kansas Teacher*

The flower of youth never appears
more beautiful than when it bends
toward the sun of righteousness. MATTHEW HENRY

Teen-Age Commandments

I. Stop and think before you drink.
II. Don't let your parents down,
they brought you up.
III. Be humble enough to obey. You
will be giving orders yourself
someday.
IV. At the first moment turn away
from unclean thinking.
V. Don't show off when driving. If
you want to race, go to Indian-
apolis.
VI. Choose a date who would make
a good mate.
VII. Go to church faithfully. The
Creator gives us a week. Give
Him back at least an hour.

VIII. Choose your companions carefully. You are what they are.

IX. Avoid following the crowd. Be an engine, not a caboose.

X. Recall the original Ten Commandments.   BY A TEENAGER

Denunciation of the young is a necessary part of the hygiene of older people and greatly assists in the circulation of their blood.   *Scholastic Teacher*

Z

Zeal

Zeal without tolerance is fanaticism.
JOHN KELMAN

SUBJECT INDEX

SUBJECT INDEX

SUBJECT INDEX

SUBJECT INDEX